War Diary

1939 - 1945

Compiled by

Alan Burns

To my wife, Norah, whose patience knew no bounds?

Ouseburn Publications
10 Ouseburn Close, Salterfen Park, Sunderland, SR2 9TJ

ISBN 978-0-9555444-0-8

CONTENTS

Bibliography

Sunderland's Blitz – Kevin Brady – The Peoples History

Sunderland: City And People Since 194 – Neil T Sinclair – Breedon Books 2004

Where Ships are Born – J. W. Smith & T.S. Holden – T. Reed & Co. Ltd. 1946.

Sunderland Municipal Handbook - County Borough of Sunderland, 1935.

Sunderland in the Blitz – Wear Books (Sunderland Leisure Department) 1990

Wearside at War – Maurice Boyle – Sunderland Echo 1984

Southwick-on Wear – Peter Gibson – Southwick Publications 1985

Southwick – Peter Gibson - The Peoples History

Wearside in Focus – The Newcastle Chronicle & Journal 1990

The Tramways of Sunderland – S. A. Staddon - Sunderland Echo 1991.

Sunderland. River, Town and People - Geoffrey Milburn and Stuart Miller Borough of Sunderland 1988

History of Sunderland - Glen Lyndon Dodds

Southwick-on-Wear – Peter Gibson – Mayfair Printers 1984

Acknowledgements

Rob Lawson, editor of the Sunderland Echo for permission to use the many photographs.

Brian Pears and his excellent website /www.bpears.org.uk

Billy McGee for his help in establishing the list of Merchant Navy men lost at sea.

The staff of the Local Studies Section of the City Library

PREFACE

This is not a history book, but a chronicle, a diary of events, taken mainly from the pages of the Sunderland Echo, which I hope will give to the reader a sense of what life was really like for residents of the County Borough of Sunderland during those dark years of World War Two.

The County Borough of Sunderland of 1939 was very different to the City of Sunderland that we know today. With a population of over 180,000 it was of course a lot smaller. South Bents, with its fishermen's cottages, in the North was still part of Boldon Rural District. The eastern boundaries extended only 3 miles from the coast with the villagers of Castletown, South Hylton, Silksworth, Rhyope and the Herrington's all in Sunderland Rural District. Alexandra Road (Queen Alexandra Road in 1941) was described as a peaceful tree-lined ring road carrying no passenger traffic. The southern boundary of the Borough was at Ryhope Grange just south of Sunderland cemetery.

Looking over the Town from Mowbray Park. The Winter Gardens are in the centre with the Victoria Hall to the right.

The diary covers the period from the outbreak of war on September 3rd 1939 to VE-Day on May 8th 1945. The war in the Far East had still to be endured for many Sunderland families and would not end until their loved ones began to return in October 1945. VE-Day, however, marked the end of the 'total war' as the Town and its habitants were no longer threatened.

In total warfare everybody, soldier, civilian, young or old, man or woman was in the front line, in fact until 1944 the civilian deaths and casualties were much higher than the military ones.

At the beginning of 1939 there were only eight shipyards on the river with only four yards open, Doxford's, Laing's, Thompson's and Crown's and only nine orders between them. This was of course reflected in the Town's unemployment figures, which in 1938 stood at 19,000.

Near full employment was achieved by the end of the war. All eight yards were working flat out with a ninth yard being opened in 1943. Conscription for the services and Essential Work Orders directing many Sunderland men and women to work in other areas of Britain the population fell to around 150,000. These yards produced over 1,600,000 tons of merchant shipping (over 25% of the UK output) as well as large amount of wartime naval construction and the many ship repairs undertaken. I have included in the diary all the ships launched during the war along with their subsequent fate.

Hudson Dock showing the Coal Staithes and Coal Conveyors with the large grain stores to the left of the picture. Top left is Greenwell's Shipyard with North Eastern Marine.yEngine Works to the right of it.

In WW2, civilians were directly affected by the conflict to a greater extent than ever before. Evacuation of the children, the rationing of food and other essentials, and the restriction of the blackout are just some examples. The Emergency Powers and Defence Acts meant the people had to endure more than 1001 interferences with personal freedom that the authorities had believed to be essential for the successful prosecution of the war.

South Dock with Bartram's shipyard top next to the Sea Lock and coal staithes along the bottom of picture

Production and Employment were regulated; conscription was in force, even if you weren't eligible for military service you were likely to have to register for war work in some form or civil defence work - fire watching for example.

With all these new regulations it was understandable that many Sunderland residents obtained a police record for such misdemeanours as breach of the blackout, wasting food, wasting fuel, absenteeism from work and bad timekeeping.

The front line was not a comfortable place to be in, and in the front line everybody had to be under military style discipline.

North Terrace f Mowbray Park

EVACUATION

The British Government was convinced that following the outbreak of war the civilian population would suffer air raids of such magnitude that they expected 100,000 deaths within the first few weeks.

Although well intended, the Government's evacuation plans were not well received. Parent were reluctant to be separated from their childr indeed, with high unemployment; many familie could not afford to kit out their children as recommended. The result was that out of a possible 24,000 eligible children only 7,910 departed by train to the rural areas of South Durham and North Yorkshire.

In the Reception Areas, the picking and choosing of evacuees resembling a Slave Market, or evacuees being 'touted' around, door-to-door, until a billet was found. Some children were greatly affected by this experience and suffered fo the rest of their lives. A clinical Psychologist, whose work involved counselling former evacuees, suggested, "it was little more than a paedophile's charter".

When the heavy bombing did not occur, mothers began to bring their children home and 1942 the Echo reported that only 1800 children remained in the Reception Areas.

RATIONING

Rationing was one of the great successes of the war. Its object being to distribute food, fairly and equally, so that everyone was sure of his or her proper share. It helped the people obtain a balanced diet and improved the health of the nation. It involved every person within the household registering with their local shop. The shopkeeper was then provided with enough food for his or her registered customers. A points rationing scheme was introduced in June 1941. The number of coupons allowed per person was at first 66 but later fell to 48. The scheme was extended in December 1941 to canned meat, fish and vegetables and later to canned fruit, condensed milk, breakfast cereals, biscuits and cornflakes. Everyone was given 16 points a month, later raised to 20, to spend as they wished at any shop that had the items wanted.

Barnes Park in the early 1930's with Humbledon Hill and the Bede Collegiate in the background

Northern Divisional Food Officer from the Ministry of Food said in 1944 "We are probably the best-fed nation in Europe and actually in better health than before the war. We cannot say that we have suffered more than inconveniences". One of these "inconveniences" was the growth of the queue habit as one of the less satisfactory features of wartime conditions.

BLACKOUT

The blackout caused serious problems for both pedestrians and car drivers. In the early months, car accidents increased and the people killed in road accidents doubled. In the first few months of the war, as many as one in five people was said to have sustained minor injuries in the darkness from bumping into people and things, tripping over kerbs or falling over sandbags. Social life changed, for many heeded the Government's advice and did not go out during the blackout period and began entertaining themselves much more. Sales of gramophone records and sheet music are greater than in any previous year. Alarming statistics revealed that 42,142 were killed by air raids on Britain during the first 24 months of war. In the same period 18,431 persons were killed in road accidents and that by May 5th, 1944, 588,000 were killed or injured in road accidents compared with 370,000 members of the forces killed or injured during the same period.

In Sunderland during 1938 there were only 11 road deaths compared with 25 in 1939, 28 in 1940 and 27 in 1941 (17 of which occurred during the blackout period).

Because of this carnage on the roads, the government was forced to change the regulations. Dipped headlights were permitted as long as the driver had headlamp covers with three horizontal slits. A 20 mph speed limit was imposed on night drivers.

To help drivers and pedestrians, white lines were painted along the middle of the road; curb edges and car bumpers were also painted white. Walls and posts, and telephone boxes where also painted white.

People were advised of the benefits of taking Vitamin A and cod liver oil capsules, for seeing in the dark and

Davison Terrace, Southwick, looking toward Marley Potts. Note the white markings on road, walls and posts. A white telephone box can be seen in the distance

recommended to wear or carry something white when out at night.

In Sunderland during the first 12 months of the war there were 750 cases of breaches of the Lighting Regulation. Many due to over officious Wardens or Police, many even believing that lighting a cigarette in the street during the blackout was an offence.

Sunderland viewed from Tunstall Hill (1937)

1939

The 'Phoney War'

Evacuees at Millfield Station

- The blitzkrieg does not happen. It heralds a period to become known as the 'Phoney War'. Not so for the many Sunderland families of serving men in the Merchant and Royal Navies and RAF.
- People are bombarded with regulations and bureaucracy.
- People stumble home in the blackout and road deaths double.
- National Registration and Identity Cards.
- Many parents suffer the heartache of sending their children to safer areas

3-Sep-1939

Alarm No. 1: 11.28 - 11.43 many, thinking it only a practice ignored the warning.

England and France declare war on Germany.

The National Services (Armed Forces) Act; all men between 18 and 41 liable for conscription.

Gas masks are to be carried at all times. Cinemas, theatres and public places are closed.

Volunteers work all weekend on Roker Beach filling sand bags.

4-Sep-1939

Retailers are warned not to raise prices of uncontrolled items such as blackout material.

5-Sep-1939

Weddings at the Sunderland Registry Office have dramatically increased, mainly of army reservists and territorials.

Laing's launch the BOLTON *CASTLE* 4897t. Sailing as part of the Russian convoy PQ-17 she was sunk by enemy aircraft on the 5th July 1942.

'SS ROYAL SCEPTRE' 4853t, built by JL. Thompson 1937, Rosario for Belfast, Torpedo and gunfire from U.48. One crewmember died but three men from Sunderland were among the survivors.

6-Sep-1939

The ordeal of being sunk by torpedo and shellfire was later related by Mr Charles Keith Temple, of 49 Pensher Street, Third Officer of the freighter Rio Claro, sunk only four days out of Sunderland

7-Sep-1939

National Registration Act passed in Britain, introduced identity cards and allowed the government to control labour. The legislation remained in place until 1952, when the Conservative Government, freshly elected to office, scrapped national registration and the national identity card as one of their first actions.

8-Sep-1939

The first offenders breaking the blackout regulations were each fined 10/-. (£20 in today's money).

St Mary's, St Benet's, Hudson Road and Moor school's parents object to Horden and South Hetton as reception areas. Horden District was abandoned but South Hetton remained a Reception Area.

9-Sep-1939

The Echo reported that police had arrested five boys, two from Hendon, two from Grangetown and one from Millfield. They were each fined 1/- (5p) for riding two up on a pedal cycle.

10-Sep-1939

7,910 older children of Sunderland were evacuated today to safer areas in South Durham and North Yorkshire. This represented only one third of the 24,000 children living in the evacuation zone.

Children evacuees from Chester Road Schools

One of the first victims of the mines laid by the U Boats was 'SS Goodwood' (2,796t), built by SP Austin in 1937, which hit a mine and sank with the loss of one of her crew off Flamborough Head. She was carrying coal from the Tyne to Bayonne. The captain H.S. Hewson of Humbledon Park, Sunderland was seriously injured and trapped. He ordered his crew to leave him and save themselves, but his plea was ignored and the crew managed to get him into a lifeboat. Other crewmembers were Mr T Broderick of Old Mill Road, Southwick and Mr T Dawsey of Howick St. Hendon.

Following yesterday's evacuation today was the turn of young mothers with babies when 1,785 were evacuated. The picture shows Southwick mothers and toddlers waiting a train to the Reception Areas.

11-Sep-1939
Catterina Kane was found dead at the bottom of stone steps in Covent Gardens, she apparently fell during the hours of darkness, a victim of the blackout.

12-Sep-1939
Many Sunderland men, now busy on the digging and construction of trench shelters, are doing their first job of work for years. Progress was slow and it was thought that most of the men might be thinking that by working quickly they were digging themselves out of a job.

13-Sep-1939
Higher freight and insurance as a consequence of the submarine warfare increases prices of basic foodstuffs. Butter up from 1/3d a pound to 1/7d; eggs have risen from 1/- to 1/3d a dozen.

Digging of Trench Shelter at Southwick Oval.

14-Sep-1939
Torches, dimmed with tissue paper, may now be used during blackout. To be pointed downwards and extinguished during an air raid.
Wm. Doxford launches the *LA ESTANCIA* 5185t. 20.10.1940 Torpedoed and sunk by U.47. Also the *RODSLEY* 5000t. Scrapped Singapore in 1982.

15-Sep-1939
Cinemas and theatres re-opened tonight. A number of people turned up without their gas masks and were turned away.

16-Sep-1939
Sunderland Transport will now have printed destination boards since the absence of the illuminated ones had created some aggravation between conductors and passengers.

Plains Farm and Marley Potts are reported to be the worst offenders of the blackout.

The Steamer Kafiristan 5,193 t, built by Short Bros. in 1924, is sunk with the loss of six crewmembers that included, Mr. T.E. Wake (Steward) of Wearmouth Drive and Mr. J. Mason (Chief Engineer) of Greta Terrace. The son of Mr. Wake was one of those rescued.

17-Sep-1939

The Sunday night parade in Crowtree Road. At 9pm it was almost impossible to get along either road or the footpath for young people many of whom were shouting or screeching, if these young people must go out on a Sunday night they should not congregate in such a narrow thoroughfare in the centre of the town. It is not difficult to imagine what would have happened had there been an air raid.

18-Sep-1939

There were eleven road accidents, one of which was fatal, in the blackout over the weekend in Sunderland and District. The victim of the fatality was Alfred Todd (34) of 3 Spring Gardens, Philadelphia; he died from his injuries received in an accident on the Sunderland/Penshaw road near Offerton.

19-Sep-1939

The Sunderland Canteen Committee, set up to provide canteen facilities as and where necessary, is appealing for donations of large pots, pans, steamers and dishes. The Guild of Help will accept donations at 4 Park Terrace.

22-Sep-1939

Petrol rationing began. Drivers were allowed so many units, each representing one gallon a month, depending on the horsepower of their cars. People with vehicles up to seven horsepower were given four gallons a month while more powerful cars were allowed anything up to ten gallons every four weeks.

A report by the Metropolitan Police Commission in London indicates that road accidents have tripled in the three weeks since the blackout began. Also, courts are packed with cases of blackout violations.

27-Sep-1939

The first budget of the war. Income tax increased from 5/6d to 7/6d. Extra taxes on beer, sugar and tobacco. Also introduced was a new Excess Profits Tax of 60 per cent on the war industries.

29-Sep-1939

The National Register taken today not only formed the basis for the issue of Ration Books and Identity Cards, but was also valuable in mobilising men and women to the greatest advantage.

Wm. Doxford launches the *BEIGNON* 5218grt. On 01.07.1940 it is torpedoed and sunk by U 30.

3-Oct-1939

River Wear Commissioners, concerned by the lack of air cover, asks Sunderland's senior Naval Officer if he considered a Balloon Barrage necessary to protect the shipyards and docks. He suggested they contact RAF Newcastle. In reply to the request, they suggest applying to the Air Ministry for a balloon barrage and additional guns.

4-Oct-1939

There is plenty of "gossip of goings-on" between Land Army girls and soldiers billeted around the farms in the area.

5-Oct-1939

A Sunderland man Ralph Burlinson (53), 2nd Engineering Officer, lost his life when a mine damaged the Anchor Brocklebank ship the 'MARWARRI' in Bristol Channel.

The 'NEWTON BEECH' 4,651t, built by Pickersgill's, sunk by the German pocket battleship the Admiral Graf Spee, is believed to have a number of Wearsiders amongst her crew. Mr J R Prior of Ridgeway Crescent is thought to be one of them.

9-Oct-1939

War conditions have allegedly brought food profiteering, with 10d steaks now at 3s 4d.

12-Oct-1939

SP. Austin launches the *LEA GRANGE* 2968t. Scrapped in Istanbul in 1973.

14-Oct-1939

JL. Thompson launches the ARGYL 1 4897t. 26.12.71 scrapped in Split.

H.M.S. Royal Oak is sunk with the loss of 833 men. Among the dead were Joseph Palfreyman of Pearl Road, Plains Farm, William Powell of Mordey Street and Frank Carrof Aylesbury Street, Millfield. A number of Wearsiders did survive.

16-Oct-1939

Home Teaching Schemes started today for 10,000 children aged between 9 and 14 years.

17-Oct-1939

Alarm No. 2: 13.57 to 15.11.

The first air raid over Sunderland turned out to be a bit of a non-event. A lone aircraft, thought to be He111, flew over Sunderland without any reaction from defence forces and without dropping bombs.
21-Oct-1939
Sunderland men in the age group 20 – 22 registered today for National Service.

22-Oct-1939

Three youths were fined 5s each for shouting and brawling in Crowtree Road during the blackout.
The 'SS WHITEMANTLE', (1,692t), was mined on route to London. It was reported Mr Richardson of Herrington Street, Hendon died within 12 hours of leaving his home.

26-Oct-1939

The Air Ministry replies to the Port Emergency Committee request for a Balloon Barrage stating, "the existing deployment of the Balloon Barrage would be modified to meet any special tactical requirement that might arise".

27-Oct-1939

Miss M Howitt, Headmistress of James William Street Girls School, reported that one month ago she weighed all the evacuees attending Croxdale, Sunderland Bridge and Hett. The results of further weighing most had put on weight. One little girl gave the reason "its all the pot pies and tatties they give us".

30-Oct-1939

Short Bros. launches the *SCORTON* 4813t. Sank in the South China Seas, following a fire, in 1967.

1-Nov-1939

Trench shelter systems are to be provided for every school before it can reopen. The Government warned that the opening of the schools was not an invitation to bring evacuated children home.

4-Nov-1939

Distribution of 150,000 ration cards begins. Registration is required at local retailers for bacon, ham, butter and sugar.

5-Nov-1939

The Ministry of Health issues instruction, prohibiting evacuees going home at weekends and holidays.

6-Nov-1939

Havelock School opened today. The school was considered to be in part of the Town that was classed as a neutral zone.

8-Nov-1939

Second evacuation of children from Sunderland today, 782 had registered but only 379 travelled.

9-Nov-1939

The public asked for tram services to revert to pre-war schedules. Being conveyed in a tram was considered far safer than groping their way home in the dark.
Laing's launch the *BEECHWOOD* 4897t. 26.08.1942 Torpedoed and sunk.

10-Nov-1939

Tenants of Plains Farm and Hylton Lane protest over eviction orders served by the landlord on persons who took part in the rent strike. Mrs Cottrell, secretary of Hylton Lane Tenants Association said that out of 28s 6d per week to keep her and her invalided husband she had to pay rent of 9s 8d "I can't keep going" she declared, "we have margarine and bread three times a day"
JL. Thompson launches the *INVERNESS* 4897t. 09/07/1941 Torpedoed and sunk by U.98.

11-Nov-1939

Crown's launches the *CORFEN* 1848t. 03/01/1942 while on voyage Sunderland to London with coal, was sunk by a mine in the Thames Estuary.

13-Nov-1939

Several clubs have tried to get Robert Gurney as a gate attraction with offers of 30s per match but he refuses and turns out for Sunderland 'A' without payment as does Hewison and Scotson who are also professionals at Roker.

14-Nov-1939

Petrol is now 1s 9$^{1}/_{2}$d per gallon, another 1$^{1}/_{2}$d on petrol from today the highest for fifteen years.

16-Nov-1939

The cost of living is reported to have risen 2.5 percent in October.
Sunderland ARP now has 2928 Wardens. In the Casualty Services 2742 have been enrolled. More volunteers are needed in First Aid Parties, AFS, Decontamination Services and the Rescue and Demolition Services.
The ARLINGTON COURT is torpedoed in the Atlantic. Two Sunderland men James Russell of 6 Coxen Street, and George Allen of 30 Norfolk Street were among those rescued by a Norwegian ship.

17-Nov-1939

Last day to obtain a Pigeon Permit. Under the Government's Pigeon Registration Scheme only registered pigeon owners may apply.

Gas masks remain Government property with penalties for damage caused by neglect.

Ernest Richardson of Hylton Road pleaded guilty to being drunk and disorderly in High Street West. He was fined 10s and ordered to pay 6s for the use of the ambulance in which he was taken to the police station.

A Group of Sunderland Wardens

18-Nov-1939

Clocks went back tonight for the end of British Summer Time. Normally done in October but new regulations put the date back to the third Saturday in November.

Wm. Doxford launches the *LA CORDILLERA* 5185t. 05/11/1942 Torpedoed and sunk by U.163 NE of Trinidad.

19-Nov-1939

The Sunderland built collier 'SS Torchbearer' (1267t), Built by J Crown in 1929, struck a mine and sank with the loss of four of her crew. One of those lost was a Sunderland man Robert Trotter of Beverley Road.

24-Nov-1939

The new Library and Mining Department of Sunderland College (Priestman Building shown opposite) is opened opposite the College in Green Terrace.

25-Nov-1939

'SS USKMOUTH' (2,483t), built by Priestman's in 1916, was sunk by torpedoes and gunfire from U 43 in the Bay of Biscay. Two of her crew died but among the survivors were two men from Sunderland.

27-Nov-1939

Bartram's launch the *HARPAGUS* 5173t. 20.05.1941 torpedoed and sunk by U 94 250m SSE of Cape Farewell. Voyage Baltimore. Halifax.

JL. Thompson launches the *ROYAL EMBLEM* 4900t. Scrapped May 1966 in Hong Kong

28-Nov-1939

Sunderland Council advises that estate tenants are not to be allowed to keep poultry in their gardens.

29-Nov-1939

A Sunderland Chief Engineer was in the water for 45 minutes when a collier was mined, he lost, amongst other papers, his National Registration Card, on returning home the authorities told him he would have to pay a shilling for the issue of a new card.

30-Nov-1939

Tuberculosis cases, which on the outbreak of war were sent home from the Infectious Diseases Hospital to free up the beds for expected casualty cases are to be returned to hospital.

Unemployment benefit for a man and wife is raised to 30s a week.

1-Dec-1939

'SS Dalryan' (4,558t) struck a mine and slowly sank, 6 miles off the East coast, watched by people on a pier. 38 crewmen were saved among them one Wearsider Mr E C Miller of Coniston Avenue Fulwell.

4-Dec-1939

Mrs Wilson a 74-year-old woman was knocked down and killed by a tramcar in Roker Avenue during the blackout.

'SS Horsted' (1,670t), a collier, on a voyage from London to Sunderland to pick up a cargo, struck a mine and sank SE of Flamborough Head. Three members of the crew that survived were from Sunderland, Mr G Ainsley of Dykelands Road, Mr M Leith of East Cross Street and Mr R Hepple whose sister lived in Water Street.

6-Dec-1939

Sunderland's unemployed now stands at 10,262.

The Town Council asks the Government to reopen the Wear yards closed by the asset stripping activities of the National Shipbuilders Security Ltd.

9-Dec-1939

Restricted but permissible lighting in the Town's shop windows is appreciated by pedestrians.

Pickersgill's launch the *DAYDAWN* 4768t. 21.11.1940 Torpedoed and sunk by U.103.

10-Dec-1939

In today's A.R.P. exercise, there was a poor response from car owners for the request for the use of their cars as 'ambulances' and 'mobile squads'

SP. Austin launches the *LEA GRANGE* 2968t. 1959 sold and renamed COSTICOS. 1973 scrapped Istanbul.

12-Dec-1939

The Mayor appeals to parents not to bring their children home for Christmas. Although the expected bombing has not as yet materialised the danger still exists.

14-Dec-1939

During the first three months of the war there were 2,975 road deaths in Britain. During the same period approximately 2,100 service personnel had lost their lives.

Short Bros. launches the *HAZELSIDE* 5297t. 28.10.1941 Torpedoed and sunk by U.68.

15-Dec-1939

The only survivor of the ten members of the crew of the HMS trawler WILLIAM HALLETT was Charles Hobson (42) of Stafford Street, Sunderland. The trawler sank in the North Sea two days ago.

16-Dec-1939

SS AMBLE (1,162t), a Dutch ship, hit a mine and sank off Sunderland.

19-Dec-1939

Robert W Robinson (71) of 34 Cumberland Street was knocked down by a tramcar in High Street West during the blackout. He died in Sunderland Royal Infirmary on the 30th.

Following the sinking of the destroyer HMS DUCHESS two Sunderland men lost their lives AB Charles Edward Flack (20) of Allison Street, Hendon and Petty Officer Donaldson of Horatio Street. However, two survivors were Harry A Moir (28) of Leechmere Road North, Grangetown and G Swinhoe of Hylton Lane Estate.

21-Dec-1939

The Town was busy with shoppers buying their turkeys, toys and decorations. There was a shortage of fruit and the deliveries of turkeys were quickly snapped up.

22-Dec-1939

Despite objection of the Authorities, 400 schoolchildren of Bede Boys and Girls Schools returned home today to spend ten days Christmas break with their families.

23-Dec-1939

The reduction of 300 full-time paid ARP personnel was announced today. Currently they are 1,007 men and 315 women on full time duty.

26-Dec-1939

For opening his fried fish business in Ocean Road, Grangetown during the holiday, Sidney Patelle, escaped conviction but was ordered to put 20s into the Poor Box.

27-Dec-1939

A quiet Christmas on Wearside the only misfortune was the none-arrival of six truckloads of beer from Scotland, which meant some pubs running out of beer.

28-Dec-1939

Vaux advises that a bottle of Double Maxim - *"gently stimulates the removal of acid wastes and it's rich constituents supply the needed nourishment, taken with the evening meal you will find that both mind and body are equipped to welcome that sound and carefree natural repose which is a due reward of a hard days work well done."*

Woodbine cigarettes cost 6d for a pack of 12 and 2s 6d for a tin of 60.

30-Dec-1939

Young skilled workers in most of the shipyard trades are exempted from military service under the schedule of reserved occupation. Before the out break of war they were not exempt below the age of twenty-one. Those young men who were mobilised with the territorial or the militia when war broke out may return on request of the employer.

31-Dec-1939

For the first time in many years there was no large gathering of people in Fawcett Street waiting for the Clock to strike midnight.

Three men from Sunderland are amongst 20 members of the crew feared lost when the steamer Boxhill hit a mine in the North Sea. They are John Clark of Wycliffe Road, William Lyle of General Graham Street and George Triggs of John Candlish Road.

1940

"...the Battle of Britain is about to begin."

"...so bear ourselves that, if the British Empire and its Commonwealth last for a thousand years, men will say, this was their finest hour".

Sunderland Station received a direct hit September 1940

- Dunkirk and the end of the Phoney War – Britain now stands alone.
- Rationing
- Creation of the Home Guard
- First bombs and first fatalities in Sunderland. 80 air raid warnings with nine fatalities.

2-Jan-1940

A survey indicates that one in five persons have had an accident in the blackout. People are advised to take Cod-liver oil and Vitamin A.

3-Jan-1940

Following completion of air raid shelters, the following schools will reopen on a part time basis; Barnes, Chester Road, Hylton Road, Diamond Hall Grange Park and Pallion.

The extreme wintry weather conditions caused a number of minor road accidents. Pedestrians also suffered from falls in the icy conditions.

4-Jan-1940

Deaths in Sunderland due to road accidents during 1939 were 25. It was recommended that pedestrians wear something luminous or white.

All merchant shipping is requisitioned for the war effort.

7-Jan-1940

The SS TOWNELEY, a 2872t a Newcastle collier struck a mine and sank in the Thames Estuary. All the crew survived. The Captain was Charles Evis of 72 Stratford Avenue Grangetown.

8-Jan-1940

Rationing regulations introduced on butter (4oz), sugar (12oz), bacon or ham uncooked (4oz) and bacon or ham cooked (3^1/$_2$oz).

9-Jan-1940

The first fatal Sunderland road accident of the year, Thomas Wilson (40) of 1 Primate Road, Plains Farm Estate, died falling from a Cleansing Department vehicle in Etterick Grove.

Wm. Doxford launches the *DERWENTHALL* 4934t. 03.02.1941 Damaged by mine Suez Canal. 1952 sold and renamed a couple of times before being scrapped in Hong Kong in 1969.

Laing's launch the *ATHELCREST* 6865t. 25.8.1940, just four months after completion, she was torpedoed by U-48. Thirty men lost their lives, among them were Sunderland men; Anthony Clark, a Greaser, aged 20: Leslie Armstrong Sanderson, Mess Room Boy, aged 16, Fulwell; Roger Tansey, Carpenter, aged 29, Southwick; Thomas Richard Wilson, Donkeyman, aged 39.

10-Jan-1940

Unlike most evacuees the children of Hylton Road School seem to be happy with their billet at Lartington Hall near Barnard Castle.

Sunderland's Food Control Authority was concerned that thousands of Ration Books lie unclaimed. The town's ration population was estimated to be 167,000 out of the census population of 182,000 but coupons provide for only 151,000 hence the concern. It was thought perhaps the population is lower than anticipated by evacuation and men joining the services.

The liner "DUNBAR CASTLE" was sunk by a mine yesterday of the Southeast coast. Sunderland survivors where Mrs A G Gleason of 16 Newcastle Road and an engineer Arnold Wolfe (30) of 100 Hawarden Crescent. Six Sunderland men are presumed dead following the sinking of the tanker BRITISH LIBERTY through striking a mine in the English Channel. Thomas Hodgson (23) of Randolph Street, Hendon and Albert Rowell (23) of Forster Street, Monkwearmouth have been buried at a French port in which 18 survivors, including several Sunderland men, were landed. Among the 20 missing men are J Hope (34) of Forbeck Road, Ford, C Robinson (32) of St. Luke's Road, Pallion, G Pace (17) of Falklands Road, Ford and G Brown (21) of East Whickham Street, Monkwearmouth.

The 'SS NORTHWOOD' (1446t) reached port today after having been attacked off the North East coast by two enemy aircraft. The master Captain I S Jones of 4 Mayswood Road, Sunderland commented "they dropped 40 bombs on us with more haste than accuracy".

11-Jan-1940

Owing to the presence of enemy aircraft, AA guns were in action, some pieces of shrapnel fell in the streets of Southwick. There were no casualties or damage. People were reminded to go to the shelter when they hear the sirens, but to stay safe indoors when the guns are heard even if the sirens have not sounded.

'SS KEYNES' (1,705t) cargo ship was bombed and sunk by German aircraft, N of Spurn Point. Mr William J Dennis, 2nd Engineer, of 65 Stratford Avenue, Grangetown was injured in the attack

12-Jan-1940

The "SS GRANTA" 2719t sank after striking a mine in the North Sea. Mr Alan Slater of Sunderland was among those picked up by a Polish vessel and landed at a North East port.

13-Jan-1940

Sir John Simon, Chancellor of the Exchequer, warns, "Let no one suppose that winning this war can be carried out without incurring immense burdens and making heavy sacrifices".

18-Jan-1940

High rental charges were blamed for the poor take-up of new allotments. A call was made for them to be rent-free for the first year of a three-year tenancy agreement.

19-Jan-1940

Wearsiders are now able to buy inferior quality bacon at reduced prices without having to spend their ration coupons. It will be sold in the East End and poorer quarters of the town.

20-Jan-1940

The Steamship BISP 1,000t built in 1889 by Sunderland S.B. Co. left Sunderland today, for Andalsnaes. Nothing more was ever heard of the ship or her crew of 16.

21-Jan-1940

The parents of Bede Secondary school pupils, at a meeting in the Cooperative Hall, Green Street, again demanded the return of their children. On hearing that the school was to open on a part time basis for non-evacuated children they felt that the school should be open to all.

23-Jan-1940

Flag Day for the Mayor's Boot Fund. Having already provided 2000 pairs it is the Mayor's desire that no child either at home or in a reception area shall go ill shod.

24-Jan-1940

Wm. Doxford launches the *CATRINE* 5218t. 29.12.1940 damaged by mine in Liverpool Bay. 30.12.1940 struck a second mine. 12/13.03.1941 bombed and damaged by aircraft Liverpool. Scrapped 9.03.1967 in Hirao.
A Sunderland man who was saved from the destroyer HMS GRENVILLE lost in the North Sea had changed watch only 45 minutes before the explosion with his friend, another Sunderland man, who is among the missing and presumed dead. The rescued man is Edward Black (20) of 60 Wearmouth Drive his friend was John Watson Jenkins (20) of 64 Bonners Field, Sunderland.

25-Jan-1940

The row regarding some ARP personnel drawing two wages continues. The ARP Committee gives one of the reasons as that of the single women of the town not pulling their weight.
Short Bros. launches the *BARNBY* 4813t. 22.05.1941 Torpedoed and sunk by U.111. 2 crewmembers were lost.

27-Jan-1940

Churchill is puzzled and worried about the "phoney war" and wonders why Britain has not been bombed yet.
A fire destroyed the eighty-year-old Long Bar in Green Street, one of Sunderland's oldest public houses and claiming to be one of the longest bars in the North of England.

29-Jan-1940

Alarm No 3: 10.13 -10.43. Enemy aircraft activity at sea. The Air Ministry announced that a number of RAF fighters were sent up and anti aircraft guns opened fire.
Bacon ration increased from 4 oz to 8 oz, it also applies to uncooked ham.
People are heeding the Governments advice and not going out during the blackout period and are entertaining themselves much more. Sales of gramophone records and sheet music are greater now than any previous year.
It has been Wearside's coldest spell since 1895 with 22 degrees of frost. It was only today that the Echo could report on the weather conditions as the Censor strictly controlled this subject.

30-Jan-1940

A national campaign is launched today to utilize almost all of the 120 million tons of household waste that are disposed of every year. Scrap iron and steel as well as waste paper are singled out as being urgently required. Housewives were asked to put their Salvage into four separate containers.

**Help put the lid on Hitler
BY SAVING YOUR
OLD METAL AND PAPER**

- Tins and Metal - For aircraft and tanks, weapons etc.
- Boiled Bones - To make glue for aircraft and glycerine for explosives.
- Kitchen Waste - For feeding pigs, goats and chickens.
- Paper - for munitions. (The newspapers of WWII were printed on a poor quality paper to save on paper).
- Rubber - for tyres.

The British Social Hygiene Council was concerned in the number girls between 14 and 18 hanging around outside armed force bases. One member commented on the number of men of the Merchant Navy who were met on landing in the blackout and convoyed to undesirable centres of the ports.
The SS ROYAL CROWN (4364t) was bombed and damaged by gunfire in an aerial attack, 15 miles South of Smith's Knoll Lightship. Able Seaman R G Agar, of Sunderland, was killed.

1-Feb-1940

The new 20 mph speed limit on roads in built up areas during the blackout comes into force tonight. Motorists were advised to gauge their speed by ear, as it was illegal to flick on the dashboard light.

Milk price were fixed at 6d per quart in rural districts and 8d per quart in urban areas.

The SS BANCREST was sunk by aircraft in the North Sea. Chief Engineer Richard Henry Wylie (60), of 32 Westlands, was among the 32 survivors.

2-Feb-1940

When the *JERRICOE ROSE* came onto the rocks north-east of Roker Pier during gales. 15 men were helped ashore by the Roker Volunteer Life Saving Brigade.

'SS PORTELET' (1,064t) sank, following a torpedo attack, With the loss of two Sunderland men. Mr Wallace Monty Allan of Ormonde Street and Mr J Waring of 19 Viewforth Drive. Among the nine-crew members rescued were, apprentice Eric Wilson, of Fulwell Road, and AB W Agar.

6-Feb-1940

The government is worried by the rising effectiveness of German U-boats, and fears that zealous reporting by the BBC will give the impression that British losses are even greater than they are.

The new Anti Gossiping Campaign The campaign was organised on the belief that women were the greatest offenders. It was left to the W.V.S. to distribute the posters throughout the town.

8-Feb-1940

Today Sunderland honoured one of the crew of HMS AJAX, which took part in the sinking of the Graf Spee, Stoker Michael Holly of Dock Street.

9-Feb-1940

Two men met for the first time today Able Seaman John Gill of Mount Road was a crewmember of the Pickersgill built *SS STREONSHALH* and George Peel of Fulwell Road a Seaman Gunner of HMS AJAX. Gill was a prisoner of war on the GRAF SPEE when attacked by British warships.

10-Feb-1940

Sunderland Higher Education Emergency and Evacuation Sub-committee rejected the Bede parent's request that the school should be brought back to Sunderland and the policy of evacuation abandoned.

14-Feb-1940

The British government announces that all British merchant ships in the North Sea will be armed.

16-Feb-1940

The absence of air raids and homesickness is attributed to the steady trickle of over 50% of evacuees returning to the town.

Mr Harry Cornell (23) of 24 Duncan Street, Pallion was a torpedo man on HMS EXETER, returned to Devonport Dockyard today.

21-Feb-1940

Emergency measures to deal with a coal shortage arising from the severe winter weather include a drastic reduction of passenger train services.

Laing's launch the *GLENWOOD* 4897t. 1948 *DURHAM TRADER*. 1958 *JAG SEVAK*. 15.07.1965 aground and abandoned.

23-Feb-1940

JL. Thompson launches the *CRAIGLAS* 4312t. 1952 LANTO. 1966 SHIA. Scrapped Hong Kong 13.2.66.

24-Feb-1940

British Summer Time clocks go forward one hour tonight.

Pickersgill's launch the *WINKLEIGH* 5468t. 1960 ST. ANTHONY. 1966 sold to Spanish breakers.

26-Feb-1940

Wm. Doxford launches the *SUTHERLAND* 5170t. In 1967 ran aground and broke in two and abandoned.

27-Feb-1940

Sunderland Education threaten to bring the Junior Technical School pupils back from Askrigg, Wenslydale, and reopen the Villiers Street school, if conditions for them did not improve.

28-Feb-1940

At least six Sunderland men, including a father and son, are among the 18 members of the crew of the Wear trader EFOS rescued after the vessel struck a half submerged wreck in the North Sea and sank almost immediately.

29th Feb-1940

Although during the past three years over 2000 Sunderland people have taken first aid courses organised by the St John Ambulance Brigade.

1-Mar-1940

The BBC estimated that six million people listened every day to the broadcasts of Lord Haw-Haw on German Radio.

2-Mar-1940

With the war now six months old, people were warned against complacency. We must not expect to be immune for the duration of the hostilities. The war on land appears to be at a standstill whereas the Royal and Merchant Navies along with the RAF have been at war since day one. For the men of these Services the term 'Phoney War' does not apply.

8-Mar-1940

Mr Allen Horn for the compulsory purchase of the land at Springwell Farm, by the Corporation, is claiming £47,000 for the value of the land and £7,000 for loss by forced sale of his pedigree Clydesdale horses.

The River Wear Commissioners, having become increasingly alarmed at the apparent defenceless state of Sunderland's docks and shipyards, and there protection, asks the Naval Officer in Charge how guns could be obtained for use against low flying aircraft. Following his advice they applied to Royal Artillery, Tynemouth. The reply was, "the matter was not for them and had passed it on to a higher authority". The "higher authority", Northern Command, York passed them on to the 7th Anti Aircraft Division, Newcastle. They said they could do nothing and suggested that the Emergency Committee write to the War Office.

9-Mar-1940

Juvenile crime in Sunderland is somewhat serious both in the number and of the gravity of the cases dealt with in court. Week after week the most astonishing depredations have unfolded.

The SS CHEVYCHASE hit a mine and sank in the North Sea. Four men from Sunderland were among those rescued; Captain John Cook of 16 Park Avenue, North Seaburn, 2nd Engineer Alfred Reed of 9 The Knoll, John Finlay (35) of Herrington Street and Bunshi Morioka (44) a seaman of Cairo Street.

11-Mar-1940

Meat Rationing introduced. Every adult will be entitled to 1s 10d worth of meat in a week and every child under the age of six by July 1st 1940 to 11d worth. Offal, rabbit, poultry, game, fish, brawn, sausages pies or paste will not require coupons.

The first case heard at Sunderland Police Court of driving a car at excessive speed during the blackout under the Emergency Powers Order of 1940. Thomas Clegg of 22 Farnham Terrace was fined £10 and his license endorsed.

13-Mar-1940

Three defendants, Thomas Sheridan (50), of Elmwood Avenue, William Gowland (54), of Yewtree Avenue, and Thomas Jones (42), of Faber Road, were all fine 10/- for using torches not properly dimmed.

14-Mar-1940

Stoker William Wright of HMS EXETER, whose home is at 7 Royle Street, Grangetown, was invited to the Town Hall today along with shipmate torpedo man Harry Cornell (23) who lives at 24 Duncan Street, Pallion.

18-Mar-1940

110 non-evacuated boys of Sunderland Bede Collegiate School went back to school today.

20-Mar-1940

A further seven defendants appeared before Magistrates for infringements of the Lighting Regulations. This makes 350 since the war began.

21-Mar-1940

The Staff and 94 boys of the Villiers Street Junior Technical School returned home today from Askrigg in Wensleydale. Efforts to find them suitable alternative accommodation in the Wensleydale Reception Area failed.

Wm. Doxford launches the *RAWNSLEY* 4996t. 8.5.1941 Bombed and damaged off Crete. 12.5.41 sank in Hierapetra Bay due to bad weather.

22-Mar-1940

The North East of England greatest walking marathon from Sunderland to Darlington, which for many years attracted the finest walkers in the Country, has been cancelled this Easter.

Bartram's launch the *HARPALYCE* 5169t. 25.08.1940 torpedoed by U.124. 37 out of a crew of 42 lost their lives.

26-Mar-1940

Many Wearsiders spent the Easter Holidays digging their newly acquired allotments under the 'Dig for Victory' campaign. The town now has more than 2,400 allotments but so far only 800 applications have been received.

28-Mar-1940

John George Parsons the 9-year-old son of John Parsons of Francis street, Fulwell died from a fractured skull when sandbags collapsed and crushed him. The accident happened near the entrance to the bus and tram depot in Fulwell Road. The Town Council later paid the family compensation of £500 (Equivalent today to £18,185.35).

3-Apr-1940

Lord Woolton becomes Minister of Food. Perhaps his most famous initiative in this office is the invention of the "Woolton Pie" This particular vegetable pie recipe was made from potatoes, swedes, carrots, parsnips and herbs. It was not widely liked.

4-Apr-1940

Sunderland, like so many big towns and cities, experienced a big rise in the number of wartime road deaths during the blackout period. During the wartime months of September to February the number in Sunderland was 17 compared with 9 in the corresponding period last year.

9-Apr-1940

A letter sent by The Town Council to the 1st Lord of the Admiralty, the Controller of Merchant Shipbuilding, the Secretary of State for War and the Air Ministry.

> "Urgent representation through the Merchant Shipbuilding of the Admiralty and the Ministry of Shipping for the provision of further and adequate defences including guns of the 'light machine gun' and 'pom-pom' type and a Balloon Barrage.
>
> In support of the application; (Notice they were careful to use the phrase "general observation").
>
> The docks and river areas have no defence against low flying aircraft. No Balloon Barrage, scarcely any guns. From a general observation the area referred to is practically defenceless. By way of contrast, by general observation, the River Tyne and its docks have been well provided for with guns and Tyne Balloon Barrage of 40 balloons.
>
> National importance of Sunderland shipbuilding. Within three miles, between harbour and Pallion there are; 8 shipbuilding yards; 5 graving docks; 12 repair and fitting out quays; a repairing slipway; an important repairing pontoon. 28 berths, each one occupied with a ship under construction and likely to be continuously occupied throughout the war. These yards will be able to provide 100 ships a year.
>
> Various repairing quays in the conversion of trawlers for minesweeping duties and the defensive armament of merchant ships, largely at the South Dock of the River Wear Commissioners, and a large ship repairing yard near the entrance to the dock.
>
> Coal staithe shipping of 5,000,000 tons per year"
>
> Letter ends

Laing's launches the *TYNEMOUTH* 4947t. Fate unknown but survived the war.

JL. Thompson launches the *THISTLEGORM* 4898t. September 1941 bombed and sunk at anchor in north of the Straits of Gubal. Later Jacques Cousteau filmed the wreck.

German invasion and occupation of Denmark and Norway.

10-Apr-1940

The appointment of Raich Carter to the Sunderland Fire Brigade caused some ill feeling in the town. The Chairman of the Watch Committee was asked to let the Council know how many late members of Sunderland AFC have got regular jobs in the Police, Specials, Fire Brigade and ARP.

Bartram's launches the *PENTRIDGE HILL* 7579t. Scrapped Belgium in 1965.

13-Apr-1940

A Sunderland man George Griffiths (26), son of Mr & Mrs G A Griffiths of 4 Cornhill Terrace, Southwick. Serving aboard the destroyer HMS COSSACK as Chief Petty Officer he was killed in action during a fight with German destroyers in Narvik.

17-Apr-1940

The proposals to have a licensed club along with Sunday afternoon tennis at the Ashbrooke ground of the Sunderland Cricket and Football Club was heavily defeated at the annual meeting.

For the second time in this war Captain Hugh Thompson, of Cymlea, Heatherlea Gardens, Alexandra Road, has been torpedoed and set adrift in an open boat. The first time was in February when he was First Officer on the SS LANGLEEFORD and today as captain of the SS SWAINBY.

18-Apr-1940

Nicholas Aiken (23) of 2 Carlyon Street, Stockton Road who is among the crew of the submarine STERLET 670 tons, which was sunk off southern Norway in Skagerrak by depth charges from German anti-submarine trawlers

19-Apr-1940

Sunderland Magistrates fined six women today for failing to observe the Shops (Allowed Hours) Regulations. They were all trading from their council house, which was against Council regulations. The women were Mary Sheraton of Harrow Square, Dorothy Ann Maddison of Flodden Road, Margaret Logan of Huntley Square, Lavinia Fitzsimmons of Peebles Road, Helen Adamson of Pancras Road and Isabella Bulmer of Hexham Road. Letter from the Secretary of State for War (Oliver Stanley) in reply to the letter of 9th April;
He appreciated the importance of Sunderland.

- Anti Aircraft gun defences have in fact already been provided.
- Points out that fighter defences of the County provide main defence.
- Reconnaissance is being carried out with a view to adding to the defences of Sunderland.

20-Apr-1940

Sunderland 0 Darlington 1. For the first time since war broke out, Sunderland today returned to serious football. They played Darlington in the War Time Cup at St. James's Park, as Roker Park was not available.

22-Apr-1940

A Searchlight Post in Yorkshire is known as 'Robson's Camp' because amongst the detachment of ten men there are four Sunderland brothers, sons of Mr Henry Robson of 37 St. Patrick's Garth, Coronation Street. In order of age they are Charles 36, Arthur 34, William 32 and George 29.

23-Apr-1940

Income Tax up to 7/6d. An extra penny on a pint of beer, whisky up by 1/9d per bottle. A packet of cigarettes now costs $8^{1}/_{2}$d. The most controversial measure, however, was the increase in postal charges, up to 2½d, an increase of 1d.

Winston Churchill's reply to the Corporation's letter dated 9th April to the Mayor, "air defences of Sunderland are receiving the immediate attention of the appropriate authorities".

SP Austin launches the *SEA FISHER* 2950t. 1967 scrapped Keelung.

Short Bros. launches the *HINDUSTAN* 5245t. 01.12.1942 bombed & damaged by aircraft at Bone. 1975 scrapped Santander, Spain.

Wm. Doxford launches the *PUTNEY HILL* 5215t. 26.06.1942 Torpedoed and gunfire by U 203.

25-Apr-1940

The Northern Redifusion Service was installing its system in Sunderland. They were criticized for not using local labour.

27-Apr-1940

Men aged 26, register for military service. It is reported that Raich Carter is one of those to register.

Darlington 1 Sunderland 3. Sunderland through to the next round 3 – 2 on aggregate.

29-Apr-1940

Paper shortage due to the German invasion of Norway meant smaller newspapers. The price of the Sunderland Echo is raised to $1^{1}/_{2}$d a copy. Comics were still produced because they brightened the lives of children.

Hopes for the safety of Sunderland officers aboard the Doxford built SS BLYTHMOOR have been raised by the safe arrival at their homes of some of the crew. Relations of the two Sunderland men on the BLYTHMOOR, Mr Norman Roche of Harlow Street and Mr Charles Feldman of Summerhill, were still without news. One Sunderland man that did come back was C H Jackson of St Cuthbert's Terrace, Deptford, the only Wearsider aboard the NORTH CORNWALL.

1-May-1940

The Amalgamated Engineering Union agrees to allow women workers in munitions factories.

3-May-1940

The findings of a Government survey seeking to standardise the sizes of women's clothing the "average girl" has the following measurements; Height 5' 5", Weight 8st 13lbs, Bust 34", Waist 26", hips 37.4" and ankles $9^{1}/_{4}$".

4-May-1940

Five members of the crew of six of a Royal Artillery Battery stationed somewhere in the Northern Command are the sons of Mr Charles William Cranmer of 8 Zion Street, Sunderland. They are Atkinson 39, Alfred 32, Charles 29, Robert 27, and Fredrick 25.

As members of the 125 Anti-Tank regiment they were all captured at the fall of Singapore in 1942. Sadly it was reported early in 1945 that Charles and Fred had died as prisoners of war while in Japanese hands.

Sunderland 0 Leeds Utd. 0 in front of a crowd of 11,226.

4-May-1940

Representatives of the 54 Polish refugees harboured at Corby Hall, Sunderland, are to present the Mayor with a framed illuminated address of their gratitude to Sunderland's hospitality in their hour of need. The address designed and executed by Mr Rudolph Ostrowski whose home is in Lwow, Poland. The Poles were from the ms PILSUDSKI a Polish liner who on their way home landed on the shores of Great Britain at the beginning of the war in 1939 and have spent the last 6 months living in Corby Hall.

6-May-1940

From today the use of flour or any milled wheat product, except for human food, is prohibited. The order from the Ministry of Food affects dog and poultry food.

7-May-1940

For the first time in many years unemployment in Sunderland fell below 10,000.

Laing's launches the *WANBY* 4947t. Torpedoed by U 47, NW of Rockall on the 19.10.1940, returning on her maiden voyage. Sank 21.10.1940

8-May-1940

Friends and neighbours welcomed home two survivors of the Norwegian campaign. 1st Class Stoker Fredrick Bainbridge, a survivor from *HMS BITTERN*, at Paton Square, Plains Farm Estate and *Able seaman Albert Hardy at Cobham Square, Southwick, a survivor of the bombed destroyer HMS ALFRIDI.*

10-May-1940

Prime Minister Neville Chamberlain resigns and is replaced by Winston Churchill, who forms a coalition government.

Germany invades Belgium, Holland and Luxembourg.

11-May-1940

Leeds United v Sunderland. Could this be Sunderland's cup year? The victory at Leeds today came as a pleasant surprise. Football, however, came to an abrupt end when Hitler invaded the Low Countries and thus ended the 'Phoney War'.

12-May-1940

Over 2,000 male Category A aliens living in coastal areas are arrested, five arrested in Sunderland. There is estimated to be 300 category B aliens on Wearside who are subject to more stringent supervision

13-May-1940

Because of the invasion of Holland and Belgium the Whit Holiday is cancelled. The Ministry of Home Security warns all Civil Defence and ARP services to be on the alert following the events in Holland and Belgium.

First speech of Winston Churchill as Prime Minister: "....blood, toil, tears and sweat"

14-May-1940

There was an immediate response in Sunderland when Mr Eden's spoke on the 6:00pm news broadcast. He asked volunteers to report to the local police stations. By 6:20pm the first volunteer from Sunderland presented himself at the Sunderland central police station for enrolment. He was Captain Slattery of Salem Street South, however he did not become a Home Guard but joined the Special Constabulary before final enrolment. Four days after volunteers kept pouring in at all hours until more than 4000 names were registered. They were called the Local Defence Volunteers and nicknamed 'Parashootists', some wags said the initials stood for Look, Duck and Vanish. On Tuesday July 23rd 1940, the name was changed to the Home Guard. It affectionately became known as "Dad's Army".

German troops invade France.

16-May-1940

The loss of Denmark and Norway and now Holland was blamed for the ration reduction of Butter, Sugar and Bacon.

17-May-1940

Motorists and garage proprietors are to ensure that cars and other motor vehicles in their charge couldn't be used by enemy parachute troops.

18-May-1940

Wm. Doxford launches the *ROOKLEY* 4998t. 1971 scrapped at Split, Yugoslavia.

22-May-1940

The new Government of Winston Churchill is granted wide ranging emergency powers. Free speech, private property, liberty of the individual to choose his/her employment – all were surrendered overnight.

Prices of goods are fixed to 1939 prices but petrol goes up by $1^1/_2$d to 1s $11^1/_2$d a gallon.

Pickersgill's launches the *STANMORE* 5969t. 01.10.43 Torpedoed by U 223 in Mediterranean. Towed into Tenes and beached, total loss.

23-May-1940

The "get you home" service for troops coming to Sunderland on leave run by the Sunderland Rotary Club and Round Table members, which had been suspended for some weeks owing to the stoppage of petrol allowances restarted tonight.

JL. Thompson launches the *ST. ESSYLT* 5634t. 04.07.1943 torpedoed and sunk by U.375. 2 dead - 397 survivors (including 321 military). Chief Engineer Wilfred Marrs was later awarded the OBE, Lloyd's Medal and War Medal.

24-May-1940

Empire Day; the significance of the Empire was never greater than at this time. "The situation is one of unexampled peril" (Churchill). Mr Duff Cooper, Minister of Information, "this country is in fearful danger today, greater danger than perhaps in the whole of her history"

HMS WESSEX was bombed and sunk off Calais by German aircraft. Stoker James Usher of 22 Friar Road, Ford Estate, was a survivor.

25-May-1940

The Ministry of Home Security has warned the War Emergency Committee that the greatest danger to be feared from air attack on the town was from incendiary bombs and the resulting fires.

27-May-1940

The sugar ration is reduced from 12oz to 8oz per head.

Restrictions on the manufacture and use of paper. Manufacture of certain classes of paper goods Handkerchiefs, serviettes, table clothes, cups, sauces and plates, book wrappers and confetti is prohibited all together.

Evacuation from Dunkirk begins. 8,000 troops rescued today

29-May-1940

There was in Sunderland more than 2000 families with members serving on ships of the Merchant Navy and some 30 or 40 of these men have already laid down their lives.

30-May-1940

All wireless receiving apparatus including the aerials must be removed from motorcars and other road vehicles, even if the vehicle is laid up. The work is to be completed by Sunday.

31-May-1940

"Message from Northern Command to ARP Controllers, "It is considered by the Chiefs of Staff that attack on this country is imminent. Enemy may use large fleets of fast motorboats simultaneous with airborne raids inland. Military commanders have been warned".

Residents of Lonsdale Street receiving Stirrup Pump training

1-Jun-1940

The Ministry of Home Security has notified the Sunderland ARP Authority of the issue of 400 stirrup pumps for use by householders and shopkeepers. Responsible people, will form groups of three and arrange for communal use of the pumps in case of fires started by air raids.

The destroyer HMS HAVANT was lost after being heavily damaged by German aircraft off Dunkirk during the evacuation of France with the loss of 8 men. Seaman Albert Fawcett 20 of Hartington Street, Roker, Seaman James Paxton 20 of Westmoor Road, Ford Estate and Stoker John Anderson of 38 Fordenbridge Road, Ford Estate were amongst the survivors.

2-Jun-1940

Second Officer James Donald, of 19 Ormonde Street, Sunderland, was one of eight survivors from the 1478t SS WINGA, which collided with a Norwegian vessel off Hartlepool.

4-June-1940

Churchill's 'We Shall Fight Them on the Beaches' speech. It was today that the people of Sunderland learned of the Dunkirk evacuation. For the people in Britain, World War Two was about to start for real. The "Phoney War" was now over. The evacuation of Dunkirk and the surrender of France meant Britain was by herself

5-Jun-1940

The Government bans all strikes.

Within 5 days, the King has honoured 3 of the original members of the County of Durham 607 Squadron of the Auxiliary Air Force. Squadron Leader J.R. Kyll (DSO), Flight Lieutenant W.F. Blackadder (DSO) and Flight Lieutenant J. Sample (DFC)

Crowns launch the *HMS HELIOTROPE* 580t Flower Class Corvette. Ended its days in Chinese Navy

7-Jun-1940

Alarm No.4: 23.43 - 23.55

The activities of German raiders were the highest since the war began. Eleven Eastern counties reported aircraft. No bombs fell on Sunderland.

Sunderland men are among the wounded veterans of The BEF in a North East War Emergency Hospital built at Ryhope. Many of the men had arrived on a hospital train a fortnight ago.

8-Jun-1940

All signposts and direction indicators that would be of use to the enemy in the event of an invasion are to be removed.

10-Jun-1940

The practice of wholesale bakers supplying bread to retailers on a sale or return basis is illegal.

Sunderland, along with other coastal areas, became a protected area and all aliens residing in them had to report to police stations to see how the new regulations affected them.

Italy declares war on France and Great Britain.

Today was the last day to comply with the order to erect delivered Anderson shelters, they must be erected and covered with 15" of earth on top and 30" at the sides or they will be taken away and penalties imposed.

Delivery and erection of Anderson Shelter at Ford Estate

In Norway the Allied campaign comes to an end. The Allies lost one carrier, two cruisers, nine destroyers and many smaller craft also many ships were damaged. The Germans lost three cruisers, 10 destroyers and several submarines. Manpower losses in the Norwegian campaign are about 5600 for the Germans and 6100 military deaths for the Allies as well as many civilian casualties.

The Germans now controlled all the western coastline of Europe's mainland. The Luftwaffe Luftflotte 5 was based in Norway and Denmark and was used for attacks against northern Britain. However in its first daylight raid on August 15th it lost one-eighth of its bomber force and one-fifth of its long-range fighters. It never made another daylight attack during the entire Battle of Britain and indeed many of its bombers were sent south were they could receive the protection from Messerschmitt 109 single-seat fighters.

Mussolini issues declarations of war to Britain and France.

11-Jun-1940

Police had to disperse demonstrators from outside the Italian owned Notarianii's ice cream shop in High Street West this afternoon. Crowds threatened anyone attempting to enter the shop.

12-Jun-1940

A recent air raid warning showed that many of the domestic air raid shelters were being used to store coal, mangles and other domestic items and in some cases even rabbits and other animals. The Corporation warned householders that inspections are to be carried out and prosecutions will be undertaken if the shelter is not properly constructed or is being misused.

'SS EARLSPARK' (5,250t) steamer, outward bound from Sunderland with a cargo of coal was sunk by U 101, NW of Cape Finisterre. Seven of her crew, including Capt. Williams, were killed and one wounded

13-Jun-1940

The ringing of church bells is prohibited, except as a warning of invasion.

18-Jun-1940

Churchill's 'This Was Their Finest Hour' speech given today. This quotation includes the famous phrase; "What General Weygand called the Battle of France is over. I expect that the Battle of Britain is about to begin. Let us therefore brace ourselves to our duties, and so bear ourselves that, if the British Empire and its Commonwealth last for a thousand years, men will say, this was their finest hour".

Civilians were told that in the event of an invasion they should "stay put" and don't give or tell a German anything, hide your food, bicycles and maps, see that they get no petrol and put all motor vehicles out of action.

19/20-Jun-1940

Alarm No.5: 23.33 - 02.51. West Hartlepool suffered its first air raid of the war along with Stockton, Billingham causing casualties, some fatal.

The housewives of Sunderland were encouraged to prepare for every emergency. The following is a list of Do's from the Chairwoman of the Housewives Bureau;

- Waste - take care what you throw into the dustbin – could it feed the neighbour's children or make compost for the garden?
- Salvage – are you sorting your refuse paper, bones, and tins ready for the collecting van? Are you sifting your cinders?
- Are you studying the Ministry of Food leaflets, which instruct you on well-balanced meal planning, and are you attending the cookery classes arranged by the Education Authority, Gas Company, Electricity Department and Housewives Bureau?
- Are your windows protected against splintering glass in air raids? Is your blackout efficient? Is your first aid kit ready at hand? Which day are you attending the lecture and film showing on how to deal with incendiary bombs?
- What are you denying yourselves so as to buy War Savings Certificates?

20-Jun-1940

Patrick Fowdy (56) of Friar Road, Ford Estate is the first person in Sunderland to be given a prison sentence for a lighting offence. The offence occurred in the early hours of yesterday when an air raid was in progress. Any householder or allotment holder can now keep pigs, hens or rabbits but no cockerels.

21-Jun-1940

River Wear Police constable Charles Peter Page 49 of 9 Queens Crescent was killed, while answering an emergency call, when the motorbike he was riding collided with the taxi of Alfred McCoombs of Elmwood Street in New Durham Road. The accident was blamed on the military stopping cars and telling the drivers to drive without lights.

Wm. Doxford launches the *TOWER GRANGE* 5226t. 18.11.1942, Torpedoed and sunk by U 154. 6 crewmembers lost.

21/22-Jun-1940

Alarm No. 6: 23.32 - 01.50. Alarm No. 7 03.36- 03.58 Sunderland had two air raid warnings during the night. Nazi bombers came over parts of the North East dropping bombs sporadically most of which were in open fields. Aircraft over northeast for more than two hours, bombs were dropped and there was heavy anti aircraft fire. Tynemouth and South Shields experience their first air raid. No casualties reported.

Bombs were dropped near Whitburn; the only casualties were two horses. A bomb fell in a grassy embankment immediately behind some newly erected cottages close to the seashore. Most of the people living in the cottages had left their homes to take cover in their Anderson shelters in their back gardens. All had high praise for the effectiveness of their Anderson shelters.

22-Jun-1940

Letter from the Mayor to Sir Arthur Lambert, Northern Regional Controller, pointing out that there were no signs of RAF fighter activity during yesterday's air raid. He thought it disturbing, considering the assurances of the Secretary of State for War (Oliver Stanley) of the 19th April.

24-Jun-1940

The habit of people going to community shelters each evening and demanding them to be opened even before an alarm is sounded is condemned. People have been advised not to leave their home until they hear an air raid warning.

25-Jun-1940

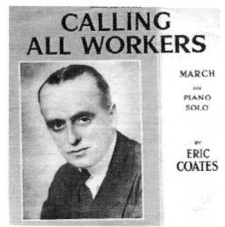

CALLING ALL WORKERS

MARCH
FOR
PIANO
SOLO

BY
ERIC COATES

The BBC's 'Music While You Work' programmes are a great success and are said to increase efficiency and therefore are an aid to war production. However, certain songs banned, like 'Deep in the Heart of Texas' because workers would stop to clap hands at the appropriate moments. 'Yes My Darling Daughter' was also discouraged, because of the foot tapping sequence at the end of each verse.

Theme tune of 'Music While You Work'

26-Jun-1940

Alarm No. 8: 00.05 - 02.25. Activity over Northumberland. No raiders over Sunderland.

Laing's launch the *CHARLTON HALL* 4897t. Sold to Karachi breakers March 1967.

27-Jun-1940

It was the duty of every household to put all waste paper and cardboard, scrap metal and bones in separate bundles to be called for by Council dustmen. Sorters were employed in the salvage dumps dealing with 92 grades of bottles, 13 grades of non-ferrous metals, various grades of paper, rag and other forms of refuse.

Scrap metal Collection

Glass bottles being sorted, maybe to be used by the Home Guard for Molotov Cocktails

28-Jun-1940

Annual report of the Sunderland probation officer reveals that although there was a big decrease in the number of juvenile delinquents from the beginning of the war until December, there was a vast increase in the months following until the end of May, thought to be due to the blackout and many fathers joining the army. Lack of schooling means that many children are hanging about from early morning without any supervision.

29-Jun-1940

Alarm No. 9: 03.55 - 04.05. Alarm probably due to mine laying activity off the coast.

So far Sunderland authority has received over 1000 applications for school children to be sent to the dominions or the United States under the government oversees evacuation scheme.

1-Jul-1940

The Control of Paper order restricts the Sunderland Echo to 36 pages a week.

The milk price is raised from 3d to 4d (1½p) per pint.

2-Jul-1940

Alarm No. 10: 17.41 - 18.05 A single aircraft caused damage and casualties at Newcastle (their first) and Jarrow.

A five-mile Defence Area is created around the coast of Britain. Persons could only enter this Defence Area for business reasons and not for mere pleasure. Sunderland, however, although within this area was initially classed as a "free zone. People would therefore be committing an offence if they stepped outside the Borough boundary for non-business reasons.

3-Jul-1940

Alarm No. 11: 13.58 - 14.36 Enemy aircraft off east coastal areas, no action reported.

A second man is sent to prison for failing to obscure a light at his home during an emergency and for being abusive with neighbours. He was Samuel Hatcheson, 50, of Knox Square, Southwick

4-Jul-1940

The new Havelock junior and infants school was opened today. The school, costing £41,000, includes the first nursery block to be attached to an elementary school in Sunderland.

5-Jul-1940

Alarm No. 12: 17.34 - 17.51 No action reported.

Because of theft and vandalism the Education Authority considers it is not worth the time, money and labour spent on the school children's allotment on the Plains Farm Estate.

Laing's launch the *WANDBY* 4947t. 19.10.1940 Torpedoed and sunk by U.46 Crew of 34 all saved.

6-Jul-1940

Alarm No. 13: 00.19 - 04.10. Alarm No. 14 14.18 - 14.35. A lone raider in the Humber area.

Volunteers required to assist in the construction of defence works, must bring their own spades.

The Parks Committee donates for scrap most of the railings around Mowbray Park, the two cannons, which "guard" the Havelock monument and the two lead statuettes in Roker Park.

7-Jul-1940

Alarm No. 15: 01.00 - 02.15. Night bombing raids began in Yorkshire and ended in the early hours at Whitley Bay.

Three trains, two from Millfield and one from Monkwearmouth yesterday carried 1,026 school children evacuees to parts of the North Riding

8-Jul-1940

Alarm No.16: 00.01 - 01.05. A Junkers Ju 88A shot down in flames during a sortie to Sunderland crashed at Hornsea in Yorkshire at 11.42.

Tea, margarine, cooking fats and cheese rationing begins; the allowance is 2oz. per week for each item. Sugar is cut to 8oz and the Government announces no more bananas, no more fresh or tinned fruit to be imported.

9-Jul-1940

JL. Thompson launches the *EMPIRE WIND* 7459t. 13.11.41 Bombed and sunk

10-Jul-1940

Bartram's launch *RICHMOND HILL* 7579t. Scrapped 1966 at Yokosuka, Japan.

11-Jul-1940

Four salvage days in the town resulted in the collection of 330 tons of old junk, today's total, despite adverse circumstances, was 77 tons 7 cwt.

12/13-Jul-1940

Alarm No. 17: 00.40 - 01.39. Off the East Coast between 23.34 hours and 01.17 hours a few raids approached Northumberland and Yorkshire and some were plotted inland. Bombs were dropped at Billingham and Thornaby.

15-Jul-1940

The Home Office bans fireworks, kite and balloon flying.

For spreading rumours and making statements, which were likely to cause "alarm or despondency" among Ford Estate residents, Harold Lampton Todd, 50, of Brookside Gardens, Sunderland, an insurance agent, was sent to prison for two months. This was the first case heard in Sunderland under this section of the Defence regulations. *'SS HEWORTH' (2,855t) steamer, London to Sunderland was sunk by German aircraft near Aldeburgh Light vessel.*

16-Jul-1940

Defensive Area Regulations were causing problems for Sunderland dog racing fans. The Boldon Dog Track is outside the Sunderland boundary. Hundreds of Sunderland townsfolk were refused admission to the track last night by the County Police. It was thought the police should have stopped people entering the 'Defence Area' in the first place, as it is not an offence to enter a dog track but it is an offence to enter a closed Defensive area without being on business.

17-Jul-1940

Two youths were each fined 20s for unlawfully entering a defence area. This was the first time the magistrates had dealt with this offence. George W Stephenson, 18 of Chestnut Crescent, Southwick, and Thomas Gardener, 19 of Mortimer Street Pallion, went for a walk to Castletown, which is in Sunderland Rural District and therefore in the Defence Area.

18-Jul-1940

Wm. Doxford launches the *DUKE OF ATHENS* 5217t. Collision-Total Loss on the 3/8/1944.

20-Jul-1940

From today, no one could buy a new motor vehicle without a licence from the Minister of Transport.

21-Jul-1940

Two bombs dropped close to Hylton Red House farm, one exploded in soft soil near the farmhouse and caused a large crater. An incendiary bomb fell in Castletown Dene not far away.
During the night 20th/21st July, enemy aircraft were reported at West Hartlepool as well as in the Sunderland area.

22-Jul-1940

The Sunderland Echo begins a campaign against the Defence Area Regulation.
Today the first batch of women conductors went into training.

23-Jul-1940

The third War Budget today raised Income Tax to 8/6d in the £1. Purchase Tax to be introduced.
Secretary of War announces Local Defence Volunteers are to be renamed the Home Guard.

24-Jul-1940

SP.Austin launches the *MOORWOOD* 2056t. 10.6.1941 torpedoed by aircraft and sunk off Hartlepool.
25-Jul-1940

Sunderland has been included in the Defence Area. This means that people of the town can now move outside the Borough boundary, as the occasion requires.
Off Sandgate, SS PORTSLADE (1,091t), built by Pickersgill's in 1936, was sunk by Stuka dive-bombers 4 miles NE of Dungerness.

26/27-Jul-1940

Alarm No. 18: 23.46 - 01.50. Between 10.30pm and 1.00am, three raids were plotted near the Tyne in the vicinity of two convoys and were probably mine laying.
There was considerable searchlight activity during the early morning and a raider, flying very low, was caught in the beams. Tracer bullets were seen and anti aircraft and machine gunfire was heard as the raider was driven off.

27-Jul-1940

SS BALZAC left Sunderland this morning with 1350 tons coal for Cowes, Isle of Wight. While anchored about 2 1/2 n. miles off Sunderland pier and waiting for the convoy (north of Hendon Rock), an explosion occurred underneath her, a little aft of amidships towards the port side. The BALZAC broke in two and sank within minutes, bow first, while listing to port. Eight members of the Norwegian crew including the Captain, lost their lives plus the Pilot Mr George Hall (33), Sunderland Pilotage Authority and son of Thomas and Isabella Hall; husband of Mary Hall, of Sunderland,

29-Jul-1940

Black's Theatre Royal reopened tonight. The north's latest luxury theatre reconstructed and specially designed for live shows with a fully licensed bar. The Royal in Bedford Street is Sunderland's oldest existing theatre having first opened in 1855.

30-Jul-1940

Sunderland's new radio Redifusion service was inaugurated tonight immediately before the 9 o'clock news. The Mayor of Sunderland broadcast to several hundred subscribers already 'hooked up' from the control centre in Bridge Street.

1-Aug-1940

Alarm No. 19: 01.15 - 01.49. Enemy mine laying.

Hospitals in Sunderland are being cleared in preparation for the reception of possible civilian casualties from air raids.

It was reported that eight enemy aliens (Italians) registered for the manufacture and sale of ice cream in Sunderland have been interned. Their business has been handed over to relations who are naturalised British subjects.

2-Aug-1940

Alarm No. 20: 00.08 - 01.42. Minelayers active during the night.

3-Aug-1940

SP.Austin launches the *CORNWOOD* a 2777t. 1972 scrapped Italy.

4-Aug-1940

Alarm No. 21: 00.08 - 00.41. Several reconnaissance raids were plotted throughout the Channel in search of convoys, but all turned back when Squadrons were scrambled.

5-Aug-1940

A new defence regulation cancelled the August Bank holiday. With the 'blitzkrieg' invasion still a threat Sunderland took August 'Blank' Holiday in its stride.

5/6-Aug-1940

Alarm No. 22: 22.44 - 01.10. The night was quiet with only a few plotted raids over Northeast coast. There were no reports of bombs being dropped.

6-Aug-1940

The Ministry of Home Security corrected widespread impression that all lights on vehicles must be extinguished when air raid warnings are sounded. This is not the case, as headlamps only should be extinguished.

Wm. Doxford launches the *FULTALA* 5051t. 1942 torpedoed and sunk by Japanese submarine I 3 west of Ceylon.

Pickersgill's launch the *EMPIRE THUNDER* 5965t. Left the Wear mid-Nov. 1940. 6.1.41 Torpedoed and sunk by U.124.

7-Aug-1940

In the first case of its kind heard by Sunderland's Magistrates, John D McBain 40 of Summerhill, East Herrington and a Sunderland lorry driver, Alfred R Budge 32 of Chester Terrace, were each fined £1 for leaving vehicles unattended without immobilising them. McBain had left his car unattended in Fawcett Street with the ignition key in the switch and doors unlocked. Budge admitted leaving his lorry outside the Barley Mow shelters during an air raid warning.

9-Aug-1940

Shortly before noon a lone raider appeared over the

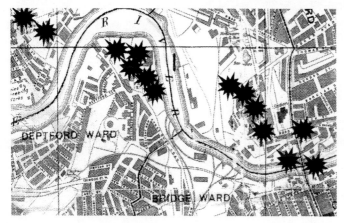

town chased by British fighters. Whether deliberately or in panic the plane dropped its full bomb load of 14 bombs. The most serious incident was at Laing's shipyard at Deptford where Richard Archer (33) of 27 Washington Street, Arthur Perry (26), of 14 Picton Street, and Thompson Reed (18) all suffered fatal injuries. Further bombs fell in the Sheepfolds area. In Richmond Street, a young woman Irene Mooney (19), of 86 Maplewood Avenue, Southwick, later died of injuries received here. The railway bridge was damaged and a lorry driver and his mate had a lucky escape. Other bombs fell in the Bonnersfield area and one into the river. A number of others also suffered injuries. The Heinkel crashed into the sea and the four crewmembers were picked up. One of the crew was carried ashore on a stretcher another with a foot injury needed assistance the remaining two crewmembers were uninjured.

A later communiqué reported, *"At 1140 hours, one He111 crossed the coast near Sunderland, but after being active over Sunderland was shot down by No 79 Squadron (Hurricanes) at 1145 hours. There is a report that 1 boat was dropped by this aircraft but there is no confirmation of the crew having been saved"*.

10-Aug-1940
Alarm No. 23: 00.00 - 02.58
Two evacuated Southwick kids who have stayed since the beginnings of the war are George 7 and Florence 5 Bowmaker. Evacuated from West Southwick School they are having a very happy time at Pickhill and their foster parents will be very reluctant for them to return to Sunderland.

11/12-Aug-1940
Alarm No. 24: 23.15 - 01.53. Raids to the north and south of the region but none in the Sunderland area. Spectacular dive-bombing by RAF planes provided plenty of 'incidents' in today's exercises. It was not difficult to imagine the panic and havoc that would have been wreaked by the low flying machines skimming the rooftops had they been dropping real bombs instead of small sugar bags filled with white powder.

2-Aug-1940
The Ministry of Food Order, preventing waste of food comes into force today. Under the order it will be an offence to waste food, which is described as everything used by man for food or drink other than water. Under the order it is forbidden to give meat to cats and dogs.

12/13-Aug-1940
Alarm No. 25: 22.39 - 01.09
During intense activity by enemy planes over Sunderland and district, a number of high explosive and incendiary bombs were dropped. There was some damage to property but casualties were few. Other bombs hit the Monsanto Chemical Works. After the raid seven families comprising 25 persons were homeless, neighbours took them in for the night. For a period of two hours raiders crossed the coast near the

The Parade, Hendon

town in relays. At times a great number of searchlights were split up in different sections of the sky. One man was killed when a shower of incendiary bombs fell on East Herrington.
Twenty-one High Explosive bombs fell in fields near Middle Herrington Farm. Little damage and no casualties.
Many people had remarkable escapes when one high explosive bomb fell to the rear of The Parade, Hendon, making a crater 45 feet across and 12 feet deep.
None of the houses had air raid shelters and the residents had taken shelter under their staircases. Despite the fact that the backrooms of a number of properties were completely demolished, the staircases were undamaged and the people sheltering under them were unhurt.

13-Aug-1940
It's official, Sunderland's Spitfire Fund is a reality and it is a Spitfire. A Hurricane had been suggested since it was the type flown by "Sunderland's Own" 607 squadron. The target is set at £5,000 the cost of one Spitfire.
'SS BRIXTON' (1,557t) collier 1551 grt and built by SP.Austin in 1927, Sunderland to London with a cargo of coal, was sunk by a mine off Aldeburgh, Suffolk.

15-Aug-1940
Alarm No. 26: 12.50 - 14.10.
A number of high explosive bombs were dropped and there was tremendous aerial activity over the North East Coast this afternoon. At Sunderland a salvo of bombs were seen to explode in the Fulwell area. Large numbers of Spitfires and Hurricanes were seen flashing in and out of the clouds engaging unseen enemy raiders. At one time many enemy planes, which could not be seen, came right over the centre of the town. The roar of the engines was so loud it was almost impossible to hear the words of a person only a foot away. The barrage put up by the ack-ack batteries in the north ceased firing while the batteries in the south took up the battle.
Many Sunderland families owe their lives to the Anderson shelter. In today's mass air raid when four people died, large numbers of people in their shelters as near as a yard of the bomb craters escaped unhurt. At Eden House, Eden Place, off Fulwell Road, three people were killed after they refused to take shelter, they were

seated at the foot of the stairs when a bomb crashed right through the roof and burst a few yards from them inflicting fatal injuries.

A bomb, which crashed through the roof, demolished the Kemps grocery store in Sea Road but all the staff and customers were in a public shelter over the road.

An express train, travelling north, was said to have been machine gunned by one of the raiders but it was more likely to have damaged by bomb splinters. Bombs were also dropped at Easington (eleven dead) and Seaham (eleven dead).

An enemy plane was reported to have been shot down into the sea off the coast at Ryhope, but no trace of the survivors or the plane has been found.

This day became known to the Luftwaffe as **"Black Thursday"** due to heavy losses suffered. The day was a turning point. German losses convinced the Luftwaffe that air superiority was essential before all-out bombing could be successful. It also marked the virtual end of Luftflotte 5's offensive usefulness; so sparing the North such heavy attacks in future. It also marks the beginning of the end of the Ju 87's usefulness as a dive-bomber and that of the Bf 110 as an escort fighter.

18-Aug-1940

During the weekend the streets in which houses were damaged on Thursday's raid has been the scene of an endless procession of sightseers.

19-Aug-1940

Alarm No. 27: 21.45 - 22.49. A lone bomber was over heard over the town, thousands of people were in the streets returning from theatres and cinemas but no bombs were heard.

Mr E J Jobling-Purser, Managing Director of the Wearside firm James A Jobling & Co. Ltd., handed over two cheques of £5,000. The gift is sufficient to provide two Spitfires.

A Bomb fell in the yards of No.'s 6/8 Viewforth Terrace causing serious damage. Another bomb completely demolished No.'s 10/12

Crowns launch the *HMS HOLLYHOCK* 580t Flower Class Corvette. Royal Navy. Commissioned 19/11/1940. Sunk by aircraft from Japanese carrier East of Ceylon.

Laing's launch the *FISHPOOL* 4947t. 1943 blew up after air attack at Syracuse.

20-Aug-1940

About 13,000 Sunderland school children, many of which have not been able to attend school since the last evacuation, go back to school tomorrow morning (60%). Eight schools, which have been opened on a part time basis during the summer vacation, open tomorrow on the basis of full time instruction. These are Pallion, Hylton Road, Barnes, Havelock, St Columba's C of E, Monkwearmouth Central Grange Park and Fulwell Junior and Infant school. The schools, which will open following improvements in the ARP shelter accommodation, are St Hilda's, Chester Road, St Andrews C of E, Redby, Stansfield Street, Thomas Street schools. Diamond Hall and High Southwick schools reopen on a half time basis for the present.

Churchill delivered his 'So Few' speech.

22-Aug-1940

It is conceivable that a person may escape from a wrecked house in night attire and lose all their other clothing. In cases like this the Assistance Board will, without delay, pay up to £10 per person for new clothing. There is in fact a very comprehensive scheme to deal with the effects of air raid damage. There are centres in which homeless people can be temporally housed and fed and stocks of temporary clothing are held at these centres. Then a Billeting Officer steps into the picture so that people can be billeted with others of the same social standing until houses can be found for them. The Council has to provide houses for all those that have lost their homes.

24-Aug-1940

At present free meals and free milk are provided where the income of the family is 25s per week or less after deducting rent.

Wm. Doxford launches the *REAVELY* 4998t. 1969 scrapped at Whampoa.

25-Aug-1940

Alarm No. 28: 01.42 - 05.00. In the morning enemy aircraft flying singly approached east and northeast coast but few penetrated far. Bombs fell in various parts of the northeast but none in Sunderland. Reported fatalities at Hebburn and South Shields.

25/26-Aug-1940

Alarm No. 29: 01.50 - 03.16.

A number of screaming bombs were dropped on Sunderland earlier today during a raid. The outcome was considerable damage to property in two residential districts on opposite sides of the town.

At Humbledon a bomb demolished 2 Seaforth Road where the residents Arthur & Margaret Taylor, along with neighbours from 30 Humbledon Park, two women named Lisle, had a lucky escape. Both houses were badly damaged. Hill House next door was also badly damaged. Mrs Thompson was injured, seriously enough to be taken to hospital.

No. 2 Seaforth Road

Bombs also fell in Huntingdon Gardens demolishing numbers 8,9 & 10; further bombs destroyed 16, 17, and 18 Hillfield Gardens. A further 100 houses were also damaged.

Bombs dropped during a period of incessant aerial activity enemy planes came in from the sea in relays, one dropped a number of parachute flares some distance north of the town they hung in the sky like Chinese lanterns for some minutes.

To the south there was heavy gunfire with flaming 'onions' mingled with the flash of exploding bombs. The raider which dropped bombs on Sunderland came in low and roared over the town for some minutes many thought that from the sound it was a British plane. In the districts where the bombs fell, houses rocked and windows were shattered most of the houses damaged are owner occupied and represented in some instances a lifetime saving.

No. 8 Huntingdon Gardens

One high explosive bomb at Warden Law and seven at Ryhope. No damage or injury.

At Fulwell, a little later, bombs fell in Prince George Avenue and Marina Avenue resulting with only minor casualties. Anderson shelters again proved their worth in one shelter a few yards from the house which was wrecked by a direct hit by a big calibre bomb Mr A Elliott and his wife, "after a smaller bomb had dropped somewhere near, Mr Elliott, of 18 Prince George Avenue, told a Echo representative "I heard a 'screamer' coming down". Next door, at No. 16, the house of Mr George Stoddard was almost razed, him and his wife had not returned home " it was lucky we had not for Mr Elliott and I would have been outside talking when the bomb fell". In a shelter in a nearby house which was considerably damaged a woman and her two daughters were asleep were awaked by the crash. Another house, which was badly damaged, was immediately opposite Mr Elliott's the elderly couple that owned it were fortunate enough to have left for a short holiday at midday yesterday.

26/27-Aug-1940

Alarm No. 30: 22.15 - 03.36. Bombs fell in coastal areas in Northumberland and Durham

Wearmouth miners voted in favour of working during air raids. Before this Wearmouth was the only lodge in the County to adopt the policy of not working during air raid alerts.

27-Aug-1940

The first batch of women conductors are under training. It is eventually hoped to employ about 60 on all bus services in the town. The 'clippers' are to wear an air force blue uniform which is similar to that worn by the woman's auxiliary air force service (WAAFS).

28-Aug-1940

Alarm No. 31: 22.06 - 22.35

The Medical Officer reported that whooping cough had replaced the measles epidemic. During the four weeks under review the cases of whooping cough was 260 compared with only two cases a year ago.

29-Aug-1940

Two canisters one smoke and one of teargas was released in Blandford Street during a gas raid exercise. Not necessary a surprise as most people in the street seemed to have their gas masks with them.

How the 'raid warnings' operate – It is explained that when enemy aircraft approach this coast observers continually report there movements to Fighter Command of the RAF. The course of the raiders is then plotted on a chart and it is possible to form a judgment of their probable course and probable objective, then follows the Yellow and Purple warnings to the area concerned and the Red warnings to the public when this is received the sirens are sounded in order that the public may take shelter. The siren is sounded only in areas where an attack is likely to develop. If all the area over which raiders flew had Red warnings it would cause serious loss of vital production. Everyone must be prepared as a civic duty to take some risk.

29/30-Aug-1940

Alarm No. 32: 21.28 - 00.29. Alarm No. 33: 02.05 - 03.52

A total of approximately two hundred and fifty enemy aircraft, flying singly and in twos and threes were over the country throughout the night. Bombs fell over a wide area in Northumberland and County Durham. None on Sunderland.

30/31-Aug-1940

Alarm No. 34: 23.59 - 00.14

The Dutch Liner 'VOLENDAM' 15,434 tons that had 320 children bound for Canada. Leaving Britain with convoy OB205. The convoy was attacked by U-boats the ship was damaged and beached on the Isle of Bute. Among the 320 children rescued were two Sunderland boys Frank 13 and Hubert 11 sons of Pastor Hubert Entwisle, pastor of the Elim Evangelical Church in Bedford Street.

After the sinking of the liner the Government were urged to provide American ships for children without further delay. "The danger of the sea crossing are known to all the 200,000 parents who registered their children for safe keeping overseas. If the parents are willing to face these risks we should not be discouraged by the torpedoing of a single ship among all the dozens, which have crossed safely over recent months".

31-Aug/1-Sep-1940

Alarm No. 35: 22.57 - 01.06. Enemy planes were reported in districts of the northeast. Raids began coming in at 10.45 p.m. with single bombers and groups of up to three.

Sightseers, after an air raid, are causing problems. From near and far they haste on foot, on bicycles, in cars in there hundreds and even thousands. Their throng soon blocks the roads around the bombed area. The damaged area should be kept free for ambulances and fire engines.

1/2-Sep-1940

Alarm No. 36: 00.25 - 03.08. Bombs fell in the North and South of the region

2/3-Sep-1940

Alarm No. 37: 22.54 - 00.15. Alarm No. 38: 00.35 - 01.14. Raids concentrated in the Northumberland and Hull areas.

The butter ration is to be cut from 6oz to 4oz.

JL. Thompson launches the *EMPIRE METEOR* 7457t. 2.10.61 ashore and broke in two Kita Daito Jima.

3/4-Sep-1940

Alarm No. 39: 22.18 - 00.00. Scattered bombing raids countrywide. Sunderland not raided.

Serious complaints about the misuse of school shelters by the general public. In some districts whole families congregate outside the shelters at dusk bringing half their household equipment with them and become abusive if the shelter is not opened up at once to allow them to 'camp out'.

Wm. Doxford launches the *ATLANTIC CITY* 5133t. 27.7.1941 torpedoed and damaged by U 141. Salvaged.1963

Short Bros. launches the *EMPIRE LIGHTNING* 6942t. 1959 Scrapped Osaka

5/6-Sep-1940

Alarm No. 40: 22.47 - 01.44.

Two Nazi bombers came to grief over the northeast last night, one a Heinkel was shot down by anti aircraft fire during an air raid over Sunderland. The machine was partially shattered by a direct hit and pieces fell some considerable distances from where the main parts of the plane crashed onto the roofs of two houses in Suffolk Street. The burning plane immediately set fire to the properties on which it crashed, one family who had stayed in their upper rooms escaped out of the burning house and another family, living at No. 55^1/$_2$, who had taken cover in a domestic surface shelter in the backyard suffered casualties. One man was seriously injured by a splinter from an anti aircraft shell while stargazing. Mrs Rachel Stormont 46 was killed and her husband John George Stormont along with daughter Jean (15) was removed to hospital with injuries. The father was severely injured but the daughter's injuries are slight (in fact she lost both hands). Happily, Jean, at 18 with special adapted limbs, began the career that she thought was lost to her as a Telephonist on the 8th June 1943.

There was little left of the Heinkel after the fire, demolition parties were left working all day digging in the mass of debris and wreckage to find if any German airmen were buried underneath. One of the dead German airmen had apparently jumped from the plane for his parachute was found partly opened. The first dead German found had fallen on top of a public shelter in the grounds of a large house formally used as a school he had been killed outright. It was sometime before they found the second body in a garden. The Heinkel's crew were buried with military honours in Castletown Cemetery.

Debris from the crashed bomber is being inspected the following day

ARP clearing the site of the crashed plane in Suffolk Street

The Feeding Centre in Herrington Street Methodist Schoolroom was put into operation at once and meals were provided for 300 people on the first day it was opened. The centre remained open for six days until the last of the 'evacuees' were able to return home.

Two hours after the Suffolk Street incident another enemy bomber dropped a number of bombs around the railway station causing considerable damage to the station.

The Town Hall had a remarkable escape although the bomb wrecked property immediately adjoining the only damage done to the Town hall was a number of broken windows, the staff shelter was partly buried in the bomb crater but no one was in it at the time.

Residents of Hendon made homeless by the crashed bomber and by unexploded bombs, which littered the area

Offices of a building society was damaged and a public reading rooms were partially demolished, these were opened as usual this morning and people were calmly reading newspapers and periodicals but in the interest of safety the authorities ordered the building closed.

The two photographs below show the Station before and after clean-up

The damage in Station Street, which ran between Union Street and Fawcett Street.

The explosion sent a piece of debris (truck wheels and axle) of several tons some 50 yards through the air and across a main road it crashed into the window of Joseph's a sports a sports outfitter's shop. The roadway outside the shop was blocked with debris for some time. The Empress Hotel, near the shop was undamaged and staff and residents sheltering in the cellar. A man named Bell, a cleaner on night duty at the Station, was at work 30 yards from where a large bomb crashed through the roof. He was blown down and taken to hospital suffering from shock and abrasions but otherwise had a remarkable escape.

7-Sep-1940

In recent air raids people have been foolish, the thrills of watching a concentrated attack upon raiding aircraft has overcome their natural caution and, instead of remaining under cover, they have come out into the open to watch. What goes up must come down and concentrated anti aircraft fire will mean that shrapnel will fall over a wide area and can inflict injury as serious as any bomb.

From 7 September 1940 to 16 May 1941, the Luftwaffe carried out an intensive bombing campaign against British cities and industries. London was attacked on fifty-seven consecutive nights between 7 September and 2 November 1940 and experienced further heavy raids in December 1940 and March, April and May 1941. Fifteen other British cities were subjected to major bombing attacks.

Some, like Coventry, suffered extensive damage. Over 41,000 British civilians were killed and 137,000 injured during the Blitz. Although the bombing caused widespread destruction, civilian morale remained high and war production was not seriously affected.

8-Sep-1940

Alarm No. 41: 13.05 - 13.42. Reconnaissance flights by enemy aircraft reported between Sunderland and The Wash.

For the second time this year Sunderland people responded readily to the King's appeal for a day of National Prayer and churches of all denominations had exceptional large attendances yesterday.

The Hurricanes of 607 Squadron left Usworth for Tangmere, a sector airfield on the South Coast of England, within 11 Group of Fighter Command. They were replaced by Hurricanes of 43 Squadron, which had suffered terribly while at Tangmere, coming north for a rest period. They saw no action but did lose four aircraft and two pilots killed in flying accidents.

Carriage wheels and part of the Station roof ended up in the front of Joseph's shop

9-Sep-1940

Alarm No. 42: 02.10 - 02.56. Alarm No. 43: 21.07 - 21.16. Enemy planes were thought to be in the vicinity of a northeast town this afternoon.

10-Sep-1940

Alarm No. 44: 02.44 - 03.45. Alarm No. 45: 04.06 - 04.15. Hull raided.

Springwell Farm comprising of 103 acres. In January 1936 the Minister of Health authorised the compulsory purchase of the land for the purposes of the Housing Act, two notices to date had been served on Mr Horn, the legal owner, and the greater part of the land had been taken over. The present application was only concerned with the farm buildings, which were not required for any purpose of housing. The corporation had erected a public house on the land (The Prospect?) and commenced the construction of an arterial road. It was contested that the original Council's notice, served on Mr Horn, did not cover the farm buildings. Lawyer (Mr Charlesworth) for the Corporation contended that the notice affected the whole of the land including the farm buildings. Mr Charlesworth wanted to get rid of the plaintiff who had caused the Corporation endless litigation, he added that it was important that the land should be put to agricultural uses by the Autumn. It was assumed that all housing on the Springwell Estate would be completed after the war. The roads and sewers were ready. Mr Horn was not in possession of the farm buildings himself they were occupied by his bailiff who was really in the nature of a trespasser. The Corporation regarded the present application as another step to delay the compulsory purchase proceedings.

11-Sep-1940

A new system of giving air raid warnings at industrial establishments, to prevent raids from interfering seriously with production, has been agreed too by representative of employers and employees and in consultation with the Government. The warning by sirens will be regarded as the alert and not as an alarm signal, work will continue until watchers on the roofs and vantage points give warning of danger when workers will take cover. It is hoped to start the scheme at once and the RAF have agreed to train watchers. The new system will combine maximum industrial output with the greatest possible protection for those at home. Working after the siren has sounded clearly involves risk but all engaged on vital production are front line troops.

12-Sep-1940

Sunderland Council agreed to the recommendation of the Transport Committee to withdraw the 2d universal fare on the trams. There was must opposition especially from those speaking for the people who have moved to the outskirts of the town. Where there are several members of the family using the trams a rise in cost of travel can mean rising cost of travel from 1s to 2s 6d is a serious matter but as to all questions there are two sides. It was considered that an economic price must be paid for a ride on a public service vehicle and just because people have moved to the outskirts it was no reason to expect preferential treatment. The lack of passengers to Roker and Seaburn and to football matches was blamed on the losses on the trams.

13-Sep-1940

It was revealed at Sunderland Police Court today by the Deputy Clerk to the Magistrates, Mr W Scott, that there had been more than 750 'lights' cases since the war began (that is a staggering 62 a month).

14-Sep-1940

Alarm No. 46: 10.40 - 11.09. During the day, many places countrywide raided, sometimes by only a single bomber although none appear to have come close to land.

15-Sep-1940

Alarm No. 47: 03.04 - 04.19. Enemy aircraft attacking shipping.

The climax of the Battle of Britain, remembered as The Battle of Britain Day. Although it is not apparent at the time or for several weeks afterward, this is the last real attempt by the Luftwaffe to destroy the resistance of Fighter Command.

16-Sep-1940

Alarm No. 48: 15.17 - 16.19. Enemy aircraft attacking shipping.

The Mayor officially closed the Spitfire Fund at a concert in The Royal the final total was £21,769 1s 9d.

17-Sep-1940

Alarm No. 49: 20.05 - 20.51. Newcastle raided.

The 'City of Benares' carrying 90 children and nine escorts to Canada, under an evacuation scheme to Canada, was torpedoed and sunk. 83 of the children and seven of their escorts were lost. Nine were from Sunderland, Peter Short (5), Dorothy Wood (9), brother and sister Ann Watson (6) and Thomas Watson (9), Maureen Dixon (10), Derek Leigh (11), Sisters Edith Smith (13) and Irene Smith (10) and George Crawford (13). There were two surviving Sunderland children Billy Short (9), brother to Peter who was lost, and Eleanor Wright (13). Plans for overseas evacuation were cancelled.

18-Sep-1940

Alarm No. 50: 20.42 - 22.21. Both the Tyne and Tees attacked.

Operation Seelöwe (Sealion) invasion is postponed yet again, this time indefinitely. The German invasion fleet began to disperse from the Channel ports. The later reports of the German navy show that 1918 barges have been assembled, of which 214 had been sunk or damaged. Similarly 21 out of 170 transports had been lost. They had been under constant day and night attack from Bomber and Coastal Command.

21/22-Sep-1940

Alarm No. 51: 21.44 - 00.38. Bombs dropped in the sea near Seaham Harbour docks around midnight. No damage and no casualties.

No October half term this year the authorities considers it is better that the children should be attending school within reach of a shelter.

Following complaints from householders in the Reception Areas about having to provide meals for parents and friends visiting their evacuated children. If any parents or friends planning to visit children today they should heed the appeal and take with them their own refreshments.

23-Sep-1940

The price of petrol rose to 2s 0½d (10p) per gallon today.

The question of 'blacking out' the old market in High Street East was before the Sunderland Estates Committee tonight. It was stated that with so much glass in the roof of the building the cost of providing material for the blackout would be in the region of £200. It was decided that no action would be taken and that the market was not to be used after dark.

THE SOWER

THE REAPER

24-Sep-1940

Alarm No. 52: 04.04 - 06.00. Whitton, Co. Durham, One bomb dropped in a ploughed field.

25-Sep-1940

The lead figures known locally as the 'babies' who have gazed across the ravine at Roker Park for a half a century or more have gone to play their part in the war effort, they are to be melted down for the lead they contain. They originally adorned the gateposts to the Stafford family mansion situated at the corner of Fulwell Road and Broad Street (now known as Roker Avenue). The figures represented the 'Sower' and the 'Reaper'

26-Sep-1940

Alarm No. 53: 22.59 - 23.37. No action recorded

28-Sep-1940

Meat ration increased to 2s 2d per head per week.

30-Sep-1-Oct-1940

Alarm No. 54: 21.41 - 22.08. Alarm No. 55: 22.29 - 22.39. Alarm No. 56: 00.04 - 00.27

Butter ration down to 2oz per head.

A volunteer Sunderland air raid warden Mr Thomas Jones, 37 of Sea Road Fulwell, is among the first batch of ARP men to receive a special commendation from the King for gallantry in action during air raids.

He won the award during daylight raids on Sunderland on August 15th. He was wounded in three places by bomb splinters and is still receiving treatment to this day.

2/3-Oct-1940
Alarm No. 57: 23.21 - 23.37. Alarm No. 58: 03.27 - 03.47. RAF Usworth attacked.

3-Oct-1940
Pickersgill's launch the *STANFORD* 5969t. Scrapped Greece Feb. 1962.

4-Oct-1940
Bartram's launch the freighter *PENTRIDGE HILL* 7579t. Scrapped March 1965 at Tamise.

5/6-Oct-1940
Alarm No. 59: 23.59 - 00.25. Mine laying suspected.

6-Oct-1940
New entertainment tax to operate from today, it will affect all prices of admission for both live and non-live entertainment. A person at present paying 1/6d hands over 3d in duty; in future 4d will go to taxation.

7-Oct-1940
Alarm No. 60: 21.13 - 22.20. Enemy aircraft were over the Sunderland area. Bombs fell in fields at Washington

Sunderland's industrial firwatcher trainees attended South Shields College today where they will learn to identify aircraft and issue warnings.

Bartram's launch the *RICHMOND HILL* 7579t. Scrapped July 1966 at Yokosuka, Japan

8-Oct-1940
Alarm No. 61: 21.15 - 21.57. Bombs fell in Cleadon.

The long running dispute between Mr Alan Horn, of Rosedeen, former owner of Springwell farm, and Sunderland Corporation finally came to an end. Work had started with the erection of The Prospect public house and roads and sewers. The work was suspended and the land put to agricultural use again.

9-Oct-1940
Alarm No. 62: 20.55 - 22.37. No action recorded.

10-Oct-1940
Alarm No. 63: 19.55 - 21.55

A tremendous barrage of anti aircraft fire drove off enemy planes, which raided Sunderland tonight They dropped four high explosive bombs near the Green at Southwick, which demolished two houses but caused only two casualties, neither of them serious. There was another raid during the early morning but no bombs were dropped. Customers at the Savoy cinema stayed seated while bombs were falling close by. The film starring Marie Wilson in the horseracing comedy "Sweepstakes Winner" must have been good.

A bomb hit a two-story house at the end of a terrace and almost cut it in half (1 Wellington Street). The occupant Mr George Lynn, a brick layer and his wife and four of their six children had amazing escapes.

Mary Taylor 66, Adam Fairley 66 were seriously injured, they were in rooms at 41 The Green (shown opposite) above a shop (Luxdon's), which received a direct hit.

1 Wellington Street

Another bomb fell at the rear of The Green and demolished an unused building

11-Oct-1940
Alarm No. 64: 20.28 - 22.27. Bombs fell in rural Co. Durham. No casualties.

12-Oct-1940
Alarm No. 65: 20.01 - 20.53.
Mine laying took place at points between the Farne Islands and the Humber.
Operation Sealion, the invasion of Britain, was formally cancelled as Hitler directed his attention towards Russia.

41 The Green

13-Oct-1940
'HM Summer Rose' (96t) a minesweeping drifter was sunk by an enemy mine off Sunderland and lies in 12 metres of water.

15-Oct-1940
The Spitfire Fund cheque for £21,769 1s 9d donated by the people of Sunderland was in a London's Carlton Club which was bombed on Monday night it was later rescued from the rubble and yesterday Mr Storey MP handed over the check to Lord Beaverbrook.

16-Oct-1940
Ministry of Food appeals again to housewives to save bones. Bones were to be used to make glue for aircraft or glycerine for explosives.

17-Oct-1940
At 0400 on the 16th, at almost full speed in murky drizzle, HMS FAME ran straight onto the beach at Whitburn

Rifle Range. HMS ASHANTI was right astern and doing 7 knots struck the Fame a glancing blow on her port quarter and ended up alongside with Fame catching fire.

Hearing all the commotion, the defence post ashore thought the invasion had started and raised the alarm, but daylight showed the destroyers so high and dry they could be walked round at low tide. Sunderland Fire Brigade manhandled their pumps and equipment over the rocks to put Fame's fire out. The Roker Volunteer Life Saving Brigade consisting of Captains N Wharton, F Albion and B Robinson and 12 men assisted them in this task. They had the dual task of putting N F S men aboard to fight the fires and after 12 hours with the weather deteriorating they brought ashore 186 men from the two vessels.

Greenwell & Co. patched and welded and sealed off what they could during the brief hours of low tide and after

a fortnight Ashanti (who had priority treatment) was re-floated and taken to Sunderland. Greenwell's made her more seaworthy for the longer tow to Swan Hunter & Wigham Richardson at Wallsend on the Tyne for complete rebuilding. Fame also lived to run again, but the affair was a closely kept secret.

20-Oct-1940
The *SS CAIRNGLEN* 5019t, built by Pickersgill's in 1926, went aground at Marsden in heavy fog. The combined power of wind and wave drove the CAIRNGLEN further inshore, where she broke her back on the reef. The Roker Volunteer Life Saving Brigade was in attendance for 22 hours and rescued 16 men from the ship's lifeboat and 35 crewmembers by breeches buoy (seen opposite). William Burton volunteered to go on board to help a sick seaman and for this act of courage was later awarded a BEM.

Local people 'rescued' her much-needed cargo of butter, bacon and tins of powdered egg.
On the 22ⁿᵈ July 1926, shortly before the launch of the CAIRNGLEN, about 100 men were climbing a gangway to start work when the gangway suddenly gave way. Fifty men were injured, three died and 15 were hospitalised.

21-Oct-1940
Purchase Tax introduced today as stated in the budget of 23ʳᵈ July 1940. The tax will be imposed on all goods except food and children's clothing.

23/24-Oct-1940

Alarm No. 66: 18.30 - 18.48. Alarm No. 67: 04.00 - 05.14. Northumberland and Yorkshire raided.

24-Oct-1940

Emergency Powers (Defence)—Summer Time dated 24th October 1940, to make the time be one hour in advance of GMT throughout the year.

26-Oct-1940

Alarm No. 68: 00.47 - 03.16

Nearly 500 men ceased work at Wearmouth colliery having completed the fortnight's notice. Shortage of trade is the reason for this payoff. In recent weeks Wearmouth colliery has worked only 2 or 3 days each week. Ministry of Food subsidises fish and chip shops to encourage potato consumption.

Following an attack by a German long-range bomber the Captain of the EMPRESS OF BRITAIN, of 42,348 tons, ordered abandon ship. With a skeleton crew still on board the ship was later torpedoed and sunk. She was the greatest loss for the Allied forces during the entire war. Mr George James Bonwick of 17 Broad Meadows a junior officer later retold the story of the attack.

27-Oct-1940

Alarm No. 69: 02.10 - 03.09. Minelaying.

Off the Yorkshire coast the cargo ship 'SS SUAVITY' (634t) en route from Sunderland to London with a cargo of wheat, hit a mine and sank.

28/29-Oct-1940

Alarm No. 70: 19.59 - 20.32. Alarm No. 71: 20.39 - 23.43

One enemy machine is believed to have been brought down off the northeast coast during several air raids last night and early today. Anti aircraft batteries put up the heaviest barrage heard so far in the area. High explosive bombs fell over a wide area of Durham County, non-in Sunderland.

Wm. Doxford launches the *EMPIRE MIST* 7241t. 1969 scrapped Hong Kong.

30-Oct-1940

Furniture stored in repositories by those who have closed their homes is now liable to be requisitioned to assist the re-housing of the homeless. Only the simplest kind of furniture will be taken, valuable antiques will not be touched. The owners will be compensated.

31-Oct-1940

An appeal is made to all landlords and house owners to give up their iron railings for war purposes. Compensation totalling £2,650 were awarded to the widows and dependant children of two riveters, Robert Durey (39), of Florida Street, Pallion and George Hill (57), of Fordham Road, Ford Estate, that were killed when a staging collapsed while working at Short Brothers Yard, Pallion on March 7th.

Short Bros. launches the *NEWBROUGH* 5255t. Scrapped Hong Kong Oct. 1969.

1-Nov-1940

Alarm No. 72: 17.45 - 18.03. Alarm No. 73: 20.15 - 20.42. Alarm No. 74: 22.12 - 22.54. Coastal convoys and trawlers attacked. Ministry of Food is now the sole importer of frozen cod fillets. Price fixed at 1s 3d per lb.

Wm. Doxford launches the *ANTAR* 5222t. 1963 scrapped at Hong Kong.

2-Nov-1940

Sunderland's War Weapons Week begins today. The task sets the Borough a target of £1,000,000; the target is sufficient to pay for two destroyers. Its two fold aim is to raise a specified amount for war funds by investment in various kinds of government securities and secondly and perhaps even more importantly, to increase and strengthen the regular saving habit for everyone. Small and local authorities around Sunderland were asked to co-operate and make it a real Wearside effort. The Mayor Councillor Myers Wayman launched the campaign from the steps of the central library.

A procession through the town and a Me109 on display at Turvey's garage at Holmeside were two of the attractions.

3-Nov-1940

Alarm No.75: 18.14 - 18.45. Otterburn Camp, Northumberland attacked.

4-Nov-1940

The Ministry of Labour launches today a big safety campaign to reduce accidents and secure greater safety in war factories. In a message to both managers and workers he stresses that accidents in factories are a bonus to the enemy. Anything that prevents disruption at work is worthwhile. Accidents in factories in 1939 totalled 193,475. In the first 6 months of the war non fatal accidents increased by 13% and fatal accidents by 42%. The maximum retail price of onions of $4^1/_2$d per lb will come into force today also the price of lemons will be controlled at a maximum of 65d per lb, equal to about 2d a lemon.

9-Nov-1940

Alarm No.76: 08.00 - 08.17. A Junkers 88 dropped a number of incendiary bombs in a north east coast district this morning.

11-Nov-1940

No ceremony today for Armistice Day. No public observance of the 2 minutes silence and no public ceremony. It was Wearside's strangest Armistice Day for the first time since 1918 the ceremony around the cenotaph seemed to lack reality even though it possessed its original sincerity. There were several hundred people around the memorial mostly women watching the Mayor and Mayoress lay a wreath.

Wearside's War Weapons Week: The total realized during the week was officially announced today as £1,038,932 11s 6d.

SS PITWINES a 932t coaster is bombed and sunk by aircraft the wreck lies 7 miles NE of The Heugh, Hartlepool. 2nd Eng. Officer Gilbert (22), lost his life. King's Commendation for Brave Conduct. Son of Mr. and Mrs. Horace Gilbert; husband of Ethel Gilbert, of Grindon, Sunderland. Awarded Lloyd's War Medal.

13-Nov-1940

Trench shelters at The Green is only for the use of Technical College students and staff and were not for use by the public until after 9-30pm.

In a ceremony conducted in the Corporation Yard at Eden Vale the Mayor presented Certificates of Commendation to members of the Rescue & Demolition Service for their bravery and devotion to duty. The two men were foreman E. Semple and assistant foreman A. Groves.

JL. Thompson launches the *EMPIRE SUNRISE* 7459t. 2.11.42 Torpedoed and sunk by U.84. Total crew 51 all saved.

'SS EMPIRE WIND' (7,459t) sunk by Focke-Wulf Condor aircraft, 250m W of Ireland. Two Wearside boys Edward Murta 14, mess room boy, of Front Street, East Boldon and Morris Edmundson 15, deck boy, of Mitford Street, Fulwell were among the crew rescued.

13/14-Nov-1940

Alarm No.77: 20.47 - 00.04. Coastal areas raided.

15-Nov-1940

The four Spitfires paid for by the townspeople of Sunderland are completed and will shortly go into service marked as Sunderland 1, 2, 3 and 4.

'SS BLUE GALLEON' (712t) cargo ship, London to Sunderland sunk by German aircraft off Aldeburgh.

16-Nov-1940

Alarm No.78: 17.53 - 18.22. Minelaying took place off the East coast.

Superintendent Thomas Bruce of the Sunderland Fire Brigade is awarded the George Cross for gallantry. When a German bomber crashed in Suffolk Street on September 6th. He led a team that rescued the Stormont family from a burning shelter.

Maximum retail prices of torch batteries fixed to prevent profiteering and speculation.

18-Nov-1940

Alarm No.79: 20.02 - 22.25. Minelaying took place off the East coast.

20-Nov-1940

Durham County War Agricultural Committee ordered Sunderland Corporation to undertake the cultivation of Springwell Farm immediately.

21-Nov-1940

Hand torches may now be used after the alert has sounded but they must show less light than before. The aperture through which the light is admitted must not be more than one inch in diameter and must be dimmed. The first Community Social Centre in Sunderland opened today on Flodden Road, Ford Estate.

22-Nov-1940

Call for the Corporation Transport Committee to keep the trams and buses running during alerts as per the District buses, which continue to run as if nothing has happened but the Corporation trams and buses stop dead in their tracks the moment the siren goes.

23-Nov-1940

Alarm No.80: 18.16 - 19.59. Minelaying off the Northumberland and Durham coastal areas.

Saving an egg; when making Yorkshire puddings or batter add a heaped teaspoon of custard powder to each quarter pound of flour used, the result will be a tasty creamy pudding.

25-Nov-1940

All departments of the Hudson Road School open today. There remain only 10 school departments in Sunderland operating on a half time basis.

26-Nov-1940

The Ministry of Labour announced last night no Bank Holiday on Boxing Day only one-day holiday over Xmas and New Year. All workers are asked to take one day off either Xmas Day or New Years Day.

27-Nov-1940

The RMS RANGITANE is attacked and sunk by the German surface raiders. The survivors were imprisoned on the raiders and were eventually released on a small tropical island. Mr John Wilson Almond, son of a Sunderland Ship Master and a junior officer on board the RANGITANE, was among those who were later rescued. He returned to Sunderland in June 1941.

28-Nov-1940

Alarm No.81: 22.11 - 22.22. Minelaying off the Northumberland and Durham coast.

Following complaints of dampness in the town's shelter accommodation the War Emergency Committee made a tour of inspection of public trench and communal shelters. The trench shelters were not that bad considering they were meant only to be used short term by people caught in the streets during the alert. A word of praise for the comfortable, tidy appearance of many of the communal shelters but a number of this type was found to be in a deplorable, filthy and disgusting state vandalised with refuse and filth scattered all over. The Corporation have carried out repairs but the same level of destruction is repeated therefore public money will no longer be wasted on the shelters in question.

29-Nov-1940

A 17-year-old apprentice electrician's "joke" in which a code, a plan, a threat of sabotage and a pro Hitler poster featured was in court today. He pleaded guilty to recording information, which might be of value to the enemy. George Anderson Garbutt of Scruton Avenue Humbledon, a Home Guardsman, was fined £20.

1-Dec-1940

The Board of Trade announces further restrictions on the purchase of luxury goods beginning today for a period up to 31st May 1941. Reductions in home trade is based on that supplied between the same period last year. The quota of corsets, garters and surgical goods will be down 50% of last years sales, mattresses and similar items at 25%, pottery at 50%, carpets at 33%, cameras, perfumery, fancy goods, goldsmiths/silversmiths wares, toys and other articles at 25%.

With the ban of silk stockings coming into force today women had been buying as many pairs as possible. The Echo however thought that there was no need to worry, as most women would be pleasantly surprised when they see the latest fine wool stockings, which were specially designed to flatter the calf line. Prohibition on silk stockings does not apply to the retailer's present stock. Only the stocks of manufacturers and wholesalers will be affected. The manufactures believe that the ban is unreasonable since huge stocks that cannot be delivered will be left on their hands.

2-Dec-1940

New ration books issued today mean that housewives who do not wish to change their retailers have no need to re-register.

A campaign is introduced telling people how to make shelters healthy and comfortable. Rules of good conduct posters were also issued.

The torpedoing of five vessels two of which two were Sunderland built. The 'LADY GLANLEY', built in 1938 by Wm. Doxford and the 'GOODLEIGH', built in 1938 by Pickersgill's.

3-Dec-1940

The list at Sunderland police court comprised of 71 cases, 44 of them concerned cyclists charged with riding without lights. Defendants were fined five shillings for having a front or rear light missing and 10 shillings for having no lights at all. Southwick and Hendon had the most cases.

8-Dec-1940

Notices for approximately 1000 employees of Silksworth Colliery expired today and the colliery will close down far an indefinite period. This is said to be due to the loss of overseas coal markets.

9-Dec-1940

The ban, which prevented visitors to the coastal areas for purposes of recreational, holidays or pleasure, has been removed. But restrictions still exist on beaches and foreshores.

10-Dec-1940

All but 86 of the redundant miners (485) of Wearmouth Colliery who recently lost their jobs because of lack of trade have been found jobs in other parts of the country.

11-Dec-1940

The first supplies of the new ration books have now been delivered. 10,000 persons in Sunderland as yet have not made their application for a new ration book; this is only six per cent of the total but they run the risk of having to go without rations. Some large families will not care however for they cannot afford to buy the authorised rations for every member of the family consequently they never take out ration books for them all.

12-Dec-1940

Alarm No.82: 15.10 - 15.22. No action recorded.

Sunderland's transport workers voted against working during alert periods after dark. They considered that they were being asked to risk their lives by working during raids.

13-Dec-1940

Lord Woolton's announcement that the only fresh fruit to escape the import ban is to be the Orange will be received with mixed feelings. On Wearside recently the Orange has been just about the most difficult of the fresh fruits to buy. It was interesting to note that while the Orange was conspicuous by its absence from Sunderland's shops they were fairly freely on sale in Newcastle. How does this happen?

14-Dec-1940

Although not officially rationed, local tobacconists have to restrict their customer's purchases as their supplies of tobacco have been cut.

Crowns launch the *HMS BURDOCK* 580t Flower Class Corvette. Royal Navy. Scrapped in August 1946.

Wm. Doxford launches the *EMPIRE DAWN* 7241t. 12.9.42 Sunk by German surface raider MICHEL.

15-Dec-1940

JL. Thompson launches the *EMPIRE MOON* 7472t. 1970 scrapped Shanghai.

16-Dec-1940

Meat rationing returned to 1s 10d as from today.

Lord Woolton's Xmas box is the doubling of allowances of sugar to 12oz and of tea to 4oz for one week only.

17-Dec-1940

Sunderland butchers opened their shops today but did not sell any meat. It was decided yesterday that this should be a meatless day because the supply of imported meat this week had been delayed through transport difficulties. Up to midday the meat had not arrived in Sunderland. It was expected by tomorrow morning, when retailers would be able to draw their allocation of imported meat. It turned up two days late.

A nice leg of lamb or a juicy breast of mutton may have to be the choice of most people on Wearside for their Xmas dinner. Next week Sunderland butchers have been informed that the allocation of meat will be 80% mutton and lamb and only 20% of beef.

Ships of two coastal convoys ran into a minefield in the Thames Estuary off Southend. Five cargo ships were sunk, including the 'SS BENEFICENT' (2,944t), built by Pickersgill's in 1932, Six crew lost

18-Dec-1940

Referees with glasses will soon be seen on football fields now that the Football Association have relaxed their ruling forbidding the registration as a referee of a person who wears spectacles.

20-Dec-1940

The Mayor appeals to Sunderland townspeople to give their support to the town's blackout road safety campaign now being conducted by the National Safety First Association.

The 2d universal return, centre of controversy in recent months, is to disappear from Sunderland's trams and buses. The Ministry of Transport has today notified the Corporation that it is prepared to agree to the request for the abolition of the 2d return fare and the substitution of $1\frac{1}{2}$d single any distance ticket available up to 9am and between 4.30 to 6pm. The last day for 2d universal return will be December 31st. At the November meeting of the town council it was stated that permission had been refused.

21-Dec-1940

Among the passengers rescued from the torpedoed liner WESTERN PRINCE *was shipbuilder Mr Cyril Thompson a director of JL Thompson and Sons Ltd at North Sands. Mr Thompson had been in America representing the Admiralty to negotiate the construction of tonnage. He introduced a JL Thompson's design that made it simpler to build a ship. This "Ocean" hull design became the basis for the Liberty Ship.*

24-Dec-1940

Final preparations for the 'make the best of it' Christmas on Wearside today. Shopkeepers are surprised at the volume of business. Toy dealers have been exceptionally busy despite the high prices of toys it would appear that there is much more money in circulation than in some years passed. Despite the big rise in the price of poultry compared with last year turkeys and ducks are in good supply but there has been a great shortage of chickens.

25-Dec-1940

A feature of Christmas Day this year is the presence in many homes of soldiers, sailors and airmen unable to reach their own home. County Durham mines have today and New Year's Day as holidays. Shipyard workers and those engaged on work of "national importance" have only today off, they will of course receive extra payment for Boxing Day and New Years Day.

27-Dec-1940

The whole scheme of air-raid precautions in Sunderland has been revised and strengthened in light of experience so tragically gained in London, Coventry and other English towns, which have withstood the full fury of the enemy air attack. One of the lessons learned is the need for prompt tackling of the incendiary menace, which the enemy uses as a preliminary to his attack with high explosives. If the incendiary bombs can be tackled at once and the flames prevented from getting a serious hold enemy airmen are deprived of this deadly aid. For tackling the firebomb menace Sunderland has ample supply from water available from a variety of sources and all have been tabulated. Loads of sand will be tipped in every street and householders will be invited to help themselves. Arrangements have been made for the training of people from every street pending in the arrival of the fire brigade or A F S. Experience, so tragically gained by other towns and cities, has shown that it is much safer to have people scattered in small shelters so the Council are pushing ahead in building domestic shelters and small communal shelters.

Short Bros. launches the *EMPIRE SUMMER* 6949t. 1984-5 Deleted from Lloyd's Register.

Pickersgill's launch the *EMPIRE CLOUD* 5969t. 21.8.42 torpedoed by U.564.

28-Dec-1940

A verdict of accidental death was returned at a Sunderland inquest on Harris Couples Logan 45, of 11 Argyle Street Sunderland who died in the Royal Infirmary on Christmas Day. On December 6th about 10:10pm an eyewitness saw a bus turn into Park Lane it was then the witness saw Logan walk right into the bus. Wm. Doxford launches the *DALTONHALL* 5175t. 1958 sold to Liberia renamed *ALTIS*

The Food Control Officer warns of meat shortages.

28-Dec-1940

To the citizens of Sunderland from the Mayor: 'We have passed through a year of very great stress and strain. To everyone in the ARP and Civil Defence I tender my warmest thanks. I would like to express my best wishes for 1941 to all of Sunderland's citizens. May the New Year bring us victory and peace and may we look forward to happier times.'

1941
Bombing Intensifies

The damaged Winter Gardens

- 115 air raid warnings with 75 fatalities.
- Binns Stores gutted by Incendiaries
- Victoria Hall demolished by Parachute Mine. The same bomb so badly damages the Winter Gardens that they have to be dismantled.

1-Jan-1941

The New Year was welcomed by another display of the rare (rare to us) phenomenon of the Northern Lights. From about 9:00pm onwards the sky in the north was illuminated by a steady glow varying in its intensity and gradually changing colour from of pale white to a dull orange. As the night progressed vivid flashers were shooting up from the Northern horizon that lit up the whole sky. The display lasted until well after 3am up and gave 1941 an impressive entrance. Let's hope it heralds a brighter year than that which has gone.

2-Jan-1941

Sunderland has nearly 500 squads of 'bomb fire' fighters but it needs another 500 if the blitz is to be tackled with real success. The town has anticipated by some months, Mr Herbert Morrison's broadcast appeal for men to train to fight the menace of the incendiary bomb and since the appeal there has been big increase in the number of volunteers.

3-Jan-1941

12 of the fatal accidents in Sunderland during 1940 occurred during blackout conditions. The number of persons killed 27 was the largest recorded for many years, 18 of the 27 were pedestrians, 5 were pedal cyclists, 1 was a motor cyclist and 3 were passengers alighting from motor vehicles. Seven children under five were among the fatal cases they were all killed during daylight hours. Two of the pedal cyclists killed were children of 13. Three older people all over 80 were killed in the blackout.

6-Jan-1941

The meat ration is to be reduced from 1s 10d per head per week to 1s 2d from today it will also include pork and most offal. Manufactured meat products such as sausages will continue to be available off the coupon. From today bacon and ham, butter and margarine, cooking fats and sugar, if a housewife is unable for any reason to buy her ration of these foods during the week for which the coupons are available she may buy them during the week immediately following. The housewife may continue to buy two week's tea ration either one week in advance or one week in arrears. The ration of meat can only be bought in the week for which the coupons are available.

SS EMPIRE THUNDER (5,965t), completed by Pickersgill only recently, suffered engine failure and was torpedoed and sunk in the North-western Approaches, with the loss of nine crewmembers.

7-Jan-1941

With the completion of the trench shelter programme all Wearside schools are open full time. The new Plains Farm School also opened yesterday.

9-Jan-1941

'The time for safety first for the individual during air raids is gone. We must all be prepared to take risks to save the community and our own homes', so said the Mayor when he made a further strong appeal for Wearsiders to organise their own local fire watching and fire fighting units.

JL. Thompson launches the *CONFIELD* 4956t. 09.10.1940 Torpedoed and sunk. 1 crewmember lost.

10-Jan-1941

Compulsory service may be the only solution to difficulties, which are arising over the Government plan for having a firebomb watcher in all substantial buildings. The order just made under the Defence Regulations provides that a firebomb fighter must be present on all premises in which more than 30 persons work and states definitely that the occupier or occupiers of the premises are responsible. The Minister of Home Security states that as the air-raid warning is now to be treated as an alert only it is open to any pedestrian to go on his way after a warning so long as he wishes but he should be prepared to take cover if he hears guns, bombs or enemy aircraft near by.

11-Jan-1941

The Air Training Corps is the new Air Ministry scheme for spare time training of boys from 16 to 18 for eventual service in the RAF and Fleet Air Arm. It will replace the existing Air Defence Cadet Corps squadron No. 111 (Sunderland) Squadron, which came into operation in April 1939 and this will be the nucleus of the local squadron of the ATC No.111.

HMS SOUTHAMPTON bombed and then sunk while escorting a convoy in the Mediterranean. Leading Seaman F Alston (33), of Sunderland, lost his life.

12-Jan-1941

Alarm No.83: 19.50 - 20.02. Reports of enemy air activity came from several parts of the northeast coast.

13-Jan-1941

Sweeping new price controls to counter food profiteering were announced today. Wholesalers and retailers have been ordered not to sell certain foods ranging from dead poultry to pickles at prices higher than those charged at the beginning of last month. More than 20 food items including coffee cocoa rice spaghetti biscuits custard and jelly are effectively frozen in price. Announcing the controls the Food Minister, Lord Woolton, revealed that growing numbers of speculators had appeared in the food industry and that these people are trying to render a bad service to the nation. They will have their fingers burned as a result of the stabilising order. More price controls are likely in the near future.

Bartram's launch the freighter *EMPIRE SURF* 6641t. 14.1.42 Torpedoed and sunk. 47 of the 53 crew lost.

14-Jan-1941

Measles are at epidemic proportions in Sunderland. The Medical Officer of Health reproached some mothers for their mistaken belief that the sooner their child caught the measles the better.

15-Jan-1941

The average working-class family in Britain lives on a weekly budget of less than £5 a week (Equivalent today to £181.85 using the retail price index).

The Hurricanes of 607 (County of Durham) Squadron of Usworth, which was formed at Usworth in September 1932, finally moved to RAF MacMurry in Scotland. From henceforth fighter defences were based at Ouston and until the end of the war Usworth was used in a training role.

16-Jan-1941

The courts were told that fines were no punishment for women that harbour alien seamen since the seamen themselves pay the fine. Annie Fitzsimmons 36, of Queen Street, who pleaded not guilty, was sentenced to prison for two months.

18-Jan-1941

Damage estimated at £16,000 was done in the early hours of this morning when Wearside's biggest wartime blaze (Binns was yet to come) gutted Ditchburn's chair factory in Warren Street.

20-Jan-1941

Fire watching is now compulsory. All men and women from 16 to 60 must register but the only requirement will be 48 hours fire watching per month by men. Compulsory fire watching and fire fighting duties can be enforced if sufficient volunteers are not available.

A new National Service Bill introduced. Because of manpower shortages those called up can opt for, or be directed to serve in, Police War Reserve, AFS or Civil Defence First Aid Parties instead of the armed forces. Currently 90% of CD workers are volunteers.

25-Jan-1941

SP.Austin launches the collier *MURDOCK* 1558t. Only days after delivery on 26.4.1941 struck a submerged wreck and sank while on voyage Sunderland to London with coal.

26-Jan-1941

Alarm No.84: 11.47 - 12.33. During day hostile aircraft dropped a bomb on Silksworth. No damage or casualties.

28-Jan-1941

You could get your false teeth repaired at Pearson's (Watchmaker) of Borough Road, which were offering a quick service. New teeth at 3/- (15p), cracks repaired at 2/6 (12.5p) and breaks at 4/- (20p about £8 in today's money)

29-Jan-1941

There are currently 3051 Sunderland children still evacuated. All distributed amongst 186 villages

30-Jan-1941

The measles epidemic continues. In the nine weeks under review there were 1539 cases of measles reported compared with 601 in the previous nine weeks and 67 in the corresponding period in 1939/1940.

31-Jan-1941

Two men were killed and two women injured when a container exploded on the beach of a Northeast coast town. The men were James Guy 47, a sergeant in the Home Guard, and William Douglas 29. The public are warned not to touch or approach objects washed up by the tide.

3-Feb-1941

Alarm No.85: 12.30 - 12.41. Single aircraft made number of daylight raids over east and southeast coasts

4-Feb-1941

The collier GWYNWOOD 1,177 tons, built by SP. Austin in 1937, sank after a parachute mine landed on her deck. Capt. Cook, eight crew and two gunners were killed. She was on a voyage from London to Sunderland.

5-Feb-1941

The Army rather prides itself on the quality of training it gives its drivers, 300 accidents every day to Army vehicles suggests further training is required.

Enemy aircraft were believed in the vicinity of Northeast England this afternoon.

6-Feb-1941

The daily expenditure on the war effort is more than double that of a year ago. We are now spending at the rate of £12,250,000 a day.

7-Feb- 1941

Small businesses are unable to find sufficient firewatchers and fire fighters. The War Emergency Committee is to form a central pool of volunteers.

8-Feb-1941

The verdict of accidental death was returned on Thomas Shearer 67 retired yeast and egg salesman of 33 Chatsworth Street who was fatally injured while crossing St. Mark's Road during the blackout on New Years Eve.

10-Feb-1941

Mr Herbert Morrison (Home Secretary) introduces a new indoor table shelter.

JL. Thompson launches the *EMPIRE SKY* 7455t. 06.11.1942 Torpedoed and sunk by U.625. Crew all lost.

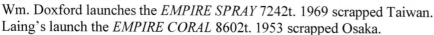

11-Feb-1941

The first of the mobile canteens for use by ARP personnel was completed at Sunderland's Transports Fulwell Road depot yesterday. An old tramcar has been converted into a mobile kitchen. Two more are now nearing completion at the depot. Two will serve the south side of the river and one the north side.

Wm. Doxford launches the *EMPIRE SPRAY* 7242t. 1969 scrapped Taiwan.

Laing's launch the *EMPIRE CORAL* 8602t. 1953 scrapped Osaka.

13-Feb- 1941

Alarm No.86: 14.26 - 14.56. Reports of enemy air activity came from several parts of the northeast coast this afternoon.

15/16-Feb-1941

Alarm No.87: 23.08 - 05.54. During the raid two people were slightly hurt in Sunderland when two bombs fell in open spaces. One raider shot down.

16-Feb-1941

Alarm No.88: 18.34 - 19.18. Four people died when bombs fell at Seaham Harbour.

Mary Johnston (70), a widow, of Fulwell Road, was killed when she stepped into the path of a tramcar during the blackout.

17-Feb-1941

Mrs Janet Ryland's became Sunderland's first woman porter at Monkwearmouth railway station.

20-Feb-1941

During the worst snowstorm in the North-East, in half a century, the Roker Volunteer Life Saving Brigade was in action again. The minesweeper *MARJORIE M HASTINGS* had struck a mine and ran ashore during the storm.

3 Tunstall Vale

There was considerable German air activity off our coast today.

21/22-Feb-1941

Picture shows snow being cleared from North Terrace of Mowbray Park

Wearside was practically at a standstill over the weekend and in danger of being cut off from the outside world. The severe winter weather, the worst in living memory, brought chaos to the town. Heavy snow blocked roads and brought down power lines. Trams and buses were unable to operate throughout Saturday.

Bombs caused some damage at Sunderland, where an electricity sub station was hit. Tyne/Tees AA guns in action.

23-Feb-1941

Alarm No. 89: 20.48 – 21.54

Two high explosive bombs at Tunstall Vale, one at Ennerdale and a large number of incendiaries fell in Hendon area. Thirty people were rendered homeless. Seven people were killed, six of the dead were women, the seventh, a six month old child, all were killed in Tunstall Vale. Eleven were seriously injured and six slightly injured.

hree people living behind a fruiterer's shop at 3 Tunstall Vale were among the dead. A mother and her two daughters were found to be dead when extracted from the debris and an 18 month old baby David Cowell was found, suffering from exposure, more than ten hours later in a bedroom marked with an arrow.

A number of people who were trapped by a bomb which fell on a house on the other side of the road at 20 Tunstall Vale completely demolishing it and doing considerable damage to the property. A mother and her 6-month-old baby died. Immediately before the high explosives were dropped the plane released a shower of incendiary bombs over the Hendon area bounded by Villette Road, Corporation Road, Spelter Works Road and Ryhope Road. These caused fires, which were quickly extinguished by stirrup-pump parties of householders and civil defence.

20 Tunstall Vale

1-Mar-1941

Since birdseed is no longer imported, substitution of oats, as bird feed was illegal.

The Government, keen to get more men into the shipyards, instruct all men with at least 12 months working experience in shipbuilding at any time during the last 15 years to register at employment exchanges. Many were reluctant because of the raw deal they have had in the past.

3/4-Mar-1941

Alarm No.90: 20.01 - 00.26

A stick of six high explosive bombs that fell on the town caused only the slightest damage and no casualties. Three fell on a slum cleared site between Back Hopper Street and Farringdon Row, another caused a small crater in a schoolyard of the Rectory Park Infants School, another hit an old wall around Gill Cemetery and the sixth fell on the corner of a trench shelter system, fortunately this part of the shelter was closed.

A large number of incendiary bombs were dropped on the East End south of Lawrence Street and east of Hudson Dock.

One high explosive bomb fell on the east side of Hudson Dock and damage was considerable in the dock area. Lying alongside the Quay, the steamship 'EMPIRE SURF', 6641tons, built by Bartram's and only launched on 13/1/1941 was damaged.

Seaman Joseph Dunn of Chapel Street Sunderland, a young gunner in the Royal Navy, in his first shot in an engagement last August (2nd August sunk off Harwich) brought down one of the four Heinkels, which bombed and sank his ship. He received the Conspicuous Gallantry Medal from the King at a recent investiture, he had also returned to the sinking trawler to search for a missing shipmate. He was previously employed by the river Wear Commissioners and is now serving on a minesweeper.

5-Mar-1941

The Essential Work Order now controls employed worker's movements.

6-Mar-1941

Alarm No.91: 20.15 - 22.38. Enemy planes were reported in the vicinity of the northeast coast but failed to penetrate far in land by the intense fire of the ground defences.

7-Mar-1941

The latest extension to the Municipal Hospital and the provision of a new entrance lodge and outpatients department at Chester Road completes the separation of the hospital from the Highfield Institution. The extension cost £15,000.

10-Mar-1941

A new order designed to reduce the amount of food in short supply consumed in catering establishments was signed by Lord Walton and takes effect from today. It is called the Food (Restrictions Of Meals In Establishments) Order and as from today it will be illegal to obtain a meal containing more than one course of the following dishes; fish, meat, poultry, game, eggs and cheese.

The cigarette shortage in Sunderland is now so acute that at least one firm with shops and kiosks in most other large towns of the north-east is refusing to supply women, even when they are buying for their men.

New order regarding the mobility of labour within the shipbuilding industry, Sunderland's yards will now work as group rather than individual concerns.

12/13-Mar-1941

Alarm No.92: 22.25 - 01.09. Many districts in the Northeast suffered bombing during the night.
Wm. Doxford launches the DAGHESTAN 7248t. Catapult Armed Merchantman Commissioned: Jul 1942. Sold Spanish breakers, 1969.
SS ESSEX LANCE 6625t freighter, damaged by bombing and gunfire from aircraft in Dover Straight. Sunderland galley boy W H Morris (20) is fatally wounded.

13-Mar-1941

If there is sufficient volunteers then Silksworth Colliery, which closed down due to lack of trade in December, is to reopen in about three weeks' time. Almost a whole of the original workforce have found work in pits in other parts of the country.

13/14-Mar-1941

Alarm No.93: 20.50 - 04.35. Defences on the northeast coast were intermittently in action during the night for the longest period since the war began. Only damage was from AA shell on a shelter.

14/15th Mar-1941

Alarm No.94: 20.22 - 02.20. Alarm No.95: 04.50 - 05.53
Four people were killed, two seriously injured and ten slightly injured when four high explosive bombs and a suspected UX fell at William Street, Roxburgh Street, Duke Street North, Francis Street and Inverness Street, Fulwell. Approximately nine houses were demolished. Three First Aid Parties and three Rescue Parties were involved.

46 Roxburgh Street

Rescue workers among the debris of 44 & 45 Francis Street

Fulwell and Roker took the brunt of this attack. The worst incident being at 46 Francis Street, Fulwell were a mother and daughter was found to be dead when extricated, a third women died at number 44.
A number were injured, some seriously, when numbers 43, 44, 45 and 46 were destroyed with other properties being badly damaged. A fourth person (Mary Atkinson) was killed when a bomb demolished number 46 Roxburgh Street and damaged others.

What remains of No.'s 30, 31 & 32 Duke Street North. Miraculously no fatalities.

Another bomb fell on Duke Street North, again people were trapped but when rescued were not seriously injured. An unexploded bomb was found in Inverness Street, Roker and people had to be evacuated. Bombs also fell in Sandringham Road and Roker Park with no serious injury.

17-Mar-1941

Alarm No.96: 20.35 - 21.32. Bombs fell in Easington Colliery, Hutton Henry and Crimdon Dene. No damage and no casualties.
The rationing of jam, treacle, and marmalade begins, 8oz per person per month allowed.
Womanpower for the war effort - that was the call today from the Minister of Labour, Ernest Bevin, as he announced the first steps in a massive mobilisation plan. Registration of 20 and 21 year-old women will begin next month with the aim of filling vital jobs in industry and the auxiliary services. Prime targets will be to get the munitions factories working round the clock but women are also desperately needed to takeover all kinds of other jobs to free men for active service. As yet,

married women with young children are exempt but those who can do war work locally will be backed up by huge expansion in day and night nurseries and child minding-systems. The drive for young women coincides with one for men of 41 and 42. Male trainees will earn £3 0s 6d, females £1.18s 0d a week.

18/19-Mar-1941

Alarm No.97: 01.03 - 03.29. Alarm sounded following a heavy raid on Hull, Estimated that 400 aircraft dropped over 300 tons of high explosive.

Ministry of Food announced today that cheese is to be rationed in the near future. Consumers must register with their grocers not later than Sunday March 29th. It is not known what the ration will be.

20-Mar-1941

Alarm No.98: 11.14 - 11.32. No action recorded

Secretary of the Boilermakers Union, Mr Mark Hodgson, commenting on the recruitment of ex-shipbuilders said 'I understand that many of our members have been reluctant to return considering the raw deal they have had in the past years.

21-Mar-1941

Sunderland's Municipal Piggery has now been established in Fulwell quarries for three weeks. There are no dwelling houses within an appreciable distance of the Piggery, which was established in an old engine house not far from Fulwell Mill. So far the herd consists of 36 pigs of about 15 weeks old. An order has been placed for 18 sucklings. The existing accommodation can take up to 100 pigs.

'SS HALO' (2,365t) a cargo ship was sunk by a mine off Beckton Pier, River Thames as she arrived from the Tyne with a cargo of coal. The Chief Officer killed in the explosion was W. Edgecombe (32) husband of Hilda Edgecombe, of Sunderland.

22-Mar-1941

The Coroner at an inquest on Thomas Collingham, a 65-year-old labourer of Frederick Street Sunderland, killed by a hit and run driver on Tuesday night at 11:10pm on the Sunderland Shields Road. Verdict given as accidental death. Charles Jude 68, a holder up of Hylton Road, was knocked down by a tramcar and after having been taken home in an ambulance he later fell down a flight of stairs at his home. Verdict of accidental death. The accident happened in Silksworth Road.

23-Mar-1941

Thomas Burton, aged 11, of 11 Forest Road, Ford Estate, died following an accident at the corner of West Moor Road, Pallion, in the blackout. While alighting from the bus he was hit by a car. The action of a Sunderland bus conductress in making up her fare sheet while passengers were alighting from the bus during the blackout was strongly criticised by the Coroner at a later inquest.

24-Mar-1941

Springwell Farm; judgment by Court of Appeal following the order on September 19th last, compensation payable by the Corporation was set at £22,700 which is less than half the amount claimed by the former owner Mr Horne. It included nothing for the loss of his horse breeding operation. The appeal was heard on the 17th 18th February last.

26-Mar-1941

Alarm No.99: 20.25 - 20.41. Enemy aircraft active off the coast.

In spite of recent air activity the homeward trickle of Sunderland's school children from reception areas continues. There are now only 2199 Wearside children evacuated.

Off Blythe, the cargo ship liner SS SOMALI 6,809t, London for the Far East, was damaged by German aircraft and sank the following day off Sunderland.

27-Mar-1941

Sunderland is not saving enough was the view of the Mayor. The level of saving is nowhere near the levels of 1940. At the Alexandra Hall meeting last night, called to consider the formation of street savings groups.

Wm. Doxford launches the *EMPIRE DAY* 7242t. Catapult Armed Merchantman. 7.8.44 Torpedoed and sunk by U.198.

28-Mar-1941

Eight business people were in court today for failing to fulfil their obligations under the Fire Prevention Order 1941. Included among the defendants were a Head Warden, a Warden and a member of the Home Guard. They were accused of not making preparations for detecting and combating fires started by enemy action.

In Sunderland last year there were 442 road accidents resulting in 28 deaths and injuries to 440 people. This compared to 561 accidents in the previous year resulting in 25 deaths and 581 injuries.

JL. Thompson launches the *EMPIRE WAVE* 7463t. 2.10.41 Torpedoed and sunk by U.562. On voyage Sunderland and Belfast Lough for Halifax. 31 crewmembers are missing.

29-Mar-1941

Rivalry between Tyne and Wear cropped up again, amusingly, today at a one-day school at Sunderland in connection with the Workers' Education Association, on the setting up of 12 regional parliaments to cover the country. When it was suggested that the north-east regional parliament would probably sit in Newcastle as the largest city it drew immediate protest from the chairman Mr Fred Williamson, 'It is not the number of people in the place that counts, but the quality of the people and Mr Williamson added 'if Lonnon hadn't been Lonnon, Sun'lan wad!.

30-Mar-1941

The body of William Thomas Springett was recovered from the South Dock today. Mr Springett, a Royal Marine from the training ship HMS Calliope, had been missing since January 21st.

31-Mar-1941

Alarm No.100: 21.31 - 22.33. Bombs dropped in the Felton area of Northumberland.

1-Apr-1941

It is reported that today's trawler men are making a lot of money due to the high demand for fish. The lowest paid member of the crew can now make £1 a day, the mate's daily earnings can average £5 and that of the skipper could equal that of a Cabinet Minister. The catch of one fishing boat, fishing in home waters, went for £4,824. The catch from larger Icelandic trawlers can fetch as much as £19,000.

2-Apr-1941

Alarm No.101: 08.53 - 09.24. Alarm No.102: 14.16 - 14.39. Shipping attacked off Northeast coast.
Parliament, on a free vote, reversed the Government's decision to permit the opening of theatres and cinemas on Sundays. 144 against the opening to 136 in favour of the opening.

3-Apr-1941

Alarm No.103: 10.50 - 11.13. Alarm No.104: 22.05 - 22.50. Shipping again attacked. Bombs fell in Yorkshire.
The auxiliary patrol vessel 'FORTUNA' (259t) was attacked and sunk by enemy aircraft off St Abbs Head.

4-Apr-1941

Laura Mary Beatrice Mason aged six was killed when a yard wall, previously damaged in an air raid, collapsed and fell on her and her four-year-old sister while playing in the street on Tuesday afternoon. She had been staying at 41 Sheepfolds since being evacuated from Gibraltar.
The Essential Work Order is introduced for shipbuilding and repair. Employees will be guaranteed a minimum wage. An employer will not be able to discharge a worker except for serious misconduct. Workers who wished to leave must obtain permission from the Regional Shipyard Controller. Cases of absenteeism and misconduct will be reviewed by Ministry of Labour and National Service.

5-Apr-1941

First Communal Feeding Centre opened in Hudson Road Schools. Prices were; soup 1d, stewed meat and dumplings with baked potato and mashed turnip for 6d and a plate of pudding with custard for 2d.

6-Apr-1941

Mrs Rebecca Laine 43, of Covent Garden, died after being knocked down by a motorcar while crossing Fawcett Street during the blackout tonight.

7-Apr-1941

Alarm No.105: 13.55 - 14.36.
The first cases against employees for failing to carry out their obligations under the Fire Prevention (Business Premises) Order were heard at Sunderland Police Court today. Richard Hutchinson 34 of Sans Street South and Norman Watson 47 of Birchfield Road were each fined £1.

7/8-Apr-1941

Alarm No.106: 21.05 - 03.14. Alarm No.107: 03.43 - 04.50

German bombers engaged last night on their most extensive raids over Britain for some weeks. The northeast got its fair share. Waves of bombers crossed the coast for hours to be met by intensive anti aircraft fire.
A high explosive bomb of small calibre fell at the junction of Cleveland Road and General Graham Street damaging two houses
Enemy planes raided several towns and villages on the northeast coast.
The Gaiety Theatre in High Street East was damaged by an anti aircraft shell returning to earth.

Workmen cleaning up in Cleveland Road

9/10-Apr-1941
Alarm No.108: 20.52 - 21.24. Alarm No.109: 23.25 - 04.51
Wearsiders today saw the sky reddened by the biggest blaze that the town had ever known. Incendiary bombs, which caused fires, large and small, had showered the centre of the town but all of them were dwarfed by the huge outbreak, which completely gutted Binns department store on both sides of Fawcett Street. For four hours, from 2am to 6am, firemen fought the blaze and prevented it
spreading to engulf the whole of the shopping centre; water from the river was pumped up into the lake in Mowbray Park to help. The flames leaping hundreds of feet into the air seemed to act as a magnet for enemy planes but they were met by a terrific barrage of anti aircraft fire and the moonlit sky was at times almost covered with flashes of shell bursts. By daylight the worst was over and people on their way to work saw the gaunt fire blackened shells of the store buildings. It would be more than a week before the debris was cleared and the street got back to 'normal'.
Part of the premises of the Sunderland Club Ltd, Fawcett Street was damaged by fire. Blackett's premises at High Street West/Union Street were damaged and a shoe warehouse completely gutted. At Messrs Steel, Holmside a stock room was gutted and a large room on the top floor was damaged. Altogether eight premises in Holmside including Northumbria Printing works and Wilkinson's garage and six in Crowtree Road were severely damaged by bombs. Blackett's premises at High Street West/Union Street were damaged and a shoe warehouse completely gutted.

Fawcett Street with the smouldering, burnt out, shells of both Binns stores

Firemen still in attendance the following morning

Two people were killed, nine seriously injured and nine slightly injured when two high explosive and many incendiary bombs fell in the Ethel Street – Brougham Street area. Five houses were demolished and over fifty people were made homeless. Incendiaries fell on to pit props stacked on the railway, starting a blaze near 300 wagons, many laden with ammunition. Railwaymen managed to remove 274 of them, thereby preventing an extremely destructive explosion. Robert Hume and John Steele were awarded the George Medal and four others; Messrs Angus, Ward, Brown and Calthorpe were awarded the British Empire Medal. Short Brothers launches the *EMPIRE SUN* 6952t for the MOWT. 7.2.42 Torpedoed and sunk by U.751. 1 crewmember was lost.

Numbers 10 & 11 Ethel Street where two people died

11-Apr-1941
No holiday today for the shipyard workers. With fish very scarce and hot cross buns unattainable and hard-boiled eggs only a memory Good Friday and Easter holidays will seem to the majority of Wearsiders rather strange.

14/15-Apr-1941
Alarm No.110: 18.24 - 18.46. Alarm No.111: 21.37 - 21.51. Alarm No.112: 22.38 - 22.49. Raid on South Shields.

15/16-Apr-1941
Alarm No.113: 22.45 - 04.58.
Eighteen people were killed, thirty-six seriously injured and seventy-nine slightly injured at about 03.00 when four Parachute Mines, High Explosives and a number of incendiaries fell at Sunderland. Three hundred people were rendered homeless. The premises of Sunderland Forge & Engineering Co (where five of the fatalities

occurred) and T.W. Greenwell& Co, South Dock were damaged and production slightly affected. An explosion in St Luke's Road demolished several houses and seriously damaged others. A bomb on the LNER line at Pallion damaged a 30 cwt crane, an electric pump and a shelter at R.W. Collin's & Co. foundry.

Mines and bombs in the area of Laura Street, Toward Road. Tavistock Place, Murton Street, Hedworth Street, South Durham Street and Hudson Road caused serious damage to dwelling houses, shops and other premises. The famous, or infamous, Victoria Hall was completely demolished. The Palatine Hotel at the corner of Borough Road and Toward Road was damaged and many houses and shops in the vicinity were either demolished or seriously damaged. The Winter Gardens (and its parrots) in Mowbray Park was hit, the Museum and Art Gallery were seriously damaged. Other explosions at South Durham Street and Hedworth Street completely demolished many houses and a small cinema called "The Victory". The incendiaries did little damage and an IB Container at the Military Camp, Grindon and another at LNER, Burdon House failed to open, no damage.

The Victoria Hall and a row of shops were wrecked by a large bomb (actually this was a parachute mine but the press were not permitted to report it as such), which exploded in Laura Street. Three firewatchers were trapped in the shops. At the Oddfellows Hall above the shops the caretaker John Hazard was extricated after a short interval but he was dead, a firewatcher Stanley Foster, of 27 Hunter Terrace South, also died. The manager of the Victoria Hall, Mr Matthew Pratt, suffered injuries and shock while two other firewatchers on duty with him had a narrow

escape. They had been in the basement for some time when Mr Pratt and one of the firewatchers went to the main door and were just about to open the door when there was a terrific explosion and a blinding flash and the doors blew in on them, they were hurled across the entrance hall and ended up against a wall with the noise of the building collapsing all around them.

Hedworth Street and South Durham Street in Hendon

The Hall was entirely wrecked; masses of stonework from the walls were flung many hundreds of yards. Also demolished is a dancehall and a hall formally used as the town's Food Office. A block of shops and houses across the way were reduced to a heap of rubble and above it the Oddfellows meeting hall. A nurse's home escaped serious damage although all of its windows were blown out and ceilings brought down, no one was hurt. The Palatine Hotel suffered extensively from the blast, the roof was damaged in several places and interior walls were blown in and every window broken but again only minor injuries were sustained. The Winter Gardens in Mowbray Park lost almost every pane of glass and rare tropical plants suffered damage however the parrots escaped injury.

A Parachute Mine fell between Hedworth Street and South Durham Street in Hendon. Again the destruction was considerable. It's hard to believe that only five died with a further ten injured. The homeless numbered 280.

Around 2.20am bombs fell in St. Luke's Road, Pallion, demolishing several houses and seriously damaging many others. Six people died at $23\frac{1}{2}$ and 25 (see opposite).

At the Forge Engineering works in Pallion some damage was caused and five workmen were killed. A third Parachute Mine exploded near the South Pier damaging Greenwell's repair yard.

Two PMs exploded in a field W of the Bents Cottages at Seaburn. No casualties.

16-Apr-1941

Alarm No.114: 22.01 - 23.03. Raiders over County Durham. Little action reported.

17-Apr-1941

Alarm No.115: 16.03 - 16.15. Alarm No.116: 22.02 - 23.42. A few aircraft over Northumberland.

18/19-Apr-1941

An enemy bomber attacked shipping off Seaham Docks.

19-Apr-1941

Alarm No.117: 16.44 - 17.24.

Enemy aircraft off the North East coast. Bombs were reported to have been dropped at Whitby.

Women born during 1920 are required to register for National Service.

20-Apr-1941

Crowns launch the *HMS CAMPION* 580t Flower Class Corvette. Royal Navy.

Commissioned 07/07/1941. Scrapped in April 1947.

21-Apr-1941

Meat ration reduced to 1s for adults and 6d for the under six.

22-Apr-1941

Alarm No.118: 21.17 - 22.07. Minelaying activity

23-Apr-1941

Mrs Churchill, wife of the Prime Minister, was on Wearside today and made a lightning tour of five shipyards in two hours. She is shown meeting veteran workers at Short's shipyard

23/24-Apr-1941

Alarm No.119: 22.31 - 01.00. Alarm No.120: 02.58 - 03.45. Parachute mines fell at Cleadon. Sunderland not attacked.

24-Apr-1941

SP.Austin launch the *CAPITOL* 1558t. 1963 sold to Belgian breakers.

25-Apr-1941

Alarm No.121: 21.52 - 23.43. Air attacks on the North East. The German High Command communiqué said, "German bomber formations successfully bombed the harbour town of Sunderland. High explosives and incendiary bombs caused considerable damage particularly on the equipment of the Deptford Wharf and in Hudson Dock. Not one bomb fell in Sunderland.

Street Saving Groups are inaugurated.

26-Apr-1941

Pickersgill's launch the *EMPIRE EVE* 5970t. 18.5.43 Sunk by U.414 while serving with R.N. 5 crew lost.

28-Apr-1941

Dr Edith Summerskill is to ask the Minister of Information whether he is aware that the poster bearing the words 'be like Dad Keep Mum' is offensive to women and is a source of irritation to housewives whose work in the home, if paid for at current rates, would make a substantial addition to the family income and whether he would have this poster withdrawn.

Wm. Doxford launches the *EMPIRE LUGARD* 7241t. 13.9.42 Torpedoed and sunk by U.558. Crew saved.

Laing's launch the *EMPIRE OPAL* 9811t. 1945 SOUTHERN OPAL. 1964 Scrapped Hamburg.

30-Apr-1941

Alarm No.123: 15.08 - 15.29. Alarm No.124: 22.14 - 23.12. Attack on Whitley Bay and later North Yorkshire.

Wm. Doxford launches the KAFIRISTAN 7250t. Built as a Catapult Armed Merchantman. Scrapped Shanghai June 1972.

1-May-1941

Alarm No.125: 23.34 - 23.49. Bombs fell in Northumberland.

2/3-May-1941

Alarm No.126: 23.30 - 00.13. Bombs fell at Newcastle and at Port Clarence and Portrack in Co Durham.

3/4-May-1941

Alarm No.127: 23.12 - 04.11

The air raid overnight was one of the heaviest Sunderland has suffered since the war began. Seventeen people were killed, fourteen seriously injured and thirteen slightly injured. Many houses were demolished and others badly smashed. Eighty-five people were rendered homeless.

Three large high explosive bombs straddled Fulwell, destroying the caretaker's cottage at Redby Schools; the school premises were also seriously damaged. In Duke Street North eight people lost their lives.

In Westcott Terrace, a street of tenemented houses, a bomb killed four people in a shelter and five others taking cover under the stairs of their homes. Fires were started, industrial damage was slight. Little damage was caused by two HEs on the South Docks and one HE at Clarke's Farm, Grangetown. Other HEs fell in the Fulwell and Roker areas, houses were demolished in Osborne Street and Fulwell Road. IBs caused damage in Hendon Road, Adelaide Place, Hedworth Terrace, Wear Street, Howick Street, Lawrence Street and Avon Street.

In Sunderland Rural District many incendiaries fell at Castletown, some explosive type, and high explosives bombs dropped between East Boldon and Castletown. Damage to house and shop windows. Incendiaries fell at Ryhope setting houses on fire. A boy sustained injury to leg. Two high explosive bombs fell at Ryhope Colliery, no damage.

Shelters were no match for the power of the bomb. In Duke Street North, six people were killed while taking cover in their backyard surface shelter.

Redby School Caretaker's cottage in Cromarty Street

5-May-1941

Alarm No.128: 00.12 - 03.45. Alarm No.129: 23.25 - 04.05. Some 386 enemy planes passed over the area in waves of about thirty every seven minutes or so, heading for Glasgow.

Two more Communal Feeding Centres in Sunderland, one at Ford Hall School and the other at West Southwick School open today without any official opening ceremony.

6/7-May-1941

Alarm No.130: 23.38 - 04.31. An attack on Northumberland and Durham areas.

The Sunderland Corporation Transport Committee have given orders that trams and bus conductresses must be dismissed on marriage. The short-sighted policy of one family one income was the governing factor of the decision.

7-May-1941

The maximum fine of £100, plus 25 guineas cost, was imposed on Joseph Clarke 35, trading as Clarke's of 205 High Street West Sunderland for selling an excessive quantity of silk stockings. Clarke was accused of making £900 profit by selling four times more than his quota permitted.

8-May-1941

Alarm No.131: 00.44 - 02.50. Bombs fell at Tynemouth, West Hartlepool, Hartlepool and Billingham.

A police raid on a house in Potts Street, Millfield discovered youths aged 15 to 19 playing cards for money. At the Borough Police Court today Ethel Newby 54 now living at Williams Street was fined £2 for using the house for the purposes of gaming.

9-May-1941

JL. Thompson launches the *EMPIRE HUDSON* 7465t MOWT. 10.9.41 Torpedoed and sunk by U.82. 4 lost.

10-May-1941

Alarm No.132: 00.39 - 04.28. Few of the enemy made landfall.

12-May-1941

Alarm No.133: 00.16 - 03.06. Five High Explosive bombs fell on a refuse tip at North Hylton causing damage to doors and windows.

Sunderland is to have six British restaurants. These restaurants are in addition to the three communal feeding centres, which are based on a cash and carry basis where people pay for the meals and take them away in their own dishes. People visiting the restaurants will eat their meals on the premises, they will be given a ticket for each course and collect the meal from the counter.

13-May-1941

Alarm No.134: 23.14 - 23.44. Machine gun attacks on West Hartlepool.

15-May-1941

Communal shelters are to be locked when not required. Reports of sanitary offences and the storing of rubbish prompted this action.

20-May-1941

Compulsory fire watching regulations now apply to Sunderland. This means that all men not exempted between the ages of 18 and 60 must register to perform as detailed fire watching duties in the Borough.

22-May-1941

"Stand firm-carry on". This message forms an introduction to a leaflet called 'Beating the Invader' more than 14 million copies of which were in the hands of the public between Tuesday May 27th and Thursday the 29th.

The two pages of advice are summed up in the final note. "Give all the help you can to our troops - do not tell the enemy anything - do not give them anything - do not help him in any way".

Beating the INVADER

24-May-1941

Alarm No.136: 06.55 - 07.06. No action recorded.

Subscribers to Sunderland's Spitfire Fund will be interested to learn that a Sunderland fighter pilot is flying one of the four Spitfires planes bearing the name of Sunderland. He is Sergeant Pilot Harold Ashton Milburn, son of Frederick Ashton Milburn and Mabel Milburn, of Sunderland. He died 09/05/1942 defending Malta.

25-May-1941

Alarm No.137: 23.12 - 00.10. No action recorded

26-May-1941

Alarm No.138: 13.18 - 14.19. There were bombs in the sea off Sunderland.

Men who have served in the Merchant Navy but who are now employed on land or are unemployed must register for the Merchant Service.

27-May-1941

Alarm No.139: 18.34 - 18.42. No action recorded.

Damage to the Winter Gardens was considered uneconomical to repair.

28-May-1941

Experimental egg rationing, the controlled distribution of eggs is announced.

Further restrictions on fish and milk; successful prosecutions under Food Control Orders now total 17,319.

29-May-1941

Alarm No.140: 17.50 - 18.19. No action recorded.

Short Bros. launches the *EMPIRE BURTON* 6966t. 19.9.41 Torpedoed and sunk by U.74. 3 crewmembers lost.

Laing's launch the *EMPIRE PEARL* 9816t. 1969 Scrapped Vinaroz, Spain.

1-Jun-1941

The Board of trade introduces Utility Scheme for retail goods.

Clothes rationing began today. Second hand clothing is not affected. Each person is to have 66 clothing coupons to last for a year. Until the new coupons are printed, margarine coupons in ration books will serve to buy clothing. People losing their clothing through enemy action will be allowed roughly two year's supply of coupons.

The number of coupons needed for some garments is shown.

Men & Boys	Adult	Child	Women & Girls	Adult	Child
Raincoat or overcoat	16	11	Mackintosh/Coat	14	11
Jacket	13	8	Coat (under 28" long)	11	8
Trousers	5	3	Woollen Dress	11	8
Shorts	5	3	Blouse, cardigan	5	3
Overalls/dungarees	6	4	Skirt	7	5
Nightshirt/pyjamas	8	6	Nightdress	6	5
Shirt, or combinations	8	6	Petticoat, slip,	4	3
Pair of socks or stockings	3	1	Corsets	3	2
Collar, tie or pair of cuffs	1	1	Pair of stockings	2	1
Pair of boots or shoes	7	3	Slippers, boots or shoes	5	3

KNITTING WOOL – 1 coupon for two ounces

2-Jun-1941

Alarm No.141: 10.38 - 11.21. Bombs at Middlesbrough.

Meat Inspectors check wholesale and retail outlets to see if meat roll, used for sandwiches, contain horseflesh.

A shop Notice saying that horseflesh is sold must be conspicuous.

2/3-Jun-1941

Alarm No.142: 22.17 - 22.34. Alarm No.143: 23.50 - 01.03. Northumberland attacked.

3-Jun-1941

Alarm No.144: 15.01 - 16.18. Northumberland again attacked.

The municipal canteens at Ford Hall and Hudson Road are evidently meeting public demand and are very popular but a third at Southwick does not seem to be hitting the mark.

6-Jun-1941

Alarm No.145: 15.19 - 15.43. In Sunderland Rural District; one high explosive bomb fell at Whitefield Pit, Penshaw, near to houses and damage was caused to about fifty of them. A male and two females sustained injuries.

7-Jun-1941

Three schools in Sunderland have been allocated, if required, as emergency hospitals, giving a total bed accommodation of 500.

SP.Austin launches the *BETTY HINDLEY* 1738t. 6-Aug-1941 she ran aground off Cromer while on passage Tyne to London and was a complete loss.

8-Jun-1941

Alarm No.146: 15.47 - 16.19. Enemy aircraft off Alnmouth sank an Admiralty vessel.

10-Jun-1941

Alarm No.147: 14.11 - 14.39. No action recorded.

The Ministry of Food announces egg rationing prices, large eggs are to be sold at 2/6 (12½p) per dozen.

JL. Thompson launches the *EMPIRE LAWRENCE* 7457t. 27.5.42 Bombed and sunk.

11-Jun-1941

The building and civil engineering industry have been brought under the Essential Work Order to help in the construction of aerodromes and war factories.

The river during June 1941; Note the Barrage Balloon on the ship but none over the town. Unlike the Tyne and the Tees, Sunderland had no Barrage Balloon protection. It only arrived after the last devastating raids of May 1943.

Laing's launch the *EMPIRE BRUCE* 7459t. 18.4.43 Torpedoed and sunk by U.123. Total crew of 49 all saved.

12-Jun-1941

The Town Council rejects the proposal to repair the Winter Garden Fernery at a cost of £306 as uneconomical.

Wm. Doxford launches the *EMPIRE RALEIGH* 7240t. 6.12.61 Wrecked Cape Spartal, near Tangier.

13-Jun-1941

Alarm No.148: 01.40 - 04.41. There was considerable activity off the northeast coast early, mine laying and attacks on shipping, and the ground defences were constantly in action. Machine-guns were heard at sea.

14-Jun-1941

Alarm No.149: 19.25 - 20.00. Enemy aircraft off the coast.

Women born in 1918 register today for industrial service. Today is expected to bring the number of women registered up to the 1 million mark.

The public were reminded that it was essential to register with retailers today for their egg ration.

15-Jun-1941

Prices of 1940 potatoes are to be substantially reduced to consumers, after today old potatoes of the cheaper grade will be available at 1d per pound in all districts.

Changes to the Preserve ration; it will be illegal for retailers to sell, or a householder to buy, more than the ration of half a pound per month.

17-Jun-1941

A frantic shop-to-shop search for cigarettes and tobacco goes on daily on Wearside as well as elsewhere. Before the war the nation smoked 195 million pounds of tobacco, now consumption is 230million pounds per year.
 It was a night of slight raids on Britain. Bombs fell in the northeast.

18-Jun-1941

Alarm No.150: 00.12 - 00.26. Alarm No.151: 13.47 - 14.05

An Air Ministry communiqué says enemy aircraft were believed to be in the vicinity of towns in the northeast of England this afternoon.

19-Jun-1941

Egg producers are not allowed to sell eggs except to recognised packaging stations or to authorised buyers.

Wearside had an unexpected visit from the King and Queen today. News of their Majesty's arrival at a large Shipbuilding Establishment flashed around Sunderland and the main streets were thronged with people as the King and Queen drove to the station to entrain for Teesside. Today their first call was at a large ammunition factory in Birtley. The King and Queen then drove to Sunderland; at Hylton Road Schools the children had been brought into the playground to see the King and Queen drive past. At the shipyard of J L Thompson & Sons two of the proudest tonight are Thomas Lawton of Enfield Street and Ralph Haswell of West Moore Road aged 15, they are apprentice fitters and turners.

The breakfast cereal 'Cheerios' is invented. These O-shaped cereals were originally called 'Cheerie Oats'.

20-Jun-1941

To save on transport, live cattle, received at abattoirs, shall be consumed in the area covered by the centre. Any surplus meat will be transferred to the nearest populated centres where there is a deficiency of home killed meat. Sunderland is a dairy farming area, which will not fare so well under the new arrangement. We shall get little or no lamb or mutton, and pork shall be mostly from sows.

"While sailing in convoy from Blyth to London on 20th/21st June 1941 the SS CORMOUNT was attacked by E-boats and aircraft and although sustaining a direct hit under the navigating bridge amidships, replied at once with defensive armament, the men on the guns went on firing despite the hail of bullets and cannon shells. Bombardier Henry Herbert Reed, aged 30, son of Henry and Annie Reed, aged 30, son of Henry and Annie Reed, was badly wounded but refused to leave his anti-aircraft gun. Then, seeing that the Chief Officer was also badly wounded, the bombardier carried him from the bridge down two ladders to the deck below and put him in a shelter, before falling dead himself. It was afterwards discovered that his stomach had been ripped open by machine gun bullets." This was the citation for the award of George Cross. Edward Johnson Scott WILLEY, Second Engineer Officer, husband of Bertha Willey, of Sunderland, later died of his wounds.

21-Jun-1941

Under the Civil Defence Duties (Compulsory Enrolment) Order 1941, 30,000 men are expected to register for fire watching over the two days, almost every male in the town between the ages of 18 and a 60.

22-Jun-1941

In the military exercise on Wearside today, some thousands of people were asked to produce their identity cards; over 25 per cent of the people challenged offered some kind of excuse for not carrying it.

23-Jun-1941

Alarm No.152: 00.13 - 00.45. No Action recorded.

Tomatoes were selling like the proverbial 'hot cakes' at 3s per pound in Sunderland shops on Saturday. Today at the controlled price of 1s 5d in operation there was scarcely a tomato to be bought in the town.

24-Jun-1941

Fire-watching duties during daylight hours are relaxed. Only one-third of approved watching personnel maybe on duty

25-Jun-1941

Alarm No.153: 01.20 - 02.40. German communiqué states that in addition to the raid on Liverpool last night air attacks were directed against port installations on Tyne and Tees estuaries.

The Chancellor of the Exchequer reveals that war expenditure is now running at £12 million per day

The first of the vegetables grown in Sunderland parks are on sale this week at shops on Wearside.

'SS Dashwood' (2,154t) cargo ship, London to Sunderland was sunk by German aircraft near Great Yarmouth.

27-Jun-1941

The grocery firm of Forster and Pickering Rock, Hendon Road, are charged with contravening regulations by selling meat, containing horseflesh, without displaying any notice to that effect.

Sugar ration is doubled for each of the next four weeks to enable householders to preserve stone fruit.

Next week's meat ration will remain at 1s 0d.

28-Jun-1941

All unexempted women born in 1917 are required to register today.

The growth of the queue habit is one of the less satisfactory features of wartime conditions. We can sympathise with the harassed housewives who have a difficult job of obtaining extra food to give their hard-working men folk. But this eternal queuing up at shops is neither the best nor fairest way of solving the problem. It represents a shocking waste of time and effort, which might be put to better use.

30-Jun-1941

Changes in rationing; Cheese increased to 2 ounces, the special ration of 8 ounces per week for underground miners, agricultural workers, and vegetarians will remain unchanged. Butter reduced from 4 ounces to 2 ounces. A new order will control the price of fish at Quay.

Wm. Doxford launches the *EMPIRE GRENFELL* 7238t. 1968 scrapped Taiwan.

1-Jul-1941

Alarm No.154: 00.21 - 01.13. No action recorded.

While out walking on the sea shore near Ryhope a schoolboy named James Browell was killed by an explosion and three of his companions injured and taken to hospital. At a later inquest held on James David Browell (12), of 16 St Bede's Terrace Sunderland, the recorded verdict was that Browell was accidentally killed by an explosion while trespassing in a prohibited area. Three of Browell's companions, William Hugh Beatty (11) of 9 Short Street Hendon, George Lennox (12) of 13 Ward Street Hendon and his brother Alexander Lennox (11) were all injured by the explosion.

'SS HOMEFIRE' (1,262t) collier, London to Sunderland in ballast, was sunk by German aircraft off Cromer with the loss of 15 of her crew of 17. S.P. Austin built the HOMEFIRE in 1925.

4-Jul-1941

Coal rationing introduced. One ton per month for householders and other non-industrial users.

5-Jul-1941

Two men were found guilty of assault and threatening behaviour in a disturbance at the junction of Hylton Road and Trimdon Street last night. George Lovell (41) of Henley Road was fined £7 10s and Stephen MacDonough (25) of Lisburn Terrace was fined £5. A crowd of 200 watched the affray.

6-Jul-1941

SP. Austin launches the *BETTY HINDLEY* 1738t. 6/8/1941 ran aground off Cromer complete loss.

8-Jul-1941

The threat of closure hangs over some fried fish shops due to lack of potatoes.

Pickersgill's launch the *EMPIRE CROMWELL* 5970t. 28.11.42 Torpedoed and sunk by U.508. 24 crewmembers lost.

JL. Thompson launches the *EMPIRE CRANMER* 7460t. 17.3.61 Aground near Novorossisk, total loss.

11-Jul-1941

Alarm No.155: 01.30 - 02.55. Bombs fell at eight places between the Tweed and the Yare in Norfolk. Utility Clothing is introduced. All clothing was stamped and labelled with the Utility mark, Civilian-Clothing 1941 (CC 41). There were general rules for the making of utility clothes, which changed from year to year. The Utility Scheme was later expanded to include other items such as furniture and soft furnishings like cushions etc and continued past the war, it was finally withdrawn in 1952.

'SS SIR RUSSELL' (1,548t) cargo ship, Sunderland to Southampton, was sunk by an E Boat near Dungeness.

14-Jul-1941

Biggest 'beer famine' in Sunderland since the last war. A number of licensed premises were closed today because they had sold out, while many others were open part time.

15-Jul-1941

Large quantities of standardised furniture and other domestic articles are being loaned to bombed out people under a Ministry of Health Scheme. Furniture, simple in design, consists of 43 separate articles, including camp beds, blankets, crockery, cutlery, cooking and cleaning utensils and table and fireside chairs.

15/16-Jul-1941

Alarm No.156: 23.53 - 00.53. Five or six raids were plotted between Newcastle and the Humber.

In a new national campaign, Sunderland is called upon to find £45,000. This figure, a 50 per cent increase on the town's present weekly savings.

17-Jul-1941

The registration of former coalminers begins today. The men required to register are those between 20 and 60 who have been employed in the industry for six months or more since the beginning of 1935. Many of the men who registered today were employed at Silksworth Colliery until it closed in December last year.

18-Jul-1941

Alarm No.157: 02.19 - 03.02. Attacks on East coast of England. No action over Sunderland.

Fruiterer Mr Frank Bell of Villette Road had to call the police when he refused to serve non-regular customer with potatoes.

19-Jul-1941

About 1200 Wearmouth miners refuse to work during alerts. The only colliery in County Durham to do so. It was pointed out that shipyards and other factories in the same vicinity of the Colliery work on under a spotting system or on the Industrial Alarm.

22/23-Jul-1941

Alarm No.158: 23.51 - 00.32.

"Last night enemy activity was on a small scale and was mainly confined to east and northeast coastal areas".

25-Jul-1941

With the start of the new football season it is anticipated to have the services of regular players such as Gorman, Hastings, Lockie, Hewitson, Gurney and Duns. It is expected that the Chief Constable will release from duties Carter, Howson, Harry Thompson and Rodgerson.

The ban on the employment of married women as conductresses is now removed provided they can guarantee regular and punctual attendance.

28-Jul-1941

Bartram's launch the *EMPIRE GILBERT* 6640t. 2.11.42 Torpedoed and sunk by U.586. 3 crewmembers P.O.W the balance of 63 lost.

Short Bros. launches the *EMPIRE WYCLIF* 6966t. 1967 scrapped Hirohata, Japan.

30-Jul-1941

Wearsiders learned today that the old Winter Gardens are to come down and the framework to go for scrap.

5-Aug-1941

Alarm No.159: 22.53 - 23.38. No action recorded.

Of the 97,000 ex-miners who have already registered, it is understood that 24,000 are willing to return to the mines. Some 10,000 have been offered to employers and 5500 have returned to work.

7-Aug-1941

Mrs Mary Elliott, of 32 Percy Terrace, Sunderland, became one of the first 'Bevin girls'. Working in a Birmingham factory she was chosen as typical of the British women whose response to the 'go for it' call and starred in the Ministry of Information film called 'A Girl Joins Up'. Mrs Elliot (22) is on holiday this week at home in Sunderland reunited with her three-year-old daughter Heather.

8-Aug-1941

Representatives of all sides of Wearside life attended the funeral today of Sir John Priestman, Baronet, who died at his home on Tuesday night. The body was brought from Harrogate this morning for a service at Bishopwearmouth Parish Church before the internment was made in the family burial ground at Sunderland cemetery.

9-Aug-1941

Clocks go back one hour tonight, end of double summer time. The experiment of manipulating the clock to suit our wartime needs was received well by the public, industry and farmers.

12-Aug-1941

The SS EAGLESCLIFFE HALL, 1900t, is attacked by aircraft 2 miles east of Sunderland, the ship puts into Sunderland for repairs. Stewart Franklin Buchanan a Donkeyman is buried in Bishopwearmouth Cemetery.

13-Aug-1941

Alarm No.160: 11.54 - 12.47. The German High Command said of today "on the east coast of Britain planes engaged in armed reconnaissance made successful low flying raids on a foundry south of Whitby and on a public utility plant in the town of Sunderland".

Three high explosive bombs fell on Mayswood Road, Fulwell. Four people were killed and two seriously and three slightly injured. Two houses demolished, and five to be demolished, eight seriously damaged and 130 slightly damaged.

Again many people had remarkable escapes.

A number of the houses damaged today had just been repaired at a considerable expense following damage from another raid about a year ago.

Crowns launch the *EMPIRE ASH* 263t Ocean going tug. 1973 Welsh Industrial & Maritime Museum, Cardiff. 1978 Restored as exhibit.

14-Aug-1941

Wm. Doxford launches the *EMPIRE LATIMER* 7244t. 1968 scrapped Mihara, Japan.

15-Aug-1941

Alarm No.161: 00.09 - 00.55. Alarm No.162: 01.57 - 02.34. Alarm No.163: 21.35 - 21.54
Raider activity over Northumberland and Co. Durham. Slight damage but no casualties.

17-Aug-1941

Alarm No.164: 01.17 - 02.03. Approximately sixty Anti personnel bombs were dropped between Washington Lane crossing and West Moor Farm, North Hylton.
Compulsory powers will be used, if necessary, for mobilising women of under 30 for war work. Choice of occupation will be more restricted. Older women are required to volunteer to replace the younger women who will be transferred elsewhere.

18-Aug-1941

The National Fire Service (N.F.S.) was formed today. It incorporated all the local fire authorities throughout England and Wales and the Auxiliary Fire Service. In 1948 responsibility for the fire service was restored by the Fire Services Act 1947 back to the local authorities.

19-Aug-1941

Alarm No.165: 01.21 - 03.35. A German communiqué said that attacks were directed by strong Luftwaffe formations in good visibility against the English shipbuilding centre of Sunderland. It was West Hartlepool that suffered.

21-Aug-1941

SP.Austin launches the *SOUND FISHER* 2950t. Capsized in 1957.

22-Aug-1941

Alarm No.166: 06.57 - 07.11. The official German news agency said that German bombers attacked the targets of military importance on the east coast of England.

23-Aug-1941

Alarm No.167: 00.41 - 00.57. Enemy aircraft off the coast looking for shipping.
JL. Thompson launches the *EMPIRE LIBERTY* 7157t. 1960 Scrapped Osaka

24/25-Aug-1941

Alarm No.168: 22.39 - 00.19. Taking advantage of low cloud, six enemy aircraft briefly attacked targets from Blyth to Teesside

25-Aug-1941

Alarm No.169: 14.44 - 15.12. Five reconnaissance aircraft crossed the North-East Coast.

Food is almost as important as armaments. This was the message given by Sir John Boyd-Orr, the eminent expert on nutrition, when he opened Sunderland's Kitchen Front and Dig for Victory, a weeks exhibition at The New Rink in Holmside.

Sunderland was the first town in the Northeast to organise such an event. Cheese allowance increased to three ounces from today.

Pickersgill's launch the *EMPIRE MARIOTT* 5970t. 1969 scrapped Bombay.

27-Aug-1941

Wm. Doxford launches the *EMPIRE SELWYN* 7167t. 1942 BELGIAN SOLDIER.7.8.42 Torpedoed and sunk.

27/28-Aug-1941

Alarm No.170: 23.05 - 23.34. Alarm No.171: 01.24 - 01.50. First major attack on Liverpool (150 bombers). Further harassing attacks over London, Midlands and northeast coast.

29-Aug-1941

Alarm No.172: 21.05 - 22.07. An Air Ministry and Ministry of Home Security communiqué stated: "a few enemy aircraft crossed the east coast.

30-Aug-1941

Alarm No.173: 22.25 - 23.39. No action recorded.
Sunderland 7 Sheffield United 1. A crowd of 10,500, at Roker Park, watched Sunderland get off to a flying start in the Northern Wartime League match

1-Sep-1941

Alarm No.174: 22.04 - 23.45. Four high explosive bombs dropped in open ground at North Hylton – no casualties but trees uprooted and damage caused to shops and houses

3-Sep-1941

Alarm No.175: 21.17 - 22.13. An Air Ministry communiqué stated: "There was slight enemy activity last night. Bombs were dropped at one or two places in Northeast England and that one of these caused some damage".

4-Sep-1941

Alarm No.176: 21.47 - 23.47. Incidents reported from the eastern coastal districts of England and Scotland.

Hendon Ward now claims that every one of its streets has its own savings group.

5-Sep-1941

Two Southwick soldiers, home on leave, struck matches during a night alert and adopted a cheeky attitude to a Warden that remonstrated with them. The soldiers Isaac Drinkald of Marley Crescent and John George Drinkald (19) of Maplewood Avenue were fined five shillings each.

6-Sep-1941

Sheffield United 0 Sunderland 1.The one change today is that Spuhler took the place of Duns at outside right.

7-Sep-1941

Alarm No.177: 22.00 - 23.50. Enemy planes spent some time in the vicinity of Sunderland. They were met by heavy gunfire as they circled round in the cloud. Eventually heavy bombs were dropped in a field near Castletown. The Germans say they bombed the Tyne and the Humber.

All sea bathing facilities withdrawn in the Wearside area from today.

9-Sep-1941

A hit and run raid by a lone Nazi plane caused 2 deaths and a number of casualties at Ryhope Pit head early hours this morning. One man John Moody (62) and a youth Joseph McLeod (19) were killed. Twenty-one others injured, mostly slight injuries, which did not require hospital treatment.

10-Sep-1941

Sunderland's Communal Feeding Committee last night appointed as manager of the British Restaurant scheme in the town Mr H Green of Sheerness. The appointment is made at a salary of £375, plus the current war bonus. Sunderland's British restaurants would have been opened some time ago if it had it been possible to obtain prompt supplies of utensils, equipment, etc which can only be supplied through the pool of The Ministry of Food which has been on order since April.

In recent months Newcastle has been visited by at least a half-a-dozen Cabinet Ministers. Lord Walton was there yesterday and Mr Attlee is expected at the weekend. Mr Alexander, Mr Morrison, Mr Margesson and Ernest Brown have all been there recently. Granted Newcastle is the administrative centre of the Northern Region yet one would think that Sunderland is sufficiently important to warrant at least a flying visit.

Laing's launch the *EMPIRE DRUID* 9813t. 1959 Scrapped Osaka.

11-Sep-1941

Alarm No.178: 20.45 - 21.43. A lone raider was sighted flying at only 200 feet; it was heading north over Hendon. It released two bombs, which fell in Hudson Dock, then turned and headed out to sea. The bombs caused little damage and no casualties. The steam trawler *WAR GREY* 246t damaged by bombs off Sunderland.

13-Sep-1941

Sunderland 0 Bradford Park Avenue 2. Unlucky in the first half and guilty of bad play in the second sums up the defeat at the hands of Bradford.

17-Sep-1941

Householders are now forced to sacrifice their iron railings for the war effort. Exceptions will be those railings having artistic merit or a historical interest.

20-Sep-1941

Bradford Park Avenue 2 Sunderland 2. Carter scored both. Shackleton converted a penalty for Bradford.

21-Sep-1941

Alarm No.179: 09.27 - 09.52. No action recorded.

23-Sep-1941

Wm. Doxford launches the *EMPIRE COWPER* 7161t. 11.4.42 Bombed and sunk.

24-Sep-1941

Crowns launch the HMS GODETIA 925t Flower Class Corvette. Royal Navy. Commissioned as HMS DART 23/02/1942. Scrapped 1947.

26-Sep-1941

All girls aged between 20 and 25 years working in retail shops (other than food stores) are to be withdrawn for war work to join the ATS or train in engineering shops.

JL. Thompson launches the *EMPIRE HALLEY* 7168t. 1959 Scrapped Osaka.

Wm. Doxford launches the *EMPIRE FIELD* 7244t. Torpedoed and sunk by U.263.

27-Sep-1941

Leeds United 1, Sunderland 3. Bill Hewison replaced Alex Lockie.

29-Sep-1941

Sunderland's Tank Week opens hoping to raise £60,000 in National Savings to buy four tanks. The Ministry of Supply's tank column, consisting of a Matilda and two Covenanter tanks was on view in the Garrison Field.

30-Sep-1941

The enemy made a sharp raid on the town last night in which one enemy plane was destroyed, the attack was over before midnight but there was considerable damage to property and some casualties.

At around 9.50pm two high explosive bombs fell at Witherwack Farm in the north-western outskirts of the Borough; one in the Corporation Playing Field and another in a field beside Southwick Cemetery. Damage was caused to the Cemetery and to greenhouses on nearby allotments. Four houses completely demolished, sixteen to be demolished and sixty less seriously damaged. Water and gas mains were fractured and sixty-one people rendered homeless.

Seven people including five from one family lost their lives when bombs were dropped on their houses in Southwick, several dwellings were demolished here and a number of others damaged. Apart from those killed there was several who needed hospital treatment after being removed from the wreckage of their homes.

The Anderson Shelter (marked by the arrow) saved the four members of the Martin family.

Damage at Shakespeare Street and Cato Street

The tragic family, living at 59 Shakespeare Street, was that of William Hackett, a 44 year-old builder's labourer, he was killed along with his wife Gladys (42), his 16 year-old son Harry, two school children Alice (10) and Thomas (5). The bomb hit the house while the family were sheltering under the stairs. The tragedy is that the Anderson shelter at the rear of the wrecked house was left intact.

At 68 Cato Street, the Hogan family were trapped and when eventually accounted for 19-year-old Nora and her 8-year-old brother Dennis had been killed, Mary (45) and Theresa (19) seriously injured and Denis (45), Mildred (12) and Terence slightly injured.

In the house with the Hogan's were Edward Wilkinson and his wife Gladys and their two-year-old son David, mother and son were taken to hospital. Rescue squads worked tirelessly.

In Dryden Street four members of another family owed their lives to the fact that they were in their Anderson shelter, they were Michael Martin (46), a Plater's helper, his wife Margaret and that their daughters Teresa (13) and Ursula (10).

2-Oct-1941

Alarm No.181: 20.03 - 22.32

Incidents of anti-aircraft shells returning to earth and exploding on contact. British Ropes suffered a loss of production due to one of these wayward shells destroying some machinery. Another fell close to British Ropes on a footpath in front of 14 Fulwell Road, damaging 13 houses and injuring two people. And yet another shell fell through the roof of 6 Gloucester Avenue, Fulwell and exploded and extensively damaging the house. South Shields suffered most in the night's raid.

Raich Carter left today to join the RAF and undergo a PT instructor's course.

4-Oct-1941

Sunderland 6 Leeds United 1. Carter dashed back from an RAF station to play his best game for many moons.

6-Oct-1941

Tank week, which ended on Saturday was intended to raise £60,000 in savings but the action of James Westoll Ltd. in investing £88,000, was a great inspiration, the week ended on £218,715.

Bartram's launch the *EMPIRE BYRON* 6645t. Torpedoed and sunk by U703 on the 7th May 1942 while sailing in the Russian convoy PQ-17. Four crewmembers were lost

7-Oct-1941
Enemy aircraft were believed to be in the vicinity of the northeast of England this afternoon.

10-Oct-1941
The Mayor, Councillor Myers Wayman, opens Sunderland's first British Restaurant in S.Durham Street Centre.

11-Oct-1941
Sunderland was reported to have been raided.
Sunderland 4 Middlesbrough 4. A game of defensive errors. The crowd was just under 9600.

12/13-Oct-1941
Alarm No.182: 23.07 - 00.35. An Air Ministry communiqué on the 13th stated: "Last night activity by the enemy was again on a small scale. The latest type of the A.A. defences (Rockets) went into action in northern England last night.
In the first months of the war juvenile delinquency rose by 41 per cent among children up to fourteen and by 22 per cent of children aged between 14 and 17.

15-Oct-1941
Wm. Doxford launches the *EASTERN CITY* 5185t. Catapult Armed Merchantman. Scrapped April 1970.

16-Oct-1941
Alarm No.183: 03.35 - 04.33. Teesmouth area raided, slight damage.
Residents of Hylton Lane, Ettrick Grove and Marley Potts bus routes will have to except a reduction in their services at peak hours to release buses to carry war workers from the docks district to their homes.

17-Oct-1941
The second British Restaurant in Sunderland at East Moor Road in Pallion opened today.

18-Oct-1941
Middlesbrough 2 Sunderland 2. Sunderland is still unbeaten away from home. Middlesbrough goalkeeper had a Guardian Angel helping him.
The collier Empire Ghyll, Sunderland to London, struck a mine and sank near Gunfleet. Five of her crew and two gunners were killed

20-Oct-1941
JL. Thompson launches the *EMPIRE JOHNSON* 7168t. 13.7.42 Torpedoed and sunk by U.255.

21-Oct-1941
Alarm No.184: 20.29 - 22.31.
Heavy batteries were in action against the raiders and night fighters roared at intervals across the starlit sky. Four miners died at Ryhope Colliery pithead and three men died at South Hylton.
Although no bombs fell on Sunderland, there were a number of incidents of rogue anti aircraft shells returning to earth.
Sunderland's third British Restaurant was opened this morning in a disused Methodist chapel in

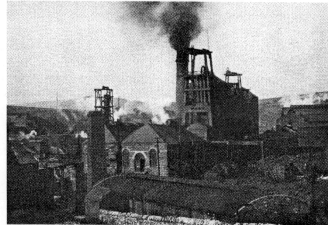
Ryhope Colliery in the 1930's

Whitburn Street, Monkwearmouth, having accommodation for 180 customers it will be the largest in the town.
Short Bros. launches the *EMPIRE NEWTON* 7037t. 1959 Scrapped Grays.
Pickersgill's launch the *STANGARTH* 5970t. 11.03.42 Departed New York on maiden voyage India via Table Bay. Not seen or heard of since. The Italian sub MOROSINI claimed to have sunk her the same day.

22-Oct-1941
Lord Beaverbrook appeals for more waste paper for shell and cartridge papers. Sunderland is urged to double its present 50 tons/month
Wm. Doxford launches the *EMPIRE DRYDEN* 7164t. 20.4.42 Torpedoed and sunk by U.572. 28 missing.

23-Oct-1940
The Regional Commissioner for Civil Defence, Sir Charles Lambert, called attention to the fact that several prosecutions have taken place lately which indicates that there are some members of the public who are not aware of the direction made by him on December 7th 1940 'that no person shall for the purpose of recreation or pleasure, or as a casual wayfarer, enter up on any beach or foreshore or enter upon any immediate approach to any such beach or foreshore'.

24-Oct-1941
The fourth British Restaurant is opened in Sunderland at Herrington Street Chapel Schoolroom. The new restaurant has a seating accommodation for about 130 customers.

25-Oct-1941

Steps have been taken by the Corporation to discourage rowdyism on the late trams and buses. There were several prosecutions arising from conduct of this nature in the Borough Police Court yesterday. In one instance a man was accused of boarding the crowded bus by opening up the emergency door in the rear. A woman used force and bad language in order to get on a full bus. The bench would not tolerate this type of behaviour and stiff fines will be imposed on future offenders.

Newcastle Utd. 1 Sunderland 1. Sunderland was unchanged. More than 22,000 people were present.

28-Oct-1941

The town's 5th British Restaurant at Carol Street in Deptford is opened. It's the smallest in the town with accommodation for only 58 persons at one sitting.

29-Oct-1941

Billy Cotton was among the guests at a Whist Drive and Dance organised last night at the New Rink by the Police Recreation Club. Billy Cotton led the band for several of the dances.

31-Oct-1941

Sunderland 6th British Restaurant was opened in Bell's Assembly Rooms in Southwick. It has accommodation for 184 persons. With the three 'cash and carry' canteens Sunderland now has nine communal feeding centres.

1-Nov-1941

Because of a shortage of matches the Board of Trade allows the manufacture and supply of 'mechanical lighters'. They must not contain more than three-quarters of an ounce of brass, and they must be marked indelibly with the letters UL (utility lighter) and must be sold at a wholesale price not exceeding five shillings. Sunderland 3 Newcastle 2.

3-Nov-1941

Rowntree announces that Black Magic chocolates will no longer be made until after the war. A new assortment is to be introduced called Cranton to be sold at 1s 8d per half pound.

4-Nov-1941

Alarm No.185: 04.25 - 05.01. Air Ministry communiqué states: "Last night there was slight coastal activity by the enemy; a single aircraft craft dropped bombs at a place on the north-east coast of England. Some damage was done and a small number of casualties have been reported".

SP. Austin launches the *LAMBTONIAN* 2781t. The 'Lambtonian" sailed as leading ship in the first merchant navy convoy to France on D-Day. A Sunderland ship captained by J E Judge, of Middleton, Teasdale, (formerly of Gloucester Avenue, Sunderland) with a crew of mostly Sunderland men. 1960 scrapped Dunston-on-Tyne.

7-Nov-1941

In a widespread raid on northeast coastal districts, Sunderland was dive-bombed in the moonlight and suffered the brunt of the attack. A number of high explosive bombs were dropped and considerable damage was done to property, mainly houses, in several parts of the town. Casualties: - Seven killed, fifteen seriously injured, thirty-nine slightly injured. Two rest centres were opened for the 100 homeless.

Berlin later said: "Strong formations of German bombers attacked the harbour and industrial installations of Sunderland in a series of waves. Visibility was good and the attacks were very successful with fires and explosions observed".

At around 10.25pm, four 500kg bombs fell in the Trimdon Street area. One damaged the water treatment plant of the Hylton Road Generating Station. The main stores were demolished and considerable damage was done to the switchgear and other buildings at the works. The station was shut down in the early hours of the 8th but was operating again by 7:30am on November 10th.

A second bomb fell on 8 Lily Street, demolishing several others and killing William Steel (74), a retired policeman, who was on his way to the backyard surface shelter. His elderly housekeeper

Mrs Hollands, who was in the shelter, was injured when the structure collapsed. In a shelter next door were two widows Mrs Pedersen and Mrs Carter. Their shelter withstood the blast but Mrs Pedersen injured herself falling into the crater when exiting the shelter.

A third bomb fell on No. 11 coal staithe of the Lambton Drops causing damage to the permanent way but causing no casualties.

The remains of what were No.'s 96 & (8 Fulwell Road

The fourth bomb of this cluster fell into allotment gardens damaging some cabins but again causing no casualties

At about the same time, four HEs fell on the other side of the river.

One partly demolished the Blue Bell Hotel, Roker Avenue shortly after closing time and only the manager and his wife and barman were on the premises. However, Joseph Cairns who was standing in the street was killed. Two other men with him were injured. A Catholic Church hall and school was damaged by the blast and flying debris.

One in Fulwell Road demolished four single-storey houses trapping several persons. One of the trapped, Joseph Gowland (46), of 108 Fulwell Road, was killed and others were taken to hospital. A brick shelter saved two families named Hadden and Richards.

One fell on the brickworks of Messrs Tyzack, Fulwell Road, killing John Barras (70), a firewatcher and damaging plant, finished products and offices. Barras lived in a street near by that had been bombed in two previous raids.

A little later four bombs near the LNER, South Dock Branch Railway. Only one of the four detonated demolishing four houses and damaging others in Whitehouse Road but caused no crater. Three were UX, one at the foot of the railway embankment and others 40' and 50' away. Three people died in this incident. Two Fireguards named Smith, mother and daughter, aged 45 and 17 and both called Madeline Louise along Edwin Smith aged 8 all died at No.1 Whitehouse Cottages.

At about the same time other bombs were heard in the region of South Dock. The first bomb dropped onto an incline railway connecting the dock bottom with a high-level railway above near No. 19 coal staithe. A locomotive was knocked over. It completely blocked the connecting incline but within 12 hours the engine was

The badly damaged the Blue Bell in Roker Avenue

removed and the bomb crater filled in and the incline opened up to traffic in again. Damage was done to the coal staithe and to a crane near by. Iron girders were hurled in all directions, with one landing on top of the spotters post on top of the staithe, a sailor in the post escaped injury.

The devastation in Whitehouse Road

The second bomb fell on the quayside between the lock gates and the South outlet this was a very near miss. As it was, it caused a critical situation for a time. A hydraulic mains supply for the sluice gates was fractured and water was escaping from the dock. If this continued the ships in the dock were threatened. Captain Chapman and others operated the gates by hand and removed the danger. A third bomb exploded in the dock itself, the Dock Masters House narrowly escaped being hit but it was damaged however along with Laing's warehouse.
8-Nov-1941
Sunderland v Bradford City. Raich Carter and Alex Hastings returned to the side. Sunderland won by a big margin.

42,142 were killed by air raids on Britain between the beginning of the war and the end of August 1941. In the same period 18,431 persons were killed in road accidents.
The collier GASLIGHT, 1696t built by Wood, Skinner & Co. Ltd., Bill Quay, damaged by bombs from aircraft 2 cables from S1 Buoy off Sunderland.

10-Nov-1941
A man was charged with contravening the blackout regulations while in fact in the process of completing his blackout procedure. The blackout time was 6:04pm and blackout had been started before that time but owing to the arrival of the police it was not completed until 6.09pm. A fine of £2 was imposed on Abraham Mersky, of

Valebrook, at his Wearside furnishing store in Crowtree Road. Mersky had been convicted on two previously occasions of blackout offences.

12-Nov-1941

Alarm No.188: 09.14 - 10.08. Bombs on Seaham Harbour.

Questions were raised in Parliament indicating that a good deal of the absenteeism was due to greyhound racing on ordinary working days and that in the interests of the country's war needs dog racing should be stopped on working days. Mr Morrison, Home Secretary, replied that greyhound racing is to be limited to one meeting per week and that afternoon meetings will only be held on Saturdays and public holidays. Greyhound racing in County Durham will only take place on Saturday afternoons.

Drastic new provisions affecting almost every section of the community, are contained in a new order, issued a by the Ministry of Supply, which comes into operation this morning. Housewives and shopkeepers are affected by the provision that no retailer should provide any paper for the packing or wrapping of goods, except foodstuff.

The Council gave consent to Northern Redifusion Service to increase their weekly rental charges from 1s 6d per week to 1s 9d per week.

13-Nov-1941

Thomas Struthers (77), former shipyard caulker, of 15 Chester Street East, was fatally injured when he was knocked down by a van in Hylton Road. The accident occurred near the junction of Hylton Road and St Marks Road at about 6:40pm on Thursday. Struthers suddenly appeared out of the dark into the light of the masked headlight.

14-Nov-1941

Alarm No.189: 12.30 - 12.42. Enemy aircraft were believed to be in the vicinity of the northeast coast during this morning.

15-Nov-1941

The Sunderland man who saved LNER ammunition trucks during a firebomb attack made on Tyne Dock has been awarded the British Empire Medal for his gallantry. He is Robert Stephen Ward (50) of 22 Yewtree Avenue Southwick. (Tragically killed on February 13th 1942).

Bradford City v Sunderland. Both Lockie and Carter could not make the journey. He phoned from Huddersfield to say that he could not make Bradford, he was given permission to play for Huddersfield.
Four survivors from the torpedoed freighter BRADFORD CITY *are Thomas Alfred Halliday (28) of Mount Road, Peter Sinkett of Church Hill Avenue, Southwick, Alfred Swan of Falmouth Square, Ford Estate and John Mason (20) of 75 Falkland Road, Ford Estate.*

17-Nov-1941

Every unmarried woman from 20 to at least 25 must accept to be called upon to help in the war effort. They're wanted for new factories and they are wanted now.
'SS BOVEY TRACEY' (1,212t) cargo ship, built in 1930 by J. Crown & Sons, Portsmouth to Sunderland, was sunk by German aircraft off Aldeburgh.

18-Nov-1941

Alarm No.190: 18.05 - 18.23. Enemy action against shipping between the Humber and the Tyne.
Laing's launch the EMPIRE AIRMAN (2) 9813t. 1959 scrapped Hong Kong.

19-Nov-1941

Wm. Doxford launches the *EMPIRE DRUM* 7244t. 24.4.42 Torpedoed and sunk by U.136. Crew of 41 all saved

21-Nov-1941

Since the start of the war there has been a serious deterioration in road behaviour by all classes of road users, largely due to wartime mentality, and to living 'dangerously' says a white paper issued by the Ministry of Transport. In a the first 12 months of the war 8358 persons were killed on the roads, a 25 per cent increase on previous years. The second 12 months of the year the number rose by a further 20% to 10,073. Abnormally large number of accidents in blackout hours occurs during the period covering the return from work especially when accompanied by air raids.

22-Nov-1941

Milk rationed; it varied between 2 to 3 pints per week. Sunderland's milk consumers may not find their strict ration of two pints of milk per week imposed at once but it will be coming into effect very shortly. The milk-rationing scheme announced this week comes into operation tomorrow but Sunderland and District dairy farmers are hoping to carry on for a few more weeks without imposing the full cut. There's no doubt however that the public must be prepared for a great reduction in milk supply.
Huddersfield 1 Sunderland 0. McMahon and Carter both missed penalties.

26-Nov-1941

After 27 months of war there are still cases of carelessness regarding the blackout regulations. Magistrates threaten imprisonment. There were a number of cases before the magistrate, which included Sarah Knowles of a Whitehall Terrace for showing a fire through a window. She was fined £2.

28-Nov-1941

Laing's launch the *EMPIRE SILVER* 8602t. 1960 Scrapped Split.

29-Nov-1941

Sunderland 6 Huddersfield 1. A poor first half but their second half domination was complete.

1-Dec-1941

Sunderland housewives raided their grocer shops this morning for their first suppliers of American tinned foods. Today the Ministry of Food's points rationing scheme, postponed for a fortnight, came into operation and there was a rush on the shops to get an early supplies of goods in the greatest demand. Nearly everyone seems to want salmon or tinned meat, particularly tongue, there's not a great demand for tinned fish or beans.

Today is what Lord Woolton, Minister of Food, called a red-letter day in the history of his ministry. Not only does the points rationing of canned foods begin but in the third year of the war consumers are to have increased rations of sugar, fat and margarine. The allowance of sugar will be increased from 8 ounces to 12 ounces per head. This increase was announced early in October but since then large quantities have been sent to Russia. The weekly fat ration is increased from 8 ounces to 10 ounces. Of this total seven ounces will consist of butter and margarine with a maximum of 2 ounces of butter. Canned fish, meat and beans will be on sale today but they are rationed and coupons have to be given up in exchange for them. The sale of these commodities has been forbidden in the past few weeks because shops did not have sufficient stocks to meet the new points coupons.

2-Dec-1941

Foreshadowing the gigantic intensification of Britain's war effort of 1942, the Premier in the Commons today outlined the new legislative demands to be made forthwith upon the Country's man and womanpower. Compulsory military service is to cover the ages from $18^1/_2$ to 51. Power is to be taken to direct men to the Home Guard in areas where it was a necessary. It is also proposed to register boys and girls between 16 and 18. Over 170,000 women are needed for the ATS and of these 100,000 are needed for the Air Defence Forces. The government is asking for compulsory powers to call up single women between 20 and 30.

For the first time in British history women are to go into action against the enemy. The first are to be the girls of the ATS who are now at work with the anti-aircraft batteries. Here they are shown receiving instruction on the use of a Predictor at the Grangetown Battery.

All single women between 20 and 30 are to be called up. Some will soon be in anti-aircraft crews along with men. Others will take over desk jobs now done by medically fit men. Up to 1,700,000 women are involved in the Government's new conscription plans. The call-up age for men is lowered to 181/2 and at the other end of the age scale men up to 50 will be liable for military service. The manpower situation is now acute in both the forces and the factories. Some conscripted women may also be put into the police and the fire services, and to meet future needs, the registration of women up to 40, both single and married will now begin. Boys and girls between 16 and 18 must also register. The idea is that these youngsters should be encouraged into suitable pre-military training after interviews with the school authorities. There will be deferment of call-up for university students and others with approved places in higher education.

The Grangetown anti-aircraft battery

3-Dec-1941

Sunderland magistrates today declined to accept a report that a Crowtree Road tradesman has been singled out by a policeman. Convicting Abraham Mersky (56) for the 4th time since the outbreak of war, they find him £10. A further 13 cases were heard with fines ranging from £5 to 10 shillings.

4-Dec-1941

The War Savings toyshop in Park Lane has proved such a marked success that its operation is to be extended for the whole of this week. The shop was opened with the dual purpose of boosting National Savings and also in helping the supply of toys, people are asked to bring to the shop old or unwanted toys for sale and were credited with the sum in savings certificates or saving stamps.

6-Dec-1941

Sunderland Scouts are to take part in the scheme arranged by the Chief Scout whereby they will co-operate with the Corporation in the collection of waste paper and for each ton collected will receive £1 for Scout funds. Today all Sunderland women aged 31 (the 1910 class) are due to register for National Service. Sunderland v York City: Arthur Wright back home from Ireland, on leave, played at left half.

7-Dec-1941

Japanese aircraft launch a surprise attack on American naval forces at Pearl Harbour, Hawaii. The Imperial Government of Japan declares war on Britain, Canada, Australia and the United States.

8-Dec-1941

Alarm No.191: 17.38 - 18.24. No action recorded.

The news of 'Sunderland's own' fighter squadron is that they are now 'bombers'. The Air Minister gave this news when he visited Newcastle at the weekend. Mentioning the 607 (County of Durham) Squadron he said 'they had fought in France and are now re equipped with Hurricanes fitted with bombing attachments'.

The Air Minister, Sir Archibald Sinclair, however, slipped up by stating that the 607 Squadron grew up under Newcastle's wing and that Newcastle supplied the whole original flying personnel. There were at least four Sunderland boys among the original pilots and there were almost certainly others.

8/9-Dec-1941

Alarm No.192: 22.11 - 00.39.

Enemy planes again crossed the coast this morning and were met with heavy gunfire from the ground defences. Several bombs fell in open spaces but caused no casualties. Bombs that fell on Seaburn Beach blew out windows of the Hotel and shops in Queens Parade. The barrage was one of the heaviest put up in the district. At times the gun flashers were so continuous that it was possible to stand in the street and read a newspaper. An anti aircraft shell fell to earth and exploded damaging walls and windows of eight houses in Westfield Grove. Near the Eye Infirmary, a bomb caused a large crater in a field, a second failed to explode. Other bombs fell into the sea off the South Docks.

9-Dec-1941

Alarm No.193: 11.08 - 11.28. A Junkers Ju 88D presumed to have been shot down by Hurricanes of 43 Squadron crashed into the sea, 10 miles off Seaham.

Lord Woolton, Minister of Food, said today there would be no additional release of food for Christmas. Rations will remain at the present rate for the rest of the month. The Ministry yesterday began the distribution of Cod-liver oil and fruit juices free to children under two.

A Sunderland youth, Wilfred Reeves (18) of Flax Square, was today sent to prison for six weeks for failing to return to work as a Fettler in a foundry at Leamington Spa. He was told that the work required of him was just as important as that of a soldier in the front line.

11-Dec-1941

About 2 million engineering and shipyard workers throughout the Country will receive a flat wage increase of five shillings per week. This applies to all adult male workers and will operate from next week. Shipyard workers will be disappointed. On time rates a Riveter earns £3 18s 6d per week. Piece workers no doubt earn more, but conditions are not as favourable as in former times, and earnings from overtime are curtailed.

13-Dec-1941

Alarm No.194: 15.41 - 16.07. An Air Ministry communiqué stated: " there was a little enemy activity, which was restricted to coastal districts".

York City 0 Sunderland 4. A week ago we saw Arthur Wright back home from Ireland on leave, at left half for Sunderland. The fact that Johnny Spuhler turned up with a suspected piece of steel in his eye, and was sent back to receive treatment, meant a reshuffling of the team at York, which involved the playing of Arthur Wright at inside left. He scored a hat trick and failed in a penalty kick. York City finished with nine men and Sunderland with 10. Sunderland's loss was Lockie who pulled a muscle in the first half and went off later in the game to prevent further aggravation.

14-Dec-1941

A Sunderland anti aircraft battery, composed of men and women, became the first such battery to have shot down an enemy aircraft in the northeast. The official confirmation of our battery's claim to have 'drawn blood' in a recent sharp attack on coastal areas has been received by the Commanding Officer.

15-Dec-1941

Mr T E Parrington, General Manager of Wearmouth Colliery Company Limited, declared when opening a new pit head canteen at Wearmouth Colliery today, "the Canteen will be open 24 hours a day and the workmen will be able to get a meal at any time whatever his shift".

16-Dec-1941

JL. Thompson launches the *EMPIRE NOMAD* 7167t. 13.10.42 Torpedoed and sunk by U.159. 6 crew lost.

17-Dec-1941

Alarm No.195: 18.03 - 20.11.

In the early part of last night there was slight enemy activity, a few bombs being dropped in the northeast and southwest. At one point in the northeast some houses were damaged and a small number of persons injured. The Press Association say that flares dropped over the northeast coast (looking for shipping) where the raiders were over one town at intervals of some time. They were met by heavy anti-aircraft fire..
Wm. Doxford launches the *TARANTIA* 7268t Anchor Line Ltd. Scrapped China 1971.
Bartram's launch the *EMPIRE BALLAD* 6700t. 1969 Scrapped at Split after grounding.

18-Dec-1941

The object of a new regulation is to remedy two weaknesses from which the Home Guard is beginning to suffer. The first is that its strength is distributed unevenly over the Country and does not always correspond to military needs. Secondly the standard of training is not uniform and with improved equipment now becoming available cannot be used with full effect by untrained men. Age for volunteers to the Home Guard remains unchanged from 17 to 65 but the age of Compulsory Enrolment will be the same as that of conscription to the regular forces between 18 and 51.

19-Dec-1941

Short Bros. launches the *EMPIRE STOREY* 7037t. 3.5.42 Ashore North West Ledge, NB.

20-Dec-1941

Alarm No.196: 17.26 - 18.10.

Alarm sounded when a lone raider came in from the sea, turned north and when near the gas works, dropped two bombs then turned and fled out to sea. The bombs caused some damage in Robinson Terrace and Short Street and blocked a railway line.
Gateshead 2 Sunderland 0.

23-Dec-1941

Christmas Day, for most people, will be a day of rest rather than festivity. Most of the important works are closing down for one-day, to give their employees a respite from months of hard toil. They will be however back into production on Friday morning. Apart from the cinemas and theatres there will be few distractions. Crowds are expected on Christmas Day at Roker Park for the return match against Gateshead. On Saturday (27th) there will be another attractive match with Middlesbrough as visitors in a League Cup tie.

24-Dec-1941

Despite restrictions on supply, Sunderland tradesmen have had one of their busiest Christmas shopping seasons. The last few days have seen the shopping centre in the town crowded with last minute present hunters. Some people must have cleaned out their last available clothing coupons. A 'Santa Clause' appearing at one department store and had 30,000 visitors over the three weeks.

A 16 year-old boy, who refused to work in the shipyard because his wage of 19 shillings per week was too small, was committed to prison for three months. He was accused of a breach of recognisance.

25-Dec-1941

Alarm No.197: 17.40 - 18.10. No action recorded.

Sunderland v Gateshead. Over 11,000 spectators watched Gateshead take maximum points from the two meetings. Len Duns was on leave and played.

27-Dec-1941

Sunderland 6 Middlesbrough 2. It was a better performance against Middlesbrough than at the one we saw beaten by Gateshead on Christmas Day. Whitelum got four of the six goals.

29-Dec-1941

Alarm No.198: 20.27 - 22.08.

An Air Ministry and Ministry of Home Security communiqué stated: during the early part of last night there was some enemy activity mainly over North East England. Three enemy bombers were destroyed. Sunderland was not attacked, however, bombs did fall at Whitburn Colliery and North Hylton, where windows of a farmhouse were broken.

Meat ration down to 1s worth with the balance made up from canned corned beef.

30-Dec-1941

The Brewers Society announced that owing to the acute shortage of labour in the malting industry and to conserve available malt, the Ministry of Food has decided that the average gravity of beer shall be reduced by five per cent. It is anticipated, in the main, that this will affect only the stronger beers and that there will be little or no change in the character of ordinary draft beers. The price of beer will not be reduced in consequence.

31-Dec-1941

Tonight we see the end of 1941 and civilians will regret its disappearance less than even its two war predecessors. It has been a great and vital year which has the war balanced wholly in our favour. It has seen Hitler making a colossal blunder in attacking Russia, thereby presenting us with a most powerful ally.

People will wait for the chime at midnight from Big Ben over the radio tonight as the signal to celebrate the coming of 1942. No longer can they celebrate in Fawcett Street under the Wearside's 'Big Ben', which has been silenced for the duration.

Anti-Aircraft Christmas dinner 1941

1942

"…. the end of the beginning"

- The year starts badly with Singapore falling to the Japanese.
- Hitler cancels planned invasion of Britain
- German and Italian armies are beaten back by the British at El Alamein in the North African desert.
- November 10, 1942. Following the Allied victory at El Alamein, Prime Minister Winston Churchill said, "This is not the end. It is not even at the beginning of the end, but it is perhaps the end of the beginning".

1-Jan-1942

Whisky production is cut by one-tenth – gold jewellery manufacture banned, except for wedding rings – the standard ring costs £1/1/-.

3-Jan-1942

Workers object to housewives and retired people taking their midday meals in restaurants.
Middlesbrough 3 Sunderland 0. Football League Cup.

'SS Corfen' (1,848t) collier, built by J. Crown & Sons Ltd in 1939, is sunk by a mine in the Thames.

HMS DELHI

4-Jan-1942

Alarm No.199: 19.50 - 20.13. No action recorded.

6-Jan-1942

Regarding Warship Week; one person wrote and asked "If I put my little bit into Sunderland's Warship Week and the cruiser HMS Delhi is adopted would I lose my money if the ship were sunk?" They were assured that is was not gifts but investments that were being requested.

9-Jan-1942

John Middlehurst (32) of Perth Road was sent to prison for one month for causing unnecessary cruelty and suffering to three ducks and 11 hens by neglecting to feed them.

10-Jan-1942

Sunderland 2 Newcastle 2. The RAF released Carter to play against Newcastle in the Football League Cup. The referee disallowed a 'winning' goal by Carter.

12-Jan-1942

From today no chocolate or sweets may be sold to the consumer at a price higher than 5d per quarter pound.

13-Jan-1942

Alarm No.200: 10.53 - 11.06. Alarm No.201: 15.36 - 15.50.

Enemy aircraft were assumed to be in the vicinity of Northeast England during the morning. Aircraft flying singularly were presumably on the lookout for shipping. No bombs were reported to have been a dropped on land.

The SS LERWICK, 5626t, built by J L Thompson & Sons in 1938, is bombed and sunk off Robin Hoods Bay. 5 crewmembers were lost.

15-Jan-1942

Alarm No.202: 17.46 - 18.56.

In hit and run raid on Sunderland. An enemy aircraft dropped four bombs, which fell in Backhouse Park causing four casualties with minor injuries and little damage. The plane then swooped low over the town, machine-gunning as it went. Many people saw a plane roaring over their heads after the sound of heavy explosions. A Theatre queue broke up as people scattered for shelter. Ryhope Road was blocked with soil and clay from the craters in the Park. Windows of the Synagogue and of the Art School were damaged by the blasts.
SP.Austin launches the *EMPIRE JILL* 739t. 1967 FARDAD, M.J. Motraghi, Iran.
Wm. Doxford launches the *EMPIRE KNIGHT* 7244t. 11.2.44 Wrecked Boon Island Ledge, Nova Scotia.

16-Jan-1942

Alarm No.203: 16.46 - 17.24. No action recorded.

25,000 Sunderland citizens are now doing some kind of voluntary service in the civil defence arrangements of the town. Special tribute was paid to the 500 boys of the Messenger Service and the progress that had been made in organising fireguards and street fire fighting parties.

17-Jan-1942

Sunderland 1 Newcastle 2. Hewitson missed the 5th consecutive penalty from which Sunderland has failed to score. Saturday's gate was just under 19,000.
Laing's launched the *EMPIRE MARVELL* 9812t. 1962 Scrapped Vigo after fire & grounding damage.

19-Jan-1942

Alarm No.204: 12.25 - 12.36. A raid on Berwick. The Duke of Kent visited Sunderland shipyards and factories. He visited a works canteen nicknamed 'The Prospect Hotel' and exchanged greetings with some hundreds of men busy with good helpings of steak and kidney pudding. At the glass works he was giving a rousing reception from hundreds of girl workers.

The Duke of Kent meets veteran workers at J.L. Thompson's shipyard. Sir Norman Thompson is on the right

22-Jan-1942

An inquest on David Neil Gibson (60), a retired shipwright, of 22 Peebles Road, a verdict of accidental death was returned. He died on Monday from the injuries after being knocked down in Durham Road last Friday (16th) night by a tramcar during the blackout.

23-Jan-1942

The Magistrates claim that a Remand Home in Sunderland is an urgent necessity. While admitting that the amount of juvenile delinquency is serious, they did not admit that the problem was that as alarming as it appeared to be.

24-Jan-1942

Women of 32 are required to register today. Married women with no children living with them will be directed into the factories. Wives of servicemen will go into industry but will not be moved away from their homes. Today Sunderland are placed 34th on of the Cup chart, 32nd place is required to qualify. They must win against Gateshead next Saturday to have any chance of qualifying.

25-Jan-1942

Alarm No.205: 11.48 - 11.59. No action recorded.

26-Jan-1942

A fine of £15 with £5 costs was imposed today on Daniel McKenna (18) of Woodbine Street for his refusal to obey a direction that he should take work in the Midlands.

30-Jan-1942

Alarm No.206: 11.21 - 11.47

Enemy aircraft were believed to be in the vicinity of the northeast coast.

Wm. Doxford launches the *TAHSINIA* 7267t. 01.10.1943, torpedo and gunfire by U.532. Crew of 48 all saved.

31-Jan-1942

Football League Cup, Gateshead 1 Sunderland 2. Sunderland's first away victory since December 15th was gained at Redheugh Park The gate of 6500 watched a poor game.

4-Feb-1942

All volunteer members of the ARP Service as with Home Guard will from today come under military style discipline. They will be required to do their 48 hours duty without fail. It will also be an offence to disobey any order or refuse to carry out any duty.

3-Feb-1942

Wearsiders woke to find snow lying nearly a foot deep and a temperature of seven degrees of frost. Where snow had drifted, it was three or four feet deep. Sunderland and South Shields Water Company had nearly 4000 burst water pipes reported to them from Sunderland residents.

6-Feb-1942

Alarm No.207: 09.43 - 09.54. Alarm No.208: 14.16 - 14.25. Enemy activity off the East coast this morning and later over the North East. Today's German communiqué said that devastating night raids were made on Newcastle/Edinburgh railway line.

7-Feb-1942

The Chief Constable reports that 186 people were charged with drunkenness during 1941. 110 were residents (96 men and 14 women) and 76 non-residents. This compared with 160 in 1940. The result showed that Sunderland rate of drunkenness was 1% of the population compared with 2% at South Shields, 2.3% at Gateshead and 3.6% at Newcastle.

8-Feb-1942

In North Africa Rommel's Afrika Korps halts its advance near Gazala. They have recaptured almost all of the territory the British had taken in 1941. The British 1st Armoured Division is in disarray and the morale of the British 8th Army is sinking.

9-Feb-1942

Soap rationing begins; the allowance is to be 4oz for household use or 2oz of toilet soap per person per month.

10-Feb-1942

Robert Longstaff (21), a labourer, of Drury Lane, was fined £20 for failing to return to his work in a munitions factory in the Midlands. The court told him that the only thing that had saved him from going to prison was the need for men at sea. Longstaff was ordered to pay the £20 in three months or go to prison for two months.

12-Feb-1942

Alarm No.209: 09.04 - 09.20. Enemy aircraft were believed to be in the vicinity of the northeast this morning.

13-Feb-1942

Robert Stephen Ward (49) 22 Yewtree Avenue Southwick was killed instantly when knocked down by a bus in Southwick last night at the junction of North Hylton Road and Carlisle Terrace. He was the yard inspector for the L.N.E.R. Company at Tyne Dock. At a later inquest it was related that as a hero of a firebomb blitz at South Shields, he was awarded, last November, the British Empire Medal for gallantry for his part in saving ammunition wagons in a railway siding, During the raid incendiary bombs were dropped among 300 wagons at the sidings setting fire to some. Ward with other men moved 274 of these wagons including those laden with ammunition. While carrying it out these tasks high explosive bombs were falling around them. The Coroner gave the verdict of accidental death.

14-Feb-1942

Sunderland Warship Week was launched today with the target of £1 million to adopt HMS Delhi. The procession, led by a Pipe Band, that marched through Sunderland today to focus public attention on the launching of the Warship Week effort was one of the biggest days on Wearside for years. It took a full half hour to pass the saluting base at the Town Hall. It was estimated that the procession was over one mile long.

Sunderland has four more games to play in the qualifying

competition, two of them at home. A convincing win today over York City, although they did concede three goals.

15-Feb-1942

Alarm No.210: 19.00 - 21.12. Raid on Northumberland.

16-Feb-1942

After today members of the Home Guard will no longer have the right to give 14 days' notice to resign. The principal provisions of the new Defence Regulations are;

Home guardsmen may now be ordered to perform training on operational duties for not more than 48 hours each four weeks.

Compulsory Enrolment will be applied in areas decided upon by the Army Council and the Ministry of Labour. The Ministry of Labour work will be responsible for the selection of men between the ages of 18 and 51.

Members can still apply for discharge on grounds such as age, medical fitness, or interference with essential civilian employment. A member may be required to serve continuously and live away from home if the threat of invasion warrants it. Military offences while on duty may be dealt with under the Army Act.

If a member, without reasonable excuse, absences himself from parade or duty he may incur a £10 fine and/or one months imprisonment.

18-Feb-1942

Miners exempted from soap rationing.

21-Feb-1942

There have been two cases this week of 'tired youths' lads of 19 who did not like to work. Each were the subject of prosecution after inducement having been made by the National Service Officer and others to get them to shoulder their responsibilities. One a miner was the despair of his father. After being sent off to work he crept back into the house by a window and went to bed.

A Wearside Plater's helper was absent for whole days and half days even after serious warnings, it was said that since December 16th he has been absent or unpunctual almost every day.

Football League Cup, Bradford 3 Sunderland 0.

23-Feb-1942

Canned fruit, tomatoes and peas are released for sale on the point's scheme today. 16 points are required for a large can of fruit, 9 points for a large can of tomatoes and four points for a large can of peas.

Ministry of Food hopes in March to distribute three eggs to each registered consumer.

24-Feb-1942

'How the call up affects the women of Britain' gave the official explanation of registration and compulsory call-up. Compulsory service may take one of two forms;

Compulsory call-up to the Women's Auxiliary Service (commonly called Conscription). The compulsory call-up to the Women's Auxiliary Services applies only to single women and widows without children, and at present to those who were born in 1920 or 1921. It may be extended to other age groups.

Compulsory call-up to work in industry (commonly called 'direction'). A compulsory direction requires a woman to go to any civilian job. If she disobeys it she is liable to prosecution.

Services and war work in which women are wanted now is the Women's Auxiliary Service, Civil Defence, Nursing Services, Women's Land Army, and Navy, Army and Air Force Institutes. Industrial work is munitions (including iron and steel, chemicals, radio and electric cables), light alloys, timber production, Post Office Engineering, domestic work in hospitals, canteens and hostels for munitions and armaments workers, Transport services including maintenance. Local jobs for those who cannot leave home to replace those who can.

25-Feb-1942

Plans estimated to cost £42,000 to provide 8000 Sunderland children a mid-day meal at school daily were provisionally approved yesterday by the Sunderland Education Committee. It was stated that a two-course lunch could be provided for the children at a cost of a between $4^1/_2$d and 5d per meal.

Sunderland's Savings Committee announce with pride that a Warship Week has resulted in the sum of £1,156,331 being raised and that the cruiser HMS DELHI has been adopted by Sunderland.

26-Feb-1942

The Medical Officer of Health to Sunderland's Health Committee reported a large increase in the number of people suffering from diphtheria and a great decrease in measles as compared with the same period last year. During the four weeks ending 21st February this year 72 cases of diphtheria were notified as compared with 21 for the corresponding four weeks of last year. Nationally one third of the children under 15 years of age had been immunised against diphtheria and in some places, Carlisle for instance, 65 per cent have been immunised while Newcastle's figure was given as 58 per cent. From information gathered Sunderland's proportion of immunised children was not above 18 per cent.

There were only seven cases of measles notified where as last year the figure was 647.

27-Feb-1942

Work is now in progress on the demolition of the old Winter Gardens.

28-Feb-1942

Sunderland 2 Bradford2. Spuhler scores from the penalty spot after five successive failures by other players.

2-Mar-1942

In the National Waste Paper contest, Keswick won the Northern Section with the salvage collection per head of population of 15lbs. Sunderland's 340 tons, from a wartime population estimated at 167,000, works out at a miserable $4^1/_2$ lbs per head.

3-Mar-1942

JL Thompson launches the *ELMWOOD* 7166t. Torpedoed by U-130 27.07.1942. All the crew were saved.

5-Mar-1942

5 million women have now registered and over 35,000 are being placed in jobs every week. Girls of 16 and 17 will shortly be registered under the youth scheme and together with the 18 and 19 age group would give a complete picture of the Womanpower available.

8-Mar-1942

Alarm No.211: 20.46 - 21.17. Alarm No.212: 21.33 - 22.21. An Air Ministry communiqué stated: "some Enemy activity last night mainly over east and northeast coasts of England".

9-Mar-1942

From today you must not throw away empty cigarette packets or screw up paper and drop it in the gutter. If you do so you are liable to a £100 fine or 3 months in jail.

Joseph Conlin (48) of Nile Street Sunderland was sent to prison for three months for leaving the employment at Wolverhampton. Robert Trotter of Zion Street was also sent to prison for three months for failing to resume employment as a factory labourer in a factory at Coventry.

12-Mar-1942

Good Friday as the usual holiday is cancelled. Events such as football are cancelled.

13-Mar-1942

A new Defence regulation. Penalties for killing or wounding homing or racing pigeons are unchanged but it is now not a sufficient defence to say, "that I did not know it was a homing pigeon". Homing pigeons are extensively used by the fighting services for carrying urgent messages when other means of communication are unpractical. The RAF has thousands of pigeons in its vital signal service. They form part of the crew of every bomber and reconnaissance aircraft operating over the seas around Britain. A pot shot at a lone pigeon and a vital operation, maybe the lives of the crew, could be jeopardised.

16-Mar-1942

The Roker Volunteer Life Saving Brigade went to the assistance of the *SS CAMEROUX I,* which had tried to enter the harbour but failed and ran ashore near the fishermen's cottages. Although the vessel lay 350 yards offshore a line was got on board and nine lives were saved.

SP.Austin launches the *FIRESIDE* 2757t. 29.12.1967 aground and broke up.

17-Mar-1942

Following the fall of Singapore on the 15th February it is only today that Sunderland hears of the capture of the 125 Anti-Tank Regiment. The Royal Artillery Regiment based on Wearside before the war as a territorial unit, and out of its total strength something like 80 per cent came from Sunderland.

Mrs Winifred Common (24) of 61 Keswick Avenue Sunderland was fatally injured last night when she was knocked down by a tramcar in Fulwell Road near Side Cliff Road junction. Miss Common was a teacher at St. Columba's CE School Southwick.

Laing's launch the *EMPIRE COLERIDGE* 9798t. 1961 Scrapped Boom, Belgium.

18-Mar-1942

Stated to have lost 651 working hours since September, Ronald Crawford ($17^1/_2$), plasterers labourer, of Woodbine Terrace was in Sunderland Police Court today given a month to improve his record with the prospect of a prison sentence as a minimum penalty for failure. Crawford is accused of failing to obey three directives of the Ministry of Labour to attend work regularly and punctually.

Pickersgill's launch the *EMPIRE CHAUCER* 5970t. 17.10.42 Torpedoed and sunk by U.504. 2 lost.

Wm. Doxford launches the *FRESNO CITY* 7250t. 12.04.1943, Torpedoed and sunk by U.706. Crew all saved.

19-Mar-1942

Work started today on the removal of unnecessary railings for scrap metal in Sunderland.

Short Bros. launches the *EMPIRE KEATS* 7035t. 1966 Scrapped Keelung.

20-Mar-1942

Fewer clothing coupons for civilians. Civilians are to have their clothes rations reduced by a quarter from June 1st; from 66 coupons to slightly over 51. The effect of the reduction will release 50,000 workers from the textile industry and there will be a substantial saving of shipping tonnage. The new coupons will be issued together in a book; the first 20 will be printed green, the next 20 brown and the third 20 in red. The 60 coupons will be issued to cover a period of 14 months. Only the first 20 of these will be available from June 1st when the new rationing years starts on October 10th. The remaining 40 together with a remaining balance of the first 20 will have to last till the end of July 1943.

21-Mar-1942

William Drew (34) of 39 South Street Sunderland was knocked down and killed by a Corporation bus at the junction of Bridge Street with West Wear Street.

Sunderland 5 Gateshead 1. Sunderland is now definitely in the draw for the Football League Cup competition.

24-Mar-1942

Crowns launch the *EMPIRE WOLD* 269t Tug. 13/11/1944 Torpedoed and sunk by U 300.

26-Mar-1942

Alarm No.213: 20.50 - 22.33. A Berlin official communiqué version of the attack on the Northeast is: "last night the Luftwaffe successfully bombed military installations and the important shipbuilding centre of Sunderland and the port at the mouth of the Humber". Sunderland was not bombed.

28-Mar-1942

On the stroke of 3pm this afternoon the gas rattles of the Wardens were heard in action for the first time and in a matter of seconds the crowded streets in the centre of town were almost clear of pedestrians. Those without respirators dived into the shops for shelter; there were many who emerged with streaming eyes when the All-Clear bells were sounded for the finish of the exercise. At least half were caught without respirators.

29-Mar-1942

Wm. Doxford launches the *HOUSTON CITY* 7262t. Scrapped Hong Kong Oct. 1968

30-Mar-1942

Two shipyard workers who refused to do specified jobs because they contended that Shipwrights should do the work, were fined £5 each today for disobeying a direction by the National Service Officer.

31-Mar-1942

Wm. Doxford launches the *VANCOUVER CITY* 7261t. 1965 wrecked at Wakayama.

2-Apr-1942

Crowns launch the *HMS FILLA* 545t Isles Class MS Trawler. Royal Navy. Sold to Italian Navy Jan. 1946.

3-Apr-1942

This will be an austerity Easter on Wearside for thousands engaged on essential war work in shipyards mines and factories. Good Friday today is an ordinary working day although most shops will be closed. Easter Monday will be a holiday.

4-Apr-1942

Fully officered with an enrolled strength of over 800 boys and youths, the 2nd (Sunderland) Cadet Battalion, DLI, is now officially in being. The battalion, with headquarters at Livingston Road Drill Hall, will become the largest Cadet Battalion in the County.

Oldham v Sunderland. Sunderland's team was in a state of uncertainty right up to kick off. The official ban on servicemen travelling during the Easter holiday badly hit football clubs all over the country.

JL. Thompson launches the *EMPIRE TRISTRAM* 7167t. 1967 scrapped at Split.

6-Apr-1942

Bread made from 85 per cent of wheat meal flour is to be known as "national wheatmeal loaf" and is to replace white bread in the national diet.

Condensed milk and breakfast cereal foods are now included in the points system.

Sunderland v Oldham. Close on 10,000 spectators for the second leg of the Football League Cup tie. Half-time score was Sunderland 1 Oldham 2. Sunderland play Bradford City in the next round of the War League Cup.

11-Apr-1942

Sunderland v Bradford. A crowd of 12,000 saw Bradford beat Sunderland by a two-goal margin.

12-Apr-1942

From today passengers of buses and trams will be required by a Ministry of Transport Order to form a queue two deep when six or more are waiting at any stopping place, whether there is a queue sign or not.

15/16-Apr-1942

Alarm No.214: 23.49 - 01.18. Middlesbrough attacked but a German communiqué said: "German bombers on the night of April 15th attacked the harbour and the shipyards of Sunderland. Extensive fires were observed after hits by bombs of heavy calibre". Not one bomb on Sunderland.

16-Apr-1942

Complaints arguing that the Council were wasting time, money and paper by going ahead with the renaming of Alexandra Road to Queen Alexandra Road.

Bartram's launch the *JERSEY CITY* 6640t. Scrapped Faslane UK Sept. 1978.

18-Apr-1942

Bradford v Sunderland. After half-time Sunderland needed four goals to win the tie. 15 minutes to go the game looked a lost but Whitelum's hat trick saw them through.

22-Apr-1942

Alarm No.215: 16.34 - 16.48. A single raider crossed the coast near Sunderland, flew to Tynemouth, and thence to Seaham Harbour, but dropped no bombs.

23-Apr-1942

Alarm No.216: 15.32 - 16.21. An enemy aircraft crossed the coast at Blyth and flew over Morpeth and Acklington. No attacks were made against land targets.

24-Apr-1942

After a domestic row in the course of which he locked his wife out of the house, James William Ewart of Hardy Square allowed some tarts baking in the oven to burn. At Sunderland Police Court today Ewart was found guilty and fined 10 shillings for wasting food.

25-Apr-1942

Sunderland versus Bradford at Bradford Park Avenue ground in the third round of the war League Cup. Team is; Heywood; Gorman and Eves; Hewison, Lockie and Hastings; Spuhler, Robinson, Gurney, Carter and McMahon. Sunderland beat Bradford by one goal.

27-Apr-1942

Tonight nearly 500 girls between 14 and 19 answered the appeal to join the Women's Junior Air Corps. The girls were disappointed when they learned that the uniforms would have to be paid for through weekly contributions.

No more canned corned meat will be issued on the meat ration after today. The order has been made prohibiting the sale. The domestic meat ration is to be cut. Lord Woolton has already indicated that it will not be possible to maintain it at its present level throughout the year. From today it will be illegal for butchers to sell canned corned meat or to use it for manufacturing purposes.

29-Apr-1942

Alarm No.217: 03.16 - 03.45. York attacked.

Wm. Doxford launches the *AVRISTAN* 7275t. Scrapped Taiwan Feb. 1970.

1-May-1942

Alarm No.218: 02.34 - 04.03.

At around 3.00am, an enemy plane, in a 'hit and run' raid, dropped four high explosive bombs on Fulwell in an area which has suffered badly in the last two previous raids. Two people, a husband-and-wife, were killed in their outdoor home-built shelter when a bomb fell at Back Mayswood Road. These were the only casualties officially reported.

The two people killed were Mr and Mrs John Swaddle of 26 Mayswood Road (opposite). Their son Leonard escaped because he had stayed in the house instead of going into the shelter with them.

Neighbours on both sides, Mrs Brown and Mrs Hornsby escaped injury.

Many of the houses damaged had just recently had repairs completed following previous damage.

Another bomb fell on Ferry's dairy farm, a pony, used for the farmer's milk round, was killed but a horse in the next stable survived.

A third bomb wrecked the billiard hall and lounge of Fulwell Workingmen's Club, the bar and the rest of the building were severely damaged.

The fourth bomb hit the corner of the fire station, which had only officially been opened less than four weeks before. The building was wrecked by the bomb, which caused a huge crater (34' x 4'). Switchboard operator, Mrs Hetty Rodgers, stayed at her post and later received the Empire Medal.

The damaged Fulwell Workingmen's Club

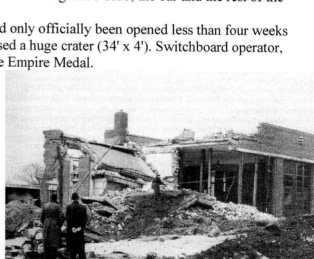

The damaged corner of the new Fulwell Fire Station

2-May-1942

Sunderland v Bradford Park Avenue, the second leg of the cup-tie. A crowd of 15,000 saw a Sunderland side with guest player Albert Stubbins (later of Liverpool) leading the attack. Sunderland draw and win the tie. Stubbins' later claim to fame was an appearance on the front cover of The Beatles' Sgt. Pepper's Lonely Hearts Club Band album, the only footballer to be given that honour.

A protest against the placing of condensed milk on the points list, it was considered as a typical London legislation. The surrender of eight points for a tin of condensed milk is a serious consideration for the northern housewife. In Durham each morning wives have to give their husbands tea and condensed milk to take to work. They don't have to do that sort of thing in the South.

Ferry's Farmyard

4-May-1942

Today witnessed the launching from Sir James Laing and Son's shipyard the new forepart of the crippled tanker Vardefjell , complete down to lifeboats and navigational lights. The bows and 200 ft of tanker slipped down into the river and were then taken in tow by tugs to Greenwell's dry dock where its other half waited. It is said that the usual naming ceremony was performed with half a bottle of champagne. Pickersgill's launch the *STANCLEEVE* 5970t. 1961 Scrapped Hirao, Japan.

8-May-1942

Relatives and friends of the men of 125 Anti-tank Regiment RA, at a well-attended meeting in St Andrew's Hall Roker last night, are to ask the International Red Cross to make contact with the men so that supplementary parcels could be provided.

9-May-1942

Lady Mountbatten, Deputy Chief Superintendent of St. Johns Ambulance Brigade, complimented all that she saw when she inspected the Brigade's personnel at Cowen Terrace and Commercial Road casualty stations. Semi-final first leg Sunderland 0 v Grimsby 0.

14-May-1942

The Home Guard celebrates its second anniversary today.
JL. Thompson launches the *EMPIRE ISEULT* 7170t. 1969 Scrapped Taiwan.

15-May-1942

Frederick Harrington, of Hardwick Street, gave evidence that Peter Costello (38), a donkeyman, of Borough Road, was drowned when he fell off a pilot ladder boarding his ship on January 11th, 1941.Verdict; accidental death.
Short Bros. launches the *EMPIRE SOUTHEY* 7041t. 1967 scrapped Taiwan.

16-May-1942

Semi-final second leg Grimsby v Sunderland at Scunthorpe. Half time: Grimsby 1 Sunderland 2. Sunderland is to meet Wolverhampton in the final on Saturday at Roker Park. Price of admission will be 1/6d.

19-May-1942

12 million tins of egg powder, equivalent to 144 million eggs, are to be made available. The tins can be purchased off the ration, at 1s 9d for a 5oz tin equivalent to 12 eggs.

22-May-1942

Sunderland Tramways warns its staff that if Saturday services are not extended to 11.0pm, beginning on June 6th for the summer period, then disciplinary action will be taken.

23-May-1942

Cup Final first leg Sunderland 1 Wolverhampton 1. 32,213 watched the game.
Raymond Glendinning gave a first class commentary of the second half but for one or two unfortunate slips. The one that really riled was his comment that what a great game the 'Tynesiders' were playing. When will the BBC learn some geography?

25-May-1942

Unlike last year when the Whitsun holiday was cancelled because of the German offensive Whitsun this year brought a welcome break for thousands working in Wearside's shipyards, engine works and collieries.

26-May-1942

Following the removal of house railings, all over the town, builders are being kept busy building low brick walls in a variety of designs and all to fence off three or four square yards of grass or even concrete. People may not be aware that the use of timber costing more than £1 for any purpose without permission is an offence.

29-May-1942

Government recommends that at least 75% of children should be immunised against diphtheria, if the disease is to be checked. Sunderland with only 16% lags far behind. All parents should take a serious view of their responsibilities in this matter.

30-May-1942

For the second leg of the Cup Final at Wolverhampton today Sunderland was unchanged. Wolverhampton Wanderers 1 Sunderland 0 at half time. Wolves deserved their triumph in front of a crowd of over 43,000. Argos criticised Heywood, Sunderland goalkeeper, and suggested that Johnny Mapson, who was watching the game, would have done better.

Sunderland supporters on the way to Wolverhampton for the Cup final had the experience of being under machine-gun fire from the air in the early hours of today.

1-Jun-1942

From today all men and youth's clothing will be subject to the following restrictions. Jackets: No double-breasted jackets – not more than three pockets – no slits or buttons on the cuffs – not more than three buttons on the front – no patch pockets – no half belt – no fancy belts and no metal or leather buttons. Waistcoats: - Plain single breasted only – no collar – not more than two pockets – not more than five buttons – no blackstrap and no chain holes. Trousers: - Maximum width of trouser bottoms 19" – plain bottoms – no permanent pleats – not more than three pockets – no side or blackstrap – no extension waistbands – no elastic in waistbands and no pleats. General: - No zip fasteners and no raised seams.

Restrictions on women's clothing include the following: -embroidery, fancy work and lace on women's and girls' underwear is banned, skirts cannot have more than three buttons, six seams, one pocket and two box pleats, double-breasted suits are out, as are pockets on pyjamas for both sexes.

Wm. Doxford launches the *HARDINGHAM* 7269t. Lost by fire and explosion 05.04.1945.

4/5-Jun-1942

Alarm No.219: 1.31am - 3.14am.

Most of the raiders were probably engaged in mine laying and in anti-shipping activities off Northeast England. There was some scattered bombing in parts of Durham and Yorkshire.

At Sunderland, two delayed-action bombs damaged a ship when they exploded on the following day, and another interfered with the loading of two coaling vessels.

During the raid four high explosive bombs were dropped in the riverside area without exploding. One exploded at 8.05am and one at 8.25am in the river West of Wearmouth Bridge damaging the 'SS Zealous' (seen below), which had to be beached. Another exploded at 11.28am seriously injuring two RNVR men and slightly injuring police and ARP personnel. One UXB remained and held up the loading of two coal carrying ships.

Incendiaries fell in the vicinity of Tunstall Poultry Farm, Tunstall & Burdon District and at Carr's Poultry Farm, Ryhope.

5-Jun-1942

5000 Wearside miners on strike, Wearmouth, Ryhope and Silksworth. Trouble has apparently risen over wages, but there was no indication of an imminent strike action until the Putters suddenly refused to descend the mine last night.

6-Jun-1942

Cooper Shanks (61), of Hallgarth Square, was fined £10 with two months to pay, for not obscuring a house light.

7-Jun-1942

Today saw the start of Sunday games in Sunderland's parks. Sunday tennis was a sad flop; in Barnes Park, only 10 games of tennis were played all day and in Mowbray Park only two. The putting greens were more popular, especially in the evenings.

8-Jun-1942

Wearmouth miners are back to work today. The strikes at Ryhope and Silksworth continue.

11-Jun-1942

A 200yd section of Seaburn beach, extending from the borough boundary to about 200 yards southwards, is to be open for bathing from 6am until 8am and from 5:00pm to 9pm in the evenings. The two shelters on the Promenade, facing this part of the beach, will be available for bathers for changing purposes.

15-Jun-1942

SP.Austin launches the *FIREDOG* 1557t. 1959 sold to Dutch breakers, but then resold for use as a sand store.

17-Jun-1942

JL. Thompson launches the *EMPIRE BARRIE* 7168t. 31.10.60 ashore in cyclone near Chittagong, total loss.

19-Jun-1942

Wearmouth Colliery 'Putters' have accepted the pay offer, a minimum wage in the industry of £4 5s a week.

22-Jun-1942

Confetti, horseshoes, wedding cake boxes, 21st birthday keys, Christmas decorations, cake ornaments, and candles. Dog collars harnesses and leads, photograph albums are to have 66.6 % Purchase Tax added.

23-Jun-1942

During their first six months working Sunderland's restaurants and canteens served 231,282 meals.
Holidays at home programme continued with a talent spotting competition at the Bede Collegiate girls' school. Winners were Miss Marjorie Holme of 12 Orchard Street (for singing); Mr W Walsh, 55 Shrewsbury Crescent (ukulele, banjo and singing); Miss Olive and Master David Elliott, of 17 Chester Street (accordion, piano, singing and dancing).

26-Jun-1942

Under the Registration of Employment Order, all men up to the age of 50 and all women up to the age of 45 must register.
Wm. Doxford launches the *COOMBE HILL* 7268t. Scrapped on the 1st November 1968 at Etajima, Japan.

27-Jun-1942

A settlement in Sunderland's tram dispute was reached today and will result in the trams running till 11 o'clock.
JL. Thompson launches the *EMPIRE GALLIARD* 7170t. 1966 Scrapped Istanbul.

29-Jun-1942

Under the Defence regulations an order prohibits the waste of Coal, Gas, Electricity and liquid fuel.
Miss Gadabout's Wartime meals: "One small teaspoon of powdered egg with two tablespoons of water makes up one egg. Put the dried egg into a bowl of water, see that at the water covers all the powder, and allow it to stand for 5 minutes until all the powder is absorbed".
Bartram's launch the *EMPIRE BANNER* 6640t. 7.2.43 torpedoed and sunk by U.77. All crew saved.
Laing's launch the *EMPIRE WORDSWORTH* 9891t. 1960 Scrapped Briton Ferry

30-Jun-1942

Wm. Doxford launches the *HARPALYCE* 7269t. Scrapped Spain Oct. 1966.
Pickersgill's launch the *STANHILL* 5970t. Abandoned after striking rocks off Ivory Coast May 1947

1-Jul-1942

Laing's launch the *EMPIRE THACKERAY* 2865t. 1946 THACKERAY. 1968 Scrapped Ystad, Sweden.

7-Jul-1942

Alarm No.220: 01.32 - 02.55. Middlesbrough attacked.
From today all children under the age of three (was two years) will be entitled to fruit juices.

8-Jul-1942

Alarm No.221: 01.40 - 02.18. Enemy aircraft last night made a short attack on a coastal area of north-eastern England. The Tees area was again attacked.

9-Jul-1942

Damage estimated at between £20,000 and £30,000 when a fire in the main storehouse of the Hendon paper works tonight.

11-Jul-1942

Sunderland has so many Home Guards that, although official sanction has now been given to the formation of a further Battalion in the town, no extra recruiting

will be necessary. The existing 9th Battalion will be divided into two to form the new battalion to be known as the 24th Durham Battalion. The Commanding Officer of the new battalion will be Lieutenant Colonel R A Bartram. The picture shows the Home Guard receiving Thompson Machine Gun training

13-Jul-1942

Butcher John Henry Grater, High Street East, was fined £300 for selling 53 cases of canned milk without a licence. On the charge of selling wet fish without a licence he was fined £50. Mayfair Confectionery Co. Ltd. of Low Row was fined £250 with 25 Guineas costs for 'hoarding' canned milk purchased from the butcher.

14-Jul-1942

The concentration of the food industry has resulted in the closure of 17 out of 22 cheese processing factories; 30 out of 40 compound lard factories; 140 out of 200 edible fat melting concerns; 13 out of 33 margarine factories.

16-Jul-1942

The present coal rationing regulations were considered grossly unfair to the average working-class family. Current allowance is for 10cwt of coal plus 20cwt of coke, however, poorer working class households are unable to burn coke, and so they are limited to 10cwt of coal to provide warmth, cooking and the supply of hot water.

Widows Pensions and Old Age Pensions to be increased by 2/6 (12½p) per week.

19-Jul-1942

A single enemy aircraft flew over Hartlepool, Seaham and Sunderland early in the morning.

20-Jul-1942

From today it will be an offence to destroy, to throw away, or abandon any rag, rope, or string. Offenders are liable to a penalty of £100 or three months in prison or both.

22-Jul-1942

Alarm No.222: 18.01 - 18.17. No action recorded.

23-Jul-1942

Serious damage amounting to several thousand pounds caused by fire in the top storey of a building belonging to Vaux's Brewery in Castle Street. It took two hours for the N.F.S. to get fire under control.

24-Jul-1942

SS CARLTON, 5,162grt (R. Chapman & Sons). Sunk in the Atlantic on the 20th December 1940 with all the crew abandoning the ship in two boats. The Captain's boat overturned in the night and 18 men drowned. The Chief Officer George W. Robinson's boat with 16 men was found 18 days later with only 4 men still alive.

Chief Officer George W Robinson OBE related the story of the experiences of the Shorts built merchant vessel's crew drifting in mid-Atlantic, which resulted in the loss of both his legs.

The picture shows four survivors in a Canadian hospital. George Robinson is as indicated.

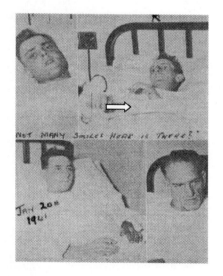

26-Jul-1942

Alarm No.223: 00.45 - 01.52. Raiders again targeted towns in the south of the region.

From today, residents of hotels and boarding houses must register individually for ration books and the establishments must use the resident's books to obtain food.

27-Jul-1942

Sweets and chocolates are rationed. A new ration book known as the Personal Ration Book is introduced. A ration of 2 ounces a week, about four or five medium to small chocolate creams or a small a slab of chocolate. They were not to come off ration until April 24th 1949, only to be rationed again from August 14th 1949 until February 4th 1953.

28-Jul-1942

The number of full time Civil Defence workers is to be reduced by 55 per cent. Those who are released will be absorbed in to the part time civil defence requirement.

Short Bros. launches the *EMPIRE WEBSTER* 7043t. 7.2.43 Torpedoed and sunk by U.77. 4 crewmembers lost.

30-Jul-1942

Due to a shortage of rubber, the Government decides that the public should not carry gas masks day-by-day. The responsibility of keeping the respirator in good order still lies with the public.

JL. Thompson launches the *THISTLEDALE* 7240t. 1959 NEDI. Scrapped Taiwan April 1967.

31-Jul-1942

The use of the car is prohibited unless the owner can prove that he is using his car for essential services. This action is due to the need to conserve manpower, fuel and tyres. Travel is to be discouraged.

Alexandro Fella trading as G Fella & Sons of Silksworth Row was fined £70 today. He was accused of using sugar supplied for manufacturing purposes in a catering establishment; of failing to keep a register of meals served; and obtaining milk contrary to the milk supply scheme.

1-Aug-1942

Furniture and many other household goods will be produced on 'utility' lines. Some 30,000 workers and big quantities of material and transport will be freed for war purposes. In addition there will be utility pottery and cooking utensils, utility of suitcases, umbrellas, cutlery, towels, sheets, tea cloths and cot blankets.

4-Aug-1942

Alarm No.224: 06.49 - 06.58. The Germans claim to have raided Leeds, Middlesbrough and Lowestoft. The 5000 or more people that saw the first performance of the Holiday at Home pageant " Cavalcade of Sunderland" in Barnes Park appeared to be very well pleased with the whole show.

7-Aug-1942

"I don't know what is the matter with women in this town", commented the Magistrate's Clerk at the Sunderland Police Court today after two assault cases had been dealt with. "The language used in these brawls is something terrible, the women are infinitely worse than the men".

8-Aug-1942

Clocks go back one hour tonight, end of double summer time.

9-Aug-1942

Alarm No.225: 23.24 - 00.43. Bombs fell over County Durham. No damage or casualties reported. A feature of the enemy air attack over points on the northeast coast tonight was the number of flares dropped by raiding planes.

11-Aug-1942

Having travelled from Bristol to Sunderland without a ticket a woman of Wellington Lane Sunderland was fined 40s with 6s 6d costs at Sunderland Police Court today. The fare she should have paid was 43s 6d.

12-Aug-1942

An inquest reopened at Catterick Hospital today into the death of a Sunderland woman Mrs Emma Wood (67), of 19 Howard Street South, Millfield, who was killed on Saturday July 25th as a result of the explosion on the road near the village of Stainton in Swaledale. Mrs Wood died when a young boy, who also died, picked up a rogue artillery shell, which exploded. Mrs Wood lived in a cottage at Stainton during the summer months and returned to Millfield in the winter.

13-Aug-1942

A Corporation Health Department driver of Scruton Avenue was sent to prison for six months for siphoning petrol from his van.

14-Aug-1942

Protesting against the penalty inflicted on him at Sunderland Police Court today the defendant George Henry Petersen (37) of Carver Terrace Jarrow. Trading as Mac's Stores in White's Market he was fined £100 for breach of Food Control Orders. He was convicted of making false statements regarding the number of points coupons handled. Petersen addressing the magistrate said, "Is that fair? I have been up three times at Whitley Bay for exactly the same thing and have only been fined £3 each time".

17-Aug-1942

More than 4000 people attended the final of the talent-spotting contest in Barnes Park. Of the 22 finalists, only one local turn appeared in the prize list she was Nancy Hill of 54 Premier Road Plains Farm who sang 'So Deep is the Night' winning £2 for her third place.

19-Aug-1942

The first case of its kind to come before Sunderland magistrates was the charge heard this morning against Michael Fagan (18) of Grindon Avenue High Ford of refusing to join a queue when boarding a tram at the North end of the station. He was fined five shillings.

25-Aug-1942

News that the LNER has decided to stop the issue of top hats. The wearing of the top hat signified the importance of the Station Master in the railway world. Until a year ago Sunderland's stationmaster was one of the select few on the LNER system that still sported the top hat. It was one of the 14 special class stations with that distinction. (I wonder where it would stand now?).

Wm Doxford launches the *TOWER HILL* 7268t. Scrapped on the 15th August 1970 Kaohsiung, Taiwan

27-Aug-1942

102 people were fined 11s 6d today for keeping a dog without a licence.

Laing's launch the *EMPIRE CAVALIER* 9891t. 1959 Scrapped Briton Ferry

28-Aug-1942

A fine of £400 was imposed on John Conley of Gladstone Street trading as a tea dealer in Roker Baths Road. He was convicted for the contravention of the tea rationing order by supplying tea without taking coupons. JL. Thompson launches the *MIDDLESEX TRADER* 7240t. Scrapped Italy 1964. Wm. Doxford launches the *HARPAGUS* 7268t. Scrapped Sept. 1960 following accident.

28/29-Aug-1942

Alarm No.227: 22.45 - 00.14. Diving over the roofs of Ryhope last night a German raider dropped its bomb load. One crashed on 11 Smith Street killing William Turnbull, asleep in his bed and wrecking five houses. A further two people were killed, Fredrick Collins and Mary Duffield, flying debris struck them while they stood on outside stairways of 5 and 6 Dinsdale Terrace.

A number of the new phosphorous incendiary bombs were dropped in Fulwell Quarries these burned themselves out harmlessly.

Woman amongst the wreckage of her home

Evidence on how the Morrison Shelter can save lives

4-Sep-1942

"It is a shame, a crying shame, that women, anxious to do their part in the national effort, should have to be sent away from Sunderland to find work in war factories", declared the Mayor presiding at the opening ceremony of Sunderland's first wartime nursery in St Mark's Vicarage, Chester Road yesterday. "It maybe said that Sunderland was a little late in opening its first nursery on the third anniversary of the outbreak of war" said the Mayor, "the answer to that", he said, "is the need for such a nursery has not been very real until now. It is rather a shame that I have to say that it is true, in spite of every effort made by the local authorities and members of parliament, we have not succeeded in bringing to Sunderland any industrial work where women matter".

5-Sep-1942

Sunderland 3 Bradford City 1.

6/7-Sep-1942

Alarm No.228: 23.41 - 00.41.

Heavy AA fire was seen to south of the Town. Anti-aircraft rockets caused damage in Alexandra Road and also to a house in Louis Avenue, Fulwell, others fell in South Hylton.

A small number of enemy aircraft flew over coastal districts of the northeast of England and bombs were dropped in a few places and some damage and a small number of casualties have been reported (Middlesbrough). A German communiqué said "during the night bombers attacked shipyards in Sunderland. A number of explosions were observed".

7-Sep-1942

It will be an offence from today to destroy or throw away any waste rubber. Max penalties for this offence will be £100 fine or three months in prison or both.

11- Sep-1942

Disclosure of wholesale thefts from allotments was made at the opening last night of the Victory Garden Show at Monkwearmouth Miners Hall. It was given as the reason for this years show was not as good as last years. Whole frames have been stripped and plots ruined.

Pickersgill's launch the *EMPIRE HUNTER* 5970t. 1964 MP-PZZ-2, Floating grain warehouse at Szczecin.

12-Sep-1942

Sunderland 0 York City 0. Sunderland's gate was 7500. It was a very poor game played out to a goalless draw. The HMS DELHI Refit Campaign ended tonight with a total of £80,131 15s 5d. The surplus is to be transferred to the 'Tanks for Attack' campaign officially launched today.

14-Sep-1942

James Geddes of Suffolk Street was accused of failing to perform his duty as firewatcher at premises in John Street on August 3rd. He pleaded not guilty and was fined £3. The fine would have been greater but for the fact that he had lost his job. It was reiterated that firewatchers should remain on watch for the whole of their term of duty without leaving.

18-Sep-1942

The Collier FERNWOOD is sunk by German aircraft at Dartmouth, Taken over by the Royal Navy and built in 1924 by Sir James Laing & Sons.

19-Sep-1942

Alarm No.229: 21.46 - 23.32. An AA shell fell and exploded in a garden at East Herrington causing slight damage.

York City 0 Sunderland 3.

23-Sep-1942

H. I. & D Berg, of High Street West, were fined £100 for selling occasional tables for 49s 6d when the price should have been 16s 6d. Also the

SS FERNWOOD at Austin's Pontoon before the war.

Sunderland firm Marshalls (Sunderland) Ltd also of High Street West received a £50 fine for displaying a woman's jumper ticketed for sale at 17s 2d when the permitted price was 16s 6d.

24-Sep-1942

SP. Austin launches the *BUSHWOOD* 2842t. 10.11.1978 arrived Inverkeithing to be broken up.

In North Africa, the British 8th Army at El Alamein launches a limited offensive.

25-Sep-1942

The King has been pleased to approve the following awards for gallantry and distinguished service in the Middle East. The Military Medal to Corporal Walter Watson of the DLI who lives at 6 Ross Street Southwick Road and Private George Robert Fearon. About a month ago Mrs Fearon who lives at 10 Woodbine Street Sunderland was officially informed that her husband was missing and since then she had no news of him. Able Seaman Arthur Lamb 38, 13 Shakespeare Street, Southwick, received a decoration posthumously. He was a member of the crew of HMS WELSHMAN, which helped beat the Malta blockade.

Short Bros launches the *EMPIRE ENVOY* 7046t. 1969 scrapped Bruges.

Wm. Doxford launches the *BARDISTAN* 7264t. Scrapped Taiwan May 1972.

26-Sep-1942

The 'Tanks for Attack' campaign ends tonight and Sunderland's name will now be emblazoned on 10 Churchill tanks.

"I am afraid you are unfortunate in having a turnip field adjoining the Ford Estate" commented Mr E Cope in Sunderland's County Police Court today when Mr George Pattinson, farmer, complained of damage done by trespassers. The farmer told magistrates that he had lost three-quarters of an acre of turnips stolen from the field. Peter Canavan (20) was fined two shillings with two shillings and sixpence costs and a nine year-old boy was dealt with in the juvenile court.

Sunderland 1 Huddersfield 3. Sunderland played Nicholson, a Tottenham Hotspur full back.

Laing's launch the *EMPIRE COLLINS* 9796t. 1964 Scrapped Karachi.

28-Sep-1942

Central heating is banned for one month under the general directions made by the Ministry of Fuel and Power, under the Control of Fuel order. No fuel is to be consumed in any central heating plant of controlled premises until after August 31st.

Fuel communiqué No. 6: "it is hoped that by the prohibition of central heating to save sufficient fuel to manufacture 1000 Spitfires. Until central heating is allowed in this district the resolute determined 'fuel saver' will co-operate by not lighting fires or stoves of coal, gas, electrical or paraffin just for heating rooms. He can save enough fuel each week to make enough bullets or cannon shells to supply a fighter pilot for 10 seconds. With this ammunition saved in your 'grate' he may shoot down one Messerschmitt and one night bomber. Not using his hot-water boiler and more than two days a week.

If everyone keeps these rules we will save 10,000 tons of fuel per week, enough to produce 100 light tanks.

29-Sep-1942

JL. Thompson launches the *THISTLEMUIR* 7237t. Scrapped Osaka April 1968.

3-Oct-1942

Huddersfield 2 Sunderland 2. In the halfback line for Sunderland was Corporal Laidman of the DLI and formerly of Everton.

5-Oct-1942

There was opposition by a number of shipbuilding and ship repairing men of Tyneside, which includes men from Wearside, to the introduction during the weekend in the alteration in the end of the pay week from Tuesday to a Sunday night.

8-Oct-1942

Fatal accidents in factories in 1941 numbered 1646 an increase of 20% over 1940, and non-fatal accidents numbered 269,652 an increase of 17%. The main increase is in accidents to adult women.

10-Oct-1942

Bradford Park Avenue 4 Sunderland 2. Sunderland found once again that Shackleton, the young Bradford inside right, is a most dangerous attacker, he scored three of Bradford's goals. Argus repeated what he said year ago of the wish to see Shackleton in a Sunderland team after the war.

11-Oct-1942

Alarm No.230: 21.06 - 22.0. The German news agency reports that Sunderland was raided saying that bombers operated at about 2200 ft over the town.

Women and children were the chief victims of the raid. Seven people, two children, four women and one man were killed, twenty-three seriously injured and fifty-four slightly injured.

Valley Road School, Hendon, (opposite) was destroyed when a 1000-kilogram high explosive bomb fell in the middle of Corporation Road blowing a crater 30 feet across (below). The bomb demolished twenty houses and damaged another 300.

A rest centre housed a considerable number of homeless people overnight. Nearly all fatalities were caught out side their shelters.

A water filled crater in Corporation Road.

Other smaller bombs fell in Back Ward Street, Burlington Road, Back Thompson Street, at the junction of Tower Street West and Bamborough Street, and in the sea E of the British Oil Store, South Dock. Slight damage was caused to residential property. There were three unexploded bombs: one in the front garden of a house in Hendon Burn Avenue, one in Back Ward Street and one which went through the roof and into the basement of a house in Athol Road.

14-Oct-1942

Stanley Lawson (44), a tramcar driver, of 204 St. Luke's Road Pallion, was fatally injured when the runaway tram ran backwards, out of control, down a hill in Rhyope Road between Grey Road and the College of Art and crashed into another tram.

15-Oct-1942

The County authority will allow children holidays from school to pick potatoes. For the next fortnight elementary school children between the ages of 12 and 14 will be released for one session each day, with the consent of their parents, for potato picking.

The Admiralty stated recently that 23 closed shipyards had been reopened. It was believed that a good many of these additional workers came from Sunderland and that was one of the reasons for not reopening Wear yards.

16-Oct-1942

Alarm No.231: 21.43 - 22.27.

"Sunderland was bombed last night," said the German news agency "the attack lasted almost an hour and fires in the port area were observed".

A blazing Nazi bomber, shot down in flames, provided a grandstand view for people of Sunderland early in the raid. One seafront onlooker said, "We saw the bomber caught and held in the beam of a searchlight. After it crashed into the sea it continued to burn for several minutes".

Fourteen people were killed, five seriously injured, eleven slightly injured, when one 500kg high explosive bomb fell in Tatham Street and another in Tavistock Place. The Education Architect's Offices were demolished and houses either demolished or damaged.

A large amount of food was lost in Moore's warehouse.

By Saturday morning only three bodies had been recovered from the devastated area. The last of the victims were got out about 1am on Sunday the 18th.

Work was kept up continuously by relays of rescue parties. The victims had apparently been killed instantly, some of them in their beds. Shelters at the rear of the houses were almost undamaged. Many of the working-class people rendered homeless were having their second experience have been bombed out on the night a parachute mine destroyed the Victoria Hall in April 1941.

A third bomb, estimated to be 1000kg, fell in Laura Street but failed to explode.

An Air Ministry and Ministry of Home Security states: "Before midnight last night a few enemy aircraft dropped bombs at places in the coastal districts of the north-east of England, there were a small number of casualties and some damage was done. One of the aircraft was destroyed".

Moore's Warehouse in Tavistock Place

14 people lost their lives at No.s 6 & 7 Tatham Street.

17-Oct-1942

Sunderland 1 Bradford Park Avenue 1. Carter like Shackleton, the Bradford forward, was playing in a command game at York. Laidman and Tuttle signed professional forms for Sunderland before the game. Tuttle got the equalising goal.

18-Oct-1942

A large crowd watched today's exercise and once the 'street fighting' had started it was almost impossible for either 'attackers' or 'defenders' to make progress through them.

The regular troops, using blank ammunition, were surrounded by swarms of children, scrambling and fighting, for their spent cartridge cases. Several boys narrowly escaped injury when thunder flashes exploded. Parents were blamed for not having control of their children and not having respect for the people who are training to defend them against possible attack.

A soldier dressed in German uniform walked the streets of Sunderland for one hour and a half today before he was detected and captured. It also included a soldier dressed in a singlet and running shorts to reconnoitre a defence position.

19-Oct-1942

The second share out of dried eggs begins today. There will be 1 tin or package (12 eggs for 1s 9d) for every owner of a general ration book, two for a child holding the green ration book RB2. You must go to the shop where you are registered for shell eggs. From today children holding ration book RB2 will not get their priority ration of fresh eggs, but will receive instead a top up ration of dried eggs. The Ministry of Food points out that there will not be many shell eggs available this winter. Only expectant mothers and invalids will obtain priority supplies from today, hopefully three eggs a week.

20-Oct-1942

Oranges is now available in the Northeast. Two pounds will be sold to the child's ration book RB2.

21-Oct-1942

Why is it that Wearside's contribution to this war effort is consistently ignored, or overlooked, by those in a position to know better? The Minister of Labour, Mr Ernest Bevin, ought to have some idea of the location of the work and the Wear workers who are tackling it. Yet in the House of Commons today, he went out of his way to praise the shipyards and workers of the Tyne and Clyde for "doing twice the shipbuilding" of the American yards. Sunderland shipyard workers, who have not been on strike over a shameful triviality, might well wonder if Mr Bevin realises that the Wear is, and has been for years, building more merchant ships than the Tyne. They might also be forgiven for wondering if Mr Bevin had read the recent speech of the First Lord of the Admiralty, that it was a Sunderland Shipbuilding firm which had designed the Liberty ship and showed the way to the American yards. Perhaps Mr Bevin labours under the common illusion that the Wear is a small insignificant tributary of the Tyne.

23-Oct-1942

William J Lowes, of South View, fined £5 for a light showing in a chemist shop in Ash Place, Newcastle Road and £1 for wasting electricity. The following people were fined £2 plus £1 for wasting electricity; Elizabeth Bousfield of Felstead Crescent; Ellen Dorian of Fourstones Road and Ralph Robson of Lawrence Street; Frederick Coombs of Cedar Crescent.

Thomas Elliott (45), a shipwright of 29 Baltic Terrace Pallion was killed in Doxford's shipyard today. At a later inquest; a verdict of accidental death was returned. A rope from a ship being launched in the next birth wrapped round a thwart on the ship on which Elliott was working and a ladder was dislodged which struck Elliott on the head fracturing his skull. He leaves a widow and nine children.

Wm. Doxford launches the *HARLESDEN* 7273t. Scrapped Taiwan Oct. 1968

24-Oct-1942

Leeds Utd. 1 Sunderland 2. They overcame a goal deficit at the interval with goals from Spuhler and Carter. Cliff Whitelum failed to join Sunderland and was replaced by Tuttle with a guy called Milsom at out side left.

At 21.40 the British offensive: "Lightfoot" begins at El Alamein, with the largest artillery bombardment since the First World war.

26-Oct-1942

Alarm No.232: 21.46 - 23.32. An enemy plane was in the vicinity of a northeast coast town in daylight this morning. No bombs were dropped. British fighters chased the raider out to sea.

Cakes are limited in price to 1s 6d per pound from today. The price of a cake is not to exceed three times the cost of the ingredients.

31-Oct-1942

John Thorburn, a merchant seaman, of 50 Old Mill Road Southwick, who was knocked down and killed by a motor van on in High Street West.

Sunderland v Leeds Utd. Leeds got rattled and beat themselves. Sunderland won.

2-Nov-1942

Housewives claimed difficulty in keeping the National bread fresh, saying it went mouldy after two days.

3-Nov-1942

For the period during the 1st November to 31st December householders were not allowed to acquire more than 15 hundredweight of coal or such less quantity that would raise their stock to over 1.5 tons.

The Government urges everyone to make their clothes and household goods last longer. The first edition of the Utility furniture had been well received.

4-Nov-1942

Local authorities must now see that each person doing fire-watching duty in business premises have a bed or a bunk and an air space of 200 cubic feet or a floor area of 20 square feet. Horizontal distance between beds must be at least six feet. A pallet pillow and where possible three blankets must be available. Adequate lighting, heating and means of cleansing should be provided. The fireguard must provide his or her own pillowcases, sheets and towels.

5-Nov-1942

The break through of the Battle of Alamein, British troops defeat Rommel's Afrika Korps and march on to Tunis. Winston Churchill was convinced that the battle of El Alamein marked the turning point in the war and ordered the ringing of church bells all over Britain. As he said later: "Before Alamein we never had a victory, after Alamein we never had a defeat."

6-Nov-1942

For wasting motor fuel, the first case of its kind in Sunderland Fredrick Barron (45) of Falklands Road Ford Estate was fined 20 shillings. His offence consisted of driving his lorry home to get his dinner. Barron was employed by Webster Co. rope makers of Deptford, complaints from the public compelled police to take action.

A mixed anti aircraft battery in the Sunderland District last night celebrated its first birthday. It was the first mixed battery in the air defence of Great Britain to go into action and during the 12 months of its existence it has been credited with shooting down three enemy planes.

7-Nov-1942

Sunderland 3 Middlesbrough 1. Half the Middlesbrough team were guest players. Sunderland had only two. Hastings scored two. Carter had a display of international standard.

9-Nov-1942

Person's accused of spreading VD will now be compelled to undergo treatment. A new Defence Regulation 33B is aimed to tackle the growing problem. During the Second World War there was a particular concern that troops were being incapacitated by venereal disease and rendered unable to fight. A notion existed that certain promiscuous individuals were acting as sources of infection for large numbers of people.

Pickersgill's launch the *STANLODGE* 5970t. Scrapped Taiwan Mar. 1967.

Bartram's launch the *EMPIRE PROSPERO* 6766t. 6.11.52 wrecked off Hook of Holland.

Wm. Doxford launches the *BRADFORD CITY* 7266t. Scrapped May 1972 Japan.

10-Nov-1942

Referring to the Egypt campaign Mr Churchill said, " We have a victory, a remarkable but definite victory. A bright gleam has covered the helmets of our soldiers and warmed and cleared all our hearts. The Germans", he said, "have received that measure of fire and steel which they so often meted out to others. This is not the end. It is not even at the beginning of the end, but it is perhaps the end of the beginning. The German Army has been defeated, it has been routed, and it has been very largely destroyed as a fighting force".

Mrs Florence Collard started working as a welder at Bartram and Sons on the 27th July 1942, and is the first woman to be admitted to the Boilermakers Society in this district. Most of the women are employed in general labouring duties, painting and a few are rivet heating.

Women shipyard workers

15-Nov-1942

After being banned for two years, Church bells are allowed to be rung to celebrate the British victory in the Battle of Egypt. There were many disappointed Wearsiders this morning, perhaps they expected too much. There are only three peels of bells in Sunderland and two of them were rung today. The bells of St. Ignatius, Hendon and those of Bishop Wearmouth. The bells of the Holy Trinity were not rung because of safety fears.

16-Nov-1942

A young soldier who used a car to teach his girl to drive resulted in him and his father both being fined. Henry Peverley, coal merchant of John Candlish Road, was fined £5 with 10 shillings cost for permitting the use of fuel for a purpose other than that specified. His son Joseph Peverley was fined £2 for aiding and abetting the offence and a further £1 for failing to produce a driving licence.

17-Nov-1942

Sir James Merchant, director of Salvage, explained the seriousness of the rubber position today, the need for rubber salvage is paramount and the contribution of every household is important. 80 elastic bands from every home would realise enough rubber to supply 1000 bombers with tyres; 50 tennis balls or 350 rubber teapot spouts is equivalent to the rubber needed for one dinghy; a pair of old Wellingtons is enough for a Mae West.

19-Nov-1942

Matthew Mather (19), of Polworth Square, a miner at Wearmouth, broke his bail conditions by working only 2 days since September. He was sent to prison for six months.

20-Nov-1942

Crowns launch *HMS GRUINARD* 560t Isles Class MS Trawler. Lent to Portugese Navy 1943-1944. Sold in June 1946.

21-Nov-1942

The "Battle for Fuel" exhibition formally opened by the Mayor in Jopling's store High Street West today proved a big attraction. It was well attended all day. Slogans written by some school children for the fuel economy campaign was used in the streets of the town by a loudspeaker van, which made a tour of many districts.

Sunderland 3 Gateshead 4. With Carter playing for the RAF, Tuttle gets another game against Gateshead; otherwise the team was unchanged from that that won at Middlesbrough. Bircham; Gorman and Eves; Bradwell, Hewison and Hastings; Spuhler, Robinson, Whitelum, Tuttle and Smallwood.

23-Nov-1942

Information from the Red Cross shows that there are now 300 men from Sunderland in enemy prison camps. SP. Austin launches the *BETTY HINDLEY* (2) of 1771t. Didn't, unfortunately, last much longer than her predecessor, struck a mine 7.10.1947 off Scarborough and sank under tow the next day. Crewmember killed. Laing's launch the *WEARFIELD* 9801t. 1.8.1960 arrived at Onomichi (Japan) to be broken up.

25-Nov-1942

The slogan competition winners were; David Brown (8) of Green Terrace School "Undress by moonlight, save your own light" are; Phyllis Chapman (9) Fulwell Junior School "Let fuel win the dual"; Marjorie Scott (8) of Grange Park Junior School "use less coal to reach our goal"; Audrey Badstevaner (8) Hudson Road Junior School "less in the bath, more in the tank"; Edna Scott (10) of Hudson Road Girls' school "careful with the fuel mother; help to beat the old Schikalgruber" Janet Spragg (10) Fulwell Junior School "Leave the firing to the forces"; Robert Thomas (12) of St. Benet's "if gas and coke and coal you save, you soon will have Hitler in his grave"; H Rowell (11) of St Joseph's " if you want to stop Hitler landing at Roker, save more fuel by hiding the poker"; Edith Hart (13) Havelock Senior Girls' School " she's a lady sweet and kind, who always has the war in mind; she saves her fuel day-by-day and so she keeps our foes at bay" ; Nancy Fisher (13) of Hendon Girls' School" saving on the fuel front means victory on the battle front"; James Higgins (13) of Hylton Road Boys' School "Save electric, gas and coal, help to score the winning goal" ; Fred Davies (13) of Commercial Road senior boys' school " if we want to win this war, we must economise even more, save electricity gas and coal and put these nazis in a hole"

26-Nov-1942

Sunderland Transport Committee tonight approved changes to bus services as requested by the Regional Transport Commissioner, which comes into force on Wednesday. On Saturday and Sunday the last bus will leave the town at 10pm instead of 10.30. There will be no bus services in the town before 1pm on Sundays except workmen's buses. From Monday-Friday bus timetables will change with reduced frequencies.

27-Nov-1942

Stated to have been late for work for 70 out of 102 working days in recent months Thomas Marchbanks (20) of Farne Square was fined £5 for being persistently late, he was employed as an apprentice core maker at Jennings Winch and Foundry Company Limited. Marchbanks said that he would have preferred a prison sentence.

28-Nov-1942

Gateshead 1 Sunderland 0.

30-Nov-1942

Alarm No.233: 21.02 - 21.31. No action recorded. A raid free night tonight meant that November was a month of quiet nights. The last bombs on Britain fell on October 31st.

Thomas Plant Robson (21) of 72 Portland Road, who was knocked down and killed by a bus near the Prospect Hotel, Durham Road, shortly after 9:00pm

1-Dec-1942

The Minister of Social Security Sir William Beveridge presents the Beveridge report. Free medical and hospital treatment of all kinds for every citizen; Pensions raised to 40s for a husband and wife upon retirement; children's allowance of 8s a week; big increases in disability rates and the abolition of the means test. In most cases the £20 funeral grant. A new charter for wives including a marriage grant, increased maternity benefit and household help in sickness. This all-in policy of social insurance based on contributions paid by employers and employees at a maximum joint payment of 7s 6d.

2-Dec-1942

Tomorrow most manual workers in Sunderland will receive income tax notices showing them what amount of tax is due from them in the next half year together with the amount to be deducted from weekly wages. The deduction will begin on February 1st and continue for six months. They are based on wages, which manual workers received during the income tax half-year March to September 1942. Some 42,000 of the notices will be sent this weekend to manual wage earners in Sunderland districts and East Durham.

3-Dec-1942

A verdict of accidental death was returned at an inquest on Thomas Plant Robson (21) of 72 Portland Road, who was knocked down and killed by a bus near the Prospect Hotel Durham Road shortly after 9:00pm on Monday night.

Crowns launch the *EMPIRE DEMON* 269t Ocean going tug. 1966 Scrapped Dublin following collision.

5-Dec-1942

Sunderland v Newcastle Utd. Carter was playing for the RAF so Potts, the Burnley forward, played at inside left. Newcastle won; it could have been a cricket score if it was not for Bircham.

7-Dec-1942

Housewives will notice the difference in the colour of sugar now been supplied. It is more yellow in colour caused by a new method of preparing the sugar, which eliminates several processes to save fuel and labour.

8-Dec-1942

The Ministry of Food has fixed prices of Christmas puddings but the prospect of any been in the shops for Christmas is not looking good.

Knocked down by a tramcar in Roker Avenue Edward Southern (60) of 24 Roker Avenue was dead on admission to the Royal Infirmary.

Short Bros. launches the *EMPIRE BARDOLPH* 7063t. 1959 Scrapped Flushing.

JL. Thompson launches the *EMPIRE BRUTUS* 7233t. 1968 scrapped Istanbul after grounding in River Parana.

10-Dec-1942

Sunday night, in the blackout, in Crowtree road is as bad as ever. Five youths were each fined 20s for shouting and brawling.

Ralph Donkin (45), a Carpenter's mate at Pickersgill's, of 304 St. Luke's Road was killed at work by a 1.5 ton baulk of timber falling from a wagon

12-Dec-1942

Alarm No.234: 04.48 - 05.52. Dawdon, Horden and Murton Colliery bombed.

The Germans stated that on 11/12th "extensive fires and destruction" was wrought by "waves of bombers" at Sunderland. The total force overland was in fact less than 10 aircraft, and although flares were dropped at Sunderland, it was not bombed at all.

Newcastle Utd. 3 Sunderland 3. Arthur Housam back home on his first leave was in Sunderland's team against Newcastle United at St James's Park today and with Lockie at centre-half the pre-war halfback line was fielded. Raich Carter promoted to the rank of sergeant this week resumes at inside left and Potts is moved to partner Spuhler. The team is Bircham; Gorman and Eves; Housam Lockie and Hastings; Spuhler, Potts, Whitelum, Carter and Smallwood. A crowd of 15,000 was the highest gate for the day.

14-Dec-1942

Alarm No.235: 20.11 - 21.09. Over a wide area of the northeast coast last night anti aircraft defences were in action against enemy raiders. Bombs, both high explosives and incendiaries, were dropped at a number of places throughout Durham County.

German High Command communiqué says, "in the fighting against Great Britain the Luftwaffe last night attacked the harbour of Hartlepool and a factory on the East Coast of England with high explosives and incendiary bombs. Considerable damage was caused to the dock installations.

With 1800 children still evacuated in country districts, Sunderland has more evacuees than any other area in Durham and North Yorkshire.

15-Dec-1942

Jean Stormont the 18 year-old Sunderland girl, who lost both her hands when a blazing German bomber crashed on her home, is soon to be back at work. She came home this week from Roehampton where she was fitted with a pair of artificial hands, which will enable her to tackle her old job at the Post Office as a telephonist.

17-Dec-1942

"There can be no question for the abolition of the blackout in urban areas", said Mr Herbert Morrison in a written reply to questions raised, which contended that the blackout contributed no security against bombing and is responsible for many casualties and hinders all air-raid precaution activities. Mr Morrison asserts that the blackout has proved its value as a defence against air attack.

Four strokes of the birch were to be given to a 13 year-old who pleaded guilty in the company of three other boys to shop breaking. One of the boys' aged 15 was sent to an approved school the other two boys were placed on probation.

18-Dec-1942

Names of Sunderland men belonging to the 125 Anti-Tank Regiment of the Royal Artillery, who were captured in the fall of Singapore and are held in Japanese prisoner of war camps, are beginning to filter through.

19-Dec-1942

Middlesbrough 2 - Sunderland 7. Sunderland's halfback line was completely changed for the game at Ayesome Park.

20-Dec-1942

Wm. Doxford launches the *JERSEY HART* 7265t. Scrapped Taiwan Nov. 1970

22-Dec-1942

Alarm No.236: 13.02 - 13.12. No action recorded.

Shipyard workers on Wearside will get the 6 shillings wage rise agreed but are by no means satisfied. That is the feeling of "time" workers who still form a large proportion of those engaged in the shipbuilding industry. Six shillings is small compared with the well-paid "piece" workers who are taking home anything up to £15 on a good week. The "time" workers for a 47 hour week, the skilled man's rate is 83s 6d a week and the labourer's rate 63s a week. Overtime does not amount to much in these short winter days.

Wm. Doxford launches the *ENGLISH PRINCE* 7275t. Scrapped Bilbao Aug 1973.

23-Dec-1942

Doxford's are now launching a ship every 23 days. Nowhere near of course to the output of the American yards but they don't have the problems of the cramped layout of old established yards, no blackout and little interruptions from the weather.

25-Dec-1942

The Ministry of Home Security allows Christmas Day church bells to be rung between 9 am and noon today.

Sunderland fielded a side of inexperienced players for the visit of Middlesbrough and was well beaten.

26-Dec-1942

Alarm No.237: 12.59 - 13.17. No action recorded.

28-Dec-1942

Sunderland's Christmas celebrations were rather subdued. Workers did enjoy a long weekend. Two football matches at Roker Park were the only outdoor events; theatres and cinemas did big business.

Sunderland's first half against Gateshead was as good as anyone would wish to see and certainly the best football seen the season. A Sunderland win.

29-Dec-1942

There is a seasonal epidemic of measles in Sunderland, 395 cases have been reported in the five weeks up to December 26th compared with 35 in the previous five weeks and only three in the corresponding period last year. Cases of diphtheria show a steady decline 40 in the five weeks against 47 and 76 respectively.

31-Dec-1942

Had the times been normal the big store sales would soon be starting. Women, instead of queuing for cakes and fish, would be queuing for bargains but alas there are few sales and fewer bargains.

Sunderland's Municipal Piggery at Fulwell now has 270 pigs every one of them fed on the kitchen waste collected by the Cleansing Department from the street bins now so widely distributed over the town.

During a dark and wet night tonight, a tramcar travelling along back Mary Street knocked down and killed William Spain (60) of 3 Spark Terrace.

1943

.....A Sting in its Tail

The new Shipbuilding Corporation Yard opened in 1943 on the old Swan Hunter Yard at Southwick

- Sunderland suffers two devastating air raids during May killing 161 people.
- All British women aged between 18 and 45 could now be forced to do war work, at least part-time. Mothers of children under 14 did not have to work.
- May 24, 1943. Germany withdrew its remaining U-boats from the North Atlantic because so many were being sunk.

1-Jan-1943

Concentrations of the soft drinks industry, 200 factories are closed. Trade names disappear. Drinks are now ordered by their coloured label. Anthony Clark (60) a docker, 6 Maud Street Lane, was rescued from the river after having accidentally walking into the river from Low Street during the blackout.

2-Jan-1943

Gateshead 5 Sunderland 4 in this League cup-tie.

4-Jan-1943

Shortage of materials and labour restricts supply of Utility Furniture to newly married and bombed out people.

Local Home Guard

5-Jan-1943

Ministry of Food warns of further tightening of belts since the food situation is unlikely to change over the next six months.

6-Jan-1943

'Potato Pete' was another character introduced to encourage the population to eat homegrown vegetables. 'Potato Pete' also had its own song amplifying its message. Vocals by Betty Driver (known by millions today as Betty Williams in Coronation Street').

The Potato Plan issued by the Ministry a Food;

- Serve potatoes for breakfast at least three days a week
- Make your main dish a potato dish at least one day a week.
- Refuse second helpings of other food until you have had more potatoes.
- Serve potatoes in other ways than plain boiled.

Pickersgill's launch the *CHERTSEY* 5996t. Deleted Lloyds Register in 1985.

7-Jan-1943

The new year has started with a heavy crop of sickness in Sunderland, apart from Measles which is still epidemic among children, there were 180 notifications last week alone, there is a good deal of influenza of a fairly serious type about.

8-Jan-1943

The company running the canteen at North Eastern Marine Engineering, North Eastern Caterers of Frederick Street, were fined £180 for selling tea and sugar at excessive prices.

9-Jan-1943

Middlesbrough v Sunderland. Qualifying round of the League Cup. Sunderland had to play Hastings at left back since Nicholson was not available and Green, a Queen of the South and DLI player, played at left half. Argos blamed the pitch at Ayesome Park for Sunderland's defeat.

13-Jan-1943

Alarm No.238: 19.53 - 20.55.

Bombs were dropped in several districts of the northeast coast during a sharp attack of enemy planes last night but no serious damage or casualties have been reported. One casualty reported was that of an 80-year-old woman in Mary Street who was injured by a falling ceiling presumably caused by fallout from anti aircraft gunfire. The barrage was heavy as the planes came in to make their attack over the town. Twice the plane came down low and two high explosive bombs, thought to be 1000kg, along with four

Firepots and two Phosphorous incendiaries were dropped near the South Docks in the vicinity of Monsanto's Works resulting in some slight damage. Incendiaries caused a few fires but were quickly attended to by Fireguards. The Nazi's said today that German fighter-bombers, during last night, attacked the town area and docks of Sunderland where large fires were observed.

The first firepot fell on the railway at the foot of Barrack Street damaging three tracks. The second fell near the railway approach, in the gardens of two houses in Railway Terrace, immediately W of Hendon Dock, doing little damage. The third fell at the base of the steam chimney of the Monsanto Works demolishing the "induced draught fan house" and causing a fire which was quickly put out. The fourth fell on the LNER Londonderry junction between the main up and down lines but caused no damage.

The first Phosphorous incendiary bomb fell on the East Quay of the South Dock, in front of Bartram's Shipyard; the resulting fire was put out immediately. The second was on the West Quay on the N end of the South Dock, near to British Oil Storage Co Ltd; it caused no damage.

The call-up age for single girls lowered to 19.

14-Jan-1943

The 10 Churchill tanks, which bear Sunderland so named, are now in action. The War Office presented a Certificate of Honour to the town in recognition of the results of the savings campaign.

In the last few days two more pedestrians have been killed in the blackout by tramcars. The tramcar having only a single headlight was blamed and thought to be in adequate.

15-Jan-1943

The Coroner returned a verdict accidental death on Gordon Wilson (12) of 13 Church Street Southwick who was knocked down and killed by a bus.

16-Jan-1943

Sunderland 7 Middlesbrough 2. Nicholson, the Tottenham fullback, partnered Gorman in Sunderland's side in today's Roker Park Cup tie. Sunderland's Cup record now reads; played 4, won 2, lost 2; goals for 20, goals against 11.

17-Jan-1943

George Hunter Thompson (67) of 72 St Luke's Terrace fell into the South Dock during the blackout this morning, he got out unaided. He said " I was on my way to Bartram's and lost my way in the blackout and walked into the dock".

18-Jan-1943

Long-service medals were presented to four members of the Roker Volunteer Life Brigade. B Robinson (Captain of the Brigade), 23 years' service; T Keenan (22 years), J McDermond (22 years) and H Atkinson (22 years).

19-Jan-1943

Improved lighting on trains but no improvement on street lighting. The Echo argues that blackout road casualties warrant its consideration.

20-Jan-1943

Mr F N Ebdon, of West Farm, Fulwell, was fined £10 for using bottles belonging to other suppliers. The Milk Vessel Recovery Unit said that Sunderland was one of the worst places in the northeast for this type of offence. A lemon, auctioned for charity, realised £1 10s 7d.

21-Jan-1943

The town council discussing the state of the railway station agreed that, although re-building was out of the question, many minor improvements could be effected, which apart from the fact there's is more light and air available to the platforms, it is in an even worse condition than pre-war when complaints were loud and long.

22-Jan-1943

Arthur Taylor (46) of The Lawn, East Herrington, proprietor of the Blue Arrow taxi company in the Littlegate, was fined £5 on each of the two charges for using motor fuel for a purpose other than specified. He used one of his own taxis for two personal trips to Newcastle.

23-Jan-1943

Alarm No.239: 20.36 - 21.02. Today's German High Command communiqué says: " German bombers during the night attacked important war installations on the estuaries of the Tees and Tyne".

York City v Sunderland in the League Cup tie. Prior to today York City had never beaten Sunderland that however was ended today in convincing style.

25-Jan-1943

When it was first suggested that women should be employed in shipyards, neither employers nor workmen took kindly to the idea. Necessity now assures the employers are ready to engage women. The numbers employed in the yards were not yet large but were steadily growing. Most of those employed are married women. They are taken on first as labourers but the most suitable are selected for training in work requiring some skill such as welding.

27-Jan-1943

There are now 572 Salvage Stewards in the town, each with the authority to report any erring bin men and to control the collection of salvage in their street or area.

28-Jan-1943

Mr Ernest Bevin, Minister of Labour, announces further controls of women and labour. The amendment of the Employment of Women (Control of Engagement) Order is to include women up to 40 (was 30). All vacancies for women aged between 18 and 40 must be filled through the Employment Exchanges. Employers are to notify the Ministry of Labour of the termination of employment to prevent loss of their services to Essential Work. A wider use of the powers of direction under Defence 58A to include part-time work. The changes mean compulsory part-time work for the majority of married women without children.

Although nearly 40% of Wearside children under the age of 15 years have now been immunised against diphtheria such treatment is needed for at least as many more if the risk of a recurrent diphtheria epidemic is to be eliminated. 6179 children under 5 years and 10,876 aged between 5 and 15 years of age have been treated. Up to the end of 1941 only 4581 children had been immunised.

29-Jan-1943

Alarm No.240: 23.35 - 23.47. No action recorded.

Fines amounting to £16 were imposed on Lawrence Shaw of Tel-el-Kebir Road on three summonses in respect to the sale of a quarter pound of sweets at his shop in Stockton Terrace Grangetown. He pleaded guilty to each of the three offences for which he was fined £5 for selling sugar confectionery under weight, £10 for being in possession of a faulty weighing machine and £1 for selling the Confectionery at an excessive price.

30-Jan-1943

Sunderland was forced to make changes for the return game against York City at Roker Park today. Sunderland's chances of appearing in the Cup competition proper are looking unlikely as York beat them.

31-Jan-1943

The ATC attended morning service at Bishopwearmouth yesterday as part of its second anniversary celebrations.

1-Feb-1943

There's nothing wrong with the youth of Sunderland when it can be said, as the probation officer said last week "There are hundreds of lads anxious to join the Merchant Navy and risk all of the perils and privations of the sea in wartime". As long as there are experienced men waiting in the 'pool' for jobs and being paid for it there is no room for the lads.

2-Feb-1943

Daniel Riddle a 20 year-old seaman of Harrison's Buildings blamed older men for getting him drunk with spirits when he was fined £1 for unlawfully wasting food. He smashed a two-pound jar of jam, emptied two tins of dried egg, threw some pasties and a loaf of bread into the fire, emptied two tins of milk into the coal house. Riddle who was of good character expressed his regret.

3-Feb-1943

Alarm No.241: 20.22 - 21.10. A delayed action bomb fell near the South and Hendon Docks and exploded shortly before 5.0am on the 4th causing considerable damage to a gas main and to No. 31 coal staithe. Incendiaries also fell between Bartram's and the South Dock.

4-Feb-1943

Statistics for drunkenness throughout the United Kingdom during 1942 showed Sunderland's figure to be only 37 per 1000 population. Much higher was Newcastle with 180 and Middlesbrough with 158 per 1000.

5-Feb-1943

Complacency was blamed for people not carrying their Identity Cards. After three years of war it ought to have become second nature.

6-Feb-1943

Sunderland v Newcastle Utd. Half time it was two all but Sunderland eventually lost.

Bartram's launch the *EMPIRE DEED* 6766t. Damaged by bombs from aircraft at Sunderland 24th May 1943. Sold to Taiwan breakers in 1966.

7-Feb-1943

Children and expectant mothers are automatically entitled to seven pints of milk per week at 2d a pint and fruit juices at 5d a bottle as well as Cod-liver at 10d a bottle. Free to both groups if on low income.

Tinned fruit is now available on points. Dried eggs 1 tin per ration book.

SS PACIFIC a 2816t collier left Sunderland in convoy for London carrying a cargo of coal. The convoy became scattered in bad weather during the night of the 8th, and at daybreak on the 9th, the Pacific and two other ships had disappeared. She carried a crew of 38.

8-Feb-1943

Something like 20,000 Sunderland householders changed their milkman over the weekend. Each milkman now has his own allotted area and customers within that area must purchase their milk from him.

Parliament voted today not to allow the opening of theatres and cinemas on a Sunday. Prayers offered up by the Lord's Day Observance Society against the Sunday opening must have worked.

9-Feb-1943

The Sunderland Corporation Bill, read in the House of Commons today, extends the time the Corporation has to exercise powers guaranteeing finances for the river Wear Commissioners, for connecting Dykelands Road and Seaburn tramlines, and for constructing a new civic centre on West Park and the widening of Burden Road.

10-Feb-1943

Sunderland, criticised by the Minister of Agriculture, argued that in a crowded industrial town Sunderland had; 4000 allotments; 60 acres of parkland now growing crops; 29 acres of potatoes; some acres of wheat on Tunstall Hills. The land is not available to create new allotments.

12-Feb-1943

William Harrison of Brougham Street, who won the Military Medal as a soldier in the Great War and went to Dunkirk in one of the little ships to rescue the BEF, was fined £10 for failing to perform his fire-watching duties in premises in Crowtree Road on January 25th.

A fine of £10 was also imposed on Jacob Warrentz of Salem Avenue for been absent for fire watching duties on January 31st; he had fallen asleep in front of the fire.

Shipyard employers were accused of deliberately transferring skilled workers from 'piece' rates too 'time' rates. Examples of members of the Boilermakers Society used to earning £10 or £11 a week being put on to time rates reducing their earnings to £4 9s a-week.

13-Feb-1943

Newcastle Utd. v Sunderland. Sunderland's victory brought them into 33rd place in the cup league table. Entry to the final stages still hang by a thread and require at least three points from Bradford to stand any chance.

15-Feb-1943

Pat, the Blue Macaw, having survived the bomb, which demolished his home in the Winter Gardens and the bombs at Backhouse Park, has finally succumbed. Most of the exotic birds have now died off, as the soft fruits on which they lived on are non-existent now.

17-Feb-1943

Mrs Mary Tough, a widow, of 12 Renoldson St. has seven sons on active service and two engaged on war work.

18-Feb-1943

One of the diseases that merchant seaman "suffer" from is an obscure nervous complaint and the patient has to smoke 50 cigarettes a day as part of the treatment. So said Mr Kirkland Bridge, Appeals Director of the Merchant Navy Comforts Service.

19-Feb-1943

All requests for AFS assistance are to be directed through fireguards.

Short Bros. launches the *EMPIRE FRIENDSHIP* 7058t. 1962 Scrapped La Seyne.

20-Feb-1943

Sunderland v Bradford Park Avenue. In today's cup-tie, Shackleton scored from an acute angle when most people expected a centre. Argus blames bad refereeing for Sunderland's draw with Bradford.

SP. Austin launches the *BOWCOMBE* 2760t. In 1958 she was still in that fleet of Stephenson Clarke Ltd.

21-Feb-1943

It is now an offence for any person to misuse or wilfully destroy a milk bottle or to keep it longer than is necessary.

22-Feb-1943

In the first case of its kind in Sunderland, Home Guard Fredrick Crann (19) of Ashwood Avenue, who had put in only seven a half hours' training since his enrolment last year, was fined £5 by absenting himself from his Home Guard duties without a reasonable excuse.

24-Feb-1943

Wm. Doxford launches the *EMPIRE BEAUTY* 7297t. 1968 scrapped Taiwan.

25-Feb-1943

Crowns launch the *HMS ETTRICK* 1370t River Class Frigate. Royal Navy. Commissioned 11/07/1943. Scrapped June 1953.

26-Feb-1943

Crowns launch the *HMS ETTRICK* 1370t River Class Frigate. Royal Navy. Commissioned 11/07/1943. Scrapped June 1953.

27-Feb-1943

Bradford Park Avenue v Sunderland; Sunderland failed to win, so fail to qualify due to inferior goal ratio. Story of the two destroyers, ASHANTI and FAME salvaged by Greenwell's from the rocks at Whitburn in the closing months of 1940 is just released by the Censor.

2-Mar-1943

Work has started on converting a shop on the corner of High Street West and Cumberland Street into a long awaited town centre British Restaurant.

3-Mar-1943

Critics considered Plains Farm Estate as one of the worst housing estates seen. "The whole layout of the estate is ugly, devoid of imagination. From the top of the 'Mile Bank' it appears as a ghastly 'red rash'. No squares have been left, no children's playgrounds constructed, no trees planted and worst of all no community centre has been provided".

Joseph Boyes (26) of Wolsley Terrace was fined £10 absenting himself from work at George Clark Ltd without reasonable cause. "He was absent a number of times, said the Magistrate, "but found no difficulty in turning up on Sunday when he got double pay".

5-Mar-1943

Plains Farm Estate's record of blackout infringements continued today when three residents were fined 40 shillings each for blackout offences. They were Mrs Mary Kirk of Primate Road, Mrs Grace Cairns and Mrs Margaret Bracebridge both of Perth Road.

6-Mar-1943

Sunderland v Gateshead. Sunderland is beaten. Argus could not recall seeing a worse display of football.

8-Mar-1943

Laing's launch the *EMPIRE ALLIANCE* 9909t. 1945 BRITISH DRAGOON. 1962 scrapped Blyth.

9-Mar-1943

Wm. Doxford launches the *EMPIRE CHEER* 7297t. 1963 Scrapped Hong Kong after engine room fire, whilst lying Aden 08.12.1962.

10-Mar-1943

The Central Agricultural Wages Board in London today decided that the minimum payment for school children under 14 working on the land should be 5d an hour.

11/12-Mar-1943

Alarm No.242: 21.40 - 22.45. Alarm No.243: 23.17 - 00.11. Two high explosive bombs were dropped at South Hylton and many hundreds of incendiaries fell at Ryhope and Silksworth in the Sunderland RDC area.

Two AA shells fell on Durham Road, one in the grounds of the Children's Hospital and the other in the front garden of 22 Humbledon Park. Both shells exploded and the latter killed Mrs Elizabeth Nicholson (59), who was apparently in the entrance of her home. A number of AA shells fell in the Monkwearmouth area and on a number of trams in the sheds at the Wheatsheaf.

12-Mar-1943

Alarm No.244: 21.13 - 22.43. Boldon Colliery suffered heavy damage in last night's raid on the northeast coast.

13-Mar-1943

Gateshead 1 Sunderland 2. Whitelum scored both goals.

14/15-Mar-1943

Alarm No.245: 23.06 - 00.14. German High Command reported, "On the night of March 14th a formation of fast bomber aircraft made a strong attack against the shipbuilding centre of Sunderland. One of our aircraft has not returned".

Sunderland suffered its worst raid of the war so far. Shortly before midnight the enemy dropped four Parachute Mines and some thirty Firepot incendiary bombs. Casualties numbered sixteen killed, thirty-one seriously injured and sixty-one slightly injured. Seventeen premises were totally demolished, 115 to be demolished, 191 untenable and 4,160 damaged.

A parachute mine fell at the junction of John Street and St Thomas's Street wrecking St Thomas's Church (opposite) and killing three civil defence workers; the vicar of St Thomas's, the Rev Leyland Orton (58), on duty as a warden, Ernest Johnson, a firewatcher on duty at the Baltic Chambers and Joseph Mutagh, a firewatcher at the River Wear Commissioner's offices. The River Wear Commissioners building on the opposite corner was severely damaged. On the other two corners of the street intersection, office buildings were destroyed.

The Havelock cinema suffered extensive damage from the blast of this bomb and would not reopen until 17th May.

Union Street as it was

Union Street after the bomb

A second parachute mine fell in Union St. destroying the New Market and demolishing part of the Empress Hotel. It was reported that the whole structure of the hotel was moved some six inches. Again many nearby buildings were severely damaged. Nearly all the shop windows in the centre of town were blown out and all the windows of the Town Hall were destroyed and the Reception Room was so badly damaged it was out of action for sometime.

A third parachute mine fell in Nora St. behind Cleveland Rd., damage to house and cottage properties was extensive and it was in Norah St., Colchester Terrace and Cleveland Rd. incident that the heaviest casualties occurred. Rescue workers did a fine job in the neighbourhood, where so many lost their homes but owed their lives to being in their shelters.

The fourth parachute mine fell in Seaforth Rd.

Humbledon Hill Causing much devastation but thankfully only one person was injured. This bomb strangely landed within a few yards of the filled in crater caused by a bomb of nearly three years ago and a house which had been rebuilt after being severely damaged was this time demolished The bomb fell in the garden of 3 Seaforth Rd. were six people, sheltering in a Morrison shelter in the dining room, were found relatively unharmed although the house was totally destroyed around them.

The Children's Hospital, opposite in Durham Road, suffered broken windows and loosened plaster but none of the patients were harmed. More than 50 children, some of them seriously ill, were carried out of the wrecked wards and air-raid shelters and evacuated by ambulance to other hospitals in the town. A Warden commented, that since a woman was killed near here, people have learnt that it is safer to go to their shelters. But for the fact that nearly everyone in this district was in their shelters we would have had scores of casualties.

30 Firepots fell across the town. In the Millfield area where the Diamond Hall Girls School and Chester Road Infants received direct hits. A number fell in the district of Otto Terrace, Broadmeadows, Thornholme Road, and Thornhill Shelters. A third stick of Firepots fell in the area of Holmlands Park North, Ashbrooke Cricket Ground, Glen Path, The Cedars, Cedars Park and Belford Terrace and Stratford Street. None caused any serious fires.

16-Mar-1943

For failing to stick regularly to his work at Wearmouth colliery Matthew Taylor (20) of Howick Street was sent to prison for three months. He was fined 40 shillings in January for absenting himself from work and he was also bound over on the basis that he stuck to his work regularly at the colliery.

17-Mar-1943

The Government warned that the shipping position was more serious than that of any period in the war despite the best efforts of the United States and our own shipbuilders, and of the efforts of our anti U-boat campaign.

19-Mar-1943

The Mayor's only son, Flight Lieutenant Myers Wayman RAFVR, is reported killed in action.

20-Mar-1943

Sunderland v Middlesbrough. Sunderland scored eight goals in beating Middlesbrough. The Castletown soldier Arthur Wright, who has been at Roker Park since he left school, showed skill and competence that amazed all.

22-Mar-1943

Alarm No.246: 22.47 - 23.47. Though bombs, both high explosive and incendiaries were scattered over a wide area of the northeast coast the damage was not heavy at any point and the casualties was surprisingly light. Heavy anti aircraft barrage met the Raiders flying in from the sea over Sunderland. Two bombs near the South Dock resulted in one death. Many houses suffered minor damage from incendiaries.

A fine of £20 was imposed on David Beck (22) of Zetland Street for absenting himself from work at Laing's shipyard without a reasonable excuse. Also a James Edward Clark (18) of Philip Square, a rivet heater at Bartram's shipyard, was fined £5 for a similar offence and also for being persistently late for work.

Pickersgill's launch the *STANRIDGE* 5977t. Scrapped India April 1965.

23-Mar-1943

The police have not confirmed the gossip and rumour of widespread looting of bombed damaged buildings following the recent air raid on the town.

JL. Thompson launches the *CHINESE PRINCE* 9485t. She was seriously damaged by a direct hit from a German bomb while still in the builders yard. 1964 scrapped at Hirao.

24/25-Mar-1943

Alarm No.247: 23.39 - 01.35. A force of raiders scattered over widely separated parts of Northern England.

27-Mar-1943

Middlesbrough v Sunderland. Middlesbrough beat Sunderland. Carter was available and Lesley Duns, currently on leave, appeared at inside right.

30-Mar-1943

Sunderland's 'Dig for Victory' Exhibition was formally opened in the New Rink this afternoon.

31-Mar-1943

The Borough Surveyor puts the plans for the building of 1500 houses in the first year of post war Sunderland forward. Houses will be built in the Springwell Farm, North Hylton Road and Southwick.

2-Apr-1943

Sunderland housewives, who spent hours in fish queues yesterday and today, did not believe the news of huge fish stocks in northern ports.

3-Apr-1943

Unless Sunderland can produce a four-goal margin at home against Bradford City next Saturday their second Cup venture, the Combined Counties Cup competition, of the season will have failed.

5-Apr-1943

SP. Austin launches the *EMPIRE JUDY* of 738t. 1977 Scrapped Lisbon.

6-Apr-1943

Sunderland magistrates dealt with 41 summonses against men and women for committing 'nuisances' (urinating) in the streets of the town. Two women were fined £3 and the 39 men £5.

7-Apr-1943

Sunderland Corporation is to purchase The Nook, which adjoins the Grindon Hall Sanatorium. The purchase included 14 acres of land at £250 per acre, house and buildings £2,500 and gatehouse and three cottages £1,000.

8-Apr-1943

The King and Queen visited Sunderland today. They were greeted warmly during their two-and-a-half-hour stay after arriving at the station in the Royal Train. Their Majesties visited the shipyards of J L Thompson & Sons and Laing's and later inspected the damage to St Thomas's church. The final event of the visit was the inspection of the Civil Defence services drawn up in John Street.

Short Bros. launches the *EMPIRE MANOR* 7017t. 27.1.44 in collision in convoy 28.1.44 broke in two, sunk by escort ship. 1973 Gold bullion cargo salvaged.

Wm. Doxford launches the *TREVELYON* 7292t. Scrapped Hong Kong Oct. 1962.

9-Apr-1943

Part of the north end of Sunderland central railway station was the scene of a spectacular fire at midday today. The roof over the main entrance was ablaze, four lift shafts were badly damaged and much damage was caused to the parcels and left luggage offices. Flames were shooting out of several points when the AFS arrived. It took firemen under an hour to get the fire under control. The roof, which was destroyed, had recently been repaired.

10-Apr-1943

Sunderland 5 Bradford City 1. Without Carter but strengthened by the return of Hastings and Lockie. Half-time Sunderland 1 Bradford City 1. With 15 minutes to go and still four goals required to win the tie. After a reshuffle, the goals soon came and the 5th and winning goal was scored two minutes from the end.

The King and Queen inspecting the damage to St Thomas's Church

Earlier at the shipyard of J.L. Thompson

12-Apr-1943

Lord Woolton, Minister of Food, admitted to a shortage of shell eggs but he does not think that the public has quite realized that in dried eggs they are getting everything of value except the shell. By bringing in dried eggs saves 2 million tons of shipping annually.

14-Apr-1943

The Post Office announces cuts in mail deliveries; currently 3 deliveries a day will be cut to 2, the post Office estimates that the release of manpower would be 5000 full time women and 2000 full time men.

A warning about the Meat situation was given by Lord Walton Minister of Food, "The simple fact is we have not got it, and nothing I can do is going to enable us to have enough meat in the Country to keep us fit for the job we have to do".

16-Apr-1943

Terence Patrick 'Tiny' Garraghan (17), of Guildford Street, received the Distinguished Service Medal (DSM) from the King, which he earned as a cabin boy on the EMPIRE GALLIARD sailing on a dangerous lone voyage to Russia. Arthur James Williams Sproxton of 19 Hutton Street is also to receive the DSM for the same trip but he is still at sea and he is yet to get his medal from the King.

17-Apr-1943

The Havelock cinema re-opens having undergone repairs and renovations following the air raid on March 15. Re-opened with George Formby in 'Get Cracking' and George Saunders in ' Quiet Please…Murder'.

Bradford Park Avenue v Sunderland. Sunderland, with a goal in hand, has an excellent chance of appearing in the final of the Combined Counties Cup.

20-Apr-1943

JL. Thompson launches the *DENEWOOD* 7240t In May 1943 Thompson's yard was heavily bombed on two successive weekends. While moored at the quayside it was sunk in the river and later refloated. Scrapped Hamburg Nov. 1964

21-Apr-1943

After 12 men had been fined £5 and a soldier £3 for committing a 'nuisance' in the streets the magistrate said, "Apparently there are men who were earning so much money that they could consume so much drink and so commit these offences in the blackout in shop doorways and church entrances".

22-Apr-1943
Church bells can now ring out on Sundays to summon people to church but not for wedding or funerals etc.
Laing's launched the *EMPIRE INVENTOR (2)* 9912t. 1959 Scrapped Savona.
Bartram's launch the *EMPIRE ROCK* 7061t. Scrapped Hamburg Aug. 1960.

24-Apr-1943
Sunderland v Bradford Park Avenue. A 6000 crowd watched the second leg of the semi-final of the Combined
Counties Cup this afternoon. A Sunderland win.

26-Apr-1943
Easter Monday. There was no evidence of paste eggs and chocolate eggs are not permitted. The only Easter
display in the town is in the foyer of the Regal with a display of giant eggs and day-old chicks in a glass case.

30-Apr-1943
Wings for Victory Week opens in Sunderland tomorrow. People will be invited to buy saving stamps to stick on
two bombs, which will later be dropped on Germany.

1-May-1943
Sunderland 8 Huddersfield 4. Clifford Whitelum broke all Sunderland's scoring records when he registered six
goals against Huddersfield. The four-goal lead is certainly a flying start for the second leg of the final.

4-May-1943
It was still costing £5 for being caught creating a 'nuisance' (urinating) in the street. The latest are William Bell
of Neal Street, John Coleman of Stobert Street and William Auld of 5 Back Half Way House.
SP. Austin launches the *EMPIRE JUDY* 738t. 1977 Scrapped Lisbon.
Wm Doxford launches the *TREVINCE* 7292t. Scrapped 1974.

8-May-1943
Huddersfield 3 Sunderland 0. Bradwell and George Robinson replaced Housam and Carter. Sunderland wins
the Combined Counties Cup. This is Billy Murray's first Cup since taking over as Manager.

10-May-1943
Sunderland passes the target set for Wings for Victory Week with a total of £1,252,563.

12-May-1943
J A Smith (17) of Hodgson's Buildings Monkwearmouth admitted at Sunderland's Police Court today that he
had been absent from his ship without leave on several occasions. When asked by the chairman why had he
acted like this? Smith replied, " I was not liked because I was the only Sunderland man on the ship. They said
they would rather have two dead men than one Sunderland man." " Were they all South Country men on board
the vessel?" asked the clerk. " They were all South Shields men", replied Smith. He further said he had been
going to sea for two and a half years and had been twice torpedoed and was anxious to get back to sea.

15-May-1943
To celebrate the third anniversary of its formation,
1500 men of the 9th Durham, 24th Durham, 7th
Durham and the 213 Anti Aircraft battery paraded
for a drumhead service at Ashbrooke

16-May-1943
Alarm No.248: 01.44 - 03.09.
The following is taken from the ARP report issued
on the 20th May.
Some 130 incidents were reported by the ARP after
the raid including 11 parachute mines, 62 high
explosive bombs, 34 firepots and many incendiary
bombs were dropped in various parts of the town
causing considerable damage to premises and
inflicting a large number of casualties both killed

*At 2.15am two bombs, one of 1000kg and the other of 250kg
caused the greatest number of casualties. Eleven died at Waterloo
Place and ten died in Whitburn Street. Monkwearmouth.*

and injured. This figure would have been considerably higher if all had exploded.
The total casualties were - seventy killed (eventually reaching seventy-five); seventy-three seriously injured and
one hundred and twenty-five slightly injured. All services were fully extended and assistance was received from
other Authorities and the Military.
It was estimated that 200 houses had been demolished or were to be demolished, and 10,000 seriously and
slightly damaged. 800 men were engaged on first aid repairs.A large number of people were evacuated owing to
unexploded bombs, some of which have not yet been cleared. Sections of the Sunderland-Newcastle road and
the Sunderland-Durham road were stopped to traffic due to the UXBs. The patients at Monkwearmouth&
Southwick Hospital were evacuated on the 17th to Cherry Knowle Hospital and Municipal Hospital owing to a
UXB in the vicinity, it was removed on Tuesday the 18th and the patients returned to the Hospital that day.

The bombs destroyed shops, pubs and Fenwick's Brewery in Low Row. The Sunderland Model Making Works and the Central Laundry were badly damaged. Incendiaries destroyed Bright Street Methodist Church, the Avenue Paint Works and the King's Theatre in Crowtree Road.

FOOD STORES:

Completely demolished - Seven retailers - three licensed premises - a Brewery - a Cafe. Seriously damaged - Two retailers - a licensed premises - a factory - a dairy. Slightly damaged - Two wholesalers - sixty-five retailers - ten licensed premises.

CHURCHES:

Damage was caused to the following Churches and Chapels:- St Maud's Mission, Sea Road - Williamson Terrace PM Chapel - Roker Congregational Church, Roker Baths Rd - Roker Wesleyan Church, Roker Park Road - Bright Street Chapel - Royalty Congregational.

THEATRES:

Serious Damage was done to the King's Theatre, Crowtree Road.

OTHER BUILDINGS:

The bombs destroyed shops, pubs and Fenwick's Brewery in Low Street. The Sunderland Model Making Works and the Central Laundry were badly damaged. Incendiaries destroyed Bright Street Methodist Church, the Avenue Paint Works and the King's Theatre in Crowtree Road.

A 1000kg bomb fell at the corner of Atkinson Road with Rosedale Road, Fulwell. 11 people died, among them a family of 6 at 90 Atkinson Road. 8 people were injured, 1 seriously.

Other premises and works damaged were:- Young's Garage, Roker - T.W. Greenwell & Co - South Dock - S.P. Austin & Co - J. Dickinson and Sons - British Ropes - Sir James Laing & Sons - Electricity Offices, Dunning St - J.L. Thompson &Sons, North Sands & Manor Quay - Fulwell Transport Depot - "Fire Queen" and three tugs in the River - Richardson Westgarth & Co.

CASUALTIES:

Assistance was also given by the Ministry of Information with their loudspeaker vans, and by Rediffusion Ltd., in allowing the Controller to broadcast over their relay system.

MORTUARIES:

Two mortuaries were opened. Seven bodies were identified at St Mark's and fifty at Hallgarth. No corpse remains unidentified.

REST AND FEEDING CENTRES:

The following Rest and Feeding Centres were opened at which 660 people were accommodated and fed: -

REST CENTRES:

Bishopwearmouth, Chester Road, Commercial Road, Simpson Street, Plains Farm, Grange Park, Dock Street, Fulwell.

FEEDING CENTRES:

Green Terrace, Chester Road, Simpson Street, Grange Park, Barbara Priestman Hall, Commercial Road, Carol Street Restaurant, Southwick Restaurant, Herrington St Restaurant.

ADMINISTRATION CENTRES:

Administration Centres were opened at St Mary's RC School, Bishopwearmouth Church Hall and Monkwearmouth Central School, Swan Street. These centres were opened to give advice to people in bombed areas on Air Raid Damage problems and the staff's were available at the Centres from 11.00 Sunday 16th. Approximately 4,000 enquiries have been made at Monkwearmouth Central and 2,000 at St Mary's and Bishopwearmouth. The following Depts were represented:- Assistance Board - Food Office - National Registration Office - Citizens' Advice Bureau - Searcher Service - Military Assistance Officer - Town Clerk's Office - Billeting Officer - Casualty Bureau - Public Assistance Office - Evacuation Department - Information Centre.

BILLETING:

1,298 homeless consisting of 550 families on the north side of the River and 678 homeless comprising 230 families on the south side have been found billeting accommodation.

WATER SUPPLY:

Considerable damage was done to water mains in different parts of the town. Repair Gangs worked continuously throughout Sunday the 16th and Monday the 17th. Most of the mains were repaired by Sunday night or early Monday. Three fractures stopped the water supply to a large part of the Roker area and water cartage was commenced at 18.00, Monday and continued until 16.00, Tuesday the 18th when the normal supply to Roker was restored.

ELECTRICITY:

Incendiary Bombs were dropped on the Hylton Road Generating Station but there was no damage.

One man died when four bombs fell in and around Alexander Park, demolishing 7 houses, seriously damaging 4 more and damaging 80 others.

At Dunning Street, incendiary bombs set fire to the offices and stores in which a stock of stationery was destroyed. Damage to EHT feeders interrupted the supply to three Industrial consumers for a short period during non-working hours, but the supply was restored on alternative feeders within one hour.

One medium pressure switch gear was lost and two transformers were damaged. In the Fulwell area, fairly extensive damage was caused to the NESCo network and the supply was off for 10 hours 50 minutes. The supply was also interrupted in the Marley Potts and High Southwick areas for 12 hours 15 minutes and 14 hours 15 minutes respectively.

Water Filled crater in Roker Park pitch

GAS MAINS:

Stoppage of gas was caused in the Roker area by water from a broken water main at the Parkside Terrace incident. About 200 houses were affected. The water was cleared and the supply restored by Tuesday evening the 18th. There was no stoppage of gas supply to Industrial works in any district.

SEWERS:

The main Low Street outfall sewer was seriously damaged for a length of about 25 yards. An overflow has been put into operation discharging into the River. One of the main trunks of the Roker Gill Sewer was fractured for a length of 30 yards in Grantham Road and the work of repair is in progress.

Other minor damage was caused to subsidiary sewers.

A 500kg bomb fell in the car park and destroyed the old Clubhouse

ARP HEADQUARTERS, "Thornholme", SUNDERLAND. 20th May 1943

Burning oil from Greenwell's punctured oil tanks was floating on the water near the gates, which form the entrance to the Hudson Dock. The whole dock system was in serious danger as the burning oil threatened to set fire to the gates.

The remains of Fenwick's Brewery in Low Street

The devastation caused by a Parachute Mine at Fulwell Crossing on the 16th May

17-May-1943
A five-year-old boy Joseph McCann, of 13 Fell Road, is drowned in a static water tank in St Luke's Road Pallion.

18-May-1943
In the House of Common's debate today on wives war savings The Chancellor was asked to ensure that a husband should not be able to claim a wife's war savings of stamps, certificates or bonds, even if she used housekeeping money for the purpose. Sir Kingsley Wood in the case of certificates and bonds only the registered owner may reclaim them, stamps however are not registered. Mr Beverley Baxter Conservative for Wood Green " Is not this question conducive to the dishonesty among wives and to perpetration of a system of housekeeping on false figures which will not be good for the husband". There was laughter.
Doxford's launch the *AVONMOOR* 7268t. Scrapped Taiwan Feb. 1968.

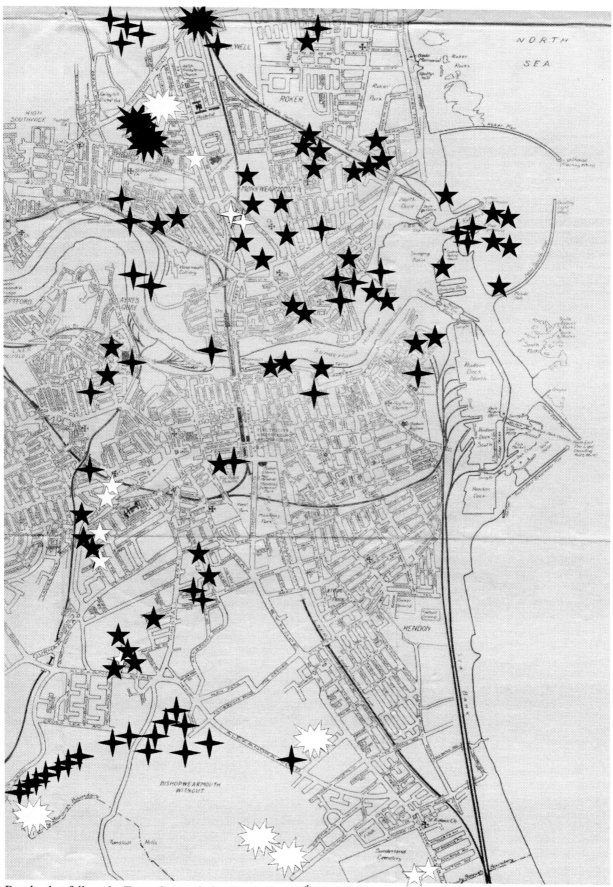

Bombs that fell on the Town Centre during the Raid of 16th May 1943 (Those shown white did not detonate)

 Parachute Mine　　　　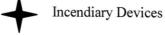 Incendiary Devices　　　　 High Explosive

20-May-1943

It was announced that signposts are to be re-erected in rural Britain as the fear of invasion recedes.

A thirteen year old boy who denied taking a man's hat from the Ritz cinema, saying "it was lying on the floor so I picked it up and took it home to see if there was a reward offered", was before the Sunderland Juvenile Court today. His mother who had admitted seeing the hat when it was brought home was fined £1. Mr F Williamson presiding magistrate commented, "we are appalled at the mentality you have shown and we think that home training is at fault"

In a case of a girl accused of looting Mr Williamson was again commenting on social behaviour, "this is an astonishing state of affairs when a man can go about the town working and scrounging for years and not contribute a penny to the upkeep of his family while the Public Assistance Committee (P.A.C.) do nothing about it and unfortunately this is not an isolated case we are getting the same story over and over again" The girl of 14 appeared on remand, the mother stated that the husband had not contributed anything towards the upkeep of the family for the past eight years and she had been forced to rely on P.A.C. allowances. The girl was placed on probation for two years.

Pickersgill's launch the *CHISWICK* 5996t. Scrapped Belgium May 1960.

21-May-1943

Many Wearsiders had seen the leaflet showered over Sunderland by German raiders last weekend headed, "Why the British Government says nothing about shipping losses". The leaflet states, " to be told of the truth about the state of the Battle of the seas would shake the belief in British naval supremacy and ultimate victory". It then proceeded to give a list of 412 ships, " ascertained to have been sent to the bottom since June 1st, 1941". Although rejected at the time, as Nazi propaganda, the Battle of the Atlantic at this time was causing great concern to the British Government.

22-May-1943

In view of the necessity for conserving supplies of textile materials, the Board of Trade will under no circumstance license the manufacture of powder puffs comprising a handkerchief of textile material greater than nine square inches in area.

24-May-1943

Alarm No.249: 02.49 - 04.07.

The German High Command communiqué reported, "that the Luftwaffe had again attacked the shipbuilding town of Sunderland with strong forces. Large fires were started in the city and harbour areas".

The following is from an ARP report on the raid. Bombs were dropped in a number of sections of the town and consisted of eleven parachute mines, four of which were unexploded, sixty-seven HEs, nine firepots, three PhIBs and approximately 600 small incediaries. These were in fact the last bombs to fall on the County Borough of Sunderland.

CASUALTIES:

The casualties were as follows:- 83 killed, 109 seriously injured and 113 slightly injured.

DAMAGED HOUSES:

It is estimated that 310 houses have been demolished or to be demolished; 1,000 seriously damaged; 10,000 slightly damaged.

1000kg fell on St. George's Square, destroying a number of houses and damaging many more. The 19 fatalities occurred at No.'s. 6 to 11. The remains of two women were never found.

FOOD STORES:

The following is a summary of the Food Stores damaged:-

Type	Total Loss	Extensively Damaged	Slightly Damaged
Retailers& Caterers	12	14	137
Wholesalers	2	1	3
Factories and Depots	2	1	3
Licensed Premises	1	7	26

The crater left by a 1000kg bomb in Dun Cow Street

Bombs began to fall around 3.00am. The Bromarsh Cinema Basement Shelter was seriously damaged, the outer wall being demolished. Three people died, and many were trapped.

Five members of the Humble family died in a shelter when a second 500Kg fell in Bonnersfield area.

In another major incident, two families were almost wiped out when a 500 Kg bomb fell in Robinson Street, demolishing a number of houses.

In High Street West J S Strother's block of shops was struck and another heavy bomb fell not far from the Empire Theatre in Dun Cow Street creating a large crater of 99 feet across by 40 feet deep. A new water main had to be laid from the Empire to the Fire Station. Damage to the Empire Theatre, however, was slight and the curtain went up on the show that Monday night.

CHURCHES:

Damage was caused to the following Churches and Chapels:- Bishopwearmouth Church - Sunderland Parish Church - St Barnabas' - St George's Presbyterian - St Ignatius Mission Hall, Burlington Road - Williamson Terrace Chapel - Newcastle Road PM Chapel - Lindsay Road Chapel.

SHELTERS:

The Bromarsh Basement Shelter was seriously damaged, the outer wall being demolished. This will entail considerable adjustment to the inside strutting. The Communal Shelter at Lodge Terrace was completely demolished.

THEATRES AND CINEMAS:

The following theatres and cinemas were damaged:- Empire Theatre, slightly - Bromarsh Cinema, Bonnersfield - Picture House, High Street West.

OTHER BUILDINGS:

Damage was also caused to important Yards and Works in the Borough. One vessel was sunk in the River and two in South Docks received damage.

At the Manor Quay a parachute mine landed on the ship DENEWOOD. She sank in the river, but was soon refloated.

The CHINESE PRINCE, another new ship, lying alongside was also damaged, and more bombs did damage to the shops and plant of the shipyard of JL. Thompson. NE Marine also sustained damage along both Hudson and Hendon Docks.

SCHOOLS:

A number of Schools were damaged and the following had to be closed:- West Park Central - Cowan Terrace - Bishopwearmouth CE - St Andrew's CE - Plains Farm - Valley Road - James William Street - Thornfield and Barbara Priestman Special Schools - St George's Domestic Science Centre.

MORTUARIES:

The following Mortuaries were opened:- St Marks - Grey School. Hallgarth Square.

REST AND FEEDING CENTRES:

Thirteen Rest Centres were opened immediately after the raid and 3,000 homeless were accommodated. At twelve Emergency Feeding Centres 3,791 persons were supplied with meals.

A 500kg bomb fell near the Almshouses, Littlegate and Church Walk

ADMINISTRATIVE CENTRES:

The Administrative Centres at St Mary's RC and St Benet's RC Schools were opened at 11.00 on Monday the 24th and remained open until 18.00 on Friday the 28th. Over 5,800 enquiries were made.

WATER SUPPLY.

Damage was caused to water mains in different parts of the town and the supply was stopped in the Hendon area. Arrangements were made for water cartage to operate on the afternoon of Monday the 24th. In some cases, temporary small by-pass pipes were fixed sufficient to restore the water supply by Tuesday the 25th. Permanent repairs in some cases cannot be put in hand until the craters are dealt with.

Three Communal Shelters were hit during the raid on the 24ᵗʰ May1943. Three people died in the Bromarsh shelter and five in the Bonnersfield shelter. The Lodge Street incident above claimed the lives of thirteen persons.

ELECTRICITY SUPPLY:
Several feeders and distribution pillars were damaged but there was no interruption in supply due to this damage. Installations at three industrial firms were damaged preventing them from resuming full supply. The supply to a number of domestic consumers was off for a number of hours but was resumed before the evening of the 24th.

GAS MAINS:
Gas mains were damaged and the supply to consumers was maintained at a lower pressure than normal for approximately 24 hours after which time the full pressure was restored.

SEWERS:
Sewers were damaged at the following points:- Lodge Terrace - Dun Cow Street - Stratford Avenue - Rickaby Street - Trinity Street - Little Gate - Mainsforth Terrace - Priory Grove. A number of subsidiary sewers may have sustained damage but there is no interference with the dry weather flow. Repair gangs are working on the sewers and assistance has been received from Newcastle, South Shields and Gateshead.

SERVICES:
All Services were fully engaged and assistance was received from Newcastle upon Tyne, Gateshead and the Northumberland and Durham County areas.

MOBILE CANTEENS:
Mobile Canteens were put into operation, all the Borough Canteens being engaged, together with others from the Durham County area.

Incidents outside the boundary included two 500kg bombs and a number of Firepots falling in Ryhope Colliery yard. A 60-year-old Firewatcher was killed and the Colliery had to close.

Three Parachute Mines falling in Silksworth caused a lot of damage but no casualties.

The Isolation Hospital (Havelock House) had to be evacuated due to an unexploded Parachute Mine.

25-May-1943
A detachment of Barrage balloons finally arrived, hardly to be used.

Miners are asked to increase coal output. If the gap between production and consumption were not closed, the war would go against us.

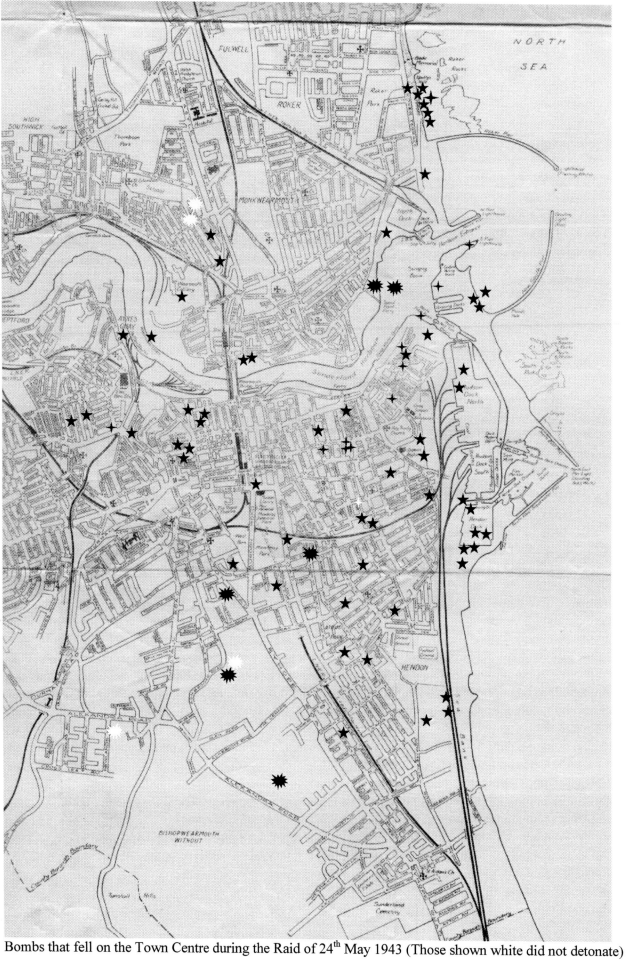

Bombs that fell on the Town Centre during the Raid of 24th May 1943 (Those shown white did not detonate)

 Parachute Mine Incendiary Devices ★ High Explosive

26-May-1943

Cases of scabies in Sunderland numbered 1828 against 1148 last year. Scabies is an unpleasant disease, borne of dirt and spread by neglect. A report suggests that parents who fail to see that their children, suffering from scabies, do not receive a proper treatment should be prosecuted for neglect. 548 school children have now been immunised against diphtheria against 2074 of the previous year.

Joseph Potts (20) of Maplewood Avenue is said to have arrived late on 17 days out of 66 and of being absent on eight of those days. Potts, an apprentice electric welder at Doxford's, was fined £5 and bound over for 12 months.

In the South Dock ,a high explosive bomb fell clean through the open hatch of a ship lying at the Coal Belts and made a hole in its bottom but the ship did not sink.

27-May-1943

Church bells may now be rung for any purpose at any time.

29-May-1943

A conscript Home Guard in an anti aircraft battery was sent to prison for two months with hard labour. He had only paraded three times since he was enrolled six months ago.

31-May-1943

Frederick Thompson (33) of back North Bridge Street and William Bond (18) of Proctor Square Humbledon were among 10 Castletown Colliery miners fined 40 shillings each for riding ponies underground.

2-Jun-1943

All of Tunstall Hills now belong to the people of Sunderland. Some years ago the town bought 29 acres, including Rocky Hill, for allotments and playing fields. Now Miss E.H. Pemberton of Ramside has presented the town with the remaining 7 acres, which includes Green Hill.

SP. Austin launches the *WRENWOOD* of 2847t. 16.4.1960 cargo of scrap iron shifted en route to Newport News; hole punched in ships side, flooded and abandoned.

JL. Thompson launches the *CAXTON* 7240t. Scrapped Taiwan July 1967.

3-Jun-1943

It is possible, in fact probable, that all ranges of men's footwear will be wooden soled. It was thought inevitable that the boot and shoe industry will have to face a period of closure.

8-Jun-1943

Sheltering in their brick surface shelter three years ago with her mother and father was Jean Stormont 15 years old a newly appointed Post Office girl probationer with dreams of becoming a Telephonist. That night a stricken Heinkel crashed into their home, trapping them in their shelter, killing her mother and injuring herself and her father. Jeans injuries were such that both hands had to be amputated. Today Jean, now 18 with special adapted limbs, began the career that she thought was lost to her as a Telephonist at Telephone House. Her father had also recovered and returned to work some time earlier.

10-Jun-1943

Seventy-five tons of debris was found in the 100,000-gallon water tank in Crown Road, Southwick when it was emptied to recover the body of 3-year-old Joan Hall of 15 Crown Road who drowned in the tank despite of several attempts to save her. The Coroner, at the inquest, said that the condition of the tank was a discredit to the people living in the neighbourhood.

11-Jun-1943

Following a disturbance in The Waterman's Tavern, Rickaby Street in the East End a "battle" involving a crowd of 500 ensued. David Elliott 37 of 24 Purley Road, Plains Farm was fined £15.

A 4-year-old boy, Derek Patrick, of 66 Coronation Street was rescued from a static water tank in Outram Street. 22 year-old Mrs Sarah Bambrough of 213 Cleveland Road gave birth to triplets in Sunderland Municipal Hospital today.

12-Jun-1943

Plains Farm residents were alarmed by a story told by a small boy of a girl falling into a static water tank and disappearing. The AFS pumped it dry but it was found to be empty apart from the usual rubbish.

14-Jun-1943

Short Bros. launches the *EMPIRE CAMP* 7052t. Scrapped Istanbul Feb. 1971.

15-Jun-1943

At the Ritz you could see Abbot & Costello in 'Money & Jam'. At the Regal Deanna Durbin was starring in 'The Amazing Mrs Holliday'. Dancing at the Rink would now cost you 1s.6d Monday and Wednesday and 2s.0d on a Saturday.

17-Jun-1943

Laing's launch the *EMPIRE GAIN* 3738t. 1967 Bombed and sunk by Israeli aircraft at south end of Suez Canal.

18-Jun-1943

Three boys, aged between 10 and 11, were in court accused of looting. They are said to have stolen ledgers to use as drawing books. They each received two years probation. Two other boys, aged 13 and 10, also accused of stealing two pairs of hair clippers, which had since been recovered, were fined £1.

19-Jun-1943

Of 322 members of the 125 Anti-Tank RA Regiment (Sunderland's Own), known to have been in Singapore when the island fell into Jap hands, 204 are now reported to be prisoners of war.

20-Jun-1943

The official opening of Sunderland's 'Holiday at Home' marks the beginning of eight weeks of special attractions. The Mayor performed the opening ceremony in Barnes Park, entertainment provided by the Blackhall Colliery Band.

21-Jun-1943

Apples and plums are plentiful with a small supply of cherries. However, regulations prevent the transport of soft fruit from the south to places north of York.
Crowns launch the *HMS BUGLOSS* 980t Flower Class Corvette. Royal Navy. Indian Navy 1945-1947. Scrapped.

COUNTY BOROUGH OF SUNDERLAND

HOLIDAYS AT HOME — JUNE TO AUGUST
If you can Sing, Dance, or Entertain
you are invited to enter for the
GRAND
TALENT SPOTTING COMPETITION
(Preliminary Show dates to be announced later).
The Audience will act as Adjudicators.
TWO SECTIONS
Juniors up to 16 years.   Seniors over 16 years.
Prizes of £10 for each Section will be given to the finalists.
Mr George Black, on behalf of Moss Empires, Ltd., has agreed to offer one week's engagement at the Sunderland Empire to the successful competitor in the Senior Section of the competition.
ENTRIES, stating age and what you do, to be sent immediately to The Secretary, Concert Committee, Town Hall, Sunderland.
WH/3.

22-Jun-1943

Thomas French (52) of Whitby Avenue, South Bents, Whitburn, was accused of having broken the Defence regulations by not handing in to authorities a propaganda leaflet dropped by aircraft. He declared that thousands of leaflets had been showered on Sunderland and were being sold at one penny apiece for the benefit of the Red Cross. The case was dismissed on payment of seven shillings.

23-Jun-1943

War Emergency Committee has finally decided that it is not prepared to pay for any further repairs to the community shelter, serving residents in High Street East Flats stating, "the louts have won".

24-Jun-1943

The junior section of a talent contest, held at Bede Girls School, was won in by Myer Robinson aged 15 (pianist) and June Howard 14 (acrobatic dancer), both from Sunderland. The adult section winners were Ernest Bailey a magician from Seaham and Nancy Hill a vocalist from Humbledon.

26-Jun-1943

A deer has been seen twice recently in Barnes Park by park gardeners but efforts to capture it has failed. Mr. R Monument of 4 Humbledon Park saw the deer cross Barnes Park Road in front of him early on Whit Monday. It disappeared into the park through the trees towards the Pemberton bowling greens.

28-Jun-1943

Four members of the A.F.S. were sentenced to nine months imprisonment having been found guilty of looting goods from the bombed premises of Henry Moat and Sons Ltd. A fifth member, because of his age (17), was fined £25.

29-Jun-1943

93 riveters from a Sunderland shipyard are accused of unlawfully taking part in a two-week strike.

30-Jun-1943

Cuthbert Ritchie, of Cornhill Road, found an incendiary bomb outside his home during an air raid. He took it to work in a munitions factory, where during an examination it exploded and blew off another man's thumb. As he had already been fined in another court for taking a bomb into a prohibited area he was acquitted with eight shillings costs.

1-Jul-1943

Wm. Doxford launches the *GREENWICH* 7292t. Caught fire and sank in North Atlantic in April 1963.
The launch by the Princess Royal is believed to be the first occasion of which a member of the royal family has performed the naming ceremony on an ordinary trader of the Merchant Navy.

2-Jul-1943

The Grocers of the town was of the opinion that the Northeast was not getting its fair share of non-rationed goods.

3-Jul-1943

"Do you realise that in any other Country your son would have been shot, such are the demands of war". So said the magistrate addressing the mother of 17 year-old Cyril Staples of 40 Wear Street, who today was sent to jail for one month for looting four doors valued at £2 4s from bombed property in Wear Street.

5-Jul-1943

Milk ration reduced from 4 to 3 pints a week. The shell egg ration is one egg a week for most.

It is feared that the story of the mystery deer, which has been roaming Barnes Park and other districts of the town ever since Whitsun, has come to an end. Rumours were that it had been shot.

Crowns launch the *EMPIRE DOLLY* 257t. 1953 THUNDERER. 1958 OCEAN OSPREY.

7-Jul-1943

Since the park lakes became honoured with the official title of NFS Static Water they seem to be doing their best to merit the title. The lakes, especially those in the Barnes and Mowbray parks are now so thickly overgrown with weeds they are almost solid let alone static. In the event of water to be required from these lakes to fight a fire, one could imagine difficulties with choked pumps and hoses.

8-Jul-1943

How a 28ft log of timber weighing 9 cwt, which fell on a Sunderland Shipwright's labourer, killing him, how the log came to be leaning against the side of the quay was not explained at an inquest on Michael Gordon (33) of 51 Friar Road. A verdict of accidental death was recorded. The accident happened on the beach below the key at the shipyard of Sir J Laing & Sons.

9-Jul-1943

Where would Television have stood today but for the war? The answer is that it would have arrived in the full sense of the word. In 1939 the price of a television set was steadily going down and for under £30 an attachment to an ordinary set could be purchased which converted into a small television receiver. Televisions with a screen size of two feet square could be purchased. The advancement in the technology was astonishing. Televisions in London were receiving outside broadcasts from Lords, Zoos and other places. Things will have to wait but when peace comes television will continue its advance in to our homes.

12-Jul-1943

Echo readers learnt of one of the most remarkable feats of ship salvage and repair jobs ever carried out in wartime. A torpedo sank the Whitby steamer STAKESBY of 7000 tons, built by Wm. Pickersgill & Sons Ltd in 1930, in August 1940. She lay for 16 months at the bottom of the sea. Following a decision to raise her she was towed round the coast to Sunderland, where Greenwell's made almost a new ship of her and renamed her EMPIRE DERWENT.

The deck of the STAKESBY before repair

The repaired STAKESBY, renamed EMPIRE DERWENT, now ready for service once more.

13-Jul-1943

Mr J W Smith, Blue Peter of the Sunderland Echo, called for the establishment of a nautical museum to help preserve the great shipping traditions of the Wear. As there were still many models, pictures and documents available to illustrate the great periods of our town he hoped that in the years after the war something on the lines of a nautical museum would be established.

16-Jul-1943

Sanction for first aid repairs only, to make the Children's Hospital weatherproof, has been received but this will not allow its reopening as a hospital.

Wm. Doxford launches the *EMPIRE CITY* 7295t. 5.8.44 Torpedoed and sunk on its maiden voyage by U.198. 2 lost. Pickersgill's launch the *EMPIRE COPPERFIELD* 6013t. 1963 Scrapped Bombay.

SS FORT FRANKLIN sunk by U-181 in the Indian Ocean; One of two crewmembers lost was David Shaw, Chief Engineering Officer, aged 44. Son of David and Margaret Hannah Shaw; husband of Elsie Shaw, of Sunderland.

17-Jul-1943

Through the generosity of Sir John Priestman's Trust, the Finchale Abbey Road House Hotel, together with its furnishing and fittings, its swimming pool and extensive grounds, was purchased in order to undertake the rehabilitation and vocational training of disabled men.

JL. Thompson launches the *EMPIRE DUKE* 7240t. 1966 Scrapped Taiwan.

Laing's launch the *THAMESFIELD* 9801t. 15.9.1966 aground on Pratas Reef, South China Sea;

Bartram's launch the *EMPIRE TOURIST* 7062t. 4.3.44 Torpedoed and sunk by U.703. Crew of 79 all saved.

18-July-1943

More than 2000 thousand people were in Barnes Park tonight to see the pantomime of Snow White and the Seven Dwarfs.

19-Jul-1943

Ringtons Ltd., for failing to reorganise its delivery operations, are band from delivering tea.

20-Jul-1943

The Minister of Labour, Mr Bevin, on the shortage of miners, warned that they might have to send 16 year olds to the mines. He admitted that he suddenly found himself a kind of 'Fuhrer' with powers to order anyone, anywhere, to do anything.

SS FORT PELLY sunk by aircraft bomb at Augusta, Sicily. Thomas Hutcheon, Able Seaman, RN was lost aged 19. Son of Robert and Janet Hutcheon, of Sunderland.

22-Jul-1943

The four Sunderland members of the N F S, recently sentenced to nine months' imprisonment for looting £7 worth of goods from H Moat and Sons bombed-out premises, failed in their appeals, but their sentences were reduced to six months.

24-Jul-1943

Admission to Barnes Park was 1/- with seats free for the Brass Band Championship contest. Tea and sandwiches for sixpence were a great attraction and there were thousands of people served.

27-Jul-1943

There is a new salvage drive going on in Sunderland, this time it is lead from the stone buttresses were railings have already been salvaged. Gangs of men are at work chipping out the lead filling which held the railings.

29-Jul-1943

The Minister of Labour, Ernie Bevin, announces that women up to age 50 must register for war work. It is an indication of the strain on labour resources in Britain resulting from mobilization for war.

Ministry of Food suggested the following packed lunches for those at work;

- Monday; Sandwiches filled with a mixture of cold mash potato, grated cheese, chutney, chopped fresh parsley and lettuce, followed by a jam turnover.
- Tuesday; Turnover filled with a mixture of chopped cooked beans, melted cheese and chopped parsley. Tomato and raw cabbage salad in a screw top jar. Chocolate pin wheels.
- Wednesday; Potato scones filled with scrambled dried egg cooked mixed vegetables and chopped parsley. Followed by prune dumplings.
- Thursday; Rissoles made with cooked meat, cooked beans and mashed potato, raw spinach and lettuce. Followed by fruit turnovers.
- Friday: Soup. Sandwiches filled with scrambled dried egg, mashed potato and chopped fried bacon. And as dessert radishes or tomatoes.
- Saturday; Turnover filled with sausage meat, cooked dried peas, herbs, parsley and chopped beet or onions. Followed by oatmeal scones and jam.

2-Aug-1943

Entries for the five-a-side football competition are open to both professional and amateur clubs and service units within a seven-mile radius of Sunderland.

Chocolates and sweets are now to be 'zoned', that is to say you are only able to buy chocolate and sweets made within that zone. The purpose again is to save rubber (tyres), transport and manpower.

9-Aug-1943

To discourage travel the return bus fares of greater than 10d are withdrawn, passengers will have to buy a single ticket each way.

All empty houses, either furnished or unfurnished, can now be requisitioned to improve the conditions of families inadequately housed. To date local authorities have been able to requisition houses only for evacuated and bombed out families and transferred war workers.

11-Aug-1943

There was a thrilling rescue on the river Wear near the Corporation quayside this afternoon when Jack Doyle (18) of 2 Wear Garth, an apprentice tug man, dived off the tug to save William Hunter (32) of 36 Henry Street who had slipped and fallen into the river.

13-Aug-1943

Hylton Colliery Juniors won the five-a-side competition; they beat the 509 Coast Regiment.

The Shipbuilding Corporation launches the *EMPIRE TRAIL* 7083t. Scrapped Japan Mar. 1963

Empire Trail was the first ship launched from the newly created Yard at Southwick, formally the site of Swan, Hunter and Wigham Richardson. J.L. Thompson's managed the yard

14-Aug-1943

Short Bros. launches the *EMPIRE DUCHESS* 7067t. 3.11.67 Wrecked on reef on Lincoln Islands.

18-Aug-1943

"After four years of blackout we still get people who either ignore or are careless at showing lights", commented the Mayor Councillor Myers Wayman at the Police Court today, when two Firewatches were fined £3 each for permitting a light to be shown from Young's Garage in Roker Avenue.

24-Aug-1943

The Holiday at Home programmes entertained 55,269 people of Sunderland. This was revealed at a supper in the Barnes Hotel to say thank you to the volunteer helpers.

27-Aug-1943

Stated to have contributed only £3 10s toward the cost of maintaining his wife in a Highfield medical ward and three children in the Cottage Homes estimated at £190 over a period of six months. Henry Mettis (34) of Dame Dorothy Street was sent to prison for one month for leaving his family chargeable to the P.A.C. Mettis who was earning £3 10s a week in addition to board and lodgings has been working in Swaledale since February and because he could neither read or write had not sent any money.

28-Aug-1943

Magistrates are concerned at the continuous stream of cases of assaults, squabbles and disorderly conduct terminating from the East End, particularly the blocks of new flats in the High Street East area. People wonder that this type of housing is really suitable for the maintenance of peace and order.

Sunderland 7 Leeds Utd. 1 in the Football League North

30-Aug-1943

After the first week Sunderland's Book Recovery totals 102,440. The campaign appeals for more volunteers to help with the sorting.

31-Aug-1943

SP. Austin launches the *CORMEAD* 2760t. Antwerp for breakers on 28/2/1971.

Wm. Doxford & Sons launched the *EMPIRE HOUSMAN* 7359t 1943 MOWT managed by Dodd, Thomson & Co. 30.12.1943 torpedoed and damaged by U 545. 3.1.44 torpedoed again by U.744 at 60.50N 22.07W 5.1.44 Sank. 1 crew lost. Total crew 45

1-Sep-1943

The first day when new clothing coupons were valid. It was almost like a peacetime sales day in Sunderland, queues four deep in many stores of women rushing to take advantage of the new reductions in coupon values. Managers were well pleased and thought there would be little of their old stock left to sell at reduced coupon value. One shoe shop had over 200 pairs of lady shoes waiting collection when the new coupons were available. Leaving their duties, five firewatchers of Short Brothers shipyard went on the river in a boat belonging to the firm on August 21st, only four of them came back. James William Proctor (22), of 74 Corporation Road, was drowned. The River police discovered the body yesterday. A verdict of accidental death was recorded.

3-Sep-1943

National Day of Prayer. The fourth year of the war was the decisive year; it showed who was going to win but not when the victory would be achieved.

Benjamin Eves (61) of 31 Stansfield Street Monkwearmouth died from injuries received in an accident at JL Thompson's shipyard where he was employed as a shipwright. He was caught by a wire rope attached to winch and was severely injured about the legs. In returning a verdict of accidental death the Coroner commented that the accident appeared identical to that which killed Sir Luke Thompson in 1941.

4-Sep-1943

Huddersfield v Sunderland. Billy Robinson, who was home on leave, played at inside right for Sunderland. A Sunderland win.

7-Sep-1943

The Sunderland Food Control Committee expresses the opinion that there is an unfair distribution of non-rationed goods, including fruit and fish, so Sunderland is not receiving a proper allocation compared with many other towns.

8-Sep-1943

Jubilation in picture houses when news of Italy's capitulation was flashed on the screen.

9-Sep-1943

Sunderland's town hall clock may be chiming and striking again after more than four years of wartime silence.

11-Sep-1943

Hartlepools Utd. 0 Sunderland 2. Sunderland remains among the elite having won every game to date.

13-Sep-1943

A call was made for the urgent repair of Sunderland's Children Hospital. While the hospital has been out of action a children's unit has been established in the Wearmouth Hospital.

14-Sep-1943

Pensioners Associations ask for the old-age pension to be raised to 30 shillings a week for all, without a means test. It was said that whenever the question was raised to increase the pension the question was always asked, "Where will the money come from?" (A question still being asked in 2007?)

15-Sep-1943

Laing's launch the *EMPIRE BERESFORD* 9804t. 1965 Scrapped Hirao.

16-Sep-1943

Corned beef is withdrawn from the weekly meat ration and consumers will receive the full 1s 2d worth of butcher's meat.

Wm Doxford launches the *EMPIRE SCEPTRE* 7359t. Scrapped Italy Feb. 1970

17-Sep-1943

With the completion of the double track on Humbledon Hill passengers on the Durham Road route still have to alight at the Gas Office and complete their journey on foot.

How a plank fell from staging and killed George Albert Hutchinson (62), of 12 Byron Street, a shipyard labourer at JL Thompson's Manor Quay yard, remained unsolved at today's inquest.

The picture, taken in 1936, shows a tram on the single track at Plains Farm. The green fields of Springwell Farm are on the right. The double track, completed September 1943, only extended to Ettrick Grove.

18-Sep-1943

Sunderland 4 Hartlepools Utd. 0. Sunderland's team today was made up of all Sunderland players. Sunderland head the northern section of the Football League on goal ratio over Blackpool and Aston Villa; all undefeated after four games.

20-Sep-1943

Accused of absenting himself from his work as a rivet catcher, James Coyne (17) of Friar Square said he didn't like the job. Fining him £10, the Magistrate said, "A lot of boys at Salerno didn't like their job but they had no option".

21-Sep-1943

Sunderland's Borough Engineer warned that the sea is encroaching on the land at the rate of at least two feet per annum at Grangetown and Hendon. The railway running along the coast is threatened and it is estimated that if the erosion was not checked the railway would be destroyed within the next 50 years.

On payment of 4s cost by each defendant, Sunderland Magistrates today dismissed summonses of unlawfully taking part in a strike against 94 riveters and holder-ups.

22-Sep-1943

Nearly 12,000 women, employed in the North-East Engineering establishments, have given their employers 14 days for which to enter into negotiations for the equitable grading of workers.

Roadblocks are being removed from roads around the district.

Mr Herbert Morrison, Home Secretary, following a recent review says that there can be no question of any amendment to the blackout. A recent amendment to the order however permits the use, by pedestrians, of undimmed torches.

23-Sep-1943

A health report shows that our health in the 4th year of the war continued to be good and in some respects even better than in peacetime, but two danger points are venereal disease and tuberculosis.

25-Sep-1943

Huddersfield Town 4 Sunderland 1. Sunderland lost their 100% record. In a 10 minute spell Huddersfield scored three times.

27-Sep-1943

"Sunderland's dance halls are so crowded that the police have told proprietors that they must limit the number attending dancers," said the Magistrate when two men were accused of assaulting police officers at Wetheralls.

28-Sep-1943

Crossing Fulwell Road, near Side Cliff Road, tonight Andrew Creighton (76) of 6 High Street East was knocked down and killed by a tramcar.

William Carr (57), a rigger, of 21 Montague Street Fulwell, died after being struck by a derrick at Austin's shipyard

29-Sep- 1943

Captain Robert Maughan, 60 The Broadway, Grindon, is awarded the OBE for bringing his badly damaged ship into port after it had been torpedoed.

Second Officer John Fuller of 35 Cleveland Road received the MBE for bringing 16 survivors of a torpedoed vessel to safety after a 34-day trip in an open lifeboat.

30-Sep-1943

Passers-by in High Street West last night helped, in the blackout, to lift a tramcar near the station in order to release Adam McConnell (57), 19 Williams Street, who was trapped under the tram.

1-Oct-1943

Bartram's launch the *EMPIRE BLESSING* 7062t. 19.3.45 Mined and sunk.

2-Oct-1943

Sunderland v Huddersfield. Huddersfield made Sunderland struggle for victory; it was a hard game against two evenly matched sides.

7-Oct-1943

Extra supply of jam will shortly be available to the general public. However the northeast has been unfortunate in being the last region to receive the vouchers, which has meant only the unpopular jams, were available.

8-Oct-1943

The first prosecution under the new Fire Guard (Business and Government Premises) Order was undertaken. Miss Annie Smith of Keswick Avenue Fulwell was fined 10 shillings for failing to perform fireguard duties as directed on September 22nd.

9-Oct- 1943

Darlington v Sunderland. Len Duns, who has been playing at out side left for West Brom in recent weeks, appeared in that position for Sunderland. Arthur Housam was also available. 11,000 spectators watched Sunderland beat Darlington.

11-Oct-1943

Wm. Doxford launches the *EMPIRE LORD* 7359t. 15.6.70. Sprang leak off Cape Palmas and beached Cape Garraway - total loss.

12-Oct-1943

A 'Good Housewife' scheme is to provide at least one good housewife in every street who was willing to prepare her home as a temporary receiving station in case of an air raid. She will be asked to provide anything from a cup of tea and a calming talk to simple first-aid.

Pickersgill's launch the *HMS LEEDS CASTLE* 1060t Castle Class Corvette. Scrapped on 5th June 1958 at Grays.

14-Oct- 1943

JL. Thompson launches the *SILVER OAK* 6597t. 1969 scrapped.

16-Oct-1943

Sunderland v Darlington. 9000 saw Sunderland beat a very capable Darlington side.

20-Oct-1943

A high number of thefts of clothing from Wearmouth colliery pithead baths were revealed when a 40 year-old man of Rainton Street was fined £5 for the theft of a shirt worth 10 shillings from the locker of Mr Richard Bradford.

21-Oct-1943

Among the prisoners of war being repatriated from Germany are Wearsiders who were on the steamer THISTLEBRAE. They were Joseph Hedgley (55), ship's carpenter, of 60 Old Mill Road Hendon; Alfred Towells (63), boatswain, of 3 Park Road; Stanley Thwaites, chief steward, of 67 Newbold Avenue. They were captured while in the port of Trondheim in April 1940.

22-Oct-1943

Included in the latest list of men known to be on their way home from Sweden in the exchange of war prisoners are Sunderland men;

William Otten, 30 Charles Street Monkwearmouth	T Mead, 41 Neale Street
A Woodward, Beechcholme Lodge The Cedars	W Cowie, 5 Wearmouth Street
H S Henderson, 44 Westlands	D Jukes, 32 Norman Street
R Peacock, 30 Cardwell Street	J Doyle, 64 Wear Garth

23-Oct-1943

Bradford Park Avenue v Sunderland. Sunderland lost their first home point against Bradford.

With 49 year-old women registering today. It has been stated by the Ministry of Labour, there is no intention to direct this class of women into domestic service.

25-Oct-1943

John Smith (47), a fire watchman on a ship, of 66$^{1}/_{2}$ Gladstone Street, died from severe head injuries caused by a fall into T W Greenwell's graving dock. The Coroner described the dock as a death trap during the blackout and in need of protection on the top of the dock.

26-Oct-1943

The first Home Guard to appear before a Sunderland Court Martial, Private Harold Woods, 2 Viewforth Terrace, Fulwell has been found guilty of using insubordinate language to a superior officer and has been sentenced to 28 days in detention to be served in a detention military barracks.

28-Oct-1943

The Court of Appeal rules that savings from housekeeping money belong to the husband.

Laing's launch the *EMPIRE RUSSELL* 3738t. 1978 Scrapped Buenos Aires.

29-Oct-1943

Workers at the yard of Short Brothers where Private Harold Woods is employed and the neighbouring yard of William Doxford held a mass protest meeting and demanded his immediate release from military detention.

Short Bros. launches the *EMPIRE STUART* 7017t. 1964 Scrapped Vado, Italy.

30-Oct-1943

Bradford City v Sunderland. With Sunderland drawing at Bradford, and the other leading teams losing, Sunderland is top with a slightly better goal ratio than Aston Villa.

31-Oct-1943

Crowns launch the *EMPIRE BELLE* 257t. 1972 Reported transferred to Italian Navy.

3-Nov-1943

The Grocers Association protest at the unfair method of distribution of the extra jam ration, which resulted in Sunderland consumers having to take the whole the supplementary ration in plum jam, which was not a favourite.

4-Nov-1943

Private Harold Woods the Sunderland Home Guard and shipyard welder returned to his home in Viewforth Terrace tonight having been released from a military prison in Yorkshire after serving 14 days of his 28 days' sentence.

5-Nov-1943

At a presentation at the George and Dragon Hotel, Mr J Ramsey Gebbie, Managing Director of Doxford's said, "Mr James Cawsey has given 45 years' service. He started work at Doxford's when they were building ship number 212 and they were now building ship number 712.

6-Nov-1943

Suitable 50-year-old women registering today will be advised to take up domestic work in hospitals or caring for the elderly, invalids or young children. Others may be asked to do lighter jobs in aircraft factories.

Sunderland v Newcastle Utd. In front of a crowd of 16,000 Sunderland beat Newcastle and still head the Football League.

9-Nov-1943

Councillor Wilton Milburn was elected Mayor of Sunderland today defeating Councillor Myers Wayman, as expected the Moderate (Conservative) vote was split and Councillor Wayman was only defeated by the Socialist member's votes.

10-Nov-1943

'Raise the Standard' campaign on November 20th the 'offensive' week in which it is hoped to raise £100,000 will be opened at 11. 30am on the steps of the Central Library building.

Crowns launch the *HMS BULLRUSH* 940t Flower Class Corvette. Royal Navy. Commissioned into Canadian Navy as *HMCS MIMICO*.

11-Nov-1943

Wm. Doxford launches the *EMPIRE GENERAL* 7359t. 1972 scrapped Scaramanga, Greece.

JL. Thompson launches the *EMPIRE WELFARE* 7083t. 1973 Scrapped Yugoslavia.

13-Nov-1943

Newcastle Utd v Sunderland. Johnny Spuhler was elected to lead Sunderland's attack in the absence of Whitelum and Flight Sergeant Collins, who has played several times for Wrexham this season, was at outside right. Clarke; Gorman and Eves; Bradwell, Lockie and Hastings; Collins, Laidman, Spuhler, Wensley and Hindmarch. In front of a crowd of 25,000 the game was ruined by tactics and poor control. There were far more incidents in the Newcastle goal mouth than in Sunderland's. Sunderland's defeat cost them the league leadership.

16-Nov-1943

The split in the Moderate group of Sunderland Town Council, over the nomination for Mayor, led to three members who supported Councillor Milburn's selection as Mayor, losing their Chairmanships to supporters of Councillor Myers Wayman. An earlier meeting of the moderate group on Saturday night, with the view to discussing the future of the group, supporters of Councillor Wayman did not attend.

17-Nov-1943

When surface workers at Ryhope Colliery learned that one of their workmates, Alexander Daglish (19) of Roselea Avenue Ryhope, had been arrested and taken to Durham jail to serve a sentence of a months imprisonment imposed on him by Sunderland County Police Court on August 14th, for refusing to obey a direction by the National Service Officer that he should work underground, they immediately downed tools and returned home. The pit remained idle for the rest of the day. Later an anonymous person paid the fine, which led to the release of the 19 year-old surface worker from Durham jail. Ryhope Miners return to work after the one-day stoppage.

18-Nov-1943

In two cases in Sunderland Money Payment Court today wives got a surprise when they learned how much their husbands were earning. A riveter earning £6 3s 3d a week gave his wife £4 a week housekeeping. A shipwright earning £7 18s 1d a week was said to allow his wife £3 10s a week.

19-Nov-1943

Something of an epidemic of influenza prevails at Sunderland.

Peter Fitzsimmons (67) of 4 Hetton Street, a coal trimmer, died following a fall of coal at Sunderland Dock.

20-Nov-1943

Sunderland beat Gateshead and is hanging on close on the heels of Blackpool with inferior goal ratio. After next Saturday Sunderland's remaining fixtures are against Middlesbrough and Hartlepool United. Sunderland have; Played 13; Won 9; Lost 2; Drawn 2; goals for 36; goals against 19; Points 20.

24-Nov-1943

Work is to begin to repair the bomb-damaged Public Reading Rooms and Juvenile Library in Fawcett Street. The cost is estimated to be £624 2s 6d.

Sunderland is likely to have modified street lighting in the centre of town during this winter.

25-Nov-1943

The death rate in Sunderland during the four weeks ending the 20th was 3.1 per cent, infant mortality was 62 per 1000 compared with 43 per 1000 for the previous four weeks. The number of births was 191 compared with 230 for the previous month. Cases of infectious diseases notified were scarlet fever 22, diphtheria 20, pneumonia 34, whooping cough 54 and Tuberculosis 53.

26-Nov-1943

Accused of leaving his employment, as a shipyard labourer, without permission of the National Service Officer, James Clark (36) of Fulwell Road appeared before magistrates today. Clarke was discharged from the forces in March 1942 and obtained employment as a salesman. Later, becoming unemployed, he accepted a post as a labourer at John Crown Limited. He commenced work at the shipyard on June 16th and on July 7th he made an application to leave the shipyard, which was refused. On August 10th he appealed against the decision but was unsuccessful. On October 21st he left his employment. The National Service Officer interviewed Clark on October 29th and asked for his reason for leaving his employment Clark said, "I considered the work unsuitable for me. I had no previous experience or knowledge, so I decided to leave". Asked if he would return to the shipyard Clark said he would not and replied, "For two-thirds of the time you're lying about in the shipyard doing nothing, that's not my idea of essential work". The case was adjourned until December 3rd.

Pickersgill's launch the *HMS* MORPETH CASTLE 1060t Castle Class Corvette. Scrapped on 9th August 1960 at Llanelly.

27-Nov-1943

Sunderland savings groups went on to bring the total 'Raise the Standard' campaign up to £133,802 10s 1d. Sunderland savings groups grew from 20 to 615 in two years and the amount saved by them during that period was more than £600,000.

Sunderland 0 Gateshead 1. The lack of first-team regulars was blamed for Sunderland's championship challenge ending.

SP. Austin launches *HMS AMBERLY CASTLE* a 1066-ton Corvette. Commissioned 24th November 1944. Converted to a weather ship in 1957.

Evacuated children have become a greater problem two social workers and those left in the bombed areas said Miss E M Carter (Social Service Welfare Officer) last night at the annual meeting of the Sunderland Council of social services. No matter how poor the home, children who have been left in the danger zones were getting a grounding of fundamental principles taught by their parents, but children who have been evacuated were now beginning to show they lacked this parental control. The child felt the needs of its parents, and no matter how well the evacuated children had been treated they all wanted to return home. In the pre-war years many families had lived in a bare existence and the parents, feeling the stress of the times had not corrected their children as they should. With the great numbers of women working away from home, the problem of giving attention to children was still present. Those women had seen a wider world and would find it difficult after the war to settle down to the old family tasks. The welfare state will provide communal help of every kind, and that would also tend to separate children from their parents. Nursery schools had done good service in their way, but they could do nothing towards the making of good citizens that could only be done at home. The home was the training ground of the community.

29-Nov-1943

The Bishop of Winchester was urging men and women of goodwill to tighten their moral belts, and if only out of fear of the consequences to others and themselves to make it clear that some kinds of conduct are no longer tolerable. Even those who are in no way morally squeamish are beginning to be appalled at the consequences of the abandonment of moral distraint and discipline in personal relationships between men and women become increasingly apparent. The increase of venereal disease, the numbers of illegitimate births, following sometimes from elicit relationships with coloured men, the number of children thus prejudiced in their upbringing from the start. The undisciplined behaviour of many persons and notably young girls and the frequent collapse of marital faithfulness under the strain of separation are acting like a cancer, gnawing at the very heart of our common life. Dare we let 1944 and the supreme tests it may bring find us morally at our worst.

30-Nov-1943

An influenza outbreak is sweeping the region and many workers are absent from work.

1-Dec-1943

Sunderland Central Station has long been a cause of bitter derision from townspeople. Our present Town Council are thinking hard at what can be done after the war to repair the error of their predecessors in permitting the station to be built as it was. It was suggested that the Council should take a good look at Monkwearmouth station before rejecting it as a solution; after all it is not so very far from the centre of the town. The Council and LNER do not appear to favour the suggestion. (Authors note; so the subsequent town councils followed their predecessor's example and made a bigger mess of the station).

The old South End of Sunderland Railway Station

2-Dec-1943

1 out of every 10 men called up between the ages of 18 and 25 will now be ordered to work in the coalmines. These men become known as the 'Bevin Boys' are to be selected by ballot. (Famous 'Bevin Boys' were Jimmy Savile, Eric Morecambe and Brian Rix the actor/manager and Mencap President).

3-Dec-1943

Since the beginning of the war Wearsiders have saved £10,109,020. The 10 million mark was topped last week when the town aimed at a target of £100,000 in 'Raise the Standard Week' and reached £133,802 10s 1d. Adjourned from November 26th in order that he might reconsider his decision James Clark (36) of Fulwell Road appeared at Sunderland Police Court today accused of leaving his employment without the permission of the National Service Officer. After consideration the court said that they had no option, no matter how sympathetic they were, he was bound over for 12 months on condition that he went back to his work or other work ordered by the National Service Officer.

4-Dec-1943

Sunderland v Hartlepools Utd. Sunderland is beaten. Clarke, Gorman, Eves, Hastings, Whitelum and Laidman were all absentees.

6-Dec-1943

Seven Hendon women were fined £5 by Sunderland magistrates today for acquiring rationed clothing from Mrs Gertrude Barnes without surrendering the appropriate number of coupons. The women fined were Mrs Lilly Banks of Fowler Terrace, Mrs Alice Dobinson of Emma Street, Mrs Gladys Mackel of Surtees Street, Mrs Margaret Carpenter of Mainsforth Terrace West, Mrs Margaret Johnson of Bramwell Street, Mrs Jenny Fowler of Emma Street and Mrs Ada Metcalfe of Page Street.

7-Dec-1943

From a Sunderland Echo Editorial - The apparent inevitability of war in August 1939, induced the nation to accept the Emergency Powers Defence Act of that year, the disastrous state of affairs in the summer of 1940 enabled the Government to gain acceptance of the second Emergency Defence Act. The necessity of defeating Nazism compelled the people to accept more than 1001 interferences with personal freedom that the authorities had believed to be essential "for the successful prosecution of the war". Now there was a suggestion of the continuance of these controls after the war. That the people at large never experienced controls those who glorify them as a short cut to the better life might have found a gullible public to follow them down the road to totalitarianism. But the public has learned what it is like to be controlled and those that have endured the experience because of emergency will not be prepared to live like this indefinitely. The continuance of some controls we shall have to accept for a period after the war; but not those we are now exercising and not indefinitely but only as a short-time as conditions may make unavoidable.

8-Dec-1943
The Deputy Divisional Food Officer said chocolate was scarce as it was being reserved with extra vitamins for distribution to children of occupied countries when they are liberated.
Wm. Doxford launches the *EMPIRE EARL* 7359t. Scrapped Whampoa Aug. 1970.

9-Dec-1943
A verdict of killed by enemy action was recorded by the Coroner at an inquest on Anthony Rennoldson (64), a blacksmith, of 1 Wilson Street. Stanley Rennoldson of Falmouth Road said his father was blown against a wall and buried in debris on May 24th when bombs were dropped near his home in an air raid.

11-Dec-1943
Hartlepools Utd. v Sunderland. Hastings, Laidman and Whitelum returned to the side. Sunderland had a hard game at Hartlepool. The pitch and the ground were in a poor condition.

13-Dec-1943
The Sunderland Amateur Operatic and Dramatic Society is formed. The nucleus of the new society are drawn from the cast of 'Merry England' who performed in the last 'Holidays at Home campaign.

14-Dec-1943
Compensation of £600 was awarded to Mrs Ellen Moat of Back Pickard Street Pallion for the loss of her husband Herbert Moat, who was killed on July 7th as a result of an accident at Steel & Co. Crown Works Pallion.
The first ballot for the selection of youths to be directed to work in the coalmines instead of service in the Armed Forces took place today.

15-Dec-1943
River Wear Commissioners returned to their offices in St. Thomas Street today having been repaired following an air raid on the night of the 14th March earlier this year when St. Thomas's Church was destroyed.

16-Dec-1943
Distribution of supplementary industrial clothing coupons begins today. Industrial workers who illegally received more than their own share of industrial clothing coupons during the previous supplementary issue will not be allowed to repeat their performance this time. Those particular industrial workers, some using threats and others financial inducements, apparently forced young apprentices to part with their ration. Entirely due to this reason many parents still await their apprentice son's supplementary clothing coupons from the last distribution.
John Thomas Lorraine (54), an electrician's labourer, of 20 Rokeby Street was killed in an accident at Dickinson's engine works today.

Started in 1942 and commissioned this month, Greenwell's conversion of an oil tanker into HMS ALEXIA an Aircraft Carrier. The yard converted it back into a tanker in 1946. Renamed IANTHINA in 1951. BU Blyth 17.9.54

17-Dec-1943
Cycle inner tubes made from synthetic rubber are introduced. The tyre manufacturers advise that they may be repaired with ordinary patches if the surface is clean and plenty of solution is applied to ensure the patch sticks.

18-Dec-1943

Sunderland 6 Middlesbrough 1. Raich Carter, home on leave, played for Sunderland against Middlesbrough at Roker Park today, but regular full backs Gorman and Eves were replaced with Wheatman and Mather.

20-Dec-1943

For failing to attend three Home Guard parades, John Britton (20) of Fell Road Ford Estate was fined £1 on each charge. Britton was ordered to do guard duty on November 10th and he turned up with his girlfriend. Britton was told to take the girl away and return in five minutes. He went away but did not return. It was the only occasion that Britton had attended guard duty since June; Britton said he had never cared for the Home Guard.

21-Dec-1943

Military authorities have asked Sunderland Watch Committee to permit the opening of cinemas in the town on Sundays. The Echo backs the campaign arguing that there should be an alternative to the public house.

23-Dec-1943

Two 15 year-old Sunderland boys accused of stealing war department stores admitted to throwing live grenades in Barnes Park. They were each fined £10.

Laing's launch *EMPIRE COMMERCE* 3722t. 30.9.43 Torpedoed and sunk by U.410. Total crew of 51 all saved.

24-Dec-1943

During January and February, charges for the repair respirators are to be suspended. Free replacement will not be available to anyone who does not produce a damage respirator for exchange. Charges for repairs and replacement will be re-imposed on March 1st.

Short Bros. launches the *EMPIRE CROMER* 7058t. 1968 Scrapped Karachi.

25-Dec-1943

Middlesbrough v Sunderland. Sunderland had several key players missing and Jenkins of Hylton Colliery Juniors made his first appearance.

26-Dec-1943

The German battleship SCHARNHORST is sunk. On the cruiser HMS NORFOLK, four Sunderland men; Leading Seaman George Wilson of Warwick Street; Leading Seaman Childs of Balmoral Terrace Grangetown; Able Seaman William Kirton of Hood Street and Able Seaman Bell of Princess Street.

29-Dec-1943

Training of the 'Bevin Boys' began at Horden Colliery today, the largest single unit pit in the country. Training will take place in the main coal seam, which has been closed since the outbreak of war owing to the number of men serving in the forces.

30-Dec-1943

Having ordered their quota of 13 hundredweight of coal for the period of November December, some Sunderland people have been informed that if it proves impossible to deliver the coal by December 31st, it will have to be foregone. It seems rather hard that consumers have to lose out. (Another little bureaucrat from the local Fuel Overseers Office dictating the regulation that forbids the carrying over the coal allowance from one period to another. This regulation was meant to curb abuses and not to impose hardship).

Sequel to an accident at Laing's shipyard in which two men fell 16 ft, as a result of which one of them died, was the inquest at Sunderland Police Buildings on Thomas Henry Graham (47), a plater's helper, of 2 Thirlwell Terrace Southwick. The Coroner recorded a verdict of accidental death. The accident occurred on December 21st.

31-Dec-1943

For the first time since the beginning of the war Wearsiders will hear the New Year chimed in on the town hall clock.

1944

THIS IS THE YEAR !

IT'S UP TO US TO LET 'EM HAVE IT !

- Sunderland receives refugees from London escaping from V1& V2 rockets.
- D-Day Allied troops storm ashore in Normandy
- Britain's Home Guard is stood down after five years.

1-Jan-1944

People believed that this year would see the end of the war. The Echo editorial also thought so. "This is the year, the Year of victory, the end of the European war, the year in which we believe all our troubles, real or imaginary, will come to an end. This is the year of our greatest hope. Compare January 1944 with January 1941, then we had only hope and determination with which to arm ourselves, compare January 1944 with January 1942, things were better than they had been earlier but the fight was still going against us, compare January 1944 with January 1943 even and the measure of our advance becomes more easily distinguished".

Sunderland v Newcastle Utd. Sunderland avenged defeat at St James's Park and is now on the road for qualifying for the first round of the League Cup.

Wm. Doxford & Sons launched the *ARABISTAN* 7360t Strick Line. 1968 aground and a total loss.

2-Jan-1944

EMPIRE HOUSEMAN, a 7359t motor freighter, built in 1943 by William Doxford's & Sons, on a voyage from the Tyne to New York, is torpedoed by U 744 forcing the crew to abandon ship. Survivors, including Gordon Broadwick (18), of 42 Ormonde Street and 5th Engineer George Bell of Dundas Street, were picked up nine hours later.

4-Jan-1944

The national figure for deaths from Influenza notified for 1943 was 5807, against 1500 for 1942.

5-Jan-1944

A nationwide petition for a change in the law regarding the wife's savings is to be presented to Parliament. Dr Edith Summerskill MP, President of the Married Women's Association, announced that the decision to launch the petition at a meeting in London today. The petition was a sequel to the case of Mrs Dorothy Blackwell who was refused leave to appeal to the House of Lords against the rejection of her claim to keep the money saved out of her housekeeping.

6-Jan-1944

Earnings today are good, but this fact is not benefiting some children in Sunderland. Indeed neglect of children in Sunderland is definitely on the increase. It is asserted as being down to women leaving their homes and children, night after night, to spend money on amusement and drink.

7-Jan-1944

Today Sunderland people heard of the revolutionary new jet propelled aeroplane the Meteor. The plane had been under development since 1940 and took its maiden test flight on March 5th, 1943. It entered service with the RAF on July 12th, 1944 and saw action for the first time in 27th July against the V1 flying bomb.

8-Jan-1944

Darlington 5 Sunderland 1. But for some fine saves by Bircham the score would have been in double figures in today's League Cup competition.

11-Jan-1944

Fines totalling £120 plus £31 costs were imposed on James Laing and Sons Ltd when found guilty of failing to keep a record showing the stock of each rationed food kept at their canteens. Gertrude Willis of Garcia Terrace was charged with aiding and abetting.

12-Jan-1944

One effect of the Workmen's compensation Act has been that people today will not, as formerly, work under difficulties caused by pain, this was stated in Sunderland County Court today at the claim for revision of compensation paid to George S Brown of Balmoral Terrace by Short Brothers Ltd. Compensation had been paid with respect to an accident on April 6th last year when Brown, working as a painter, slipped from a ladder and suffered spinal injuries. Compensation was to be £2 13s a week.

14-Jan-1944

Frank Pucci of Coronation Street was find £15 plus £5 cost for making and selling ice cream. His claim that it was made with saccharin and therefore not ice cream was dismissed.

15-Jan-1944

Sunderland v Darlington. The loss of Hastings, who was sent off, was too great a handicap and Sunderland conceded five goals.

18-Jan-1944

Mr Hugh Dalton, President of the Board of Trade, said in the House of Commons today that British wireless sets were being put on the market as they were being completed. 18,000 American sets have arrived in this country and prices would be controlled.

Young men from all parts of the country, and from all walks of life, this morning turned out to learn how to be mine workers. Most of them did not want to serve in the mines, for like those that are already in the pits they would much rather be in one or other of the services.

20-Jan-1944

Wilful and widespread damage to emergency water supplies prompts the Ministry of Home Security to make an appeal for the public to report at once anyone seen tampering with or throwing things into the tanks. Parents are to stop their children from playing around the Tanks. Nationally last year 54 children were drowned in them. Water is our first line of defence should heavy raids reoccur.

SS FORT BUCKINGHAM is sunk by torpedo from U-188 northwest of Maldive Islands. The Master, 30 crew and 7 gunners were lost. One of the gunners lost was Henry Laverick, Able Seaman RN. Age 21. Son of H. and Ellen Agnes Laverick, of Southwick.

21-Jan-1944

Because of enemy bombing, Sunderland housing shortage is now acute. Many families are experiencing considerable hardship. There are Sunderland residents who have had to leave the town to get a roof over their heads.

22-Jan-1944

Sunderland v Hartlepools Utd. On paper, at any rate, Sunderland had a strengthened side to oppose Hartlepool but was beaten. Bob Gurney played and did his best but really he is past his best.

25-Jan-1944

SP. Austin launches the collier *HAWKWOOD* of 2850t. 14.7.1969 arrived Hamburg to be broken up.

26-Jan-1944

John David Reay Doyle (19), tugboat apprentice of Wear Garth, received the parchment of the Royal Humane Society in the Gaiety Theatre tonight in recognition of his rescue of a man from the River Wear in August.
Bartram's launch the *INDIAN CITY* 7320t. Scrapped Istanbul May 1972.
Pickersgill's launch the *HMS NUNNERY CASTLE* 1060t Castle Class Corvette. Served with the Canadian Navy as *BOWMANVILLE (K493)* in 1944. Transferred to Chinese as *KUANO CHOU* in 1951.

28-Jan-1944

JL. Thompson launches the *EMPIRE PITT* 7086t. 11.11.46 Aground and wrecked in Seine Estuary.

29-Jan-1944

Hartlepools Utd v Sunderland. One win in six Cup games, that is Sunderland's record, Hartlepool completed the double over Sunderland. Sunderland is eighth from bottom and is unlikely to qualify for the League Cup competition proper.

31-Jan-1944

Riveters and Holder-ups employed in Wear shipyards, gave a week's notice that it was their intention to work only on time rates. A big increase in the oddments of scattered work has meant that their earnings on piecework are down to little more than time rates.

2-Feb-1944

There were 17 fatal accidents in Sunderland last year compared with 29 in 1942, 27 in 1941, 28 in1940, 25 in 1939 and 11 in 1930. Of those killed 12 were pedestrians, 2 pedal cyclists and 3 were passengers in public service vehicles.

5-Feb-1944

Gateshead v Sunderland. In the absence of Lockie, Stokoe took over the centre-half position. Sunderland's Cup hopes completely disappear. Seven goals are scored against them.

8-Feb-1944

Sunderland's latest British Restaurant (the 7th) is to be opened today. Most centrally situated of all the local restaurants it should prove a boon to those that work in the centre of the town. In keeping with other British Restaurants prices are very modest, and a three-course lunch can be had for 1s with a cup of tea to follow for a 1d. The rooms are beautifully decorated in blue and cream and there is seating accommodation for 200 people in the large room, which looks out into High Street. An innovation will be the serving of suppers, as well as dinner and tea. Tea, consisting of sandwiches and tea, will be provided for 4d and supper will cost 6d.
Concern was expressed over the pilfering of knives forks and spoons from the restaurants.
Wm. Doxford launches the *TREVETHOE* 7355t. Scrapped Taiwan Aug. 1969

9-Feb-1944

Demand of military operations for coal on a mass scale are putting an acute strain on transport, this is aggravating the fuel position, which is already critical. It is crucial that industry reduces, still further, their daily coal consumption and set rail trucks free with the least possible delay.

10-Feb-1944

50 convictions for drunkenness in the Borough last year are the lowest on record. In past years it had been as high as 530. However Magistrates were concerned about the amount of under 18 drinking.

12-Feb-1944

Sunderland v Gateshead. When Darlington, Hartlepool and Gateshead can take all the points against Sunderland there is something wrong. To get goals against the Sunderland defence in recent weeks has been as easy as shelling peas, 33 in eight games.

Crowns launch the *EMPIRE PHYLLIS* 257t Tug. MOWT, naval work - Ceylon / India. 1982 scrapped.

13-Feb-1944

Issued by the Ministry of Health: Venereal diseases of syphilis and gonorrhoea have increased by 120 per cent since the war and are still increasing; about 80,000 new cases are now occurring yearly amongst civilians alone. Venereal disease destroys health, endangers life, wrecks happiness, ruins careers, injures innocent people and imperils the future of the race. By knowing the facts, and seeing that those about us know them too, you can all help to check the spread of this loathsome disease.

16-Feb-1944

An explosion at the Monsanto Chemical establishment this morning injured 16 men. Thomas McMahon, Frederic Morritt and Thomas Sloan were reported rather poorly.

19-Feb-1944

More than 1000 boys and girls were welcomed to the new Junior Club at the Havelock Picture House today. Sunderland v Middlesbrough. More changes were made in the Sunderland team that met Middlesbrough today. Victory over Middlesbrough by three goals.

21-Feb-1944

Sunderland has failed badly during the past year in its 'Penny a Week' Red Cross house-to-house collection scheme. Sunderland was only collecting £500/month, the average for the size of the town, should be nearer £1,500. (Authors note: My wife, Norah Taylor then aged 10, along with friends Margaret Thompson and Mary McGlaughlan, all of Plains Farm, were keen to help and began collecting house to house in the Humbledon area. A police detective living on Durham Road decided to confiscate the collecting tins because the children had no official authority. My wife still, to this day, wonders what happened to the two collecting tins, and if the Red Cross benefited?).

22-Feb-1944

Supplies of Portuguese sardines received in Britain are nearly 50 per cent higher than last year. The normal size tin will cost 1/- and require six points.

24-Feb-1944

Church halls are being used as dance halls, as many as two or three times a week. The behaviour of some from the dances in the churchyard has been very regrettable.

Shipbuilding Corporation launches the *EMPIRE GLADSTONE* 7090t. 5.9.50 Ashore near Sydney - total loss.

25-Feb-1944

657 rats were destroyed on 42 vessels visiting in the port. A further 1,675 were killed in buildings on the riverside.

Laing's launch the *EMPIRE PARAGON* 9892t. 1969 Scrapped Taiwan.

26-Feb-1944

Middlesbrough 4 Sunderland 5. Housam was back in the team and Lorenson of Blackpool was a new edition. However, both clubs are the only two of the six Northeast clubs to fail to qualify for the later stages of the League Cup.

28-Feb-1944

The total number of children and young persons, over 8 and under 17 years, who appeared before the juvenile court on indictable offences during 1943 was 246 as compared with 224 in 1938 and 232 in 1942.

29-Feb-1944

Seville oranges in Wearside are not selling well. The lack of sugar is blamed for the poor sales of these bitter marmalade oranges. Originally offered for sale at 9d a pound but because of low demand now at 3d a pound.

1-Mar-1944

The fuel position gets no easier as the war proceeds and no help is envisaged.

2-Mar-1944

The mass transfer of married men to the munitions factory in the Midlands and the South is having an adverse effect upon Sunderland married life. In many cases the husband has succumbed to the temptation surrounding him in his new environment and the wife no longer shares either his affections or his wages.

A target of £1,250,000 is set for 'Salute the Soldier' week. This would be the fourth major saving effort that the town has attempted since the war began.

3-Mar-1944

Accused of employing two 15 year olds for 13 hours a day, John Oliver, of Lyndhurst Terrace, was fined £16 on each of the four charges with seven shillings cost. The offences took place at a muffin factory trading as William Allan and Sons.

British civilian casualties now total 50,324 dead; military deaths: 50,103.

4-Mar-1944

Sunderland v Middlesbrough. In front of a gate of only 2,300, Sunderland beats Middlesbrough.

Men born between April 1st and June 30th, 1926 are due to register today. These men will be able to opt for coalmine working.

6-Mar-1944

A report indicates that 6398 families in Sunderland are overcrowded and that 1199 more houses are needed to re-house those families whose houses have been destroyed by bombing.

8-Mar-1944

Believed to be the only Sunderland man serving on Sunderland's adopted ship, HMS Delhi, is able Seaman Ronald Blackett of Colchester Terrace.

Ralph Heppell, licensee of the Saltgrass Inn, made application on behalf of C Vaux & Co. to remove the current licence to St Marks Vicarage in Chester Road, currently let to the Corporation for a wartime nursery. It is proposed to build after the war a modern hotel to be named 'The Chesters'. The request was denied.

9-Mar-1944

"It's the pictures that does it. They want to stop pictures for kids under 14 ", said a father who was fined £1 in the juvenile court today for non-compliance with the school attendance order made against him for his child. There were 11 other defendants charged with the same offence and all were fined £1.

10-Mar-1944

Both Houses of Parliament pass resolutions authorising Sunday cinema openings in Sunderland.

11-Mar-1944

Middlesbrough v Sunderland. Half time Middlesbrough 1 Sunderland 2, both Sunderland goals scored by Hodges (Arsenal). Sunderland has met Middlesbrough six times this season, Sunderland has won five and they are still friends.

13-Mar-1944

Utility furniture now available to those married on or after September 1st, 1943.

14-Mar-1944

A year ago tonight Sunderland endured the first of three of the heaviest air raids on the town. The destruction was greater than on any previous raid. Union Street and John Street were blocked for hours. St Thomas's Church along with the vicarage together with neighbouring parts of John Street were demolished. The Empress Hotel and the New Market were among the buildings destroyed. West Enders will not forget the 'blockbuster' that fell near Colchester Terrace, which wrecked many houses and caused damage within the range of quarter of a mile. Another heavy bomb dropped at Humbledon did such damage to the Children's Hospital that it had to be evacuated. It was a miracle that none of the children were killed or hurt.

The cleared site in Union Street became a Market (shown opposite) followed by a Bus Station.

15-Mar-1944

John Cable (30), a horse keeper of 26 Chilton Street, was fatally injured at Wearmouth colliery today. A later inquest failed to find a reason for the accident and assumed that the untrained pony must have reared.

16-Mar-1944

18,000 cases of lemons arrive on Wearside.

18-Mar-1944

Sunderland 3 Gateshead 0. Now that we are out of the Cup we are winning matches.

20-Mar-1944

Opening performance tonight of "Merrie England" by members the Sunderland Amateur Operatic and Dramatic Society. Those that quibbled over the seat prices must give credit to the cast for effort and quality of performance.

21-Mar-1944

R A Butler, President of the Board of Education, gave the pledge that the school leaving age will be raised to 15 shortly. Not done until April 1947.

22-Mar-1944

Sunday opening of cinemas in Sunderland is likely to begin in a month's time. The Watch Committee is still discussing the terms and conditions on which cinemas will be permitted to open.

23-Mar-1944

Wm. Doxford launches the *LCT 7068* and *LCT 7067* 640 ton Tank Landing Crafts for the Royal Navy.

25-Mar-1944

Hartlepools Utd. v Sunderland. In their 8th meeting of the season Sunderland are beaten by Hartlepool.

27-Mar-1944

Contraventions of food rationing laws, including conspiracy and fictitious transactions when handling cocoa butter and cocoa beans, were alleged in a case, which opened before Magistrates today. Four companies and eight persons answered 123 summonses. Companies are Dunn & Co. (Sunderland) Ltd., Mayfair Dairies Ltd., Mayfair Confectionery Ltd. And St John's Malting Company (Newcastle). On Thursday 30th March all the defendants concerned were committed for trial at Newcastle Assizes in June.

28-Mar-1944

Double sugar and preserves ration. For six coupons people could get 2lbs of sugar and 2lbs of jam, or 3lbs of sugar and no jam or 6lbs of jam and no sugar.

Tyneside shipyard and engineering apprentices strike over being directed to the mines on call-up.

Short Brothers launches the landing craft *LCT 7081* 640t for the Royal Navy.

JL. Thompson launches the *LCT 7065* and *LCT 7066*

Pickersgill's launch the *LCT 7057.* Lost cause and place unknown, 16th July 1944.

29-Mar-1944

Losses of cutlery from British Restaurants has become so heavy it has forced the Corporation to take special measures to check them. Each customer will be given a knife, fork and spoon, no matter what his/her requirement, and will be expected, on leaving the restaurant, to give them up. This system started it in the Green Street restaurant today.

30-Mar-1944

The response to the appeal for lorry-drivers to assist in the second front has been very satisfactory. In the Sunderland area 83 men and five women have volunteered.

The Highway Committee accepts the offer from the Electrical Committee to provide 'star' lighting with about 500 more lamps in practically all the main streets of the Borough.

31-Mar-1944

Alarm No.250: 05.26 - 05.43. While on his way to work as a winding engineman at Ryhope Colliery Mr George Heads (58), of 8 South View, was killed instantly when he was struck by debris from a Halifax bomber, which crashed near Ryhope Pit earlier today. Pilot Officer Barton (22) who died before he was admitted to hospital was posthumously awarded the VC. Three members of the crew were injured, one seriously. Before it crashed, the plane did considerable damage to two houses near the pit. In 1985 a plaque was erected on Ryhope's war memorial in honour of PO Barton's bravery.

The recent Porter Award stipulated that miners' working a Bank Holiday must be paid 'double time'. Could this have had some bearing on the decision of the coal owners to declare Good Friday this year as a Holiday? In 1942 and 1943 it was a working day.

Pickersgill's launch the Tank Landing Craft *LCT 7058.*

1-Apr-1944

Only 4cwt of coal per month will be allowed during the months of April and March.

2-Apr-1944

Cheese ration cut from 3 ounces to 2 ounces per head per week. The ration of 12 ounces for those engaged in heavy industry remains the same.

At a meeting of Wearside apprentices, held in the Cooperative Hall, it was unanimously decided not to join in the Tyneside apprentice's strike. It is now believed that the Apprentice Guilds on Tyneside and Wearside that political agitators, belonging to the Militant Workers' Federation had infiltrated the movement.

3-Apr-1944

Collieries in County Durham will work on Good Friday and Saturday and Easter Monday will be a holiday. Double time rates will be paid for Good Friday to all.

6-Apr-1944

Today is the first day of the Pay As You Earn income tax scheme. The scheme will relieve the burden of finding lumps sums and the onus for collecting the tax is placed directly on the employer.

LCT 7080 a 640 ton Tank Landing Craft launched by SP. Austin.

7-Apr-1944

Today on Good Friday morning for the first time since the war began, thousands of Sunday school children met in Fawcett Street and sang hymns and then moved in procession to their own church. It marks the resumption of a Wearside tradition and acts as an omen of the peace to come.

8-Apr-1944

Housewives again had to queue for fish. Many were disappointed.

Sunderland 1 Gateshead 1. The gate was about 9000. Gateshead continues to be Sunderland's bogy team.

10-Apr-1944

The Watch Committee recommends that cinemas on Wearside will open from 4:30pm to 9:30pm on Sundays.

11-Apr-1944

After the two-day break many workers failed to report. One shipyard reported an absentee list of 25 per cent, which had a serious effect on production.

Short Bros. launches the *EMPIRE PENDENNIS* 7058t 1966 Scrapped Taiwan.

12-Apr-1944

The Manager, George Hancock, of the Olive Branch Hotel Howick Street was fined £10 for offences against the licensing laws. For consuming beer during non permitted hours, Robert Holder, of Netherburn Road; John Bambrough, of Summerhill; Margaret Vitch, of Howick Place; Mary Dean, of Zetland Street; James Lewins, of Nelson Street were each fined 40 shillings and Beatrice Duncan, of the Social Tavern, Charles Street and Mary Sutherland, of Howick Place were each fined £5.

Doxford & Sons launches the *WELSH PRINCE* 7381t for the Rio Cape Line. 1971 scrapped on Whampoa Island (China)

13-Apr-1944

James Bainbridge (23) of Paton Square was fined £10 and bound over for failing to attend Home Guard parades on three dates. William Burns (20) of Richmond Road was fined £5 for two absences.

15-Apr-1944

Sunderland v Newcastle Utd. The first stage of the semi-final of the Tyne, Wear and Tees Cup competition. There is a 'slight' suspicion that Sunderland has completed their cup of misfortune by being knocked out of the Tyne, Wear and Tees Cup competition. They start the return game at Newcastle three goals in arrears.

16-Apr-1944

Black's Regal Theatre cinema opened tonight (Sunday) showing Bette Davis and Herbert Marshall in The Letter and on the stage, T Arnold Eagle and orchestra and artists. (All the other cinemas began Sunday schedules on the 23rd April).

17-Apr-1944

The Mayor opens Sunderland's second Red Cross shop. The new premises at Havelock Buildings, High Street West, were offered to Sunderland's Town Women's Guilds free of rent by H Samuel Ltd.

18-Apr-1944

The new defence regulation gives the Government powers to deal with people who are responsible for inciting strikes or lockouts, which interfere with essential services.

19-Apr-1944

588,742 persons have been killed or injured on the roads of Great Britain since the start of the war, which is substantially in excess of all British military and air-raid casualties combined.

British engineering ingenuity has produced an electrical machine not only for washing the family clothes but the dirty dishes as well. It will be mass-produced as soon as conditions allow and the proposed price is £14.

21-Apr-1944

To save on gas and electricity the Shipyards and engineering unions agree to a $51^{1}/_{4}$ hour week (Winter) instead of the normal $56^{1}/_{2}$ Summer average. No overtime will be worked during the week but two Sundays out of three will be worked.

22-Apr-1944

Newcastle Utd. v Sunderland. Without their service players, Sunderland's displays must be giving the manager, Mr Murray, some headaches. Apart from Bircham, Hindmarch and possibly Boyd it was difficult to see any of the younger players making the grade.

Bartram's launch the *STANREALM* 7062t. Scrapped Hong Kong June 1963.

24-Apr-1944

For military reasons, travel to all destinations overseas has been suspended. These restrictions will remain in force until further notice.

25-Apr-1944

James MacIntyre (18), of Murton Street, was sent to prison for one month for failing to comply with the instruction to work down a mine.

Budget Day: very few tax changes; big tax relief's for post-war reconstruction; prices have risen 28% against pre-war; wages now up 37%.

Wm Doxford launches the *TREVOSE* 7360t. Scrapped Whampoa Feb. 1971.

26-Apr-1944

19 Home Guardsmen appeared at Sunderland Police Court today on accusations of absenteeism from their duties without a reasonable excuse. Sentences range from two months imprisonment to £10 fines.

A report says that 28,000 children were examined for cleanliness during 1943 and the percentage of unclean children was 13.8 per cent compared with 16 per cent in 1942.

27-Apr-1944

Pickersgill's launch the Tank Landing Craft *LCT 7059*

29-Apr-1944

Sunderland 3 Middlesbrough 3.

3-May-1944

Magistrates dealt with a further batch of men today for failing to perform Home Guard duties without reasonable excuse.

4-May-1944

The total killed and wounded altogether on the fighting fronts as a result of all the efforts of Hitler's war machine is 370,000; and on the road since the war began 586,000. This is a great social problem.

5-May-1944

Robert Thwaites (20), apprentice plater, of 5 Pit Row Silksworth, was injured at work while working on a counter-sinking machine for J L Thompson's shipyard. He died from a fractured spine on May 12th.

6-May-1944

Middlesbrough v Sunderland. Sunderland's league games came to an end they finished 9th with 23 points out of 18 games.

7-May-1944

Weekly Milk Ration raised to 3 pints (was $2^1/_2$).

The 4th anniversary of the formation of the Home Guard was celebrated with a parade at Whitburn today.

8-May-1944

The first woman Guard to set a train away from Sunderland was Mrs Catherine Sanders of 48 Westheath Avenue. Mrs Ruth Davis of 8 Flax Square, who is also trained to act as a railway guard, accompanied her.

Crowns launch the *EMPIRE NICHOLAS* a 258 Tug for MOWT used by the Admiralty for naval work Japan / East Indies. 1947 ASTA, Indonesia. 1961 LAUT ARAFURA, Tanjung Priok Port Authority, Indonesia.

Pickersgill's launch the Tank Landing Craft LCT 7060

9-May-1944

Accidental death was the verdict recorded by the Coroner at the inquest today on Ernest Keenan (47), foreman turner, of Chapman Street who was employed by George Clark (1938) Ltd. He was crushed by falling plate at his work on February 9th.

14-May-1944

Two apprentices were drowned in the river Wear near South Hylton yesterday, when the racing skiff in which they went for a row with three other youths was capsized by a wave. They were William Rowland Stephenson (18), of 6 Grindon Terrace Sunderland, an apprentice engineer at Sunderland Forge and Ernest Tate (20) of 9 Ford Oval, South Hylton, an apprentice fitter at Forster's Forge, South Hylton. Two of the others John Moore Russell (18) of 36 Elgin Street, South Hylton and William Arthur Giles (18) of 3 Sunniside, South Hylton managed to struggle ashore. The fifth apprentice, Alexander Wilson (19), of 15 Sunniside, South Hylton, was rescued by a man in a boat. All five were members of the South Hylton Rowing Club. Tate's body was recovered after about three hours search; Stephenson's body was not discovered until much later.

17-May-1944

Alfred Jones (19) of St Patrick's Garth was again in court. Fined £10 on March 10th and bound over to attend Home Guard duties regularly, Jones had attended only one parade since and had only paid £1 of the £10 pound fine. He was put on probation.

18-May-1944

Frederick Ebdon, of West Farm, Fulwell. He was fined £5 for breach of control regulations. It was said he had sold 730 gallons when his authorized weekly total was only 529 gallons.

19-May-1944

Thomas Johnson, of Johnson Street was fine £4 for supplying and delivering 5cwt of coal and John Connolly, manager of the Ship Isis Hotel, was fined £6 for receiving it. The court heard seven other charges involving the same offence. Very few people were aware that it is illegal to acquire more than 28lbs of coal from any body except a licensed dealer. If your neighbour runs short of coal you would be breaking the law if you give or sell them more than 28lbs. The regulations say that you cannot, over the limit of two stones (28lbs), neither sell, giveaway nor buy coal except from a licensed merchant.

20-May-1944

Laing's launch the tanker *EMPIRE SALISBURY* 8197t. 1963 scrapped Singapore

21-May-1944

3500 members of Sunderland's youth organisations paraded today to celebrate Empire Youth Day. With several bands they marched along Newcastle Road, Roker Avenue, Fulwell Road and Roker Baths Road to Roker Park where a service was held.

22-May-1944

Drastic cuts in mainline and local train services have been made throughout the country. 48 trains have been withdrawn from Sunderland Schedule. Workmen's trains were not affected as most curtailments apply between 10.0am and 4.0pm.
The first of Sunderland's 'Holiday at Home' events began tonight when Open Air Dancing took place on tennis courts in Barnes Park. Dancing is to continue every Monday, Wednesdays and Fridays until June 16th.
Sunderland Drama Club gave a performance of 'Danger Point' in St Benet's Hall tonight. Out standing in the cast were Harold Pointer, Muriel Patterson and Ernest Walker. Others taking part were Lewis Hinckley, George Frankton, Percy Bell, Charles Stewart, Howard Wood, Betty Carter and Jean Elsdon. The stage-manager was Mr John Goss.
SP. Austin launches the collier *ROGATE* of 2871t. On a voyage from Sunderland to London, the *SS ROGATE* was one of the last ships to be sunk by E-Boats on the east coast route. She was torpedoed off Lowestoft on 19/03/1945 with the loss of two lives.
JL. Thompson launches the *EMPIRE DYNASTY* 9905t. 1969 Scrapped Taiwan.

23-May-1944

The Chief Constable officially installed Clive Boy's club in the new parish hall in Cato Street, Southwick tonight.
Shipbuilding Corporation launches the *EMPIRE TUDOR* 7069t. 1.9.64 broke moorings and grounded, total loss.

24-May-1944

Mr J Bowman held a property sale in the Palatine Hotel today and the following houses were sold; 22 Henry Street for £80; 43 Henry Street East for £50; 44 Bramwell Street for £105, and 8 Cromwell Street for £285.
Pickersgill's launch the landing craft LCT 7061

25-May-1944

"Young men so directed must work in the mines", said Mr Bevin, the Minister of Labour, in the Commons today. "If the war effort is not to be impeded by a lack of coal there can be no question of a revision of the Government's decision to direct young men to the mines". "As regard to the ballot scheme", said Mr Bevin, "there is no doubt that on the whole it was working well and the system of the ballot is the fairest that can be devised".

29-May-1944

Alarm No.251: 03.00 - 03.29. No action recorded

31-May-1944

In the early hours today two Sunderland men completed their journey home from German prison camps via Barcelona. They were Private Robert Davis (39), of the Seaforth Highlanders, living at 2 Mafeking Street Pallion and fusilier Joseph Whinfield (31), R N F, of 36 Moor Street Hendon.

2-Jun-1944

The Estates Committee felt compelled, in the interest of public safety, to recommend the removal of the 384 trees at Ford Estate. Ford Estate residents object. Let's have a greener Sunderland plea.

3-Jun-1944

Field Marshall Lord Birdwood said, " We know the Germans have promised not to use gas, but when faced with defeat they may well go 'Mad Dog' and resort to gas warfare. So take care of your gas masks and don't let children play football with them".

6-Jun-1944

Before dawn, the Allied Expeditionary Force of British, American, Canadian, Polish, and Free French troops begins Operation Overlord, the long-awaited invasion of France.

7-June-1944

Eleven more absentee Sunderland Home Guardsmen appeared before magistrates. One was sent to prison for one month and the second was fined £15. Others on their first offence were fined £5.

10-Jun-1944

The freedom of the Borough to the Durham Light Infantry was given today. Huge crowds gathered to see the 'Salute the Soldier' parade. Te procession arranged was one of the biggest yet held.

At the inquest today a verdict of accidental death was recorded on John Sloanes (44), a steel erector, of Falmouth Square. He died on Wednesday following an accident at the Pallion Crown Works of Steel's. He was caught and crushed by an electric crane. Steel & Co. Crown Works Pallion were fined £75 for contravening the Factories Act (1927).

12-Jun-1944

An inspection of the Ford Estate trees by the Chairman and members of the Estates Committee, and the blowing down of one of the trees by the wind, confirmed the Superintendents report and the Committee felt compelled, in the interest of public safety, to recommend the removal of the trees.

On the Ford Estate alone 1161 new trees have been planted. Considerable damage is unfortunately done to the trees, flowers and the parks generally, by children and others and is one of the main causes for the loss of these trees.

Wm Doxford launches the *FLORISTAN* 7368t. Gutted by engine room fire whilst lying in Antwerp Docks. Sold to Spanish breakers 23.10.1973. Pickersgill's launch the Tank Landing Craft LCT 7062

The Estates Committee inspecting damaged trees in Ford Estate

13-Jun-1944

Reference was made to the black market when Abraham Winson, of Seaburn Close, was fined £200 with £100 cost; Stanley Boyd, of Cleadon, was fined £300. The firm of Dunn & Co. (Sunderland) Ltd. was fined £1,500 with £200 costs. Mayfair Dairies Ltd, Mayfair Confectionery Company Limited and St John's Malting Company Limited were all fined £300 with £200 costs.

14-Jun-1944

In a statement prepared by the Town Clerk: there are now 348 families in requisitioned houses, 484 families officially billeted with other householders and 81 families evacuated to other towns (A total of 2687 persons).

15-Jun-1944

Plans to build a clothing factory at Southwick, which would provide 1500 jobs. Objections by some Southwick councillors because the 17 acres of land near North Hylton Road had been earmarked for new houses.

Stated to having been fined for a similar offence in 1942, Joan Winrow (18), of Louis Avenue, was fined £5 for allowing an un-obscured light after blackout plus £1 for wasting electricity. Christine Lowry, of Grey Road, was fined 10 shillings for allowing an un-obscured light.

16-Jun-1944

Sunderland folk hear today that the enemy is now using pilot less planes for raids on this country. (V 1's)

17-Jun-1944

The final figure for Sunderland's 'Salute to Soldiers' week, which ended tonight, was announced to be £1,251,687 11s 2d.

19-Jun-1944

John Pullen (17), of at St Leonard's Street, along with three juveniles aged 10, 11 and 12, were accused of throwing stones in Back Hedworth Street. All were fined £1 each.

20-Jun-1944

J. L. Thompson launches the *EMPIRE HALDANE* 7087t for MOWT managed by J.Morrison & Son. 8.11.65 aground 40m north of Mukho, Korea - total loss.

Wm Doxford launches the *BROCKLEYMOOR* 7368t. 1959 RESTORMEL, Orders & Handford SS Co. (John Cory Ltd). 1964 Beached in Ambelika Bay, after engine room fire, which burned for three days. Total Loss.

21-Jun-1944

The Ministry of Labour and National Service pays tribute to the contribution made by the women of the country. Over 90% of the single women and the 80% of the married women aged 18 to 40, without children under 14, were in the forces, Civil Defence or industry. In some factories 85% of the workers are women.

24-Jun-1944

More household goods are becoming available. Chamois leather, dish mops and feather dusters, are easily obtained. Metal and floor polish, night-lights, and house cloths are also in the shops again.

26-Jun-1944

A deputation from residents of Ford Estate met members of the Estates Committee of the Town Council in the Town Hall to protest against the removal from Ford Estate of 384 trees.

27-Jun-1944

Sunderland's death rate of 16.1 last year is the highest recorded since 1929, states the annual report of the Medical Officer of Health. More deaths from bronchitis, influenza and pneumonia were the cause of this high rate.

3-Jul-1944

Men of the Sunderland Rescue Services are now demolishing the Bromarsh cinema wrecked by bombs.

5-Jul-1944

Stated by his mother to be suffering from some peculiar complaint whereby he could sleep for 30 hours at the time, George Stephenson (18), of Dame Dorothy Street, appeared before Sunderland magistrates today for breach of bail. He had been fined £5 for been absent from Home Guard duty and a breach of bail but the case had been adjourned for one month.

6-Jul-1944

The Estate Committee today inspected the trees, which have been condemned at Ford Estate. They singled out Fordham Square and the Haig Homes as fine examples of a well-kept community with bushes and gardens in excellent condition. There was a marked difference in various parts of the estate and even in different parts of the same street.

The opening night of the 'Taming Of the Shrew', performed by the Sunderland Drama Club, in Barnes Park, which was postponed from last night.

7-Jul-1944

Laing's launch the tanker *EMPIRE CREST* 3738t 1961 Scrapped Singapore.

10-Jul-1944

A fine of £20 was imposed on Robert Jones (48), of Park Gate, Roker, accused of allowing an unobscured light during blackout at Steel & Co. Holmeside. He had forgotten to turn the mains off.

Three workmen from Ryhope Colliery were accused of absenteeism. Ryhope Colliery was stated to have the worst percentage absenteeism in Durham County. The men were Thomas Davie (22), of Commercial Road, Grangetown, David Carden (24), of Haddon Road, Sunderland and Thomas Ayre (22), of Seaview, Sunderland. They were all fined £5.

Bartram & Sons launches *HMS MULLION COVE* Repair Ship of the Moray Firth Class. Royal Navy. In 1968, renamed, she caught fire on a voyage from the Philippines to Korea and was scrapped in Korea.

11-Jul-1944

To date 479 people (211 families) have found accommodation in the town to escape the V1 bombing. Most of the arrivals were people who had left the town years ago and were returning to friends and relations.

In all 5438 evacuees were accommodated in Sunderland during the war despite the fact that 366 Sunderland families were still living in requisitioned houses with a number of other families billeted elsewhere out side the Borough.

Modern dwelling houses are bringing higher prices these days. An exceptional figure of £2,725 was paid for 31 Barnes View aT the sale by Barnes, Welch and Barnes today.

12-Jul-1944

Several hundred men and women at the wire rope factories of Glaholm & Robson and Dawson & Usher stopped work today over a wage dispute. They returned the following day.

The popularity of the make-do-and-mend exhibition in the Sunderland Art Gallery is shown in the attendance figures that today totalled more than 10,000. Women were encouraged to repair and remake their family's old clothes. Old curtains were cut up to make skirts and dresses. Unwanted jumpers were unravelled and knitted into something else or the wool used to darn socks.

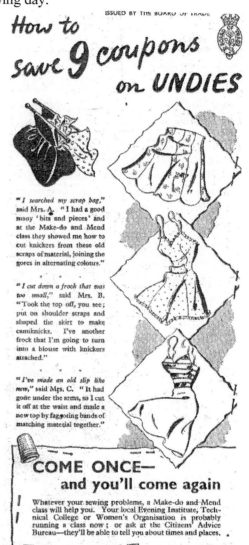

15-Jul-1944

The matinee performance of "Peter the Pied Piper" attracted large crowds today and the talented young players were greeted with enthusiasm. Irene Hopkins as the Pied Piper impressed with her personal charm and in the part of the spokesman Caspar Wheley Jnr. made an excellent master of ceremonies. The show is to be repeated on the evening and continues every night next week until Friday.

18-Jul-1944

Sunderland watchers closely to the persistent efforts of Tyneside's leaders to get the Admiralty to open closed shipyards on the Tyne. Protesters are concerned about the 40 years sterilisation of closed shipyard sites acquired by the National Shipbuilders Security. We on the Wear have a direct concern in the aspect of this case.

A Wearsider played an important part in the "GAY VIKING" that made the first successful dash through to the Skagerrak, Sweden to pick up vital war supplies. He was radio officer T H Ruben (19), of 16 Rolandson Terrace Sunderland.

19-Jul-1944

Parents who failed to send their children to school regularly suffered fines of £1 plus 4s costs. (£36 today using the retail price index).

John Turnbull (65), of 3 Zetland Street, a watchman employed by J L Thompson and Sons Ltd, was found crushed by steel plates at the shipyard tonight. How six steel plates, used in shipbuilding and weighing 15 and half tons, came to keel over remained a mystery following a later inquest. A verdict of accidental death was recorded.

20-Jul-1944

What is the cause of juvenile delinquency and the widespread wanton destruction by children? These were the questions discussed at a meeting tonight. Suggestions put forward were; publication of names of juvenile offenders or their parents; the imposing of higher penalties so that parents would feel more disposed to discipline their children; the clergy to be given offenders' names so that clergymen can visit their parents and emphasise their responsibilities for the children; bomb damage sites should be cleared of the 'ammunition' and converted into playgrounds; more playing-fields should be provided; the appointment of estate's managers.

A plea to clean out the Boating Lake in Roker Park, which is in a bad state with more weeds than water to be seen. Any sailing of model boats is completely out of the question.

SP. Austin launches the FIREGLOW 1549t. 1965 sold to Dutch breakers.

21-Jul-1944

Accused to stealing timber valued at five shillings, the property of Sunderland Corporation, Hector Hill (22) of Harold Street was fined 40s. He admitted taking three pieces of timber, none of which were over 3 ft in length, to his father's house in Worcester Terrace to be used as firewood.

23-Jul-1944

Durham County brass band championship held in Barnes Park, for the second year in succession, the bands competed for four cups valued at £235. First prize went to Horden Colliery Band other prize winners were the Colliery bands of Craghead, Thornley and Crookhall.

25-Jul-1944

Up to April this year no fewer than 36,000 persons have been killed and over 550,000 injured on British roads since the outbreak of war. 588,742 killed or injured, a total substantially greater than that of all British military and air casualties up to that date.

26-Jul-1944

Fines amounting to £300 were imposed in cases on which the wartime restrictions of £100 maximum for building work without a licence. Hector Grabham, Managing Director of a firm of painters and decorators, was fined £200; Samuel Talbot, managing director of Samuel Talbot Ltd. (heating engineers), was fined £50 and the Company a further £50, all pleaded guilty. Mr Grabham bought 7 The Cedars in June 1942, and embarked upon an extensive redecoration, which included the central heating costing £113 17s 10d.

28-Jul-1944

For the second time in three weeks the wire rope workers of Sunderland are on strike.

29-Jul-1944

An expert, hired by Ford Estate residents, contradicts the Corporation regarding the state of the trees on Ford Estate. Of the 160 trees adjoining Hylton Road only a dozen need removal. Of the 50 trees in Ford Hall Drive only nine needed to be removed on the grounds of safety. Trees at the back of Fordenbridge Road and Front Road have suffered considerable damage by children and few worth keeping. Dealing with the trees in the Ford Hall School grounds, less than 25 per cent need to be removed.

31-Jul-1944

The strikers of wire rope workers employed in Sunderland went back to work today after being out since Friday.

1-Aug-1944

The Estates Committee are to seek a further expert opinion on the question of the trees on Ford Estate and meanwhile will postpone the felling of the trees.**4-Aug-1944**

The Education Committee's decided to bring the juniors back to Valley Road Schools following refurbishment and leave the infants at Commercial Road School. It is a long way for the infants and a good many have to take the bus. With winter coming it was thought a better idea to have the juniors going to Commercial Road.

5-Aug-1944

Sunderland had every appearance of being on holiday today. There were crowds for everything, trams, buses, pictures, cafes, and queues were the order of the day. It seemed that everyone wanted to enjoy the last public holiday of the year.

7-Aug-1944

Everyone was out to enjoy themselves as they did yesterday and on Saturday. Reminiscent of pre-war days there were queues for hot water. The cafes lining the Promenade did a roaring trade. In fact the only thing that seemed to be missing were the ice-cream vendors. Many public houses were on short rations all last week and many had to observe short hours yesterday and some even closed today. Almost every public house in the town was closed long before the usual closing time.

8-Aug-1944

A scheme by the Seaside Development Committee proposes the development of a miniature railway on land at Seaburn at an estimated cost of £500. The Parks Committee also agreed to the application from the Sunderland Model Boating Club to run a small gauge railway track, to run model engines, on the disused tennis courts near the Parks Superintendent's house in Roker Park.

9-Aug-1944

Seaburn has become so popular these past few days that it has set a problem for the residents. The buses that were introduced for their use, when the trams stopped running along the seafront, are so full that many residents are finding it hard to get on them.

As usual, after Bank Holidays, attendances at shipyards and workplaces were below normal. Miners again were slow to respond and at Wearmouth Colliery, almost one-third of the men were absent yesterday.

Richard Irving, of Bramwell Street, appeared in court today for being absent from work. He had been absent from June 15th and had been consistently late before that. The defendant was employed as a Bevin Boy at Hylton Colliery. The case was adjourned for a month.

Wm Doxford launches the *REGISTAN* 7360t. 1954 capsized and sank in heavy weather.

Seaburn Beach was almost as busy as a peacetime August Bank Holiday

10-Aug-1944

The Council agreed to provide a wartime nursery in George Street, to supply the needs of Grangetown and the East End. A maximum of 48 children of two to five years of age will be accommodated from 7 am to 7pm daily.

11-Aug-1944

Thomas Kelly, of Gower Street, Southwick, was summoned today for leaving his employment without permission. Kelly was employed at a shipyard on the Thames but returned to Sunderland in May. He had complained of the lack of accommodation for himself and his wife. The case was adjourned for two weeks to allow Kelly to think again and return to the south to work.

Tomorrow's matinee and evening performance of Tom Jones in Barnes Park will be the last of a two-week run. Almost 5000 people attended the seven performances up to Wednesday night.

12-Aug-1944

Civilian admissions to hospital have been restricted by order of the military and Ministry of Health in order to ensure adequate accommodation for service casualties. This restriction had been in force for some time but hospitals were asked to observe secrecy. Waiting lists of non-urgent cases are therefore growing.

Sunderland has been allocated 1600 evacuees from London and the South. Sunderland has already received 1143 adults and 1756 children. In addition the town, because of the Blitz last year, had 1295 persons living in requisitioned houses, 318 living in billets and 202 persons billeted out side the Borough.

14-Aug-1944

An observation that there were not sufficient public conveniences in Sunderland was made at Sunderland Police Court today when five women were bound over for six months each with a fine of 40s plus 4s costs when they appeared for committing a 'nuisance' in Back Pallion Road.

15-Aug-1944

The allies launch Operation 'Dragoon', a combined assault on the South coast of France from Toulon to Nice. 9,000 airborne troops are landed, along with 90,000 by sea. The operation came 10 weeks after the bigger Normandy invasion of June 6th, 1944 and pushed German troops into a closing Allied pincer movement. Soldiers from America, Britain and Africa liberated southern France in one of the Second World War's most flawless battles. Then, history forgot them.

In Normandy, six towns and 2,000 prisoners are taken. About 200,000 Germans (23 divisions) are in the 40-mile long, 11-mile wide (at narrowest point) Argentan-Falaise gap, but start to pull out as Anglo-Canadian troops resume the attack to the North.

Adolf Hitler describes this as 'The worst day of my life'.

16-Aug-1944

Allegations made at Sunderland County Court today against a company that it had received pram hoods and covers to be repaired, together with money for the work, and had not returned the goods. Mrs Olivia Wilson, of Osborne Street, made a claim against the Stockton Pram Hood Company for the return of her pram cover or alternatively £5. At the shop, opened in Norfolk Street, scores of Sunderland people, estimated to be around 200, had left pram hoods for repair and a large majority of them never got them back.

At the sale by auction, held in Sunderland today, Charles Bell and Sons sold 15 and 17 St Marks Road for £257.10 shillings, 19 and 21 St Marks Road also for £257.10 shillings and 34 Alfred Street for £170.

18-Aug-1944

The supply of beer is at present only 50 per cent of normal. It was said the demand had increased significantly. For being absent from work on two occasions since early this year John Robson (21) of James Armitage Street, who was remanded for medical examination on Monday, was fined £2.10 shillings for each charge and bound over for 12 months.

19-Aug-1944

Shipbuilding Corporation launches the *EMPIRE COWDRAY* 7072t. 1960 scrapped Barrow.

21-Aug-1944

Opening the beaches at Seaburn, Seaham and Marsden has been the salvation of the Holidays at Home programme this summer. For almost five years the beaches have been closed.

22-Aug-1944

44 Sunderland elementary schools will reopen today. It is expected that the big influx of evacuated children will be absorbed into the schools nearest their homes.

23-Aug-1944

Thomas Anderson (22) was sent to prison for three months for failing to attend Home Guard duties after he had been working. Others fined were John Montgomery, of Hardwick Street, Thomas Naisbitt, of High Street West, Septimus McPhee (28), of Ogden Street and Robert Cockburn, of Barrie Square.

Peter Calvert (29), of Peebles Road, was fined £5 or one month in prison for leaving his employment without permission.

News that French forces have liberated Paris is another milestone in the United Nations march to complete victory.

25-Aug-1944

Carelessness in regards to observance of the blackout is becoming much too common for of the peace of mind of law-abiding householders.

26-Aug-1944

The Wire rope workers, at a meeting today, rejected the employers' offer of an extra three shillings a week, a long way short of the workers demand for eleven shillings a week. At a later meeting by a majority of one vote, union delegates accepted the employer's offer of an increase of four shillings a week.

Sunderland 0 Middlesbrough 0. There was a crowd approaching 12,000 for the opening game of the season.

28-Aug-1944

Although the new miniature railway at Seaburn has proved an outstanding success with children. The steam engine, which was acquired with the rolling stock, has not been as efficient as was hoped and another engine, this one petrol-driven, has been put into use pending repairs.

29-Aug-1944

Northern England and Scotland would have to depend on Northern Ireland this season for a supply of apples, which will be principally the Bramley cooking apple. Eating apples will be scarce.

30-Aug-1944

Since 1938, wages of workers in this country have nearly doubled. The average weekly earnings of 6 million workers were; men £6 4s 2d; women £3 4s 6d; youths and boys £2 6s 11d; girls £1 14s 3d.

Wm Doxford launches the *ROYBANK* 7368t. 1962 SILVER LAKE, Panama. Scrapped Taiwan April 1968.

Struggling to port with a ship, which had been torpedoed, with a hole in its side big enough to drive a bus through, Captain Richard Humble, of 56 Stratford Avenue. (In the Gulf of Aden the Italian submarine I-27 torpedoes and damages the 7126 ton British Liberty ship FORT CAMOSON on the 3rd December 1943).31-Aug-1944

31-Aug-1944

The British 11th Armoured Division captures Amiens and takes the German bridge across the Somme in surprise attack. Montpellier, Beziers, Narbonne and Nice all taken.

1-Sep-1944

Work is to begin on the new clothing factory at Southwick, between the river and North Hylton Road. (The factory occupied by Rego Clothiers opened in April 1946. It closed soon after and was taken over by Ericsson's, which later became Plessey).

The site of the other new factory is between the trading estate and the river at Pallion.

The first and most destructive phase of the V1 campaign, the bombardment of the United Kingdom from bases in the Pas de Calais, came to an end with the launch of the final weapon at 0400hrs. Between 13 June and 1 September 1944, no fewer than 8,617 V1s had been fired at the United Kingdom from Northern France.

2-Sep-1944
Middlesbrough 1 Sunderland 5. There was an unchanged eleven at Middlesbrough. Attendance was about 3000.

4-Sep-1944
Two months notice is given to two thirds of Sunderland's full-time paid wardens.
Short Bros. launches *HMS DULLISK COVE* 7058t Repair Ship of the Moray Firth Class. Royal Navy.
Laing's launch the *EMPIRE CHANCELLOR* 9917t. 1960 Scrapped Piraeus.

5-Sep-1944
It was thought unfair that evacuee families had to be separated when the Harrison Buildings in Salem Street was standing empty? One of the first places to be repaired after the last air raid and has stood empty ever since with rooms for 14 families.

6-Sep-1944
Sunderland asks for an extra allocation of food, in view of the large number of evacuees in the town.

7-Sep-1944
Sunderland town centre is under 'master switch' control and therefore could benefit from new lighting that is 1000 times brighter than 'star lighting'. 91 of the lamps in the central part of the town will be lit with these lights.

8-Sep-1944
Accused of absenting himself from work without leave, Thomas Kelly, of Gower Street, Southwick, who was stated, to have been working at Erith, Kent was today fined £10 or two months in jail. The case had been twice adjourned for him to return to work.

9-Sep-1944
Leeds Utd. 0 Sunderland 1. Sunderland's five points out of six from the opening games is on a par with last season when they were leading the championship up to early November. Then came the slump.

11-Sep-1944
Compulsory drills of the Home Guard, including assistance to civil defence, will be discontinued. Such operational duties as are now required of the Home Guard will be carried out on a voluntary basis. These arrangements will take effect from today. All recruitment to the Home Guard is suspended.

12-Sep-1944
From today all daylight fire guard duties will be abolished, and night fire guard duties will end in a very large part of the country. Throughout most of Britain the Civil Defence will be on a part time basis.

14-Sep-1944
Authority has been received to remove all roadblocks and pillboxes.

15-Sep-1944
Summoned for selling short measures of gin, Norman Boucher, of the Alexandria Hotel, Grangetown, was fined £5 for each of the three offences. The North Eastern Breweries, Castle Street, Sunderland were fined £10 for each offence.

16-Sep-1944
Start of Merchant Navy Week. It is hoped to raise £10,000 to be divided among various local organisations. Because of poor response it was decided to continue until the target was reached.
Sunderland 5 Leeds Utd. 1. Sunderland seven points out of eight and 11 goals for with two against.

17-Sep-1944
Britain's blackout was greatly eased from today ordinary peacetime curtains and blinds may be used. Street lighting of a much higher standard was allowed.
Cheers were raised in Fawcett Street tonight when five years of blackout ended by the switching on of the new and better-modified lighting in the centre of the town. Many people came into town just to see the lights go on.

18-Sep-1944
Sunderland welcome home repatriated prisoners of war. Warrant Officer George Davison, RAF, of 53 Forster Street, Roker. Archie Donaldson, a wireless operator air gunner, of 72 Ridley Street, Southwick. Private Thomas Pratt, of 70 Hood Street, Monkwearmouth. Fusilier H R Clarke (36) of 20 Marley Crescent, Southwick.
JL. Thompson launches the *EMPIRE GANGES* 3744t. Scrapped Spezia in 1978.

19-Sep-1944
Riveters at the shipyard of John Crown and Sons Ltd are now on strike over piecework rates saying it was not possible on piecework to earn as much as would have been paid on time rate.

20-Sep-1944
Sunderland's total savings since the outbreak of war has reached £12,500,000.
Ex-P.o.W Private J A Hutchinson (31), of 14 Drury Lane is now at home He was captured during the fall of France.

Private R Eccleston (24), Green Howards, of 33 Leechmere Road South, has also been repatriated but he is at present in hospital.

21-Sep-1944

Riveters of John Crown and Sons Ltd resumed work today after a five-day stoppage.

22-Sep-1944

19 parents were summoned at the Juvenile Court today for failing to send their children regularly to school. Orders to attend school were made in all of the cases.

23-Sep-1944

Sunderland 2 Newcastle Utd 0. Sunderland's goal ratio gives them second place in the league championship. Huddersfield is yet to drop a point.

25-Sep-1944

95 per cent of the full-time members of the Northern Region Civil Defence Service and approximately 50 per cent of part-time workers are to be released,

26-Sep-1944

The weekly rates of National Insurance contributions are announced; employed men 3s 10d plus 3s 1d by employer; employed women 3s plus 2s 3d by employer; Self employed men 4s 2d; self-employed women 3s 6d.

27-Sep-1944

A verdict of accidental death returned an inquest today on Matthew Thirwell a 15 year-old apprentice electric welder, of 12 Catherine Street, who was severely injured at work at W Doxford's and Sons Ltd.

28-Sep-1944

Sunderland people are accused of forgetting the debt that the country owes to the gallant men of the Merchant Navy. To date only £1,705 has been raised of the target of £10,000.

29-Sep-1944

Many Sunderland parents and wives must feel a debt of gratitude to the Prime Minister for his special reference yesterday to the Burma campaign. Feelings were that the Far East war was the forgotten war.

30-Sep-1944

Newcastle Utd. 1 Sunderland 5. Sunderland leads the Football League (North) on goal difference.
Part demobilization of National Fire Service.
The new factory which, which is being built at Pallion, has a floor space of 160,000 square feet and will provide employment for a considerable amount of female labour.

2-Oct-1944

In Sunderland in 1943, there were 295 accidents, 17 fatalities and 17 injured. Drivers of all types of vehicles, from hand carts to motor vehicles, were responsible for 117 and 160 were traced to some fault on the part of the pedestrian. There were 18 accidents due to miscellaneous causes such as wind etc. Oddly enough there seems to be more caution on everyone's part at dusk. During 1943, 5 people were killed and 73 injured during the blackout and 12 killed and 244 injured during daylight. Sunderland Safety Week will be held from October 16th to the 21st.
SP. Austin launches the *CORMOUNT* 2871t. 10.1974 broken up at Split.
Wm Doxford launches the *EMPIRE TAVOY* 7381t. 1975 scrapped Shanghai.

3-Oct-1944

The Minister of Fuel told the House today that the increase in coal output expected following the wages agreement with the miners had not materialised. Output per man has fallen by 5 cwt a week, mainly owing to an increase of 25 per cent in voluntary absenteeism.
Pickersgill's launch the *HMS LARGO BAY* 1600t Bay Class Frigate. Ex - Loch Fionn. Broken up 1958.

5-Oct-1944

The acute shortage of houses in Sunderland was evidence today when, in answer to an advertisement 150 people, from all parts of the town, queued up at Fullwelll in the hope of becoming tenants of an upstairs flat comprising four rooms and the use of a bath at a house in Maud Street. The queue was so long that it overflowed into the Sea Road shopping thoroughfare. None of the people in the queue got the rooms; they had been let the previous night.

6-Oct-1944

Sunderland's Invasion Committee is disbanded. Regional Commissioner agrees with the military that they were no longer required.
Margaret Lownds, of Norfolk Street, was fined a total of 30s for failing to show the price of the crabs she was selling and for selling them at an excessive price. When told the maximum price of crabs was 10d a pound she replied, " How can I sell crabs at ten pence, I pay more than that for them?" she had sold crabs for many years and had the never weighed them.

7-Oct-1944

Bradford City v Sunderland. Four positional changes knocked the bottom out of the attack. Whitelum scored then Bradford City equalised.

Men of 35 years of age and over are not to be called up. The Services now have sufficient trained men.

10-Oct-1944

The House of Commons discusses the boundary changes for towns that suffered most from German bombing. Samuel Storey illustrated the case for Sunderland. Sunderland before the war had a density of population of 26 to the acre, against an average in all County Boroughs of 15. It has 1.45 families per dwelling, and only 50 per cent of families are in undivided possession of their own homes. The position has been aggravated by the fact that nine per cent of the houses have been either destroyed of very seriously damaged, and 81 per cent had been damaged to some extent. Sunderland will require 12,500 houses to deal with the slum clearance and overcrowding and one third of those must be built outside the County Borough. Sunderland must also provide schools, playgrounds, and playing fields to meet the requirements of the Minister of Education and will need 600 acres when the school leaving age is raised to 15 and 700 acres when it is raised to 16. Already Sunderland has had to put out side the Borough boundaries schools, which cater for children living within the Borough. There is a third reason Sunderland depends largely upon the receipt of coal and shipbuilding. It is essential to the future development than it should have new light industries, which can be best allocated in the clearance areas in the Borough where facilities are available.

11-Oct-1944

Chairman of the Seaburn Development Committee said that 16,750 persons have been carried on the miniature railway at Seaburn with the engine obtained two days after opening the railway. The Committee promised to do their best to get the beaches on the south side of the town free from restrictions.

12-Oct-1944

Part-time members of the Civil Defence services, including the NFS and fireguards, shall be allowed to retain their authorised uniform, including great coats and leather boots/shoes on demobilisation. However the N.F.S. tunic must be surrendered for security reasons.

14-Oct-1944

Sunderland 2 Bradford City 1. Scorers Spuhler and Whitelum.

16-Oct-1944

A fine of 40 shillings was imposed on Lionel Davis, of Barnes View and Maurice Davis, of Ashwood Terrace, for the unlawful use of motor fuel.

17-Oct-1944

Among the British prisoners of war rescued by the Allies after the sinking of a Japanese ship are two members of the 125 Anti-tank Regiment. Gunner T Smith, of 42 Elmwood Avenue Southwick and Gunner C Perry, formally of 1 Hendon Road but whose wife now lives at Tavistock Crescent, London. His parents live at 38 Alderson Street, Deptford.

18-Oct-1944

The Duchess of Kent visited the town where she received Sunderland's donation for the Greek Red Cross at the New Rink. Restrictions are eased on weather reporting. So the Echo was able to describe that the weather was fine and sunny for the visit of the Duchess of Kent.

Robert Anthony Watson, of 25 Trimdon Street, was bound over for 12 months for being persistently late for work. He started working February this year at North Eastern Marine and since that date up until August 17th he had been late 107 times out of 115.

JL. Thompson launches the *EMPIRE ALLENBY* 9904t. 1959 scrapped Hong Kong.

19-Oct-1944

A shortage of cigarettes in Sunderland thought, by tobacconist, to be suffering more than other towns. People visiting the Lake District report an abundance of most things in the shops that are not available in Sunderland.

21-Oct-1944

Sunderland's Merchant Navy Week and up to last night the total raised was only £5,170. This afternoon a procession of the forces, Merchant Navy men and pre-service units paraded through the town.

Hartlepools United 2 Sunderland 6. Bradford and Huddersfield sharing the points strengthened Sunderland's hold on the leadership. The Roker side has scored 27 goals against seven conceded.

24-Oct-1944

The quarterly report of the Chief Constable, revealed a considerable decrease in crime compared with the corresponding period last year. Drunkenness, however, showed an increase of three to seventeen.   .

27-Oct-1944

At a sale by auction, by Barnes, Welch & Barnes, 30 St Vincent Street was sold for £340.

Joiners and Apprentices employed at William Doxford and Sons ceased work for a few hours today because of a wage grievance.

28-Oct-1944

Sunderland 4 Hartlepools Utd 2. Eddie Burbanks played today, his first appearance since Sunderland resumed League football. Walshaw therefore moved into the inside position and Harry Bell partnered Spuhler.

29-Oct-1944

Sunderland's Piggery at Fulwell Quarry has developed into a thriving little industry and it now consists of several acres. The herd of pigs now number 327.

Shipbuilding Corporation launches the *EMPIRE MANDALAY* 7086t. 1961 scrapped Hong Kong.

30-Oct-1944

Announced today, the Home Guard is to stand down on Wednesday but will remain in reserve.

Michael Brewster (34), of Hendon Road, was summoned on two counts of selling combs at prices exceeding the maximum price. He was fined £25 on each offence. He had sold combs at 2/6 and 2/- when the maximum price of the combs of that length was 1/-.

Bartram's launch the *EMPIRE MAURITIUS* 7310t. Scrapped in 1985.

31-Oct-1944

Lazy Sunderland mothers were blamed for the low take up rate of orange juice (42%), cod liver oil (16%) and vitamin tablets (38%).

Short Bros. launches *HMS SOLWAY FIRTH* 7058t Repair Ship of the Moray Firth Class. Royal Navy

1-Nov-1944

In the Casualty Service, about 80 of the full-time staff of the Ambulance Depots are to be released along with about 165 of the part-time staff. Of the First Aid personnel, 53 full-time and 300 part-time are to be released. The Ambulance Service is to be cut by half. Of the 2000 part-time air raid wardens 50 have asked to be released on health grounds. Of the original 120 full-time wardens only 18 will be retained after November 15th.

James Semple (48), of 40 Lee Street, a plater, died tonight from injuries received when he fell into the hold of a ship he was working on at Bartram's shipyard, South Docks. At an inquest held on November 4th, the mystery of how he fell from a staging at the yard and received injuries from which he died later in the day at the Royal Infirmary, was unsolved. Death was due to fractured skull and a verdict of accidental death was returned.

Pickersgill's launch the *HMS MORCAMBE BAY* 1600t Bay Class Frigate. Ex – Loch Heilen.

2-Nov-1944

Sunderland Civil Defence workers, who are being released, are for the most part finding other jobs fairly easy. November 15th is the date fixed for the release, but those with jobs are released immediately. The Rescue Service is retaining its 400 part-time personal but only 20 of its full-time workers. During the past months the Rescue Service has earned for itself the name of 'handymen' of the Civil Defence. They are now engaged on the destruction of roadblocks as well as demolition, construction and maintenance of houses.

3-Nov-1944

The house, 'West Bank', Ashbrooke Road was sold at auction at the Palatine Hotel yesterday for £1,600.

4-Nov-1944

Huddersfield 3 Sunderland 0. Sunderland's team that visited Huddersfield today was; Heywood; Gorman and Eves; Wallbanks, Lockie and Hastings; Spuhler, H Bell, Whitelum, A N Other and Burbanks.

5-Nov-1944

From today, the milk allowance reduced from two-and-half pints to two pints.

Single deck tramcar on the Villette Road route

6-Nov-1944

The 14 year-old schoolboy George William Charlton, of 6 Salisbury Street, Hendon, recently awarded a testimonial on vellum from the Royal Humane Society, has been recognised by the Boy Scout Association by awarding him their silver cross and certificate for gallantry. Lord Barnard the County Commissioner presented the award.

7-Nov-1944

Sunderland has seen the last of its 'covered wagons', otherwise the single deck tramcar No. 85, which earned its nickname on the Villette Road route. It is the last of a dozen single deckers, which the Corporation one time owned, and went out of use some years ago when the railway bridge at the bottom of Tatham Street was heightened so that double-deck cars could run on this route. Now the Corporation has sold the 'covered wagon' to Leeds for £375.

Mr Storey the Sunderland MP voiced his surprise at the poor showing of Sunderland's Merchant Navy Week total. He thought that Sunderland of all places would have produced £10,000 for the Merchant Navy without any difficulty and urged everyone to continue until the £10,000 was reached.

8-Nov-1944

"I am quite satisfied, from the evidence I have heard, that this man lost his life in consequence of their having been no light in No. 2 hold. The lack of light cost this man his life". The Coroner recorded a verdict of accidental death at the inquest later on Joseph McKenna (42), of 39 Bramwell Street, a joiner for the North-eastern Marine Engineering Company. McKenna was found today at the bottom of No. 2 hold of a ship under construction at Bartram and Sons shipyard by Walter Wilkinson an apprentice fitter.

9-Nov-1944

Councillor John Young was elected Mayor of Sunderland today.

The badly bombed towns and cities of England, including Sunderland, are the first to have their claims for boundary extensions considered when the Boundary Commission is set up. The seven-bombed towns Sunderland, Plymouth, Hull, Portsmouth, Bristol, Dover and a Great Yarmouth, will have precedence and the Commission will be instructed to deal with them first.

10-Nov-1944

More than 2000 workers crowded into Doxford's Canteen to see and hear Henry Hall and his Orchestra in today's 'Break for Music' the radio show on the BBC Home Service.

11-Nov-1944

John Lilley, played at inside right for Sunderland against Huddersfield at Roker Park today, he is on Grimsby's books. In the absence of Whitelum, Ken Walshaw will lead the attack but Carter and Burbanks are definitely not able to come. The team is expected to be; Heywood; Gorman and Eves; Wallbanks, Lockie and Hastings; Spuhler, Lilley, Walshaw, H Bell and A Dixon. Argus considered Huddersfield the best side he'd seen since the beginning of the war. Sunderland's makeshift attack was blamed for not putting up a better show. Walshaw helps to make one goal and scored the other. There were 21,000 present.

13-Nov-1944

There were 81 summonses at Sunderland Magistrates Court today for failing to have a dog licence. Six were withdrawn and the remaining 75 were each fined 11s 6d.

14-Nov-1944

In May this year the Sunderland built ship EMPIRE CITY built by Wm Doxford and Sons was torpedoed in the Indian Ocean within a year of leaving the Wear on her maiden trip. All the Sunderland members of the crew along with three from Seaham Harbour escaped. Now all are back at home. The Sunderland men are, Geoffrey Hall of Ford Estate; Alan Adamson of 27 Frederick Street; J Brooke of 28 The Parade; J Pringle of 108 Burleigh Garth; A Colling of 157 Canon Cockin Street; R Taylor of 97 Fordfield Road; A W Donald of the Manor Hotel; N Robson of 1 Beverley Road; T Wilkinson of 12 Sans Street South; Maurice Edmundson of 12 Mitford Street; James Smith of 7 Suddick Street; F Green of 32 Ridley Terrace; E Mackay of the Hendon Station Hotel; S Barry of 40 Allison Street; A Devine of 30 Walton Garth and J G Carr of 30 Thorburn Street Fulwell.

15-Nov-1944

The Secretary of State for War in Parliament today took the opportunity in correcting any misunderstanding that might be about the present position regarding Home Guard uniforms. The instructions so far issued is of the standing down of the Home Guard and not its disbandonment. Members of the Home Guard are liable for recall if the need arises. The instructions make it clear that should the Home Guard be required for active duty, members will report for duty complete with the articles of clothing and equipment, which they have been allowed to retain. It will not be until actual disbandonment that members will be allowed to dispose of or have their khaki trousers and great coats dyed for use as civilian clothes.

Wm Doxford launches the *EMPIRE SINGAPORE* 7381t. Sold Chinese mainland breakers 11.11.1970.

16-Nov-1944

Mr and Mrs N Andrews, a 54 Neale Street, Fulwell, have received word that their son Kenneth, who was an apprentice aboard the *THISTLEBRAE* when she was captured at Trondheim in April 1940 and has since been a POW in Germany, has been successful in passing an examination for his Second Mate Certificate. Kenneth had been taking a correspondence course under the Prisoners of War Department of the Red Cross.

18-Nov-1944

Sunderland met York City today at York, it was the first wartime journey by motor coach. The team was; Heywood; Stelling and Eves; Wallbanks, Lockie and Hastings; Spuhler, Potts, Whitelum, Carter and Burbanks.

Sunderland beat York. A Sunderland win (half time Sunderland 4 – York City 1.The defeat of Everton gives Sunderland and Huddersfield a two-point lead in their joint leadership of the league.

20-Nov-1944

A greater effort is still needed if the target of £10,000 for Sunderland's Merchant Navy Week is to be reached. The latest figure is £8,694 13s.

21-Nov-1944

Manufacturers are beginning to change over to the manufacture of items for domestic requirements. Steel has been allocated for the manufacturer of wringers, mangles, lawnmowers, kettles, water heaters and cookers.

22-Nov-1944

Sunderland people were warned not to be alarmed on hearing the works buzzers, blowing at 7:30am, it is mainly that shipbuilding firms on the river have now received permission to sound the works buzzers at starting and finishing times. Workmen will no longer be able to excuse themselves for finishing 15 minutes before time. Laing's launches the *EMPIRE MARS* 8199t. 1946 WAVE DUKE, Royal Fleet Auxiliary. 1969 Scrapped.

23-Nov-1944

Mr Corquedale of the Ministry of Labour and National Service made high praise for the work done by Wearside shipyard workers, both men and women, during the war. He emphasised the absence of industrial strife for Wearside, when he toured a number of shipyards today. He spoke briefly to the workers of Short Brothers and again when he addressed hundreds of workers in the canteen of Doxford and Sons, " I could not leave Wearside without speaking of the splendid record of the Sunderland shipyard workers. Good, if not better than any group of workers in the country for production. It had not been possible to tell the full story of Wear shipbuilding production, but when it could be told, the workers would have the satisfaction of knowing that their work had been second to none of any of the great shipbuilding centres in this country or abroad. As fee or record for the absence of industrial strife and industrial disputes, that is the finest in the country. Mr Bevin asked me specially to congratulate you on your record. There is no doubt but for the fact that the women of this country were prepared to come forward in our hour of need and do work, which had always been supposedly too hard for them, we should not be in so good a position as we are today. We men, owe more than we can say to the magnificent way the women, of this country, of this town, and of this firm, have come forward and done such good work".

For the past week there has been almost continuous rainfall. Nearly four inches has fell over the last month.

25-Nov-1944

Sunderland v York City. Sunderland was without Gorman, Burbanks and Carter. Sunderland draw. Sunderland is second in the league, one point behind Huddersfield who has 23 points.

26-Nov-1944

£30,000 of damage was caused by a fire, which completely gutted Ditchburn's furniture factory in Villiers Street
The last official transport of about 180 children, evacuated from Sunderland during the war years, today returned home by bus to the reception centre at Cowen Terrace.

28-Nov-1944

Work started on a new factory at Pallion. Sadly the completed factory lay empty for 18 months before Cosmos took up the lease to manufacture radio valves. Cosmos closed in the 60's. The Pallion Retail Park now occupies the site.

In 1975 the Cosmos site was popular to Wearside bargain hunters when it opened as a Sunday Market

30-Nov-1944

The London farewell parade to mark the stand down of the Home Guard to take place on Sunday will include representatives from Home Guard Units throughout the country.
Representing the Sunderland Home Guard are; -

- For the 24th Durham (Sunderland) Home Guard Battalion - Private E W Cooper, Private J E Gladwin and Private E C Harrison.
- For the 9th Durham (Sunderland) Home Guard Battalion - Lance corporal R P Elliott, Private N Harrison, and Private G F Robinson.
- For the 103rd Durham Home Guard Rocket AA Battery - Sergeant A Ferguson and Private J Hearn.

Wm Doxford launches the *WEYBANK* 7268t. Scrapped Taiwan April 1968.

1-Dec-1944

A call to reopen Newcastle Road Baths, to ease overcrowding at High Street Baths. They reopened on 14th May 1945.

2-Dec-1944

Darlington 1 Sunderland 3.

Crowns launch the *EMPIRE PHYLLIS* 257t tug for MOWT 1982 Italian Navy at Messina, later scrapped.

3-Dec-1944

Britain's Home Guard is officially stood down after five years. King George VI declares, "You have fulfilled your charge". In Sunderland and District some thousands of men, have for more than four years, given solid service to this wartime Citizens' Army. They did not repel an enemy invasion, nor round-up enemy paratroopers, nor did they capture a single German spy, and the 'Z' Battery have only once had the occasion to fire their rocket guns in anger, but they have all been ready and fit to play their part.

The London Home Guard Standown Parade

The local parade of the Home Guard was probably one of the most impressive parades of the war. The 9th and 24th battalions and 103rd County Durham Rocket Battery attended a non-denominational service at the Roker Park football ground at 10:45am before parading through the town.

On May 17th, 1940 the LDV groups for Durham County were drawn up. On May 18th a meeting held in Sunderland in which the 24th Group of the LDV was formed with Colonel L Laing as Commanding Officer. Initially formed into platoons at works and factories they volunteered to turn out for nightly duty at the place of their employment well before the fireguards scheme had come into operation. Companies with more experienced men were formed with their 'battle' positions at Hendon gasworks, Humbledon Hill, Dykelands Road and Southwick. Every shipyard and engineering works had its company or platoon, so had the railway company, the docks the River Wear Commissioners, Wearmouth Colliery, Post Office and other large concerns. The Post Office Company was organised as, and continued to be, part of the separate Post Office Battalion the 13th Northumberland.

After Mr Churchill had changed the name from the LDV's to that of the Home Guard, the volunteer citizen army became in to closer liaison with the regular military forces and was reorganised on more military lines. Sunderland's battalion became the 9th Battalion Home Guard. In the early days three or four battalions were formed into Groups, which came under the command of the Zone Commander. For a considerable time the Sunderland battalion was in number 2 Group.

In August 1942, the service changed from voluntary to compulsory and the Sunderland Battalion, with vastly increased numbers, divided into two with one based on the south side and the other on the north side of the river. The south side Battalion, with Colonel Laing, remained as the 9th Durham Battalion DLI Home Guard and the north side became the 24th Durham Battalion DLI Home Guard with Colonel Bartram as commander. Most of the officers and men which formed the 103rd 'Z' Battery were recruited from the 9th and 24th of battalions.

4-Dec-1944

Sunderland central railway station, long criticised as one of the most dowdy in Britain, is at last being improved. Because of the war it is to be a brighter and better station through the erection of umbrella glass roofing over each platform in place of the massive overall roof, which was largely demolished by enemy action.

5-Dec-1944

Chester Road is the longest road in Sunderland, from the Borough boundary to Low Row; its length is 2.7 miles (6 miles today). Durham Road comes next at 2.69 miles (7.5 miles today). Newcastle road is only 1.96 miles.

7-Dec-1944

The Home Office states that from Saturday evening it will not be necessary to blackout premises when an alert sounds. Public service vehicles need not reduce their interior lighting during an alert.

8-Dec-1944

After seeing improvements to the platforms of Sunderland Station, what about some improvement to the North Hall of the Station especially the lighting. For five years the hall has been in a condition that must be the gloomiest, most depressing place on the L N E R system by day as well as by night.

9-Dec-1944

Sunderland 6, Darlington 2. The next two games will decide who wins the Football League (North).

Huddersfield lead with 27 points, Sunderland are second with 26 points and Derby are third with 25 points.

10-Dec-1944

Britain's brighter Christmas budget. An extra ounce of tea each week for persons over 70. An additional half-pound of sweets for every one between six months and 18 years. An extra half-pound of margarine. Meat ration increased to 1s 10d on the week preceding Christmas.

11-Dec-1944

The Health Committee reports that the Corporation may not receive the type of temporary bungalows they prefer. The Estate Committee recommend the rent for these temporary bungalows should be 10 shillings per week, exclusive of rates, but with estimated water charges of 4s 1d. There were four types of temporary bungalows approved; Portal; Arcon Mark V; Uni-Seco and the Tarran. They all provide a living room, two bedrooms, kitchen, bathroom, WC, entrance porch and outside shed. The sites recommended for the temporary

bungalows are; 300 at High Southwick estate; 14 at Wellfield Recreation Ground; 24 at Southwick Oval; 9 at; Millburn Place Southwick; 6 at Maud Street Fulwell; 21 at Duke Street; 12 at Black Road Colliery Square; 10 at Gladstone Street; 17 at Williamson Terrace; 24 on the Town Moor; 25 at Hedworth Terrace; 11 at D'arcy Street; 55 at Whitehouse Road; 20 in Corporation Road; 15 at Percy Terrace allotments; 16 at South Johnson Street; 14 Carlyon Street and Tunstall Vale; 36 on land in Elms Street; 221 open space at Diamond Hall; 19 in Cleveland Road; 18 at Flodden Road frontage; 190 on land adjacent to The Nook; 8 in Hunter's Hall Road; 22 on Bede School playing fields and 180 on land to the west of Plains Farm Estate.

Sunderland Town Council adopted the provision of temporary houses under the Government's scheme as recommended by the Health Committee. It is now proposed to reduce the number on High Southwick Estate from 300 to 150 and at the Plains Farm Estate from 180 to 100 and build a 100 on the Springwell Farm Estate.

12-Dec-1944

Women's hats may be cheaper after March 1st, if the scheme is approved, manufactures hope to bring women back to the habit of wearing a smart hat instead of scarves and bandeaus.

Traders forecast that, this the 6th Christmas of the war, will see little relief from the Spartan menus.

14-Dec-1944

Mr Morrison, Home Secretary, told the Commons today that of nearly 16,000, youths picked by ballot and directed for training for under ground coal-mining, 148 had been sentenced to imprisonment for failing to comply or for leaving without consent. Some thought that it was an injustice that an 18 year-old should now be carrying the stigma of having a prison sentence just because they preferred to join the armed forces and fight for his country rather than dig for coal.

15-Dec-1944

In a sale by Richard Crow No. 29 Ewesley Road went for £855, while 10 cottages in Duncan Street, Pallion was sold for £150 each. Seven cottages in Brady Street, Pallion realised £140 each and bidding for four cottages in

Regent Terrace, Grangetown stopped at £130 each. Numbers 11-13 at the Green, Southwick raised £700.

Police, transport authority and the public give the thumbs-up to the tram barriers erected in Fawcett Street. Barriers are still to be erected in Derwent Street and at the Gas Office corner.

16-Dec-1944

Eating apples are in short supply and the first batch of nuts from Sunderland is fast running out. There was a chance of oranges for Christmas. Parents claimed that the quality of toys available this Christmas was poorer than it was last Christmas and the prices were higher.

Tram queue barriers in Fawcett Street

JL. Thompson launches the *EMPIRE ENSIGN* 3758t. 1966 scrapped Singapore with boiler damage.

Gateshead 1 Sunderland 2. Sunderland were still without Alex Hastings when they met Gateshead at Roker Park today but Jimmy Gorman returned to the team, and with Walshaw playing for Northern Command, Harry Bell moved over to out side left to make room for Lilley. The team was Heywood; Gorman and Eves;

Wallbanks, Lockie and J Bell; Spuhler Lilly Whitelum Laidman and H Bell. Conditions for the game was poor but Sunderland scraped a win, Whitelum and Harry Bell scored.

The German Army in the West begins 'Operation Wacht am Rhein' (Watch at the Rhine), with the objective of splitting the allied forces and capturing the strategic port of Antwerp. The attacking forces pouring forth from the Ardennes forest comprise of the 6th SS Panzer Army, 5th Panzer Army and the 7th Army providing flank support to the south of the line of advance. The German offensive manages to breakthrough the American front on a 70-mile front. (The Battle of the Bulge)

18-Dec-1944

There is a body of Wearside men, all volunteers, who receive no reward other than the feeling that they have done their duty, and of whom little have been seen or heard during the five years of war. Yet they have brought ashore from ships, by the aid of the rocket apparatus and breeches buoy, no fewer than 368 sailors. This is a record behind the work of the Roker Volunteer Life Saving Brigade. The Brigade is back 'home' tonight. Naval, military and RAF personnel have occupied the Brigade House since the beginning of the war and tonight the Brigade celebrated the handing back of their headquarters by a supper/smoker.

19-Dec-1944

Sunderland's lifeboat, the motor driven Edward and Isabella Erwin, has been launched 21 times and saved 21 people since the beginning of the war.

20-Dec-1944

Sunderland's Book Recovery drive ends with 341,000 collected. 326,260 went for salvage; 13,877 to the forces; 775 to hospitals and 86 to libraries.

Shortage of festive birds on Wearside. Rabbits are also in short supply. One dealer, before the war, was supplying 1000 rabbits a week but last week he had only 40 for sale.

21-Dec-1944

Officers of the 103rd Home Guard Rocket AA Battery held at their stand down dinner at the Bay Hotel tonight. Captain Alex Hastings on behalf of the officers and men of the battery presented a silver tankard to Major J Victor Thompson, commander of the Battery since March last year.

The 103rd Home Guard Rocket Anti Aircraft battery was formed at the beginning of November 1942, with Major J Y McLean as Commanding Officer. When in March of the following year Major McLean resigned owing to other duties, he was succeeded by Major J Victor Thompson, who was in fact the first Home Guard officer of the 9th Durham Battalion to be enrolled in the 'Z' Battery. At first it was known as the 'Z' Battery but later and more accurately known as a Rocket Battery. More than 2300 men were enrolled in the Battery between 1942 and the 'stand down' last September when the number on the roll was 1400. Almost 90 per cent were shipyard workers. The Battery started off with a batch of 500 men and two months later a second batch of 500 arrived. The build-up continued continually until March 8th this year when No. 8 relief were able to man all the projectors of the battery. The only occasion when the batty fired a salvo at the enemy was on May 23rd, 1943 when number 2 Relief was on duty during a vicious air raid on Sunderland. Many shift workers who had enrolled had to be discharged because of the difficulty in fitting in their work with the demands of the Battery and a number of other men who caused a good deal of trouble by their unwillingness to train and qualify. Some undeserved notoriety came to the Battery due to a Gunner being court-martialled on a charge of using insubordinate language to his superior officer. He received 28 days' detention, but served only half his sentence before rejoining the battery.

22-Dec-1944

Christmas holiday entertainment in Sunderland includes the pantomime Cinderella at the Empire beginning tomorrow for three weeks. A Christmas fair is being held in the Garrison Field. Cinemas will be open Christmas Day and Boxing Day. Dancers at Seaburn Hall and the New Rink. The Shipyards will be off Christmas Day Boxing Day and New Years Day. Wearmouth Colliery will only have Christmas Day and New Years Day as holiday.

The 2000 toys with a similar number of sweets from America have been distributed among the poorer children.

23-Dec-1944

Sunderland v Gateshead. A poor gate at Roker Park, under 20,000, saw Sunderland win.

24-Dec-1944

Alarm No.251: 05.59 – 06.15

A formation of specially adapted HE111 bombers approached the Northeast coast this morning. Under each of these bombers sat a deadly weapon - a V1 flying bomb, better known to us as a 'Doodlebug' or 'Buzz-bomb'. Thirty V1s were launched from positions over the North Sea between Skegness and Bridlington. The intended target was Manchester but their accuracy was such that only one reached its target with most falling throughout the North of England. Just after 6.00am eleven people were injured when a V1 landed on the cricket field at Tudhoe, Co. Durham. There was severe damage to 22 houses and slight damage to 368 other houses.

25-Dec-1944

Almost 400 wounded soldiers from Wearside hospitals will receive a Christmas parcel, contributed by Sunderland people, to make them feel that they had not been forgotten.

26-Dec-1944

Urgent operational necessity now require the use of unmasked headlamps on all service motor vehicles is announced by the Ministry of Home Security. Therefore the government has decided to extend the relaxation to civilian motor vehicles. The requirement that headlamps on motor vehicles should be fitted with a mask will be withdrawn, and may be used unobscured. With effect from today all restrictions on the sidelights and rear lights on motor vehicles and on the front lights of pedal cycles will be withdrawn.

Newcastle 3 Sunderland 1. Huddersfield are champions. All we're now interested in is the League Cup. Attendance 40,000.

29-Dec-1944

Preparations are now ready for what promises to be one of the brightest wartime New Year holidays Sunderland has experienced. Most popular outdoor attraction will be the football at Roker Park between Sunderland and Newcastle. Collieries and shipyards are to have Monday as a holiday. Most shops will be closed Monday but butcher shops will close for three days. There is a shortage of beer and spirits in the town because of the Christmas rush and this is likely to continue over the weekend. Cigarettes are also scarce although tobacco is freely available.

30-Dec-1944

Houses more than 200 miles apart were rocked and people tipped out of their beds early today by the worst earthquake shock that Britain had experienced for years. Northern England was the area chiefly affected but the shocks were felt in districts as far apart as Carlisle and Cromer and Wearsiders reported feeling tremors. Mrs Doreen Work, of 13 Roker Park Road, said, "I heard a noise like a distant explosion, the bed seemed to rock from side to side. It continued for some seconds and then died down. I thought it was a flying bomb." The general opinion was that the tremors were not as pronounced as that of the one 13 years ago.

Sunderland v Newcastle Utd. Under 20,000, half that at Newcastle. High scoring game which Sunderland just edges. Whitelum scored three.

31-Dec-1944

The Home Guard is disbanded. From today the Home Guard ceases to exist.

The Government expected 150,000 men to volunteer when Anthony Eden made his broadcast on 14th May 1940. Within 24 hours of the broadcast, 250,000 men had put down their names and by the end of May 1940 the number was between 300,000 and 400,000. By the end of June, 1940 the number of volunteers was just under 1½ million. The number peaked at 1.8 million in March 1943 and never fell below 1 million until the Home Guard was disbanded. Members of the Home Guard, aged between 17 and 65, were either in reserved occupations, too young or too old to serve in the normal army.

1945

Crowds in Fawcett Street to hear the Mayor's announcement that the war in Europe is over.

- VE-Day (Victory-in-Europe Day).
- VJ-Day (Victory-in-Japan Day) would not be declared until August 15.

1-Jan-1945

It was not intended to hold a watch night service at Sunderland Parish Church, but so many people were in the church at midnight that the Reverend R S Troop made a last minute decision to hold a service. For the first time in six years the bells of this church heralded in the New Year.

As in former years a large crowd gathered outside the town hall to welcome in the New Year.

Sunderland police report a quiet weekend and that for the first time in living memory; no person was locked up for drunkenness during the Christmas and the New Year holidays.

2-Jan-1945

In the first batch of men who arrived home this morning for a seven-day leave from the Continent, were two Sunderland men, Lance-corporal Sidney Teasdale of Easington Street, Monkwearmouth, and Private B B Charlton of Ocean Road, Grangetown.

Concrete from the demolished roadblocks is being dumped on the foreshore of Hendon to help to arrest the inroads of the sea.

3-Jan-1945

In 1943 the number of people killed in road accidents in the town were 17, whereas last year there were 19 fatal accidents when 10 adults and 9 children lost their lives. The greatest hazard to life would seem to be the boarding and dismounting from moving vehicles, as last year four people were killed and 68 injured performing this action.

4-Jan-1945

Although no frost was registered in Sunderland today, snow fell heavily in the afternoon and evening.

East Enders will, perhaps some time this year, lose another piece of the Town Moor, for the Corporation has decided to erect 24 of the 450 houses promised to the Borough on a site which fronts onto Wear Terrace and the Quadrant.

6-Jan-1945

Road conditions have been very difficult these last few days with snow, sleet and frost. Drivers have complained of lack of gritting done by the Corporation. On Durham Road at Humbledon yesterday police stopped horse-drawn vehicles until the horse's hooves had been covered. Ettrick Grove has been closed to horse-drawn traffic for a few days.

Sunderland v Darlington. Sunderland has scored only one goal from the last eight penalty kicks. Sunderland drew.

8-Jan-1945

Jaffa oranges and grapefruit were on sale in Sunderland today in the proportion of one pound of oranges and one pound of grapefruit for each ration book holder.

'Bevin Boys' and regular miners taking unauthorised longer holidays caused the substantial loss of coal in the Durham region over the Christmas and New Year holidays. More than 1100 trainees absented themselves from work far beyond the Christmas and New Year holidays and 85 per cent of them took five days or more in excess of the recognised holidays.

9-Jan-1945

The Sunderland wing of the Air Training Corps is to lose three of its six squadrons. Cadets from Squadrons 373, 1198, and 1882 will be absorbed into Squadrons 111 and 1863. Squadron 2000 will remain as it is. Over 1000 cadets have passed through the six Squadrons since they were formed.

10-Jan-1945

Chief Constable reported to today that 134 crimes had been committed in the quarter ending December 31st, 1944, an increase of 55 and the corresponding period in 1943. Of the accused 39 were juveniles compared with 52 in 1943

11-Jan-1945

Shopping snapshots: vacuum flasks have appeared in shop windows; Wooden soled shoes, now down to two coupons, are becoming scarce; Half coupon sales are being held in many stores; slightly soiled coats and costumes are reduced from 18 to 9 coupons; tinned marmalade (8 points) and tinned sausage meat (12 points) are plentiful again.

12-Jan-1945

SP. Austin launches the *PINEWOOD* 2853t. 1967 to Sweden and later converted to a lighter.

After lasting 13 weeks, the dispute at the Walker Naval yard on the Tyne, in which 520 Boilermaker's are at present involved, was ended today. Work will resume on Monday on the piecework rates they were on when taking strike action. They had wanted daywork rates.

13-Jan-1945

Darlington v Sunderland. Sunderland hold 38th place in the Cup qualifying competition, with three points out of a possible eight. Sunderland had a two-goal lead at half time but eventually lost.

15-Jan-1945

The parents of Gunner Sinclair White, of 28 Offerton Street, of the 125 Anti-tank Regiment RA and who was captured at Singapore, have learned that he has died while a prisoner of war.

160 people, almost all those present, enrolled at the first annual meeting of the Grangetown Community Association, held in St Aidan's Church Hall tonight. The following committee members were elected; Mr G Bolton, Chairman; Mr C Stocks, Vice Chairman; Mr D D Haswell, Secretary; Mr C Pickard, Treasurer; Mr S C Stocks, Press Secretary. Section Officers were; Mr W Bolton, Social; Mr T Burke, Hobbies; Mrs T Bolton, Education and Mrs T Gibbs, Youth (Girls).

17-Jan-1945

Sergeant Cyril Towell, of 8 Grange Crescent, Stockton Road, and a member of the 125 Anti-tank Regiment, has been officially reported as having died of his wounds while as a prisoner of war in Japanese hands. He is the third brother to be lost in the family, one of his brothers was killed at Dunkirk, during the evacuation, and the other in France five days after the invasion began.

18-Jan-1945

The A F S continues to pump out all the water tanks throughout the town in readiness for their disposal.

19-Jan-1945

Gales reaching 80 to 100 mph in some parts of the country swept Britain during the night causing considerable damage to property. The storm in Sunderland, accompanied by blinding snow and frost, did considerable damage to property but the greatest inconvenience came this morning when the electricity supply failed for several hours. The breakdown for two periods was blamed on the failure of the grid system as an area from the Tyne to North Yorkshire was affected.

20-Jan-1945

Sunderland v Middlesbrough. Sunderland had Lloyd at out side left against a Middlesbrough at Roker Park today and he had Horton as his partner. The team; Bircham; Gorman and Eves; Wallbanks, Lockie and Hastings; Spuhler, Laidman, Whitelum, Horton and Lloyd. Close on 6000 real football fans faced the elements and saw the game on Saturday made possible by the hard work of manager and staff on the pitch prior to kick-off. Sunderland won.

22-Jan-1945

Death of members of the 125 regiment reported to have died while in Japanese hands: - Gunner G Brennan, of 20 Holly Terrace. Gunner F Donkin, of 7 Friar Square, Ford Estate, missing at sea whilst a prisoner of war.

Officers of 13th Battalion Durham (South Hylton) Home Guard were entertained to dinner by their commanding officer Colonel A Allan at the Grand Hotel Sunderland on Saturday night. In his address Colonel Alan said that the battalion had been involved in a greater operational role than any other battalion in the County. They were the first Battalion to provide personnel for naval guns and for 'A' Troop of the Heavy Anti Aircraft.

Mr E H Sinclair, Clerk to the Sunderland Rural District Council, gave a summary of the harm done by enemy bombing in raids over Sunderland Rural Areas. There were 20 raids. Almost 3500 houses were damaged and all have now been repaired. When a number of houses were destroyed in Ryhope rescue workers found £500 in money. In all the raids no deaths occurred in any of the shelters provided. There have been a dozen deaths but most of them were the result of people not staying in their shelters.

23-Jan-1945

The Ministry of Food's announcement that we may have an official rationing of potatoes in the north-east within the next fortnight brings to a head the many stories and complaints of late about the shortage of potatoes. The past week or two an unofficial rationing has been in force in many parts of Sunderland and so far there's no sign of any improvement.

24-Jan-1945

Sunderland's Housing Exhibition, held in the Museum and Art Gallery, opened today to February 7th. Visitors will have the opportunity of seeing, in wood instead of steel, as it will be when erected, the Ministry of Works Portal house. The Portal will be erected in various parts of town as previously announced.

Sunderland experienced its coldest day for sometime today when the temperature fell to 16 degrees Fahrenheit. Milk froze solid on the doorstep. Plains Farm school had to be closed because of a failure in the heating system. The Wear froze at South Hylton, a rare happening.

Charged with being absent from work on two occasions without a reasonable excuse, James Olsen (21), of Sans Street South, an apprentice riveter at Short Brothers shipyard, was fined £5 on the first charge and bound over on the second. On a further charge of being persistently late Olsen, was also fined £5. Records showed that out of 69 days he was absent on 37 days and late on 32. John George Hind (19), of Fell Road, also an apprentice riveter, suffered the same penalties for being absent and persistently late. Out of 48 working days he was absent on 15 occasions and late on 32.

25-Jan-1945

There was very little improvement in weather conditions in Sunderland today. Ponds and streams remained frozen over and there were skating on the park's lakes.

26-Jan-1945

'Hill View' in Alexandra Road was sold last night to Mr Luigi Maggiore, of 137 Rhyope Road, for £1,800. The house, sold with vacant possession, is a semi-detached villa with an entrance hall, two reception rooms, kitchen, three bedrooms, garden and outbuildings including garage.

Tomorrow's football at Middlesbrough is called off because of weather conditions.

HMS MANNERS was hit and sunk by a torpedo with the loss of four officers and 39 ratings, while 15 others were injured. One of the injured who later died was W Cheal (18) of Sunderland whose was buried in Bishopwearmouth Cemetery.

"Every German must except the fact that this is the final showdown" so said Hitler's own newspaper Voelkischer Beobachter today, adding; "About one third of Germany has become a bombed area, and sometimes looks likes a scene in the immediate rear of the frontline".

27-Jan-1945

Three Sunderland sisters, daughters of Mr and Mrs J Barkes, of 63 Balmoral Terrace, Grangetown, are among the many North Country girls now employed in the Midlands. Lillian (22) was previously employed in the hosiery department of Jopling's; Susan (25) worked for Kemp's Stores Ltd., and Marjorie (39) for F W Woolworth's & Co. Ltd. Now they all work in a tube shop of an aircraft factory. Their brother John of the DLI is a prisoner of war in Germany.

A tramcar proceeding south along Bridge Street jumped to the points at Mackie's corner and crashed into another tram coming in the opposite direction. No one was injured, but the conductress of one tram, Lillian Hay (24), of 34 Sandringham Road, suffered slight shock. Both trams were badly damaged and had to be withdrawn from service.

29-Jan-1945

Snowstorms in Sunderland and District have caused widespread damage. The Cleansing Department have been busily engaged, both night and day, clearing snow. 300 men and staff, reinforced by another 100 men supplied by the Employment Exchanges, have been working on Sunderland's main roads and streets. Conditions in the area around Sunderland have been very bad, and roads running inland from the coast have been completely blocked.

30-Jan-1945

The controversy over the proposed felling of trees at Ford Estate has started up again. The long awaited report from an expert of the Forestry Commission recommends that 198 trees should be removed, in addition to 25, which are already dead.

The Ford Hall School grounds, states the report, should be virtually cleared of the elm trees and a few other trees which are very near to the caretaker's house. Also to be taken away are some near the school itself, which have been damaged by building work. There is no serious problem in the Havelock school grounds and only a little thinning is proposed. Between Front Road and Felstead Crescent the damage done is so great that complete tree felling is recommended.

It was recommended that 31 trees at Ford Hall School and four at Havelock School, 53 in Hylton Road, Fordham Road and Fordenbridge Crescent, 10 in Friar Road, 92 in Front Road and Felstead Crescent, three in General Havelock Road and three in the gardens of Fordham Road, Front Road and Fordfield Road this is a total of 198 the idea trees plus of course the 25 that are already dead.

1-Feb-1945

Charles Bell and Sons a sold a double-fronted four-room cottage, 27 Ridley Terrace, Hendon, for £352 10s. The self-contained flats 13, 14, 15 and 16 Marion Street, Villette Road, each comprising four rooms, scullery and bathroom on the ground floor, and five rooms, scullery and bathroom on the first floor were sold for £652 10s. The dwelling-house 16 Dunelm, Durham Road, comprising six rooms, kitchen and bathroom realised £702 10s.

2-Feb-1945

Paper bags and wrapping paper, stain, varnish and lacquer, opera glasses and binoculars, and infant feeding bottles and teats have been added to the list of price-regulated goods.

Mr Herbert Morrison in Parliament today said that in view of the reduced risks of heavy incendiary attacks he felt justified in authorising the N.F.S. to begin removing emergency water installations.

3-Feb-1945

Gateshead 2 Sunderland 1. Sunderland was without Eves, who was suffering from bronchial trouble, at Gateshead today and Whitelum was getting married. The team was Bircham; Gorman and Stelling; Wallbanks, Lockie and Hastings; Spuhler, Laidman, Walshaw, Bell and Burbanks. History repeated itself at Gateshead, Sunderland lost in the last two minutes of the game. Gateshead played better on the treacherous conditions.

The old Eye Infirmary building in Stockton Road has been taken over by Price's (Tailor's) Ltd., who will use the premises for training personnel for their new clothing factory, which there are to occupy in Sunderland.

5-Feb-1945

Jean Pounder, 11 year-old, of 32 Catherine Street, is another of Sunderland's budding stars. Jean, who attends Diamond Hall School, has appeared in the shipyard canteens, where she entertained the workers with her dancing and singing.

6-Feb-1945

In an effort to relieve the housing shortage, seven Nissans huts, built close to the old barrage balloon sites to house the balloon crews, have been taken over and passed for habitation. The seven are situated in the Ewesley Street, Mount Road, Mowbray Park, Silksworth Row, Backhouse Park, Hendon sports field, and one near the Boy's Orphanage. Seven families now occupy them. Two of them, one in Mount Road and that in Hendon sports field are occupied by evacuees from the South and at the other five have Sunderland families who have lost their homes from air raids.

7-Feb-1945

At a Housing Brains Trust held in the town hall, mention was made that the erection of a Phoenix prefabricated house would be started in Sunderland next week. The question was asked, "would anyone other than service men be able to obtain a house?" As a shipyard worker was making his contribution to the war effort and it was not his fault that he was not in the services. Another question was why the houses could not be built with rounded corners. Councillor Mrs Huggins observed that as a housewife she thought that they should have rounded corners and they should not mind any increase in the cost too much. All the members of the trust said that they favoured electricity for household purposes, but Mrs Huggins and Alderman Cohen declared a that they would like to see at least one coal fire in each house.

8-Feb-1945

From today oranges will be on sale in Sunderland at the rate of one pound per head.
50,000 British and Canadians troops with 500 tanks and 1,034 guns launch a new offensive into the Reichswald, to the Southeast of Nijmegen.

9-Feb-1945

Sunderland Port Health Authority had only six cases of infectious diseases to deal with last year, and in no case did the infectious disease spread from the Port to the Borough. They were, however, 92 British and 48 foreign seamen treated at the VD clinic. The number of visits paid to vessels in connection with the destruction of rats was 815 and the number of rats destroyed was 610. In warehouses, wharfs and industrial premises on the docks and riverside, 1834 rats were destroyed and in addition 4199 poison baits were laid at various points where trapping was conceded futile, the results of which cannot be properly estimated.

10-Feb-1945

Horatio Carter played for Sunderland at Roker Park today against Gateshead. Walshaw led the attack. Eves was still in the doctor's hands. The team was Bircham; Gorman and Stelling; Wallbanks, Lockie and Hastings; Spuhler, Carter, Walshaw, Laidman and Burbanks. Carter made the journey from the Midlands on a 48-hour pass. The 14,000 plus at the game gave him a tremendous welcome. Sunderland won by three clear goals.
Wm Doxford launches the MEADOWBANK 7307t. Scrapped Taiwan Sept. 1968

11-Feb-1945

The Housing Exhibition closed today and 30,274 people had seen it. The prefabricated house in the show came in for much more praise than criticism. Women were greatly impressed with the labour-saving kitchen equipment on view. Pickersgill's launches the LST 3033 4175t for the Royal Navy. Renamed EMPIRE SHEARWATER in 1956. Scrapped in 1963.

Tank Landing Craft LST3033 in Hendon Dock

12-Feb-1945

Initial operations have begun on the erection of 30 Phoenix type prefabricated houses in Johnson Street. Workmen are busy clearing the site, which was formerly occupied by homes demolished under a slum clearance order. The clearing of the site, which includes the demolishing of a brick emergency water supply basin, and the laying of foundations are expected to take about a fortnight.

13-Feb-1945

The Education Committee's proposal to convert John Priestman's old house on the Seaburn front into a remand home for " 12 naughty girls" and spend £3,000 to do so, caused a lot of criticism. If wooden huts had been good enough to house our sick and wounded of the last war why is it that 12 delinquent girls must have something more palatial. The opening of a rehabilitation unit for our own wounded was thought to be a better proposal for this fine house in such a pleasant spot. The proposal was defeated by 30 votes to 21

Bartram's launch the EMPIRE ADEN 7308t. 1967 aground Okinawa, total loss, scrapped.

Beginning of the bombing of Dresden. Over the days of the 13th and 14th, between 35,000 and 135,000 people were killed. The real figure will never be known as the City contained many refugees.

15-Feb-1945

If you wanted to hire a taxi in 1945 the fare was 1s 3d up to a mile and then 6d for every additional half-mile or part. Double fares were permitted for hire between 12 midnight and 7.0am.

Mr Bevin, Minister of Labour, told Parliament today that, between March 1st, 1944 and January 27th, 1945, 18,796 men were directed to the mines, and of these 17,293 have actually entered training. On the policy of directing boys by ballot, Mr Bevin stated, that it would remain unchanged until the war with Germany is over.

16-Feb-1945

The policy of the Estates Committee in letting the temporary prefabricated bungalows erected in the Borough was explained. The Committee has allocated 40% to bombed out people, 40% to discharged servicemen and Merchant Navy and 20% to hardship cases. Although there are many applicants for these bungalows the Council is restricted by the size of the applicant's families. They can't be let to families of more than four persons including children.

17-Feb-1945

Whitelum was again leader of Sunderland's attack against Hartlepools United at Roker Park today in the League Cup game. This is the only change in the side that won against Gateshead. Bircham; Gorman and Stelling; Wallbanks, Lockie and Hastings; Spuhler, Laidman, Whitelum, Walshaw and Burbanks. Two more points from the four to be played for may place Sunderland in the first round of the competition proper. At the moment they hold 28th place. Middlesbrough, our last game, cannot possibly qualify. Sunderland scored six goals between the 6th and 17th minute of the second half.

19-Feb-1945

Dixon Walton (31), of East Cross Street, charged at Sunderland Magistrate's Court today with being absent from work at Silksworth Colliery on September 11th, 15th and 20th, was sent to prison for three months on each charge, with sentences to run concurrently. He pleaded guilty. He had appeared before the court before for the same offence and had been fined by the Pit production committee.

20-Feb-1945

Apples were the main attraction for shoppers today, there were queues of up to 300 strong. Mackintosh Reds and Winesnap, American apples, crowded the shop windows yesterday when sales started. Fruiterers were busy coping with the crowds from early-morning. Queues were so long that policemen were needed to keep the footpaths clear. There were enough apples in the town to provide everyone with a pound per head.

21-Feb-1945

A plea for the return of silk stockings for women factory workers, as soon as possible. " Bare legs of our working women and girls in the 6th winter of the war were a tribute to their grit and determination".

22-Feb-1945

Barnes, Welch and Barnes sold by auction today a four-roomed house, 2 Tunstall Terrace, for £570.

23-Feb-1945

Today being the 2000th day of the war. 1000 days ago the Germans were on the Caucasus hoping to join hands with the Japanese. Now the defenders of Stalingrad are close to Berlin, the defenders of Alexandria are battling with the Germans on the Rhine and MacArthur is back in Manila.

24-Feb-1945

Hartlepools Utd. 3 Sunderland 1. Housam was drafted into the attack at inside right. Walshaw led the attack. Bircham; Gorman and Stelling; Wallbanks, Lockie and Hastings; Spuhler Housam Walshaw, Laidman and Burbanks.

26-Feb-1945

With labour and materials not yet as plentiful as had been hoped. The Government means to push on with production of the temporary bungalows until permanent house building gets into its stride.

27-Feb-1945

Sunderland and District Trade Council stressed their support in the campaign to keep the Ford Estate trees. Wm Doxford launches the *PUNDAU* 7295t. Scrapped Singapore Oct 1973.

28-Feb-1945

Sunderland Town Council is to be asked by the Estates Committee to open Newcastle Road plunge baths this summer, along with a proposal to increase admission charges from 2d to 4d for children. This should not make much difference as children have the opportunity of going once a week, with the school, free of charge. There are now some 13,000 children in youth organisations in Sunderland and there is obvious overcrowding at High Street of Baths.

1-Mar-1945

A Sunderland shoe shop displays a notice warning customers that they cannot be allowed to try on shoes unless they are wearing stockings. Much of the stock, says the notice, has been soiled by people trying on shoes in their bare feet.

Allegations made against Mr and Mrs Eggleston, of Percy Terrace, that they had made considerable profits on hairnets, hairpins, combs, elastic and similar articles from a stall in Darlington market. Mr Eggleston was fined £25 and his wife £17. A hairnet was sold for 6d (legal price $4^{1}/_{2}$d), a packet of 24 hairpins for 4d (legal price 21 for 2d), three yards off elastic for 2s (legal price $4^{1}/_{2}$d) and a tail comb for 2s 6d (legal charge 8d).

Shipbuilding Corporation Ltd launches the *EMPIRE PROME* 7086t 1970 Scrapped Istanbul.

2-Mar-1945

A number of defendants at the Magistrates Court pleaded guilty to trespassing in a prohibited area. Alderman Cairns said Hendon beach is still a prohibited area and dangerous for people to go there. On the morning of February 12th a Police Reserve Constable N Walsh apprehended the defendants on the beach, all defendants had sacks filled with wood and coke. Jane Sanderson (44) of Robinson Terrace; Sarah Lurch (28) of Robinson Terrace; Sarah Greene (39) of Winchester Terrace; Hannah Smith (41) of the Boys Orphanage; Ralphetta Iley (37) of Henry Street and five juveniles were each ordered to pay four shillings costs.

3-Mar-1945

Sunderland v Gateshead. Whitelum, Walshaw and Laidman were not available to meet Gateshead at Roker Park in the league cup match. The team was; Bircham; Gorman and Stelling; Housam, Wallbanks J, and Hastings; Spuhler, Lilley, Wallbanks H, Taylor and Burbanks. With Gateshead winning Sunderland must win at Middlesbrough on March 17th to have any chance of qualifying for the final stages of the Cup competition.

4-Mar-1945

Alarm No.253: 01.07 - 02.37. In the early hours of the morning, seventy night fighters roamed over eastern England for 3½ hours. Targets included some in Northumberland, County Durham and Yorkshire. The Luftwaffe mounted Operation Gisella on this night, sending approximately 200 night fighters to follow the various bomber forces to England. This move took the British defences partly by surprise and the Germans shot down 20 bombers - 8 Halifaxes of No 4 Group, 2 Lancasters of No 5 Group, 3 Halifaxes, 1 Fortress and 1 Mosquito of No 100 Group and 3 Lancasters and 2 Halifaxes from the Heavy Conversion Units which had been taking part in the diversionary sweep. 3 of the German fighters crashed, through flying too low; the German fighter which crashed near Elvington airfield was the last Luftwaffe aircraft to crash on English soil during the war.

Judging for the 'Miss Venus 1945' at the Havelock Theatre resulted in Miss Evelyn Richmond of 33 Rosedale Street being declared the winner. Runners up were; Miss Ethel Johnson of 71 Dame Dorothy Street; Miss Betty Middleton of 10 Salisbury Street and Miss Angela Gourley of 21 Elmwood Street.

5-Mar-1945

George Wimpy and Co., of Newcastle, are given the contract for the advance preparation of housing sites for road and sewer works at Springwell Farm Estate at a cost of £49,799 10d and J W Wight (Contractors) Ltd, Sunderland was given the contract for the Southwick estate with their tender of £13,305 7s 5d.

Mr Charles Jude sold, with vacant possession, the dwelling house of 7 Exeter Street for £425. The property comprises three rooms with scullery, bath, yard and out houses.

6-Mar-1945

Anticipating the opening of Sunderland's beaches, the Corporation have allowed for the additional income of £1,000 from the hire of tents and deck chairs, £350 from the boating pool and £270 from the miniature railway. Last year only that portion from the north boundary to the Seaburn Hotel was available to the public.

7-Mar-1945

Sunderland trams are expected to be running to Seaburn by the old route from Roker this summer. Seaburn residents have got used to the buses as a quicker means of transport.

8-Mar-1945

A large number of chairs have been stolen from St Mary Magdalene Church, Millfield. Systematic thieving has been going on over a long period from this church, a valuable blue carpet having disappeared from St Francis Chapel a few months ago.

Charles Bell and Sons sold by auction 6 Robert Street, Millfield, for £440.

9-Mar-1945

Sunderland magistrates granted an application from C Vaux & Co. to transfer a licence from the Walworth Castle, in Walworth Street, to a new public house that the firm proposed to erect on the site, which was formally St Marks Vicarage in Chester Road purchased for £2,500. It was proposed to build a licensed premise that will have every modern convenience and will include an indoor bowling green. The district in which the new premise will serve has a population of approximately 9000 and the nearest licensed premise to the west of the site was the Grindon Mill Inn.

George Rogers, of 8 Lawson Crescent, was admitted to Monkwearmouth hospital today suffering from head injuries received when he fell 20 ft down a ship's hold at the Shipbuilding Corporation yard at Southwick. Robert Bell (18), of 12 Rainton Street, was also admitted with injuries received while working for the firm of J L Thompson and Sons Ltd.

10-Mar-1945

The whole of the bus services run by the Northern General Transport Company Limited were suspended this morning when drivers, conductors and conductresses came out on strike. About 400 vehicles are standing idle and about 3000 men and women employees are involved. The cause of the dispute was that later bus services were due tonight to be instituted on the Company's routes.

Sunderland v Darlington. Sunderland was without Hastings, Gorman and Burbanks. Had it not been for Alex Lockie and Stelling, Darlington might have got into double figures.

12-Mar-1945

The only buses running from Sunderland today is the Economic Company service to South Shields, the Triumph service to Middlesbrough and the ABC service to Darlington.

Lieutenant Colonel R H. Bartram, opening the 24th Durham (Sunderland) Home Guard Rifle Club at the Seaburn Drill Hall, wished the members a happy future and the continuance of the spirit of comradeship that had existed in the battalion since its inception. So far the membership is 120.

13-Mar-1945

In view of the difference of opinion among the experts, on the question of the removal of the trees at Ford Estate, the Chairman of the Estates Committee was asked if he would recommend acceptance of the report, obtained by the residents, from Mr Booth. Councillor J W Wilkinson assured Ford Estate residents that they would leave as many trees as possible standing and even go as far as to accept the Booth report, providing that it did not commit the Corporation to any liabilities.

On Wearside, army lorries continue to take miners and war workers to and from their places of employment.

JL. Thompson launches the *EMPIRE JOY* for MOWT. 1967 Scrapped Taiwan after fire damage.

14-Mar-1945

The wartime output of merchant ships from the Wear shipbuilding yards has exceeded 1,500,000 gross tons. Between September 1939 and September 1944 245^1/$_2$ new vessels have been built and launched from the nine Sunderland yards, which includes an entirely new yard at Southwick opened in 1943. The figures, supplied by the Wear Shipbuilders Association (and released by the censor for publication), give some indication to the great effort by the Wear shipbuilding firms and the people in keeping open the nation's ocean lifelines.

This total does not include the naval construction or work done in repairer's yards. Not only was an entirely new yard with three births constructed, owned by the British Shipbuilding Corporation on a derelict site at Southwick, but three other new berths have been constructed at existing yards on the river. The increase in welding has gone on apace.

Compulsory purchase proposed of 248 acres of land west of Grindon Lane for Borough housing.

Eldon House, Chester Road, together with two cottages and 12 stables was sold for £1,525. 22 Clanny Street for £150 and 14 John Candlish Road for £340.

Laing's launch the *BEECHWOOD* 8197t. Nov.1973 broken up Kaohsiung.

15-Mar-1945

The boating pool at Seaburn is being cleaned out and so far 250 tons of rubbish has been removed. It was hoped to get the 'speedboats' into use again this summer, but as yet it was not known if petrol, to run the boats, would be available.

In his annual report the Probation Service says, "The number of youths in the town between the ages of 15 and 21 who will neither work regularly nor serve the Country in any way is increasing."

16-Mar-1945

For selling bread and cakes to unregistered persons, fines and costs totalling £82 were imposed on Smith and Stephenson Ltd., of Dundas Street and three of its customers; Harry King, of Association Road, Andrew Bainbridge, of Barnet's buildings, Southwick, and Sarah Davison, of Dean Terrace.

17-Mar-1945

Middlesbrough 2 Sunderland 1. By beating Sunderland, Middlesbrough made sure that for the third successive year Sunderland would not qualify for the Cup competition proper.

20-Mar-1945

30 per cent of Sunderland's quota of temporary houses will have to be taken in the American type of temporary house. The remaining will be of the Phoenix type. The American style is a wooden structure faced with asbestos sheeting on the outside and is somewhat smaller than the Phoenix House. It was thought that the interior fittings were inferior to that in the Phoenix House.

21-Mar-1945

The first permanent housing after the war will probably have to be built without baths, to be added later when materials become more available.

22-Mar-1945

Only people who need vacuum flasks for work will now be able to buy them, according to a Board of Trade order. Priority certificates will have to be produced before purchasing a flask. Other goods requiring a priority certificate are blankets and lino.

23-Mar-1945

The Northeast bus strike has now officially ended. At midnight tonight the Workmen services will be restarted and normal passenger service will resume tomorrow morning.

24-Mar-1945

Sunderland 2 Gateshead 2. In their league game against Gateshead at Roker Park today, Sunderland was without Hastings and Spuhler. The team was; Bircham; Gorman and Stelling; Fleck, Lockie and Housam; Purvis, Taylor, Whitelum, Laidman and Burbanks. The official attendance at Roker Park on Saturday was 3200. Sunderland had a two-goal lead after 35 minutes but the game ended as a two-goal draw.

The comparison of earnings by shipyard workers in a typical week in July 1944, with earnings in October 1938

	1944	1938
Men	£7.4s	£6.6s
Boys	£2.8s	£1.15s
Women	£3.12s	No women worked

A table of hours worked showed that in 1938 the average hours worked by men was 45, a figure which rose to 53.5 last year. Boys and Youths worked 47.4 hours weekly last year compared with 44.9 before the war. Women's hours last year was 44.8.

Montgomery's 21st Army Group attacks across the Rhine, 15 miles North of Duisberg in the Wesel area, after 3,500-gun barrage. 16,870 paratroops land across the river Rhine in Operation 'Plunder' and succeed in linking up with advancing British troops and establishing four bridgeheads.

26-Mar-1945

Sunderland Corporation faced opposition from ex-shopkeepers when they announced their intention to use the site of the small shopping centre at the junction of Fulwell Road and Laburnum Terrace, for the purpose of erecting temporary bungalows. The Parachute Mine that fell on May 16 1943 destroyed these properties.

27-Mar-1945

SP. Austin launches the *EMPIRE MAYA* 394t. 1947 *MERLIMAU*, Straits SS Co. 9.6.59 Capsized and sunk by tidal wave off Dwarka.

The last V2 rocket to fall on Britain falls at Orpington in Kent at 1645hrs

28-Mar-1945

Residents of Ford Estate have 'won the day'. It means that of a total of 160 trees in the belt adjoining Hylton Road, only about a dozen will be felled; 9 of the 50 trees in Ford Hall Drive will go; almost all of those at the back of Front Road; and some 28 in the interests of safety will be removed from Ford Hall School grounds.

29-Mar-1945

The whole of the beaches from the north to the south boundary are now open to the public. Bathers are warned that they enter the water at their own risk. The Corporation can accept no responsibility for any injury, which may occur. Barbwire has lain submerged for almost six years, and this cannot all be cleared in a short time. There's also a danger of explosives being brought in by the tide.

Shipyards will be closed for the whole of the holiday weekend for the first time since the war began.

Wm Doxford launches the *AMBASSADOR* 7312t. Disabled with engine trouble 18.02.1964 in North Atlantic. Abandoned by crew, later re-boarded. Taken in tow but sank.

Laing's launch the *BORUS* 3735t. Scrapped 1968.

31-Mar-1945

Sunderland Corporation Transport dispute is to be placed in the hands of the Conciliation Officer of the Ministry of Labour and if the result is not satisfactory more than 600 bus and tram workers will strike tomorrow night. A new running Schedule is due to come into operation on Tuesday.

Gateshead 4 Sunderland 2. After being two down at half-time Sunderland got to two goals all then lost the match in the last eight minutes.

1-Apr-1945

Today, Easter Sunday, is the real opening of the ice cream season this year. It is the beginning of a new rationing period with 30,000 small ice-cream firms, 90 per cent of the trade, now able to make ice cream again. These firms used fresh milk before the war, but now have to use skimmed milk powder and margarine. To replace the use of fresh milk, the reconstituted milk has first to be made from the skimmed milk powder, margarine and sugar.

Clocks are to be forward one hour tonight as Double Summer Time comes into force. It will continue till July 15th.

2-Apr-1945

Today Sunderland people had to make the most of the Easter Monday Bank Holiday without the convenience of the town's transport service. This is the first tramless Bank Holiday since the service was started nearly 50 years ago. Tomorrow the effects will be more serious as the absence of Transport will be a definite handicap to thousands of workers. The Echo reports that the cause of the stoppage was of a matter of five minutes, more or less, in running time on two tram routes and called the striker's action irresponsible.

Newcastle Utd. 0 Sunderland 3. Sunderland's fortunes changed at Newcastle today. They won 3 - 0, assisted by a first goal from Brown, the Brentford forward, and two by Cliff Whitelum.

3-Apr-1945

Sir Arthur Lambert (ex Regional Commissioner) was asked why the northeast had escaped from more widespread destruction, he answered, that in his opinion this was due to, among other things, to the strong anti aircraft defences and the natural industrial haze, which constantly obscured vital targets.

5-Apr-1945

The deadlock in Sunderland's transport workers strike continues but there was some improvement in the transport situation for Wearsiders this morning, when the Ministry of Transport arranged army lorries to run from outlying districts to the shipyards. 25 lorries, driven by servicemen, will take approximately 1000 shipyard workers to their homes tonight.

Shipyard workers are arriving from a quarter to a half hour late, the management are not quite sure if it's due to the lack of transport or whether the men are feeling the effect of Double Summer Time and the consequent early rising.

6-Apr-1945

Sunderland Corporation trams and buses will be running again tomorrow, much to the relief of Wearsiders, who for five days have had to walk instead of ride. The men and women Transport employees at a mass meeting tonight decided to accept the arbitration offer from the Transport Committee. The return to work is the result of the Mayor of Sunderland, Councillor John Young, intervening and relieving the deadlock.

7-Apr-1945

Sunderland 0 York City 0. Argos thought that the game today was the worst game he had witnessed at Roker Park since it opened in September 1898. York City was not good enough to score. Sunderland's attack did not perform well and Eddie Maguire was so much out of condition, from his return from the Middle East, that he should never had played, as for the rest of Sunderland's attack, the least said the sooner mended. They would not have scored if they had played at all night.

9-Apr-1945

The hire of tents and chairs at Seaburn is to cost 50% more. The new scale of charges are; chairs (all day) from 3d to 6d; tents (all day) 2/- to 2/6d.

10-Apr-1945

The draw for first round of the Tyne-Wear-Tees competition was Sunderland verses Hartlepools United; York City verses Darlington; Middlesbrough versus Huddersfield, with Gateshead getting a bye. Games will be played on a home and away basis starting April 21st.

Churchill reveals British Empire casualty figures up to this point as 306,984 killed. Total casualties are 1,126,802, merchant navy losing 34,161 dead or captured. Civilian casualties are 59,793 killed and 84,749 injured.

11-Apr-1945

The school medical officer, Dr A S Hepplethwaite, in his report for 1944, said that the nutrition of school children had not appeared to have been affected by wartime conditions. As regards cleanliness, the report says that 25,000 children were examined and 3,325 (13.3%) were found to be unclean. In all cases of cleanliness the home conditions are investigated and there is a follow up by a school nurse until the children present a cleaner appearance. There were 1500 cases of scabies. Only 44% (80% is recommended) of children between 5 and 15 in Sunderland have been immunised against diphtheria. For children between one year and five years old the percentage is 68%.

12-Apr-1945

"The damage to trees, grass and flowers in our parks is so extensive that the Borough Parks Committee and the Watch Committee recently held a joint meeting to see what steps could be taken to stop it", said Mr F Williamson, presiding in the Sunderland Juvenile Court today, when 36 children, whose ages ranged from eight to 15, were accused of trespassing in Barnes Park between March 21st and the 23rd. All the children admitted the offence and also admitted that they had been warned at school against trespassing. There were each fined 15 shillings. Two of the juveniles who did not appear were fined the maximum penalty of £1. Magistrates at Sunderland juvenile court today had one of the busiest days for a considerable time. There were, in total, 64 children, whose ages ranged from eight to 16, and almost £50 was collected in fines and other costs.
SP. Austin launches *EMPIRE MAYMOUNT* 394t. 1947 MELUAN, Straits SS Co. 1955 ashore and abandoned Gopinath, India - total loss.
Pickersgill's launch *HMS LUCE BAY* a Bay Class Frigate. Ex – Loch Glass

13-Apr-1945

Grindon Lane Estate is to be turned into a model 'neighbourhood unit' housing estate of 1600 houses. The plans exhibited show the estate designed as a self contained small township with a community centre, bowling green, tennis courts, three secondary schools, two junior schools, to infant schools, four nursery schools, public baths, library, Fire Station, churches, health centre, two public houses, police houses, a major shopping centre, and two subsidiary shopping centres. It was proposed to have no front fences and the carriage way will be flanked by wide grass margins.

14-Apr-1945

York City 4 Sunderland 2. Sunderland's defeat was not unexpected in view of the lack of experience in the defence.
The promised 3 pints a week is under threat if the Milk Vessel Recovery Unit is unable recover the thousands of '*lost*' milk bottles.
It is now more than 15 days since any V bomb or any other enemy air activity was reported over England.

16-Apr-1945

Wearside had its warmest day of the year today when the temperature rose to 72 degrees.
At an inquest on Gordon Bramley Clayton (23), plater, of 38 Annie Street, Fulwell, a verdict of accidental death was recorded. He was killed on Thursday when a steel plate fell on him fracturing his skull. He was employed at George Clark's Southwick engine works.

18-Apr-1945

Vandalism and hooliganism are the latest terms to be applied to the bad behaviour of some of Sunderland's children and young people. It is the minority that is guilty of this anti-social conduct, but the few can make matters very unpleasant for the many. Some months ago a conference was held and there was much talk and many suggestions but nothing much seems to have happened. The complaints of bad conduct and damage have continued just as numerous. Last year £800 in fines and damages were ordered by magistrates to be paid by children and their parents, but still the evil goes on. Children often leave the court smiling at the leniency of their punishment.
The Police report on juvenile crime stated that last year, 121 boys and 13 girls were proceeded against for larceny; 94 boys and three girls for house and shop breaking; 11 boys and three girls for other indictable offences; 88 boys and seven girls proceeded against for wilful damage; 87 boys and five girls for disorderly behaviour in the streets; 41 boys were dealt with for other non indictable offences. These figures give a total of 431 boys and 29 girls proceeded against during 1944.
It was officially announced today that the total of prisoners taken on the Western front since D-Day and up to Monday was 2,055,565.

19-Apr-1945

The cigarette shortage, which had been acute in Sunderland for the last fortnight, will be relieved today, as a large consignment of cigarettes has just reached the town after a long delay. A railway truck containing 117 cases, some 3 million cigarettes, was dispatched by rail, from the manufacturer in Nottingham, on March 27th.

Beaches were crowded and almost reached pre-war attendance levels, while ice-cream and cool drinks were in great demand

20-Apr-1945

Licensing Magistrates today granted C Vaux and Sons the exchange of licence from the Walworth Castle, Walworth Street, to their newly required premises at St Mark's Vicarage, Chester Road. St Mark's Vicarage premises were required for £2,500. An indoor bowling green has been tried at the Alexandra Hotel, Grangetown, and had proved most successful.

Mr Charles Jude sold, with vacant possession, 27 Hurstwood Road, comprising five rooms, kitchenette and bathroom, for £865.

21-Apr-1945

Sunderland 5 Hartlepools Utd. 0. The introduction of Cyril Brown, newly signed from Brentford, made all the difference to the attack. Wallbanks also played very well at outside left.

23-Apr-1945

All restrictions on the display of lights from shops and houses will end today, but dim-out will continue in a five-mile belt around the coast.

24-Apr-1945

From the beginning of the war to the end of 1944, shipyards in the United Kingdom completed 1240 new merchant ships totalling 5,722,532 gross tons. The Wear's contribution to this total was well over one and a half million tons (26 per cent) and William Doxford's and Sons came second in the list of firms of the whole kingdom with the highest individual output. The total of 71 ships of 470,304 gross tons was only exceeded by Lithgows on the Clyde, who built 80 ships of 506,968 gross tons. Harland and Wolff of Belfast came third with 434,335 gross tons. J L Thompson and Sons were 5th with 291,210 gross tons.

25-Apr-1945

Following the introduction of the new Education Act, the Sunderland Education Committee adopted recommendations to the town council that 17 schools be renamed 'Modern School' and two others to be renamed 'Grammar School'. The Bede Collegiate Boys school becomes the Bede Boys Grammar school and the Bede Girls become the Bede Girls Grammar school.

An order from the Ministry of Home Security defines the Durham area as included in the five mile coastal dim out as follows; South Shields, Sunderland, West Hartlepool, Hartlepool, and Jarrow. The Urban Districts of Boldon, Hebburn, Hetton, Houghton-le-Spring, and Seaham. The Rural Districts of Easington and Sunderland. In the Rural District of Durham the parish of Shadforth.

26-Apr-1945

Released prisoners of war at gradually reaching their Sunderland homes Lieutenant Ditchburn, Lieutenant Geoffrey Browell, and Lieutenant Mitchell arrived home this evening. Others who have reached home are trooper Frank Jopling (32) who was captured in 1942 in Libya; Private T H Dorrian (28), of 10 Booth Street, who was captured at Dunkirk in 1940; Private A V Albert, of 63 Falkland Road; Private D B Muir (27) of 4 Elgin Street, captured at Dunkirk; Private J T Cairns (26) captured at Dunkirk; Corporal Pat Bartram (35) has return to his home in 3 Renoldson Street having been a prisoner for nearly five years.

All restrictions on the interior lighting of tramcars, trolley vehicles and public service vehicles are removed. When an eight year-old Sunderland boy, charged on remand with housebreaking, was asked in Court today, if he would like to return to the South Hetton Remand Home for three weeks, he said he would rather go for four weeks as he was doing a job there and wanted to finish it. The boy has spent the last three-week at the remand home and a report from the Superintendent revealed that when he entered the Remand Home and a knife and fork was placed before him he didn't know what to do with them.

Wm Doxford launches the *MORAYBANK* 7307t. Scrapped Hong Kong Dec. 1969.

Short Bros. launches the *EMPIRE DOMINICA* 7319t. 1966 Scrapped Hong Kong.

German troops at Bremen surrender to the British and Canadians. Allied troops now line the Swiss border from Basle to Lake Constance. The U.S. Third Army takes Regensburg on the Danube. Goering's fall from grace announced in Germany, General Ritter von Greim is to replace him.

27-Apr-1945

Personal gas masks should be preserved until instructions are given for their disposal.

Mr Charles Jude at an auction held in the Palatine Hotel. Sold 24 Olive Street, comprising six rooms, two attics and a scullery for £400; 24 Stewart Street, a cottage with three rooms realised £260, while a £150 was paid for 18 Mable Terrace, a house with three rooms and a scullery downstairs and three upstairs rooms.

JL. Thompson launches *EMPIRE ARROW* 3766t. This was the last ship to be launched on the Wear before VE Day. 1981 scrapped Kynosoura, Greece.

28-Apr-1945

After considering the claim of the bombed out shopkeepers at the junction of Laburnum Road and Fulwell Road to be allowed to re-establish their shops on the site, Sunderland Health Committee have decided to give up the idea of erecting two temporary houses on the site and instead to permit the owners of the old premises to build five temporary shops, to remain for a period of 10 years. The reason being the area is subject to town planning.

Hartlepools Utd. 0 Sunderland 2. Sunderland, Gateshead, York City and Huddersfield are the four clubs into the semi-finals of the Tyne-Wear-Tees Cup. Goals by Brown and Cliff Whitelum gave Sunderland a 2 – 0 victory at Hartlepool and 7 – 0 lead on the tie.

29-Apr-1945

German forces in Italy surrender.

30-Apr-1945

Houses destroyed in Cleveland Road and Colchester Terrace by a parachute mine, which fell in the Spring raids of 1943 are to be rebuilt, under a cost of works payment, by the War Damage Commission. The cottages in Nora Street and Kitchener Street, demolished by the same bomb, are not to be rebuilt. The War Damage Commission's policy is to rebuild in cases where properties had up to date amenities, such as bathrooms, hot water supply, indoor sanitation and so on. The cottages referred to apparently have not these amenities. Where homeowners wish to improve on their properties, they are required to pay the extra cost, as the Commission is only required to pay for the reinstatement of the property, as it existed before the war. A deputation of residents from Nora Street is to meet with the War Damage Commission in Newcastle.

Adolf Hitler and Eva Braun, whom he had recently married, commit suicide in the air raid shelter in the Chancellery in Berlin and their bodies are burnt

1-May-1945

The Ministry of Food gave the following advice as regard food trade arrangements for VE Day and VE +1 day. Grocers should remain open on VE Day for at least one hour after the announcement has been made. Dairymen must deliver milk on VE Day and VE + 1 day. Restaurants are asked to stay open on these days.

Britain's remaining ARP workers given one month's notice.

2-May-1945

The Ministry of Home Security announces that the National Air-raid Warning System and the Industrial Alarm system are to be discontinued from midday today. The Control of Noise Regulation, which prevented the use of sirens, hooters, rattles, etc except to give air-raid warning have been rescinded and such instruments may again be put to their peacetime uses. Vehicle lighting from now on will be subject to peacetime regulation even in the coastal areas, with the exception that interior lighting on public service vehicles and trains will, for the time being, be kept at its present standard. The restrictions on torches and hand lamps have also been removed throughout the whole country.

Berlin surrenders to Soviet army.

3-May-1945

Communal air raid shelters are to close. Free issued Anderson and Morrison shelters may be purchased from the Corporation. Shelters may be dismantled, and the parts collected and stored, as the materials are Government property. It is not proposed to repurchase shelters sold to householders.

4-May-1945

Bonfires and floodlighting are banned in Sunderland for VE Day celebrations, as the Borough is within the five-mile dim out belt.

Barnes, Welch and Barnes sold 23 Woodbine Street, Hendon, for £83 and 7 Merle Terrace, Pallion, for £245.

5-May-1945

Neither Spuhler nor Burbanks were available, through injuries, to play at York today in the second round of the Tyne-Wear-Tees Cup. Another junior was introduced to the outside right position. Hetherington, who was signed this week as an amateur for next season. He plays inside right for Shiney Row St. Oswald's and Silksworth Juniors. The selected eleven was Bircham; Stelling and Eves; Laidman, Lockie and Housam; Hetherington, Brown, Whitelum, White and Wallbanks. By a margin of one goal by which York's City led Sunderland in the first leg of the Tyne and Wear Tees Cup should not worry Sunderland when the teams meet at Roker Park on Saturday. York won 2 - 1. (Later results; the second leg on the 12th May, Sunderland 6 York City 1. Semi final on the 19th May Huddersfield 1 Sunderland 0, in the second leg on the Whit Monday Sunderland 2 Huddersfield 0. Sunderland wins with a 2 – 1 aggregate. Sunderland met Gateshead in the final at St. James's Park on Saturday 26th May and lost.)

7-May-1945

All anti-gas precautions may be relaxed from today.

The German Chief-of-Staff, General Jodl, signs Germany's unconditional surrender to the western allies and Russia at 2:41am. Operations are to cease at 1 minute after midnight (GMT) on the 8th May. British troops enter Utrecht to a tumultuous reception.

8-May-1945

Hostilities will officially cease one minute after midnight tonight. The Prime Minister paid tribute to the men and women who had laid down their lives for victory as well as to all others who had fought valiantly on land, sea and in the air. In his speech, Mr Churchill said, "We may allow ourselves a brief period of rejoicing; but let us not forget for a moment the toil and efforts that lie ahead. Japan with all her treachery and greed, remains unsubdued. We must now devote all our strength and resources to the completion of our task, both at home and abroad.

Heralded by a fanfare of trumpets, the Mayor, Councillor John Young, spoke from the steps of the Town Hall one hour after the beginning of the broadcast by the Prime Minister announcing the end of hostilities in Europe. Theatres, cinemas and music halls are expected to remain open to the usual hour. Places with licence for dancing will be allowed to remain open later than normal. Half-an-hour extension has been granted in Sunderland.

Shortly after Mr Churchill's broadcast, several families had a nasty shock when 20 mm cannon shells burst through their roofs, making holes in ceilings and floors. It was thought to be down to the over exuberance of a crew of a ship on the Wear. Shells fell in Roker and Fulwell but fortunately no one was injured. Three shells fell in the House of Mrs Ellen Chambers at 68 Inverness Street.

9-May-1945

VE Day + 1 was not a good day for Sunderland football team. A crowd of nearly a 11,000 saw them beaten 5 – 0 at Newcastle

VE Day Party in Perth Road, Plains Farm Estate

10-May-1945

The end of a long list of Defence Regulations is announced, including the one that made it an offence to spread alarm and despondency. Rationing, however, would continue well into the 1950's.

So ended 'Sunderland's' war. World War Two would continue until August but the town and its people would no longer be threatened.

Next to Hull, with its casualty list of 1200 killed and 3000 injured, Sunderland was the most heavily bombed town in the northeast. Since the first bombs were dropped on Whitburn Bents on June 22nd, 1940 there have been 1267 casualties, 267 persons killed, 362 seriously injured, and 638 less seriously injured.

Some 34,500 houses were damaged, and 1013 have been a total loss. This is a high proportion, about 90 per cent, for the total number of houses in the town.

Many dwellings of course were only slightly damaged but just over 2000 were seriously damaged. Altogether 251 alerts have been sounded in Sunderland during the war. Bombs dropped on the town include 384 high explosives, 39 parachute mines, 36 firepots, 23 phosphorus and thousands of small incendiaries. High explosives ranged from 50 to 1000 kilogram, the majority being of the 500 or 1000 kilogram.

Part of the estimated crowd of 10,000 in Fawcett Street to hear the Mayor's announcement

Civilian Deaths due to Enemy Action

09/08/1940

Richard Archer
> *Laing's Shipyard*

Irene Mooney
> *Richmond St.*

Arthur Perry
> *Laing's Shipyard*

Thompson Reed
> *Laing's Shipyard*

15/08/1940

John S Henderson
> *Cardwell St.*

Elsie Parr Holt
> *Eden House, Eden Place*

Doris Jobling
> *Eden House, Eden Place*

George Todd
> *Eden House, Eden Place*

05/09/1940

Rachel Stormont
> *55 1/2 Suffolk St.*

23/02/1941

Violet Temple Cowell
> *3 Tunstall Vale*

Amelia Sharp
> *3 Tunstall Vale*

Irene Sharp
> *3 Tunstall Vale*

Mary Thompson
> *7 Tunstall Vale*

Margaret Armstrong
> *20 Tunstall Vale*

Antoinette Sloan
> *20 Tunstall Vale*

Joyce Sloan
> *20 Tunstall Vale*

14/03/1941

Mary Atkinson
> *46 Roxburgh St.*

Rose Pennell
> *46 Francis St*

Sarah Pennell
> *46 Francis St*

Lewis Viner
> *44 Francis St.*

10/04/1941

John Bowe
> *10 Ethel St.*

Laura Sinclair
> *11 Ethel St.*

16/04/1941

Stanley Foster
> *Laura St.*

Thomas Hazard
> *Oddfellows, Laura St.*

Doreen Henderson
> *25 St Luke's Rd.*

Margaret Henderson
> *25 St Luke's Rd.*

Brenda Clarke
> *25 St. Luke's Rd.*

John Clarke
> *25 St. Luke's Rd.*

Francis South
> *23 1/2 St. Luke's Rd.*

Rosina Clarke
> *St. Luke's Rd.*

Edward Bland
> *59 South Durham St.*

Jane Chapman
> *60 South Durham St.*

John Cheek
> *59 South Durham St.*

Ernest Harrison
> *Sunderland Forge*

Francis Home
> *Sunderland Forge*

John Boddy
> *Sunderland Forge*

George Nottingham
> *Sunderland Forge*

William Saint
> *Sunderland Forge*

Isabella Stephenson
> *60 South Durham St.*

Joseph Stephenson
> *60 South Durham St.*

04/05/1941

Fredrick Foster
> *5 Duke St. Nth.*

Margaret Foster
> *5 Duke St. Nth.*

Edith Storey
> *5 Duke St. North*

Anthony Storey
> *5 Duke St. North*

Audrey Storey
> *5 Duke St. North*

Edith Storey
> *5 Duke St. North*

Louisa Flett
> *5 Duke St. Nth.*

Alice Spanton
> *6 Duke St. North*

James Turnbull
> *4 Westcott Terr.*

Joan Turnbull
> *4 Westcott Terr.*

Margaret Turnbull
> *4 Westcott Terr.*

Maurice Turnbull
> *4 Westcott Terr.*

Anne Harvey
> *5 Westcott Terr.*

Mary Harvey
> *5 Westcott Terr.*

Elizabeth Moore
> *5 Westcott Terr.*

Margaret Moore
> *5 Westcott Terr.*

Mary Usher
> *7 Westcott Terr.*

13/08/1941

Douglas Easby
> *40 Mayswood Rd*

Isabella Easby
> *40 Mayswood Rd.*

John Robson
> *38 Mayswood Rd.*

Dorothy Forster
> *38 Mayswood Rd.*

09/09/1941

Joseph McLeod
> *Ryhope Pit Head*

John Moody
> *Ryhope Pit Head*

30/09/1941

Alice Hackett
> *59 Shakespeare St.*

Gladys Hackett
> *59 Shakespeare St.*

Harry Hackett
> *59 Shakespeare St.*

Thomas Hackett
> *59 Shakespeare St*

William Hackett
> *59 Shakespeare St.*

Denis Hogan
> *68 Cato St.*

Norah Hogan
> *68 Cato St.*

21/10/1941

James Hudson
> *14 John St.*

George Moses
> *14 John St.*

John Moses
> *14 John St.*

Aaron Bainbridge
> *Pit Head Ryhope*

David Connolly
> *Pit Head Ryhope*

William Dodds
> *Pit Head Ryhope*

James Ridley
> *Pit Head Ryhope*

07/11/1941
Joseph Gowland
108 Fulwell Rd.
John Barras
Tyzack's, Fulwell Rd.
Joseph Cairns
Roker Av.
Joyce Armstrong
Whitehouse Cottages
Madeline Smith
1 Whitehouse Cottages
Edwin Smith
1 Whitehouse Cottages
Madeline Smith (Dau.)
1 Whitehouse Cottages
William Steel
8 Lily St.
01/05/1942
Edith Swaddle
26 Mayswood Rd.
John Swaddle
26 Mayswood Rd.
28/08/1942
Frederick Collins
5 Dinsdale Terr. Ryhope
Mary Duffield
6 Dinsdale Terr. Ryhope
William Turnbull
11 Smith St. Ryhope
11/10/1942
Agnes Nottingham
5 Corporation Rd.
June Wilson
6 Corporation Rd.
Joan Doyle
7 Corporation Rd.
Alice Stoker
7 Corporation Rd.
Thomas Stoker
7 Corporation Rd.
Sarah Colvin
11 Corporation Rd.
Ernest Miller
12 Canon Cockin St
16/10/1942
Robert Leadbitter
Tatham St.
Walter Devenport
Tatham St.
Brian Monaghan
Tatham St. Canteen
Edward Carter
Tatham St. Canteen
Diane Borreson
6 Tatham St.
Gwendoline Cook
6 Tatham St.

James Landers
6 Tatham St.
Doreen Wardle
6 Tatham St.
Joyce Wardle
6 Tatham St.
Margaret Wardle
6 Tatham St.
Mary Wardle (aka Cook)
6 Tatham St.
Eileen Halverson
7 Tatham St.
Ida Halverson
7 Tatham St.
Septimus Carter
7 Tatham St.
19/10/1942
Elizabeth Nicholson
22 Humbledon Park
14/03/1943
Mary Bewley
2 Nora St.
William Durrant
4 Nora St.
Catherine Moorhead
6 Nora St.
Anthony Smith
15 Nora St.
John Fowler
Cleveland Rd.
Jane Cromie
207 Cleveland Rd.
Ann Riley
207 Cleveland Rd.
William Dixon
68 Colchester Terr.
Ernest Johnson
Baltic Chambers, John St.
Joseph Mutagh
St. Thomas St.
James Orton
St. Thomas Church
Thomas Robertson
Central Railway Station
James Morrison
White's Market
John Simpson
South St.
Alfred Munro
Young's Garage, South St
William Walton
Young's Garage, South St
22/03/1943
William Hume
South Dock
16/05/1943
Robert Goldsmith
Atkinson Rd.

Edith Airey
88 Atkinson Rd.
James Craig
88 Atkinson Rd.
Alan Miller
90 Atkinson Rd.
Dennis Miller
90 Atkinson Rd.
Eric Miller
90 Atkinson Rd.
Gladys Miller
90 Atkinson Rd.
Gordon Miller
90 Atkinson Rd.
James Miller
90 Atkinson Rd.
Alice Phillips
123 Atkinson Rd.
Meggie Chell
123 Atkinson Rd.
Mary Evans
71 Cairns Rd.
John Wilson
73 Cairns Rd.
Evelyn Briggs
32 Gladstone St.
Michael Briggs
32 Gladstone St.
Thomas Briggs
32 Gladstone St.
Watts Warne
32 Gladstone St
Emma Warne
32 Gladstone St
Lilian Sinclair
34 Gladstone St.
Florence Evans
36 Gladstone St.
June Evans
36 Gladstone St.
Samuel Johnson
36 Gladstone St.
David Haswell
1 Parkside Terr.
George Haswell
1 Parkside Terr.
Gladys Haswell
1 Parkside Terr.
Norman Haswell
1 Parkside Terr.
Isabella Coxon
4 Parkside Terr.
Lancelot Slawther
Roker Baths Rd.
William Kennard
79 Cooper St.
Walter Phillips
6 Netherburn Rd.

Evelyn Thwaites
        2 Waterloo Place
Mary Thwaites
        2 Waterloo Place
Sarah Thwaites
        2 Waterloo Place
Patricia Robson
        3 Waterloo Place
Elizabeth Laidler
        3 Waterloo Place
John Feeney
        4 Waterloo Place
Mary Feeney
        4 Waterloo Place
Edward Innins
        5 Waterloo Place
Albert Alcock
        5 Waterloo Place
Emily Alcock
        5 Waterloo Place
Mary Alcock
        5 Waterloo Place
Lilian Kirtley
        Whitburn St.
Florence Henderson
        90 Whitburn St.
Elspeth Matthew
        91 Whitburn St
Jane Matthew
        91 Whitburn St
William Matthew
        91 Whitburn St
Ellen Matthews
        92 Whitburn St
Eleanor Taylor
        91 Whitburn St.
Henry Taylor
        91 Whitburn St.
Mary Swalwell
        92 Whitburn St.
John Shovelin
        94 Whitburn St.
Abraham Dixon
        Tug 'Wexford'
James Taylor
        2 Livingstone Rd.
Robert Metcalf
        10 Hetton St.
Mary Bainbridge
        Lewis Cottages, Roper St.
Emma Byers
        9 Abingdon St.
Luke Winter
        2 Allonby St.
Mary Nelson
        Sunderland
Richard Rogerson
        Sunderland

Oswald Skeen
        Sunderland
Margaret Walton
        Sunderland
Jean Suffield
        10 Azalea Ave.
Lucy Suffield
        10 Azalea Ave.
Elsie Salter
        12 Azalea Av.
Leonard Salter
        12 Azalea Av.
Elizabeth Howard
        17 Barrack St.
John Howard
        17 Barrack St.
Doris Thompson
        2 Barracks Cottages
George Thompson
        2 Barracks Cottages
George Thompson Jnr.
        2 Barracks Cottages
Mary Thompson
        2 Barracks Cottages
Joseph Taylor
        25 Alexandra Park
Mary Martin
        149 Perth Rd.
Annie Bates
        151 Perth Rd.
Jane Harvey
        15 Miners Cottages
24/05/1943
Ethel Brown
        6 St. George's Sq.
Elizabeth Fallen
        6 St. George's Sq.
Leonora Garrick
        7 St. George's Sq.
Sarah Garrick
        7 St. George's Sq.
Fredrick Hunter
        8 St. George's Sq.
Annie Hunter
        8 St. George's Sq.
Margaret Coffey
        8 St. George's Sq.
Eve Pigg
        8 St. George's Sq.
John Pigg
        8 St. George's Sq.
Joyce Pigg
        8 St. George's Sq.
Margaret Pigg
        8 St. George's Sq.
Norman Pigg
        8 St. George's Sq.

Ellen Simmons
        8 St. George's Sq.
Anna Rae
        9 St. George's Sq.
Elizabeth Smith
        9 St. George's Sq.
Elizabeth Forster
        11 St. George's Sq.
Winifred Cowe
        11 St. George's Sq.
Thomas Gaffney
        12 St. George's Sq.
Norma Thompson
        12 St. George's Sq.
George Forster
        Lodge Terr. Shelter
Margaret Foster
        Lodge Terr. Shelter
Annie Gisby
        Lodge Terr. Shelter
Susan Hall
        Lodge Terr. Shelter
Alice Harris
        Lodge Terr. Shelter
Kathleen Harris
        Lodge Terr. Shelter
Anne Huntley
        Lodge Terr. Shelter
Alan Hutchinson
        Lodge Terr. Shelter
Ronald Hutchinson
        Lodge Terr. Shelter
David Lorenson
        Lodge Terr. Shelter
Ronald McArdle
        Lodge Terr. Shelter
Agnes O'Neill
        Lodge Terr. Shelter
Catherine Telfer
        Lodge Terr. Shelter
Eva Thorne
        Lodge Terr. Shelter
Hannah Warde
        Lodge Terr. Shelter
Doris Humble
        Bonners Field Shelter
Fredrick Humble
        Bonners Field Shelter
Jean Humble
        Bonners Field Shelter
Marjorie Humble
        Bonners Field Shelter
Mildred Humble
        Bonners Field Shelter
William Middlemiss
        3 Bonners Field
Joseph Jobling
        Bonners Field

George Brown
Bromarsh Shelter
Ellen Morgans
Bromarsh Shelter
John Murtha
Bromarsh Shelter
Marjorie Leng
6 Robinson St.
Ruth Leng
6 Robinson St.
William Leng
6 Robinson St.
William Leng Jnr.
6 Robinson St.
Milly Michaelson
6 Robinson St.
Lilian Swales
6 Robinson St.
Olive Swales
6 Robinson St.
David Bergson
6 Robinson St.
Miriam Bergson
6 Robinson St.
Arnold Bergson
6 Robinson St.
James Leng
6 Robinson St.
Kenneth Leng
6 Robinson St.
Thomas Jackson
8 Robinson St.
Dorothy Bickford
5 Salem Ave.
Maurice Gallerstein
8 Salem Ave.
Charles Thompson
6 Salem St
Margaret Thompson
6 Salem St
Winifred Tuddenham
6 Salem St
John Annison
Ravensworth St.
Thomas Watson
41 Ravensworth St.
Sarah Watson
41 Ravensworth St.
John Atkinson
42 Ravensworth St.
Mary Briggs
23 Hedley St
Christina Price
24 Hedley St.
Ethel Tate
24 Hedley St.
Anthony Rennoldson
5 Somali St.

Thomas Taylor
63 Wear St.
Walter Miller
73 Wear St.
Annie Sillett
14 Abbs St.
John Sillett
14 Abbs St.
Ernest Goldsworthy
15 Abbs St.
Mary Hughes
4 Devonshire St.
John Simpson
4 Devonshire St.
Robert Scott
Hendon
George Whittle
Running St.
Robert Lowes
38 Henry St. East
Thomas Ramshaw
Sunderland
John Huggins
Sunderland
John Burnip
8 Carlyon St
Hannah Thompson
71 Alexandra Rd.
Thomas Thompson
71 Alexandra Rd.
Thomas Eves
Alexandra Bridge
Robert Ward
8 Ashmore Terr.
Percy Stoker
17 West Terr. Ryhope
George Heads
Ryhope Coll. Gangway

Sunderland Members of the 125 Anti Tank Royal Artillery

Names of Sunderland men belonging to the 125 Anti-Tank Regiment of the Royal Artillery, who were captured in the fall of Singapore and held in Japanese prisoner of war camps, began to filter through early in 1943.

Those members who sadly died in captivity are in bold with the date of death

A J Ainslie
36 Inverness St.
L/Sgt. Aird   15.10.43
70 Kirkstone Av.
G Alcock
23 Brandling St.
F Allan   7.7.43
31 St Patrick's Garth
G Allen   26.9.43
Hendon Gardens Hotel
Sgt C F Anan   8.9.45
30 St Leonard St.
W Arnold   12.7.43
38 Joan Avenue
W E Arthur
25 Sea Road
J Askew
78 Beechwood Cres.
R Austin
77 Dock St. East
B W L Bailey
Not Known
Sgt Bainbridge
36 Askrigg Av.
J Baldridge
4 Cecil Street
L Barker   12.9.44
58 Chester Road
Sgt R A Beattie
35 Winhurst Grindon.
L/Sgt. F Bell
12 Monk Street
Lt. G Bell
Park Avenue North
L/Bdr. H Bell
9 Chester St. East.
R Bell
9 Eden Vale
G H Black
30 Croft Avenue
L Blakeman   12.9.44
122 Wayman Street
Bdr A B Bogie
21 Lorne Terr.
Bdr.A Bogle
6 Harrogate Street
L/Bdr S Bowden 6.10.43
32 Oswald Terrace
R Boyce
34 Millum Terr.
P Boylen   21.2.45
Not Known
H Braley
39 James Armitage St.
R Brand
28 Ross Street
B Brennan   25.6.43
34 Henry Street
G Brennan   22.6.43
20 Holly Terrace
S Britton
late of Coronation St
J Brodie
10 Bell St.
C Brooks
10 Queen's St. West.

J T Brown
35 Shaftsbury Av.
T D Brown
31 Blandford Street
Sgt N Burnikell
129 Harrington Street
Sgt. J Burnett
76 Atkinson Road
Sgt N Burnikell   6.8.43
129 Harrington Street
C Bdr J A Cameron
65 St Leonard St.
F Carling
26 Nth. Millburn St.
C Carney
5 Swinbank Street
L/Bdr G Carney 9.12.42
65 Alexandra Road
Sgt J J Carney
55 Q. Alexandra Rd.
Lt. W Carter
2 Ashbrooke Crescent.
L/Bdr J Cessford
108 Westheath Av.
R Chambers   21.7.43
42 Chester Road
E P Chapman   12.9.44
69 Rutland Street
Lt. R Charman
108 Side Cliff Road
Ddr H Chatt
15 Violet St.
F Cheeseborough
36 Hendon St
L/Bdr. J Clarke
37 Offerton Street.
T H Cleghorn
Mainsforth Terr.
Bdr. Clingly
55 Chester Road.
Coates R W   28.12.43
Not Known
Coleman P
26 Sth. Durham St.
W Common
6 Enderby Road
M Conlin
31 Eyre Street
R Cook
29 Camden St.
J Coulson   27.9.44
48 Lawrence Street
J Cowie
19 Franklin Street
A Cranmer
23a Covent Garden
C W Cranmer   8.6.43
8 Zion Street.
F Cranmer   1.7.43
22 Zion Street
R Cranmer
3 Annie Street East
E W Crawford 29.11.42
108 Cairo Street
J J Crawford   8.9.45
34 Leechmere Road

J Crompton
30 Wellington St.
S Crosby   4.7.43
6 Chester Road
A Crouthers
28 Guildford Street
A H Curry
8 Belle Vue Cres.
D L/Bdr. J Daglish
325 Hylton Road.
L/Bdr. D Davis   16.6.43
35 Belle Vue Park
W Davison
5 Premier Road
Sgt W Defty
20 Ewesley Road
Sgt T P Denton
82 Ormonde Street
Bdr. C Dick
187 Fulwell Road
F Donkin
7 Friar Square
W Doran
24$^1/_2$ Whitehouse Rd.
A E Duell   29.12.44
Not Known
J T Dunn
39 Pilgrim Street
E E Elliott
3 St Patrick's Garth
Bdr T Elliott
6 Thompson Road
F M Feechan
4 Salem Terrace
Cpl Fenwick
The Terrace, S/wick
L/Bdr. R Forster
10 Chester Road
A Fowler
1 Azalea North.
G R France
37 Tatham Street
G Bdr. L Gibson
10 North Millburn St.
C E Gilbertson
81 Burleigh Garth
R Gilhespy
16 Westburn Terrace
J Glancey
11 Stratfield Street
B H Gooderick 13.2.42
Not Known
S Goodfellow
4 Princess Gardens
Lt. M Goodyear
17 Roker Baths Rd.
J Greaves
3 Fordenbridge Cres.
Captain W Greenwell
24 Marina Avenue
R Gregory
6 Walton Garth
H N Hannon
6 Beverley Road
Bdr. E H Harrison
26 East Whickham St.

H A Harvey   31.7.43
         10 St Leonard's Street
     Maj J P Havard
                        Durham Rd.
     Bdr. D Herbert 15.10.42
         The Nook South Cliffe
     C Hill
                26 Hamilton Street
     J W Hodgson
                        17 Eldon St.
     J Hossack
                93 Victor Street
     A Howey
                2 Nelson Street
     N Howey
                54 Perth Road
     M Howey
                26 Gladstone St.
     M Howey
                26 Gladstone St.
     R W Hubbard
                9¹/₂ Salisbury St.
     J Huggins
                19 Hollywood Av.
     Sgt K M Hunter
                5 Meadow Gardens
     N L Hutchinson
                92 Fulwell Road
J A Jamesson   9.7.43
                38 Atkinson Road
     L/Sgt W N Jefferson
                44 Bond Street
     L Johnson
                40 Ripon Street
     Lt N L Jones
                20 Belle Vue Park
     L/Sgt A Judson
                18 Dinsdale Road
K Sgt E H Kent
                158 Durham Rd.
     Driver E Kidd
                74 Queens Crescent
L Bdr. F Laidlaw
                20 John Street
     D P Lang
                10 Drury Lane
     L/Bdr. Langley
                31 Western Hill
     E Lawson
                1 Ryhope St.
     E H Lawson
                18 Ocean Road
     E R Lawson   26.7.43
                63 Ewesley Road
     L/Sgt W Lawson
                49 Eglinton Street
     Bdr J A Lawson
                1 Peacock Street
     J T Lee
                2 Whitehall Terrace
     R Lee
                143 Premier Road
     D Linden
                        Trinity Place
     Bdr. P Lindley
     15 Liddell Terr.

M Sgt S Maddison
                5 Fordham Square
     J Madgwick   4.10.43
                        Not Known
     J H Magrill   12.9.44
                1 The Oaks.
     J J Marlborough
                22 Mable Street
     Bdr. R Marshall
                162 Cleveland Road.
     J R Marshall
                81 Hawarden Cres.
     Sgt E Mason   30.5.43
                4 Halfway Houses
     J R McCready
                52 Ancona Street
     W McCready
                13 Belle Vue Cres.
     L/Bdr. S McCully
                49 Frederick Street
     D McKenna
                7 Avenue Terrace
     A McManus
                207 Hastings Street
     D Macintosh
                7 Old Mill Rd.
     Sgt. J Mawood
                34 Hunter Terr. Sth.
     A Metcalf
                50 Hylton Road.
     M Metcalf
                149 Victor Street
     R P Milburn   21.9.44
                89 Cowell Terrace
     Lt. G Miller
                        Ewesley Road
     Sgt Mincovitch
                17 Belle Vue Park
     Sgt E Minto
                176 St. Lukes Road
     Lt. G Moore
                147 Alexandra Road
     J G Morgan
                        8 Lee St.
     W L Morgan   12.9.44
                15 Marlborough St.
     BQMS J T Morrison
                32 Pancras Road.
     T Mulvaney
                32 South Durham St
     D S Mustard
                7 Grey Terrace
N V Nanson
                23 Sea Road
     E A Nelson
                20 Beachville Street
     Bdr R A Nevill   9.4.45
                25 Ford Street
     Bdr. S Nicholson
                36 Pearl Road
     BSM C Nicklas
                31 Ayre's Quay St.
     L/Cpl M Nixon
                        Bedford Street.
O L/Bdr. T Old
     7 Huntcliffe Av.

P A Page
                53 Felstead Crescent
     BQMS F Pain
                        Aubrey Terrace.
     Sgt A Pattison
                1 Exhibition Terr.
     Bdr. E Pearlman
                6 Belvedere Rd.
     C Perry
                38 Alderson Street
     B Philp
                55 Sea Road
     Bdr. L Plummer 14.2.43
                7 Sorley Street
     C Plunkett
                32 Dunsmore Av.
     Bdr. E Porter
                15 Keswick Avenue
R L/Sgt F Raine
                9 Gillside Grove
     G Raine   12.9.44
                1 Sydenham Terrace
     L/Sgt W Raine   19.11.42
                1 Sydenham Terrace
     J G Reed
                26 Beverley Road
     L/Bdr. H Reed
                5 Guisborough
     G Reeves   1.5.43
                        Not Known
     Lt. E H Rich   25.2.44
                64 Chatsworth St Sth.
     F Riddell
                3 Mayfield Court
     G W Riddell   13.12.43
                45 Robinson Street
     T S Ridley
                156 Alexandra Road.
     R Roberts
                69 Faber Road
     Sgt J Robinson
                246 Fulwell Road.
     W B Robson   25.10.43
                63 Laburnum Road
     J L Rochester   21.9.44
                7 Harlow Street
     J W T Ross
                66 Fordbeck Road
     Bdr. W Routledge
                1 Fern St.
     L/Bdr. Rowntree
                68 Roker Avenue
S A Scott
                33 Tatham St.
     F Scott
                22 Netherburn Road
     L/Bdr. J Scott
                126 Durham Road.
     R Slingsby
                30 Perry Street
     Bdr. J Smith
                22 Fawcett Street
     Sgt J Smith
                6 Ashbrooke Mount
     J Smith
     Churchill Avenue

S **S G Smith**   **12.9.44**
33 Westheath Road
T Smith
42 Elmwood Avenue
Sgt J Sneddon
3 St. Andrew's Terr.
A H Spraggon
88 Brandling St.
M T G Stacey
40 The Green, S/wick
R Stephenson 12.9.44
16 Friar Road
W Stoker
12 Windsor Terrace
J Sugden
84 Coniston Av.
J Sullivan   **2.5.43**
39 Croft Avenue
A Sumby
193 Cleveland Rd.
F G Swan   **26.10.44**
Not Known
Sgt. W Swanson
41 Perth Road

T BSM R Tait
Willowpond Inn
Lt. A Tate   **18.12.43**
Eastfields Street
E Tate
30 Athol Road
Sgt. N D Taylor   **4.2.42**
Not Known
R Thirlbeck
20 Oaklands Cres.
A Thompson
56 Falkland Rd
E Thompson
26 Kitchener Terrace
Bdr. A Timney
11 Warwick Street
L/Bdr. G Timney
11 Warwick Street
Sgt C Towell
8 Grange Crescent
G N Trotter   **24.9.43**
104 Victor Street
W Tuddenham   **23.6.43**
45 Colchester Terrace
E Tutin
91 Newcastle Rd.

W G E Wainwright
37 The Parade
G Walker
11 Ettrick Grove
W Walker
52 Tweed Street
L/Bdr. T Wallace
40 Croft Av.
L/Bdr. J W Wallace
3 East St.
Lt. M Walsh
5 Woodside
L/Bdr. D Wand
8 Princes Avenue

D Wandless
155 Hastings Street
G Ward
6 The Green
R Wardell
8 Hawthorne Street
G Waterworth
4 Forebeck Road
A Watson   **17.5.45**
11 Bower Street
R Welch   **7.9.44**
101 Cleveland Road
Welsh J E
9 Sans St. Sth.
L/Bdr. R White
36 Hendon Road
W S White
28 Offerton Street
L/Bdr. R H Wight
36 Henderson Rd.
E Williams   **12.9.44**
24 Wear Street.
P Williams
2 Roker Park Road
Bdr. W Wilson
3 Pallion Road
K Wolfe
18 Westheath Avenue
Driver C Wright
70 Nora Street
Bdr. T Wrightson
104 Eglinton St
BSM R Wylde   **12.9.44**
3 Hollyoake Terrace

Y **W Young**   **11.12.42**
3 St Mark's Street

Roll of Honour

Sunderland Members of the Merchant Navy who lost their lives due to Enemy Action

AGAR, Ronald George, Able Seaman, S.S. Royal Crown. 30th January 1940. Age 20. Son of Arthur Ernest and Ann Hannah Agar, of 31 Harwarden Crescent, Sunderland. Buried Sunderland (Bishopwearmouth) Cemetery.

ALLAN, Arthur, Second Officer, S.S. Deptford. 13th December 1939. Age 32. Son of Walter James Allan and Lucy Elisa Allan; husband of Vera Allan, of Sunderland.

ALLAN, Wallace, Second Engineer Officer, S.S. Kildale. 3rd February 1940. Age 49. Son of James and Priscilla Allan, of Sunderland; husband of Florence Allan, of Sunderland. Buried Cleethorpes Cemetery.

ALLEN, Arthur Cousins, Third Officer, S.S. Dayrose. 14/01/1942. Age 28. Son of Henry and Violet Allen; husband of Freda Allen, of New Silksworth, Co. Durham.

ALLEN, William Henry, Second Engineer Officer, S.S. Tunisia. 4th August 1941. Age 34. Son of Arthur Reading Allen and Louisa Grace Allen; husband of Violet Allen, of Millfield, Sunderland.

ALLINSON, George Frank, Chief Engineer Officer, S.S. Lackenby. 25th January 1943. Age 40. Husband of M. Allinson, of Sunderland.

ALLISON, Joseph, Cabin Boy, S.S. Empire Bison. 1st November 1940. Age 16. Son of John Thomas Allison and Agnes Allison, of Fulwell, Sunderland.

AMISS, Charles Leslie, Second Engineer Officer, M.V. Narragansett. 25th March 1942. Age 28. Son of Charles Harrison Amiss and Ellen Amiss, of Sunderland; stepson of Mrs. C. Amiss, of Sunderland.

ANDERSON, Andrew Dalrymple, Boatswain (Bosun), S.S. Stangarth. 16/03/1942. Husband of L. Anderson, of Castletown, Co. Durham.

ANDERSON, Arthur James, Chief Officer, S.S. Roxby. 7th November 1942. Age 36. Husband of Annie Anderson, of Sunderland.

ANDERSON, George Frederick, Chief Engineer Officer, S.S. Belvedere. 17th December 1940. Age 60. Son of George Fredrick and Catherine Jane Anderson; husband of Margery Ann Anderson, of Sunderland.

ANDERSON, James Henry, Chief Engineer Officer, S.S. Zurichmoor. 24th May 1942. Age 44. Son of James Robert and Ellen Anderson; husband of Alice Archbold Anderson, of Sunderland.

ANDERSON, Thomas Henry Smelt, Chief Officer, S.S. Sheaf Mount. 24th August 1942. Age 27. Son of Gordon Palmer Anderson and Dorothy Murray Anderson; husband of Elsie Anderson, of Monkwearmouth, Sunderland.

ANDERSON, Wallace, Able Seaman, S.S. Royal Crown. 30th January 1940. Age 24. Son of William Johnson Anderson and Dorothy Anderson, of Hendon, Sunderland. Buried Sunderland (Ryhope) Cemetery.

ARMSTRONG, Joseph, Fireman and Trimmer, S.S. Empire Dryden. 23rd April 1942. Age 22. Son of Joseph Armstrong, and of Mary Jane Armstrong, of Hendon, Sunderland.

ARCHER, William, Fireman, H.M.S. Registan, Naval Auxiliary Personnel (Merchant Navy). 28 May 1941. Age 37. Son of George and Mary Archer; husband of Elizabeth Archer, of Sunderland, Co. Durham.

ATKIN, John Robert, Fourth Engineer Officer, S.S. Rio Azul. 29th June 1941. Age 26. Son of William and E. S. Atkin, of Sunderland.

ATKINSON, Francis Devitt, Fireman and Trimmer, S.S. Harpalyce. 25th August 1940. Age 26. Son of John William and Mary Elizabeth Atkinson, of Sunderland.

ATKINSON, Frederick Thomas, Third Engineer Officer, S.S. Sabor. 7th March 1943. Age 24. Son of Frederick Thomas Atkinson and Mary Jane Wilson Atkinson; nephew of Albert E. Hurst, of Fulwell, Sunderland.

ATKINSON, George William, Galley Boy, M.V. Fishpool. 14th November 1940. Age 17. Son of Christopher Byers Atkinson and Agnes Atkinson, of Hendon, Sunderland. His brother Stanley also died on service. Rothesay Cemetery.

ATKINSON, Herbert, Chief Engineer Officer, S.S. Thistlegarth. 15th October 1940. Age 50. Husband of Hilda Atkinson, of Roker, Sunderland.

ATKINSON, Joseph Horace, Third Engineer Officer, S.S. St. Sunniva. 22/01/1943. Age 22. Son of William Ismay Atkinson and Dorothy Jean Atkinson, of Cleadon, Co. Durham.

ATKINSON, Stanley, Cabin Boy, M.V. Fishpool. 14th November 1940. Age 18. Son of Christopher Byers Atkinson, and of Agnes Atkinson, of Hendon, Sunderland. His brother George William also died on service.

ATKINSON, Thomas Proudlock, Second Officer, S.S. Glenlea. 07/11/1942. Son of Thomas Proudlock Atkinson and Cordelia Atkinson, of Marsden, Co. Durham.

BAKER, Robert Anthony, Steward, S.S. Waziristan. 02/01/1942. Age 37. Son of William Hunter Baker and Margaret Baker; husband of Jane Ridley Baker, of Cleadon, Co. Durham.

BALL, Harold M., Steward, S.S. Eastwood. 24th December 1941. Age 19. Son of Samuel Ball, and of Lily Ball, of Grangetown, Sunderland.

BANKS, John, Boy, S.S. Empire Gold. 18th April 1945. Age 17. Son of Mr. and Mrs. Thomas Banks, of Southwick, Sunderland.

BEADNELL, Robert, Apprentice, S.S. Empire Heath, 13th May 1944. Aged 17. Son of Robert and Mary Beadnell, of Fulwell, Co. Durham.

BECK, Julius Christian, Fireman and Trimmer, S.S. Ashby. 30/11/1941. 6 William Street, High Street West, Sunderland.

BELL, Thomas, Lieutenant (E), H.M.S. Chakdina, Royal Naval Reserve. 5 December 1941. Age 37. Son of Thomas and Margaret Bell, of Castletown, Co. Durham.

BELL, Thomas, Chief Engineer Officer, M.V. Tricula. 3rd August 1942. Age 56. Son of William and Elizabeth Anne Bell; husband of Jessie Bell, of Sunderland.

BICKER, Sidney, Able Seaman, S.S. Lambtonian. 10/09/1947. Age 36. (Buried Sunderland (Bishopwearmouth) Cemetery).

BIRLISON, Ralph, Second Engineer Officer, S.S. Marwarri. 5th October 1939. Age 43. Husband of Wilhelmina Alberta Birlison, of Sunderland. Buried Sunderland (Bishopwearmouth) Cemetery.

BODDINGTON, Cyril Harold, Cook, S.S. Sourabaya. 27th October 1942. Age 31. Son of Harold Gustavus Boddington and Daisy Olive Boddington, of Corona Del Mar, California, U.S.A.; husband of Mary Boddington, of Sunderland.

BOYACK, Thomas B., Fifth Engineer Officer, M.V. Harpa. 22/12/1941. Age 26. Son of Lawrence Bernard and Mary Agnes Boyack, of 20 The New Arcade, Sunderland. Buried at Kuala Lumpur (Cherus Road) Malasia

BRACK, Norman, Cook Steward, S.S. Stronsa Firth. 28th November 1944. Age 32. Son of Norman and Mabel Brack; husband of Jane Brack, of Roker, Sunderland.

BROADLEY, Albert Edward, Chief Engineer Officer, S.S. Empire Light. 8th May 1941. Age 39. Son of Capt. John Broadley, M.M., and Clara Broadley; husband of Isobel Broadley, of Roker, Sunderland.

BROWN, David Webster, Master, OBE, S.S. Dagenham. 22nd August 1944. Age 63. Husband of Evelyn Brown, of Sunderland. Buried Sunderland (Mere Knolls) Cemetery.

BROWN, George, Cook, M.V. British Liberty. 6th January 1940. Age 21. Son of James and Elizabeth Brown, of Roker, Sunderland.

BROWN, Thomas Henry, Fifth Engineer Officer, S.S. Virginia. 24th November 1941. Age 36. Son of Matthew and Mary Brown; nephew of Alfred G. Cowen, of Sunderland.

BUCHANAN, Stuart Franklin, Donkeyman, S.S. Eaglescliffe Hall. 12th August 1941. Age 34. Buried Sunderland (Ryhope) Cemetery.

BURDON, John, Chief Engineer Officer, M.V. King Malcolm. 31st October 1941. Age 39. Son of John and Isabella Burdon; husband of Margaret Millicent Burdon, of Fulwell, Sunderland.

BURNHAM, Alfred, Chief Engineer Officer, S.S. Holystone. 15th February 1941. Age 46. Son of Thomas Proder Burnham and Elizabeth Jane Burnham; husband of Ada Mary Burnham, of Sunderland.

BYRON, Ernest, Fireman and Trimmer, S.S. Garlinge. 10th November 1942. Age 29. Son of Ernest and Elizabeth Byron; husband of Elizabeth Byron, of Sunderland.

CAIN, Cyril, Fireman, S.S. Thistlegarth. 15th October 1940. Age 22. Son of Mrs. B. Cain, of Southwick, Sunderland.

CAIN, Cyril, Chief Cook, S.S. San Fabian. 28th August 1942. Age 29. Husband of Annie Cain, of Seaburn, Sunderland.

CALDWELL, Sub-Lieutenant, HUGH COCHRANE, H.M.S. Lipis, Royal Naval Reserve. Died ashore 12 December 1942. Age 39. Husband of M. A. Caldwell, of Fulwell, Sunderland.

CANEY, Albert Austin, Third Engineer Officer, S.S. Knitsley. 12th December 1942. Age 47. Husband of Henrietta Caney, of Millfield, Sunderland.

CARNES, William Davie, Second Officer, S.S. Euphorbia. 14th December 1940. Age 32. Husband of Agnes Caroline Carnes, of Sunderland.

CARR, John, Third Engineer Officer, S.S. British Chancellor. 10/07/1940. 22 Regent Terrace, Grangetown

CARTER, Henry, Chief Engineer Officer, S.S. King Idwal. 23rd November 1940. Age 58. Husband of Barbara Carter, of Fulwell, Sunderland.

CARTER, Oliver Elston, Lamp Trimmer, S.S. Almeda Star. 17th January 1941. Age 32. Son of George Carter, and of Sarah E. Carter, of Sunderland.

CHARLTON, Joseph Polley, Steward, S.S. Heworth. 15th July 1940. Age 47. Son of Georgina Charlton, of Sunderland.

CHARLTON, Thomas, Fourth Engineer Officer, S.S. Anglo Peruvian. 23rd February 1941. Age 22. Son of William and Mary Isabell Charlton, of Sunderland.

CHEAL, William, Able Seaman, S.S. Tynehome. 08/01/1940. Age 39. Page Street, Hendon, Sunderland.

CHRISTIANSEN, John Christian, Able Seaman, S.S. Norman Monarch (Glasgow). Merchant Navy. Lost in S.S. Harpagus (London). 20th May 1941. Age 52. Son of Olaf and Christina Christiansen; husband of Elizabeth Grierson Christiansen, of Fulwell, Sunderland.

CLARK, Anthony, Greaser, M.V. Athelcrest. 25th August 1940. Age 20. Son of George and Jane A. Clark, of Sunderland.

CLARK, Eric Alexander Doctor, Able Seaman, S.S. Hartlebury. 07/07/1942. Husband of Hannah Blackett Surtees Clark, of 27 Wilfred Street, Pallion, Sunderland.

CLARK, George, Fourth Engineer Officer, S.S. Empire Lawrence. 27th May 1942. Age 21. Son of Edward and Margery Smith Clark, of Sunderland.

CLARK, John, Second Officer, S.S. Box Hill. 31/12/1939. Age 26. 8 Wycliffe Road, High Barnes, Sunderland.

CLARK, Robert Hodge, Chief Engineer Officer, S.S. Glenlea. 7th November 1942. Age 59. Husband of Ellen Clark, of Grindon, Sunderland.

CLARKE, William John Albert, Carpenter, S.S. Zurichmoor. 24th May 1942. Age 45. Husband of Mary Elizabeth Clarke, of Sunderland.

COOK, Albert E., Fireman and Trimmer, S.S. Queensbury. 6th June 1941. Age 39. Husband of Dorothy Cook, of 3 Broomshields Avenue, Fulwell, Sunderland.

COOK, Harry Wilson, Chief Engineer Officer, S.S. Ocean Crusader. 26th November 1942. Age 53. Husband of Annie Graham Cook, of 23 Mount Road West, Sunderland.

COOK, Thomas, Third Officer, S.S. Ocean Crusader. 26th November 1942. Age 22. Son of Mrs. A. Cook, of Fulwell, Sunderland.

COOMBS, Charles Calvert, Third Engineer Officer, S.S. Housatonic. 19th February 1941. Age 33. Husband of Jane Louisa Coombs, of Hendon, Sunderland.

COOPER, James Purse, Deck Boy, S.S. Homeside. 28th January 1941. Age 17. Son of Robert William and E. W. Cooper, of Millfield, Sunderland.

CORBETT, Henry, Third Engineer Officer, S.S. Harpathian. 26th August 1941. Age 38. Son of Henry and Barbara Corbett, of Sunderland; husband of Hannah Corbett, of Sunderland. Buried Sunderland (Ryhope Road) Cemetery.

CROUCH, George, Second Engineer Officer, M.V. British Courage. 11th October 1944. Age 42. Son of Samuel and Ann Crouch, of Sunderland; husband of Sarah Jane Crouch, of Fulwell, Sunderland. Buried Sunderland (Bishopwearmouth) Cemetery.

CURTIS, John Redpath, Cook, S.S. North Britain. 5th May 1943. Age 23. Son of Margaret Curtis, and stepson of Martin Carabine, of Sunderland.

DALBY, Douglas Haig, Deck Hand, S.S. Empire Mersey. 14th October 1942. Age 24. Son of Robert and Margaret Elizabeth Dalby, of Southwick, Sunderland.

DAYMOND, William, Fireman and Trimmer, S.S. Garlinge. 10th November 1942. Age 31. Son of Mr. and Mrs. G. Daymond, of Hendon, Sunderland.

DE GRUCHY, Ralph Sydney, Master, S.S. Sheaf Mount. 24th August 1942. Age 40. Son of Sydney and Blanche De Gruchy; husband of Louisa M. De Gruchy, of Fulwell, Sunderland.

DENTON, William Nesbitt, Chief Engineer Officer, S.S. Sea Glory. 11th July 1940. Age 55. Husband of Georgina Denton, of Sunderland.

DEVINE, Andrew, Sailor, S.S. Harpalyce. 25th August 1940. Age 19. Son of John William and Sarah Jane Devine, of Humbledon, Sunderland.

DICKSON, James, First Engineer, S.S. Tynehome. 8th January 1940. Age 44. Son of William and Mary H. Dickson, of Seaham, Co. Durham; husband of Jane Hedworth Dickson, of Sunderland.

DITCH, John, Fireman and Trimmer, S.S. Baron Blythswood. 20th September 1940. Age 31. Husband of Florence Ditch, of Sunderland.

DIXON, Basil Renwick, Third Radio Officer, S.S. Waziristan. 02/01/1942. Age 17. The Limes, Sunderland

DIXON, Geoffrey, Able Seaman, S.S. Hartlebury. 07/07/1942. Age 34. 37 Fawn Road, Ford Estate, Sunderland

DIXON, John, Boatswain (Bosun), S.S. Empire Wave. 2nd October 1941. Age 45. Husband of A. C. Dixon, of Sunderland.

DIXON, Thomas Cruickshanks, Deck Boy, S.S. Empire Wave. 18th October 1941. Age 15. Son of John Dixon, and of Ann Cooper Dixon, of Sunderland. Buried Reykjavik (Fossvogur) Cemetery.

DOCHERTY, Charles, Galley Boy, S.S. Empire Thunder. 6th January 1941. Age 16. Son of Mrs. M. Docherty, of Sunderland.

DODDS, Frederick, Pilot, Sunderland. Pilotage Authority. 7th November 1941. Age 59.

DODDS, Victor, Fifth Engineer Officer, S.S. Empire Heron. 15th October 1941. Age 20. Son of Thomas and Jane Dodds, of Fulwell, Sunderland.

DONACHIE, Robert, Third Engineer Officer, S.S. Pacific. 9th February 1943. Age 54. Husband of Lily Donachie, of Southwick, Sunderland.

DONALD, Raymond, Third Engineer Officer, S.S. Empire Newcomen. 30th November 1941. Age 27. Husband of F. Donald, of Sunderland.

DOUGLASS, William, Second Engineer Officer, M.V. Empire Dawn. 12th September 1942. Age 29. Son of William and Martha Douglass, of Sunderland. Obtained a Carnegie Hero Fund Trust Award for life saving.

DRAPER, Joseph Norman, Third Engineer Officer, M.V. Beignon. 1st July 1940. Age 36. Husband of S. Draper, of South Hylton, Co. Durham.

DUGAN, Edward, Third Engineer Officer, S.S. N. C. Monberg. 15th December 1940. Age 46. Husband of Annie M. Dugan, of Monkwearmouth, Sunderland.

DUNN, Robert, Chief Engineer Officer, S.S. Langleegorse. 23rd January 1941. Age 57. Son of Mr. and Mrs. David Dunn, of Belfast, Northern Ireland; husband of Esther L. Dunn, of Fulwell, Sunderland.

DUNVILLE, Edward, Second Engineer Officer, S.S. Creofield. 31st January 1940. Age 30. Son of Edward and Isabella Dunville; husband of Sarah Jane Dunville, of Sunderland.

DURY, Henri, Donkeyman, S.S. Harpalyce. 25th August 1940. Age 45. Son of Eugene and Dorothy Dury; husband of Mary Ann Dury, of Sunderland.

EAGLE, Arnold William, Apprentice, S.S. Warkworth. 10/10/1941. Age 17. Of 19 Hillside Gardens, Sunderland.

ECHEBARRIA, Manuel, Fireman, S.S. Assuan. 17th October 1943. Age 31. Husband of M. Echebarria, of Fulwell, Sunderland.

EDGECOMBE, William, Chief Officer, S.S. Halo. 21st March 1941. Age 32. Son of William and Lily Edgecombe, of Folkestone, Kent; husband of Hilda Edgecombe, of Sunderland. Buried Sunderland (Bishopwearmouth) Cemetery.

ELLIOTT, Arnold David, Sailor, S.S. Stanwold. 27th February 1941. Age 17. Son of William and Agnes C. Elliott, of Sunderland.

EMBLETON, William, Master, S.S. Westbury. 12th February 1941. Age 41. Husband of Louisa Embleton, of Roker, Sunderland.

FAITH, Stewart T. Age 26. Of 11 Gordon Terrace (late of Burntland Avenue).

FARNIE, Henry, Steward, S.S. Ullapool (West Hartlepool). Merchant Navy. 13th March 1941. Age 40. Son of Mark Frederick and Eliza Farnie; husband of E. M. Farnie, of Sunderland.

FENN, Ernest James, Chief Officer, O B E, S.S. Chulmleigh. 9th November 1942. Age 45. Husband of Margaret Fenn, of Southwick, Sunderland. Awarded Lloyd's Medal.

FINKLE, Norman, Chief Engineer Officer, S.S. Lunula. 9th April 1941. Age 54. Husband of Ethel Finkle, of Roker, Sunderland.

FINKLE, Charles Henry, Second Radio Officer, S.S. Empire Sky. 06/11/1942. Age 23
2 Netherburn Road, Sunderland.

FISHER, Lindsay Mathieson, Chief Officer, S.S. Empire Ghyll. 18th October 1941. Age 41. Son of Jessie M. Fisher, of Grangetown, Sunderland.

FLEMING, Leslie Wallace, Ordinary Seaman, S.S. Empire Gilbert. 2nd November 1942. Age 19. Son of Wallace Fleming, and of Ruth Wallace Fleming, of 32 Goschen Street, Southwick, Sunderland.

FLOYD, William, Able Seaman, S.S. Ilse. 7th October 1942. Age 42. Son of Thomas Henry and Isabella Floyd; nephew of Dora Bates, of Sunderland.

FORREST, Anthony Thomas, Fireman and Trimmer, S.S. Ashby. 30th November 1941. Age 36. Son of Joseph T. and Annie Forrest, of Sunderland.

FORSTER, Lancelot Edwin, Second Radio Officer, S.S. Empire Airman. 21st September 1940. Age 18. Son of Lancelot Edwin and Kate Chell Forster, of Sunderlandurham.

FOSTER, Charles, Able Seaman, S.S. Thistlegarth. 15th October 1940. Age 41. Son of Charles and Mary Foster; husband of Mary Elsie Foster, of Humbledon, Sunderland.

FOWLE, John William Wright, Chief Engineer Officer, S.S. Dalewood. 20/08/1941. Age 44. Buried Sunderland (Bishopwearmouth) Cemetery.

FRAME, George Alexander, Able Seaman, BEM, S.S. Fireglow. 16th August 1944. Age 37. Son of Mary Agnes Frame, of Sunderland; husband of Florence Frame, of Sunderland. Buried Sunderland (Ryhope Road) Cemetery.

GENT, William Thomas, Fireman, S.S. Westbury. 14th February 1947. Age 48. Husband of Ellen Gent, of Sunderland. Buried Sunderland (Mere Knolls) Cemetery.

GILBERT, Owen F.H., Second Engineer Officer, S.S. Pitwines. 8th November 1940. Age 22. King's Commendation for Brave Conduct. Son of Mr. and Mrs. Horace Gilbert; husband of Ethel Gilbert, of Grindon, Sunderland. Awarded Lloyd's War Medal. Buried Sunderland (Bishopwearmouth) Cemetery.

GILL, John Henry, Able Seaman, S.S. Streonshall. 5th March 1942. Age 23. Son of Lawrence and Catherine Gill, of Sunderland. Buried Sunderland (Bishopwearmouth) Cemetery.

GIBSON, Ernest, Able Seaman, S.S. Empire Dryden. 23rd April 1942. Age 35. Son of David and Margaret Gibson; husband of Emma Gibson, of Sunderland.

GIBSON, Ernest, Chief Engineer Officer, M.V. San Victorio. 16th May 1942. Age 43. Son of Timothy and Sarah Gibson; husband of P. E. Gibson, of Sunderland.

GIBSON, James, Second Radio Officer, S.S. Empire Springbuck. 10th September 1941. Age 26. Son of Francis Miller Gibson and Elspeth Ross Gibson, of Monkwearmouth, Sunderland.

GOODFELLOW, Harry, Chief Engineer Officer, M.V. Aldington Court. 31st October 1942. Age 43. Son of James and Jane Goodfellow; husband of Mildred B. Goodfellow, of Fulwell, Sunderland.

GRAHAM, John Foster, Apprentice, M.V. Jedmoor. 16th September 1941. Age 20. Son of John Foster Graham and Mary Graham, of Sunderland.

GRAHAM, John George, Boatswain (Bosun), S.S. Camberwell. 18/05/1942. Age 48. Son of James and Mary Jane Graham; husband of Elizabeth Hannah Graham, of Hastings Square, Hylton. Buried Sunderland (Bishopwearmouth) Cemetery.

GRAY, F Aged 30 of 13 Boughton Street died in hospital.

GREEN, John, Third Engineer Officer, S.S. Jersey City. 31st July 1940. Age 28. Son of Harriet Arm Green, of Millfield, Sunderland.

GREEN, James, Second Engineer Officer, S.S. Samsip. 7th December 1944. Age 35. Son of Edward and Elizabeth Green; husband of Margaret Robinson Green, of Sunderland.

GREGORY, Frederick Rogerson, Fireman and Trimmer, S.S. Harpalyce. 25th August 1940. Age 21. Son of Robert Donnison Annison Gregory, and of Mary Elizabeth Gregory, of East End, Sunderland. His father perished with him.

GREGORY, Robert Donnison Annison, Greaser, S.S. Harpalyce. 25th August 1940. Age 57. Husband of Mary Elizabeth Gregory, of East End, Sunderland. His son Frederick Rogerson Gregory perished with him.

GREGSON, Robert Mitford, Second Engineer Officer, S.S. Fort Athabaska. 02/12/1943. Age 37. Son of Robert Mitford Gregson and Margaret Elizabeth Gregson; husband of Emily Gregson, of 10 Blackett Terrace, Sunderland. (late of 30 Rainton Street, New Seaham).

HALL, Douglas Haig, Second Engineer Officer, S.S. Baron Kinnaird. 12th March 1943. Age 24. Son of Alice Hall; husband of Rebecca Urwin Hall, of Southwick, Sunderland.

HALL, George, Pilot, S.S. Balzac. Pilotage Authority. 26th July 1940. Age 33. Son of Thomas and Isabella Hall; husband of Mary Hall, of Sunderland.

HALLIDAY, Ernest Hay, Master, S.S. Leadgate. 11th March 1943. Age 39. Son of Thomas Halliday, and of Miriam D. Halliday, of Sunderland. Awarded Lloyd's Silver Medal for Gallantry.

HALLIDAY, James, O B E, Chief Engineer Officer, S.S. Zouave. 17th March 1943. Age 60. Son of James and Martha Halliday; husband of Mary Marie Halliday, of Seaburn, Sunderland.

HANSEN, Jens Christian, Able Seaman, S.S. Harklebury. 7th July 1942. Age 42. Son of Peter and Sofia Hansen; husband of Frances Hansen, of Hendon, Sunderland.

HARRISON, Maurice, Cadet, S.S. Thistlegarth. 15th October 1940. Age 17. Son of Elizabeth Harrison, of Sunderland.

HELLENS, Henderson Miller, Trimmer, S.S. Zaan. 4th December 1942. Age 18. Son of Henderson Miller Hellens, D.S.M., and Ellen Hellens, of Sunderland. Buried Bone War Cemetery, Algeria.

HELLENS, John Millar, Able Seaman, S.S. Eston. 28th January 1940. Age 47. Son of Robert and Elizabeth Hellens; husband of Mary Ann Hellens, of 53 Hadleigh Road, Hylton Lane Estate, Sunderland.

HELM, George Mewse, Chief Engineer Officer, S.S. British Emperor. 7th May 1941. Age 45. Husband of Elizabeth Helm, of Sunderland.

HENDERSON, Walter George, Cook Steward, M.V. Williamstown. 13th August 1940. Age 46. Son of George Edward and Elizebeth Henderson; husband of Dora Leonie Henderson, of Sunderland. Buried Southampton (Hollybrook) Cemetery.

HESLOP, John, Chief Engineer Officer, M.V. Narragansett. 25th March 1942. Age 33. Husband of Jane Heslop, of Southwick, Sunderland.

HESLOP, Joseph William, Third Engineer Officer, S.S. Scottish Chief. 20th November 1942. Age 34. Husband of Nora Heslop, of Fulwell, Sunderland.

HIND, Herbert, Able Seaman, S.S. Effna. 1st March 1941. Age 30. Husband of Lily Agnes Hind, of Sunderland.

HODGSON, Thomas Webster, Steward, M.V. British Liberty. 6th January 1940. Age 22. Son of Thomas Webster Hodgson and Georgina Hodgson, of Hendon, Sunderland. Buried Calais Southern Cemetery.

HOFFMAN, Frederick James, Third Engineer Officer, S.S. Cyprian Prince. 6th April 1941. Age 26. Son of Frederick and Ada Dorothy Hoffman, of Sunderland.

HOPE, John, Carpenter, M.V. British Liberty. 6th January 1940. Age 33. Husband of Isabella Bellamy Hope, of Sunderland.

HOPPER, John William Dawson, Second Engineer Officer, M.V. Cornish City. 29th July 1943. Age 25. Son of William and Sarah Hopper, of 112 Sorley Street, Sunderland.

HOPPER, Richard Henry, Donkeyman, S.S. Gasray. 5th April 1945. Age 61. Husband of Mary Hannah Hopper, of Sunderland.

HORN, David, Chief Officer, S.S. Kildale. 15th January 1940. Age 38. Son of James and Christiania Horn; husband of Irene Marcia Horn, of Sunderland.

HOWARD, Charles Edward, Master, S.S. Koranton. 28/03/1941. Age 31. Only son of Mrs and the late Mr C Howard of Mansfield Crescent, Roker, Sunderland

HOWARD, Gordon, Electrician, S.S. Svend Foyn. 21st March 1943. Age 28. Husband of Mary Wilhelmina Howard, of Felstead Square, Ford Estate, Sunderland.

HOWIE, Alexander, Third Officer, S.S. Euphorbia. 14th December 1940. Age 29. Son of James M. and Mary Howie, of South Shields, Co. Durham; husband of Marion Howie, of Castletown, Co. Durham.

HOWLISTON, Ernest, Engineer Officer (Seventh), S.S. Inverlee. 19th October 1941. Age 20. Son of John Thomas Howliston, and of Mary Ann Howliston, of Sunderland.

HUDSON, Robert Burton, Second Officer, M.V. San Emiliano. 9th August 1942. Age 27. King's Commendation for Brave Conduct. Son of Albert James Hudson and Mary Alice Hudson; husband of Evelyn Beatrice Hudson, of Sunderland.

HUGHES, Edward, Chief Steward, S.S. British Viscount. 3rd April 1941. Age 34. Son of Edward and Amelia Hughes, of Sunderland.

HUMBLE, Richard Cowell, Able Seaman, S.S. Norman Queen. 8th March 1941. Age 43. Son of Richard and Aida Lavina Humble; husband of Margaret Lettice Humble, of Sunderland

HUME, William Howard, Second Officer, M.V. Chama. 23rd March 1941. Age 23. Son of Thomas William Hume, and of Elizabeth Hume, of Sunderland.

HUNNAM, George, Chief Engineer Officer, S.S. Adams Beck (London). Merchant Navy. 9th August 1947. Age 64. Son of Robert and Martha Hunnam, of Sunderland; husband of Elizabeth Beatrice Hunnam, of Fulwell, Sunderland. (Mere Knolls) Cemetery.

HUNTLEY, William Henry, Greaser, M.V. Shelbrit I. 19th September 1940. Age 30. Husband of I. Huntley, of Sunderland.

HUTCHINSON, Henry, Fireman and Trimmer, S.S. Hartlebury. 7th July 1942. Age 38. Husband of C. Hutchinson, of Humbledon, Sunderland.

HUTCHINSON, George Race, Apprentice, S.S. Langleegorse. 23rd January 1941. Age 18. Son of Charles and Margaret Hutchinson, of Whitburn, Co. Durham.

IRVING, Claude H., Fireman and Trimmer, S.S. Queensbury. 6th June 1941. Age 32. Son of Charles Archibald Irving and Ellen Irving, husband of Grace Wooton Irving, of Whitburn. Buried Sunderland (Southwick) Cemetery.

INGLIS, George, Able Seaman, S.S. Ilse. 20/06/1941. Age 27. Buried Sunderland (Ryhope Road) Cemetery.
IRVING, Claude H., Fireman and Trimmer, S.S. Queensbury. 06/06/1941. Age 32. Son of Charles Archibald Irving and Ellen Irving, husband of Grace Wooton Irving, of Whitburn.

ISHERWOOD, James, Greaser, S.S. Empire Cloud. 9th May 1941. Age 32. Husband of L. Isherwood, of Millfield, Sunderland.

JACKSON, William Hardy, Chief Officer, S.S. Knitsley. 12th December 1942. Age 56. Son of William Hardy Jackson and Elizabeth Jane Jackson; husband of Jane Jackson, of Sunderland.

JAMESON, Thomas, Steward, S.S. Joseph Swan. 4th September 1940. Age 35. Son of William and Elizabeth Jameson, of Sunderland; husband of Margaret Jameson, of Calton, Staffordshire.

JOHANSSON, John William Ingvar, Third Engineer Officer, S.S. Empire Tristram. 23rd June 1944. Age 25. Son of John Ingvar Johansson and Elizabeth Ann Johansson, of 66 Kirkstone Avenue, Fulwell, Sunderland. Commemorated Newcastle (West Road) Cremetorium.

JOHNSON, Dennis, Junior Engineer Officer, M.V. Northmoor. 17th May 1943. Age 22. Son of F. and Ann Johnson, of Fulwell, Sunderland.

JOHNSON, William George, Donkeyman, S.S. Empire Dryden. 23rd April 1942. Age 41. Husband of Ada Isabela Johnson, of Sunderland.

JONES, Alfred, Second Engineer Officer, S.S. Spanker. 7th September 1946. Age 72. Son of William and Helen Jones husband of Alice Jones, of Fulwell. Sunderland. (Mere Knolls) Cemetery.

KINDER, Thomas Hedley, Steward, S.S. Homeside. 28th January 1941. Age 37. Husband of Jane Elizabeth Kinder, of Sunderland.

KIRBY, William Edward, Chief Engineer Officer, M.V. Glenmoor. 28th November 1940. Age 44. Son of William and Louisa Mary Kirby; husband of Elizabeth May Kirby, of Sunderland. Awarded a Testimonial of the Royal Humane Society.

KIRTON, Edgar, Second Officer, S.S. Leadgate. 11th March 1943. Age 21. Son of Edgar and Margaret Kirton, of Fulwell, Sunderland.

KNOWLES, John, Chief Engineer Officer, S.S. Holmelea. 28th February 1941. Age 54. Husband of Florence Laura Knowles, of Seaburn, Sunderland.

LAWTON, Herbert, O B E, Chief Engineer Officer, S.S. Riverton. 20th January 1946. Age 70. Husband of Catherine Ann Lawton, of Sunderland. Buried Sunderland (Bishopwearmouth) Cemetery.

LOCKEY, Frederick Gray, Sailor, S.S. Ashmun J. Clough. 6th December 1943. Age 30. Son of Frederick Gray Lockey and Mary Ann Lockey, of Sunderland; husband of Ethel May Lockey, of Sunderland. Buried Sunderland (Bishopwearmouth) Cemetery.

LONSDALE, Harold Gordon, Deck Hand, S.S. Craster. 21st January 1947. Age 23. Husband of Sarah Ann Lonsdale, of Hendon, Sunderland. Buried Sunderland (Ryhope) Cemetery.

LONSDALE, Richard Grozier, Chief Engineer Officer, S.S. Empire Heath. 13th May 1944. Age 61. Husband of Mary Lonsdale, of Sunderland.

LOVELL, Edgar Lindsey, Donkeyman, S.S. Ashmun J. Clough. 26th August 1944. Age 32. Son of Edgar and Caroline Lovell; husband of Margaret H. Lovell, of 12 Sea View, Grangetown, Sunderland.

LUDLOW, Edgar Ramsay, Third Engineer Officer, M.V. Pacific Skipper. 12th May 1947. Age 48. Son of George and Annie H. Ludlow, of Sunderland. Buried Sunderland (Bishopwearmouth) Cemetery.

LUMSDEN, William Gordon, Able Seaman, M.V. Derwent Hall. 11th March 1947. Age 46. Son of James and Margaret Lumsden, of Sunderland; husband of Emma Lumsden, of Millfield, Sunderland. Buried Sunderland (Bishopwearmouth) Cemetery.

LYALL, William, Second Engineer Officer, S.S. Box Hill. 31st December 1939. Age 64. Husband of Margaret Jane Lyall, of Sunderland.

LYNCH, John, Fireman and Trimmer, S.S. Harpalyce. 25th August 1940. Age 50. Husband of M. A. Lynch, of East End, Sunderland.

LYNCH, Matthew, Fireman, S.S. Tynehome. 08/01/1940. Age 44. Nelson Street, Ryhope.

MADDEN, Bernard, Chief Engineer, M.V. Ryal. 24th November 1940. Age 30. Son of Bernard and Ethel A. Madden, of Sunderland.

MAHONEY, Edward John, Second Officer, S.S. Avonwood. 12th December 1942. Age 22. Son of Frederick Patrick and Susan Mahoney; husband of Violet Mahoney, of Sunderland.

MALLEN, Edward, Greaser, S.S. Hindpool. 8th March 1941. Age 41. Son of Edward and Winifred Mallen, of Sunderland.

MALLIN, Edward Gordon, Galley Boy, S.S. Hartlebury. 7th July 1942. Age 17. Son of Patrick and Margaret Mallin, of Hendon, Sunderland.

MASON, John James, Chief Engineer Officer, S.S. Kafiristan. 17th September 1939. Age 53. Husband of Hannah Mason, of Sunderland.

MATTHEWSON, Ralph, Second Engineer Officer, M.V. Silvercedar. 15th October 1941. Age 32. Son of Ralph Nunn Matthewson and Dinah Matthewson, of Sunderland.

MELLENTIN, Robert Charles, Second Officer, S.S. Rio Azul. 29th June 1941. Age 31. Son of Robert and Charlotte Isabella Mellentin; husband of Jane Morris Nixon Mellentin, of Hendon, Sunderland.

METCALF, Ernest Gordon, Apprentice, M.V. Silverbeech. 28th March 1943. Age 17. Son of William Henry and Janet Metcalf, of Chatsworth Street, Sunderland. His brothers, John Callum Metcalf and William Metcalf, also fell.

METCALF, George Shaw, Second Engineer Officer, S.S. Chelsea. 30th August 1940. Age 54. Son of Thomas and Margaret Metcalf; husband of Lily May Metcalf, of Seaburn. Sunderland.

METCALF, John Callum, Third Officer, S.S. Rowanbank. 31st January 1941. Age 22. Son of William Henry and Janet Metcalf, of Grindon, Sunderland. His brothers William and Ernest Gordon also fell.

METCALF, William, Apprentice, M.V. Diala. 15th January 1942. Age 18. Son of William Henry and Janet Metcalf, of Grindon, Sunderland. His brothers, John Callum Metcalf and Ernest Gordon Metcalf, also fell.

MILBANKE, George, Master, S.S. Tia Juana. 16th February 1942. Age 56. Husband of Margaret Milbanke, of Sunderland.

MILBURN, Edward Chilton, Able Seaman, S.S. Empire Thunder. 6th January 1941. Age 26. Son of Ethel Atkinson, of Grangetown, Sunderland.

MILLER, Arthur Herbert, Third Engineer Officer, S.S. Holystone. 15th February 1941. Age 30. Son of Arthur Herbert and Susanna Miller; husband of Alice Miller, of Sunderland.

MITCHELL, Laurence Porter, Chief Officer, S.S. Eston. 28/01/1940. Age 40. Born in Hatfield, Hertfordshire. Now a Widower living with his Sister-in-law, Mrs Moat, at Ivanhoe Crescent, Sunderland.

MORDEY, John George, Carpenter, M.V. Fishpool. 14th November 1940. Age 21. Son of John George and Grace Mordey, of Hendon, Sunderland.

MORRIS, William Henry, Galley Boy, S.S. Essex Lance. 14/03/1941. Age 20. Son of Henry Hunter Morris and Ethel May Morris, of Grangetown. Sunderland.

McALLISTER, Kenneth, Third Radio Officer, S.S. Dayrose. 14th January 1942. Age 20. Son of David and Margaret McAllister, of Sunderland.

McCALL, John Strong, Junior Engineer Officer, M.V. Melbourne Star. 2nd April 1943. Age 23. Son of Brian and Kate McCall, of Cleadon, Sunderland.

McCREE, Cyril, Fifth Engineer Officer, S.S. Turakina. 20th August 1940. Age 26. Son of Frederick Joseph and Sarah Milburn McCree, of Sunderland.

McFARLANE, Junior Engineer, NINIAN LYLE, H.M.S. Registan, Naval Auxiliary Personnel (Merchant Navy). 28 May 1941. Age 23. Son of Robert Oley McFarlane and Margaret Ellen McFarlane, of Southwick, Sunderland.

McMURROUGH, John Robert, Fourth Engineer Officer, S.S. Coulmore. 9th March 1943. Age 28. Son of Eliza Stokoe, of 47 Newcastle Road, Sunderland.

McNAUGHTON, Adam, Chief Engineer Officer, S.S. Eastlea. 30th March 1941. Age 66. Husband of Ruby McNaughton, of Sunderland.

McQUE, Edward, Fourth Engineer Officer, S.S. Cree. 21st November 1940. Age 30. Son of Edward and Elizabeth McQue; husband of Jane Ann McQue, of Sunderland.

NELSON, Frederick Milbank, Chief Engineer Officer, S.S. Whitford Point. 20th October 1940. Age 37. Son of Charles and Elizabeth Nelson; husband of Florence Margaret D. Nelson, of Fulwell, Sunderland.

NEWMAN, Thomas, Junior Engineer Officer, S.S. Napier Star. 18th December 1940. Age 22. Son of Mary Lucy Newman, of Whitburn, Co. Durham.

NEWTON, Peter Telford, Second Engineer Officer, S.S. Hertford. 16th April 1943. Age 36. Son of Alfred Nicholson Newton and Florence Leconby Newton, of Sunderland; husband of Carolyne Newton, of Sunderland. Buried Halifax (Camp Hill) Cemetery. Nova Scotia.

NICOL, Garth Douglas Herbert, Third Engineer Officer, M.V. Neptunian. 7th September 1940. Age 29. Son of Quintin A. and M. H. Nicol, of Sunderland.

O'FLAHERTY, Nicholas Patrick, Fireman, S.S. Lindisfarne (Newcastle). Merchant Navy. 12th March 1942. Age 53. Son of Peter and Ann O'Flaherty; husband of Ann O'Flaherty, of Roker, Buried Sunderland. (Mere Knolls) Cemetery.

OGILVIE, William, Second Engineer Officer, S.S. Giralda. 30/01/1940. Chester Terrace, Sunderland

OLIVER, Douglas, Second Officer, S.S. Gwynwood. 4th February 1941. Age 22. Son of Walter J. and Phyllis L. Oliver, of Sunderland.

OLIVER, George William, Deck Hand, GEORGE WILLIAM, S.S. Stanwold. 27th February 1941. Age 23. Son of John Edward and Elizabeth Oliver, of Sunderland, Co. Durham. Buried Seaford Cemetery.

OWEN, Thomas William, Fireman, S.S. Galacum. 29th March 1943. Age 30. Son of Rowland and Grace Owen; husband of Marion Owen, of Sunderland. Buried Sunderland (Ryhope) Cemetery.

PACE, George Albert, Chief Engineer Officer, S.S. Dalveen. 28th September 1940. Age 42. Son of William and Jane Ann Pace; husband of Edith Pace, of Fulwell, Sunderland.

PALMER, Guy Mordey, Second Engineer Officer, S.S. Benlomond. 24th November 1942. Age 38. Son of Richard and Alice Palmer, of Sunderland; husband of Kathleen Palmer, of Petts Wood, Kent.

PARKIN, Carpenter, JAMES WILLIAM, 90658, H.M.S. Registan, Naval Auxiliary Personnel (Merchant Navy). 28 May 1941. Age 36. Husband of Marjorie Parkin, of Sunderland.

PARKINSON, David William P., Fourth Engineer Officer, S.S. Hartlebury. 7th July 1942. Age 20. Son of Thomas A. and Frances A. Parkinson, of Southwick, Sunderland.

PEACE, George Atkinson, Ordinary Seaman, M.V. British Liberty. 6th January 1940. Age 17. Son of Albert and Ellen May Peace, of Sunderland.

PERCIVAL, William Henry, Electrician, M.V. Melbourne Star. 3rd April 1943. Age 27. Son of Charles and Annie Percival; husband of Mary Lydia Percival, of 17 Marion Street, Sunderland.

PETRIE, Gordon, Fourth Engineer Officer, S.S. Effna. Merchant Navy. 1st March 1941. Age 20. Son of William and Isabella Petrie, of Sunderland.

PETTERSEN, Charles Arthur Hudspith, Third Officer, S.S. Empire Engineer. 2nd February 1941. Age 21. Son of Charles Magnus Pettersen, and of Minnie Pettersen, of Sunderland.

PEVERLEY, John, Fireman and Trimmer, S.S. Empire. 10/09/1941. Age 45. 13 Aiden Square, Hylton Estate.

PICKERING, Francis Courtney, Able Seaman, S.S. Westburn. 11th June 1941. Age 24. Son of Richard Curtis Pickering and Katherine Pickering; grandson of Mrs. C. Pickering, of Sunderland.

PIGGFORD, Charles, Second Engineer Officer, S.S. Aelybryn (London). Merchant Navy. 11th March 1943. Age 51. Husband of L. I. Piggford, of 20 Prengarth Avenue, Fulwell, Sunderland.

PINKNEY, Cyril, Second Engineer Officer, S.S. Thistlegarth. 15th October 1940. Age 36. Son of Thomas William and Frances Harriet Pinkney; husband of Dora Pinkney, of Sunderland.

POOLE, John Thomas, Junior Engineer Officer, M.V. Jedmoor. 16th September 1941. Age 21. Son of Mr. and Mrs. J. T. Poole, of Sunderland.

POWLEY, Robert, Master, S.S. Empire Dryden. 23rd April 1942. Age 35. Son of Wilfred and Mary Powley; husband of Mary Powley, of Sunderland.

PRICE, Charles, Able Seaman, S.S. Harpalyce. 25th August 1940. Age 20. Son of William Price, and of Elizabeth Price, of Southwick, Sunderland.

PRITCHARD G. W. Age 24. Of 63 Carley Road, Sunderland. (died in hospital).

PURVIS, John, Chief Cook, M.V. San Cipriano (London). Merchant Navy. 10th January 1943. Age 27. Son of Albert and Elizabeth Purvis; husband of Edith Purvis, of Fulwell, Sunderland.

RAMSHAW, Arthur Edmund, Chief Officer, S.S. Domingo de Larrinaga. 23rd October 1940. Age 41. Son of William and Mary Elizabeth Ramshaw; husband of Emmeline Margaret Ramshaw, of Sunderland.

RANEE, Leslie Mathsall, Cook, S.S. Taber Park. 13th March 1945. Age 20. Son of Mr. and Mrs. M. Ranee, of Sunderland.

RATCLIFFE, Luke Kelly, Fireman and Trimmer, S.S. Hartlebury. 7th July 1942. Age 28. Husband of Ethel Elfreda Ratcliffe, of Sunderland.

REED, Charles Holloway, Chief Engineer Officer, S.S. Belcrest. 15th February 1941. Age 52. Son of Arthur Ray and Anne Stevens Reed; husband of Hilda Reed, of Sunderland.

REED, Fireman, JOHN THOMAS, 292, H.M.S. Rajputana, Naval Auxiliary Personnel (Merchant Navy). 6 November 1940. Age 46. Son of John William and Margaret Ellen Reed, of Sunderland; husband of Mrs. M. Reed.

REED, Robert, Able Seaman, S.S. Empire Thunder. 6th January 1941. Age 21. Son of Thomas and Sarah Ann Reed, of Sunderland.

REYNOLDS, John Joseph, Second Engineer Officer, S.S. Euphorbia. 14th December 1940. Age 48. Son of Joseph and Elisabeth Reynolds; husband of Lottie Reynolds, of Humbledon, Sunderland.

RICHARDSON, Edward W., Second Engineer Officer, S.S. Whitemantle. 22/10/1939. Age 50. Husband of Annie Peters Richardson, of Whitburn, Co. Durham.

RICHARDSON, Walton, Apprentice, S.S. Whitecrest. 24/02/1942. Age 17. Son of Thomas and Margaret Richardson, of Ryhope, Co. Durham.

RIGG, Albert Dobson, Third Engineer Officer, S.S. Rio Azul. 29th June 1941. Age 30. Son of David and Jane Rigg; husband of Edith Catherine Rigg, of Grangetown, Sunderland.

ROBERTSON, Charles Edwin, Able Seaman, M.V. British Liberty. 06/01/1940. Age 31. 16 St Luke's Road, Pallion, Sunderland.

ROBINSON, Michael Hindmarsh, Fireman and Trimmer, S.S. Harpalyce. 25th August 1940. Age 37. Son of Mr. and Mrs. T. Robinson, of Sunderland.

ROBSON, David, Junior Engineer Officer, M.V. Siamese Prince. 17th February 1941. Age 21. Son of Noble Giles Robson and Jane Robson, of Southwick, Sunderland.

ROBSON, George Alwyn, Third Engineer Officer, M.V. Siamese Prince. 17th February 1941. Age 26. Son of George and Jessie Robson, of Pallion, Sunderland.

ROBSON, John George, Second Engineer Officer, S.S. Bradfyne. 22nd November 1940. Age 30. Son of Edward E. and Mary J. Robson; husband of Norah Robson, of Fulwell.

ROBSON, Nathaniel, Chief Engineer Officer, M.V. Bardistan. 27th February 1946. Age 56. Son of Henry and Elizabeth Robson, of Sunderland; husband of Annie Chrystal Robson, of Fulwell, Sunderland. Buried Gibraltar (North Front) Cemetery.

RODENBY, Stanley, Fourth Engineer Officer, S.S. Westpool. 3rd April 1941. Age 21. Son of Sarah Rodenby; grandson of Eliza Rodenby, of Sunderland.

RODENBY, William Rain, Junior Engineer Officer, S.S. Victoria City. 2nd December 1940. Age 20. Son of Thomas Bird and Edith May Rodenby, of Sunderland.

ROLFE, George, Fourth Engineer Officer, S.S. River Afton. 4th July 1942. Age 21. Son of George Coulson Rolfe and Annie Rolfe, of East End, Sunderland.

ROLFE, Joseph Munroe, Ordinary Seaman, S.S. Thistle Gorm. 6th October 1941. Age 17. Son of Samuel Richard and Eliza Munroe Rolfe, of 17 Lucknow Street, Hendon, Sunderland.

ROSE, Stephen, Second Engineer Officer, S.S. Empire Eve. 18th May 1943. Age 59. Husband of E. C. Rose, of Sunderland.

ROSS, Senior Third Engineer Officer, ERNEST WILLIAM, M.V. Scottish Maiden (London). Merchant Navy. 5th November 1940. Age 25. Son of Alexander and Jane V. Ross, of Sunderland.

ROUTLEDGE, Fireman, CHARLES ERNEST, S.S. Thistlegarth (Sunderland). Merchant Navy. 15th October 1940. Age 24. Son of Elizabeth A. Routledge, of Monkwearmouth, Sunderland.

ROWELL, Albert Edward, Steward, M.V. British Liberty. 6th January 1940. Age 23. Son of Albert Edward and Mry Rowell, of Roker, Sunderland, Co. Durham. Buried Calais Southern Cemetery.

ROWNTREE, Chief Engineer Officer, JOHN, M.V. Lucellum (Liverpool). Merchant Navy. 19th December 1941. Age 42. Son of John and Mary Rowntree; husband of Elsie Rowntree, of Sunderland.

RYLES, Chief Engineer Officer, WALTER, S.S. Homeside (Newcastle-on-Tyne). Merchant Navy. 28th January 1941. Age 63. Son of Elijah and Alma Ryles; husband of Pol]ie Ryles, of Sunderland.

SAMPSON, Able Seaman, JOHN WILLIAM, S.S. Harpalyce (London). Merchant Navy. 25th August 1940. Age 24. Son of Mrs. M. Sampson, of Fulwell, Sunderland.

SANDERSON, Steward, ALAN, S.S. Inverness (Newcastle-on-Tyne). Merchant Navy. 9th July 1941. Age 27. Son of Margaret Sanderson, of Fulwell, Sunderland.

SANDERSON, Leslie Armstrong, Mess Room Boy, M.V. Athelcrest. 25th August 1940. Age 16. Son of Armstrong and Rosanna Sanderson, of Fulwell, Sunderland.

SCAIFE, Thomas, Second Engineer Officer, S.S. Nirpura. 3rd March 1943. Age 42. Son of Thomas and Margaret Scaife; husband of Florence Elizabeth Scaife, of 23 Ewesley Road, Sunderland.

SCHOLEFIELD, William, Chief Engineer Officer, S.S. Joseph Swan. 4th September 1940. Age 56. Husband of A. Scholefield, of Fulwell, Sunderland.

SCOTT, William H., Able Seaman, S.S. Stanwold. 27th February 1941. Age 19. Son of William Henry and Emma Scott nephew of Mrs. E. M. Edmundson, of Sunderland. Buried Sunderland (Southwick) Cemetery.

SEERY, Michael, Electrician, S.S. British Premier. 24th December 1940. Age 36. Husband of Doris Seery, of Fulwell, Sunderland.

SELLARS, George Waite Steel, Able Seaman, S.S. Empire Dryden. 23rd April 1942. Age 52. Son of George Waite Steel Sellars and Mary Jane Sellars; husband of Elizabeth Ann Sellars, of Sunderland.

SHAW, David, Chief Engineer Officer, S.S. Fort Franklin. 16th July 1943. Age 44. Son of David and Margaret Hannah Shaw; husband of Elsie Shaw, of 1 Sydenham Terrace, Sunderland.

SHIELDS, William, Donkeyman, S.S. Empire Gilbert. 2nd November 1942. Age 34. Son of Francis and Margaret Shields; husband of Sarah Shields, of 16 Halstead Square, Sunderland.

SIMEY, Edward George, Fourth Engineer Officer, S.S. Empire Dew. 11th June 1941. Age 26. Son of George and Mary Simey; husband of Cora Ruth Simey, of Hendon, Sunderland.

SKINNER, Richard, Boatswain, S.S. Stanbank, 05/05/1942. Age 42. Of 14 St. Mark's Road, Sunderland

SLIMIN, Lieutenant (E), JAMES ROY, Mentioned in Despatches, H.M.S. Malvernian, Royal Naval Reserve. 1 July 1941. Age 29. Son of James and Jane Slimin; husband of Lilian May Slimin, of Sunderland.

SMITH, Arthur Richard, Third Officer (Supy.). S.S. British General. 6th October 1940. Age 22. Son of Arthur Crosby Smith and Lilian Smith, of Fulwell, Sunderland.

SMITH, Harris Thompson, Able Seaman, S.S. Empire Rosebery. 24/08/1944. Age 34. Of 7 Summerhill, Sunderland.

SMITH, Robert Morrison, Apprentice, S.S. Castlemoor. 25th February 1940. Age 19. Son of Robert Morrison Smith and Rebecca Tate Smith, of Whitburn, Sunderland.

SMITH, Walter, Second Officer, M.V. Harpagus. 20th May 1941. Age 27. Son of Alfred and Lizzie Smith; husband of Margery Manser Smith, of Sunderland.

SMITH, William Henry. Second Engineer Officer, M.V. Fishpool. 26/07/1943. Age 29. Of 12 Priory Grove, Sunderland.

SMITH, William John, Cabin Boy, S.S. Tredinnick. 25th March 1942. Age 18. Son of James and Jennie Smith, of Sunderland.

SPROATES, James, Fireman and Trimmer, S.S. Hartlebury. 7th July 1942. Age 32. Son of James and Ethel Sproates, of Hendon, Sunderland.

SPROUL, Richard John, Master, S.S. Empire Lake. 15/07/1943. Age 37. Son of Charles Daniel and Alice Sproul; husband of Elizabeth Sproul, of 19 Elmsleigh Gardens, Cleadon, Co. Durham.

STAFFORD, Frederick, Carpenter, S.S. Hartlebury. 7th July 1942. Age 35. Son of John and Cathrine Stafford; husband of Mary Eveline Stafford, of Fulwell, Sunderland.

STANGER, Norman, Cabin Boy, S.S. Empire Thunder. 6th January 1941. Age 19. Son of Norman Stanger, and of Ivy Wayman Stanger, of Millfield, Sunderland.

STEPHENSON, John Charles, Able Seaman, S.S. Oxshott. 6th August 1941. Age 48. Husband of H. Stephenson, of Sunderland. Buried Sunderland (Ryhope) Cemetery.

STONEMAN, Aubrey Robert, Boatswain, S.S. Harpalyce. 25th August 1940. Age 48. Husband of Lydia Stoneman, of Hendon, Sunderland.

STOREY, John Watson, Second Engineer Officer, S.S. Garmula. 23/07/1942. Age 39. 129 Side Cliffe Road, Roker, Sunderland

STRUTT, Robert, O B E, Master, S.S. Lea Grange. 12th February 1947. Age 54. Son of William Robert and Dorothy Ann Strutt, of Sunderland; husband of Florence May Strutt, of Roker. Buried Sunderland. (Mere Knolls) Cemetery.

STUART, James Smith, Master, M.V. Pacific President. 2nd December 1940. Age 44. Husband of H. Stuart, of Sunderland.

SUMMERS, Douglas Haig, Able Seaman, S.S. Stangarth. 16th March 1942. Age 23. Son of Stanley Summers, and of Miriam Elizabeth Summers, of Sunderland.

TANSEY, Roger, Carpenter, M.V. Athelcrest. 25th August 1940. Age 29. Son of Thomas and Aris Tansey; husband of M. Tansey, of Southwick, Sunderland.

TAYLOR, Martin, Third Officer, S.S. White Crest. 24th February 1942. Age 31. Son of James and Sarah Ann Taylor; husband of N. Taylor, of Humbledon, Sunderland.

TAYLOR, Sydney Allison, Chief Officer, S.S. Tabaristan. 29th May 1941. Age 28. Son of Gilbert and Mildred Taylor, of Seaburn, Sunderland. Master Mariner, Merchant Navy.

TAYLOR, Samuel Herbert, Second Officer, M.V. Shelbrit I. 19th September 1940. Age 56. Husband of I. S. Taylor, of Sunderland.

TAYLOR, William, Third Officer, S.S. Empire Wave. 2nd October 1941. Age 24. Son of William Taylor, and of Anne W. Taylor, of Sunderland.

TELFORD, Frederick, Fireman and Trimmer, S.S. Thistleglen. 10th September 1941. Age 37. Husband of A. Telford, of Hendon, Sunderland.

THACKRAY, James Mills, Chief Engineer Officer, S.S. Glynn. 12th October 1941. Age 49. Husband of Ellen Thackray, of Sunderland.

THOMPSON, Charles, Able Seaman, M.V. British Vigilance. 3rd January 1943. Age 22. Son of Charles Frederick Thompson, and of Isabella Thompson, of 8 Raby Street, Sunderland. His father Charles Frederick perished with him.

THOMPSON, Charles Frederick, Boatswain, M.V. British Vigilance. 3rd January 1943. Age 65. Husband of Isabella Thompson, of 8 Raby Street, Sunderland. His son Charles perished with him.

THOMPSON, William Arnold, Chief Steward, M.V. Silverbeech. 28/03/1943. Age 38. Of Burnville Road South, Sunderland.

THORNE, Henry, Chief Engineer Officer, M.V. Silverpalm. 9th June 1941. Age 50. Husband of Mary Elizabeth Thorne, of Seaburn, Sunderland.

TILLEY, John Leonard, Second Engineer Officer, S.S. Holmelea. 28th February 1941. Age 50. Husband of Mary Alice Tilley, of Southwick, Sunderland.

TIVNEN, Joseph Patrick, Ordinary Seaman, S.S. Harpalyce. 25th August 1940. Age 25. Son of Thomas and Jane Ann Tivnen, of Sunderland.

TODD, Lawrence, Chief Engineer Officer, M.V. Fishpool. 26/07/1943. Age 57. Of 2 Irene Avenue, Grangetown, Sunderland.

TOPLIFF, John William, Fireman and Trimmer, S.S. Harpalyce. 25th August 1940. Age 37. Husband of Jane Ann Topliff, of Sunderland.

TRETT, Robert Thirlwell, Able Seaman, M.V. Empire Drum. 6th August 1944. Age 43. Son of John Thomas Trett and Hannah Trett; husband of Barbara Trett, of Southwick, Sunderland. Buried Sunderland (Southwick) Cemetery.

TRIGGS, George, Third Engineer Officer, S.S. Box Hill. 31/12/1939. Age 25. 31 John Candlish Road, Sunderland.

TROTTER, Robert Lawson, Steward, S.S. Torchbearer. 19th November 1939. Age 34. Son of Septimus and Martha Trotter; husband of Doris Trotter, of Hendon, Sunderland.

TRUEMAN, John Milburn, Third Engineer Officer, S.S. Waziristan. 2nd January 1942. Age 25. Son of James and Elizabeth Trueman, of Hendon, Sunderland.

TURNBULL, Robert, Chief Steward, S.S. Gurden Gates. 24th June 1944. Age 35. Son of Charles and Jessy Turnbull, husband of Ethel Maud Turnbull, of Sunderland. Buried Sunderland (Bishopwearmouth) Cemetery.

UNDERWOOD, John George, Sailor, S.S. Stangarth. 16th March 1942. Age 21. Son of William Underwood, and of Louisa Underwood, of East End, Sunderland.

WALKER, Cyril, Fourth Engineer Officer, S.S. Kirkpool. 10th April 1942. Age 26. Son of Thomas Wilkinson Walker and Jane Bell Walker, of Grangetown, Sunderland.

WARD, Herbert Ralph, Third Officer, M.V. Silveray. 4th February 1942. Age 21. Son of Jennie Ward, of 5 Mary Street, Southwick, Sunderland.

WARING, Joshua, First Engineer, S.S. Kildale. 03/02/1940. 19 Viewforth Drive, Fulwell, Sunderland.

WATSON, Charles, Fireman and Trimmer, S.S. Harpalyce. 25th August 1940. Age 39. Son of Charles and Gracie Watson; husband of C. Watson, of Sunderland.

WATSON, John Woodrow, Second Engineer Officer, S.S. Tiberton. 14th February 1940. Age 26. Son of James and Jessie Watson, of Sunderland. His brother Ernest also fell.

WATSON, Michael Hooks, Chief Officer, S.S. Parkhill. 17th November 1939. Age 39. Son of John and Ellen Watson; husband of Dora Watson (nee Angus), of Sunderland.

WAUGH, Joseph, Steward, S.S. Betty Hindley. 26/04/1946. Age 46. Son of Joseph and Isabel Waugh, of Sunderland; husband of Marguerite B. Waugh. of Hylton.

WELLS, Ernest Vivian, Fireman and Trimmer, S.S. Lackenby. 25th January 1943. Age 22. Son of Ernest Vivian and Mary Jane Wells, of Whitburn, Co. Durham.

WELLS, Lancelot Ormston, Sailor, S.S. Hartlebury. 07/07/1942. Age 20. Son of Thomas Henry and Beatrice Ormston Wells of 36 Chatsworth Street, Sunderland

WHITE, Albert, Chief Engineer Officer, S.S. Empire Sky. 6th November 1942. Age 49. King's Commendation for Brave Conduct. Son of William and Sophia White; husband of Winifred Blanche White, of 50 Hathaway Gardens, Durham Road, Sunderland.

WHITE, George Henry, Fifth Engineer Officer, S.S. Harpalyce. 25th August 1940. Age 21. Son of G. H. and Margarat White, of Sunderland.

WHITE, William Albert, Second Engineer Officer, S.S. Indian Prince. 26th January 1945. Age 35. Son of Charles William and Susannah White, of Sunderland; husband of Virginia White, of Fulwell, Buried Sunderland (Mere Knolls) Cemetery.

WILKIE, Henry, Fireman and Trimmer, S.S. Baron Blythswood. 20th September 1940. Age 33. Husband of Jane Wilkie, of Monkwearmouth, Sunderland.

WILLEY, Edward Johnson Scott, Second Engineer Officer, S.S. Cormount. 28th September 1941. Age 58. Son of Robert William and Martha Matilda Willey, of Sunderland; husband of Bertha Willey, of Sunderland. Buried Sunderland (Bishopwearmouth) Cemetery.

WILLIAMS, Frederick, Chief Engineer Officer, S.S. Horseferry. 11th March 1942. Age 42. Son of William John and Harriet Williams; husband of Florence Williams, of Sunderland.

WILLIAMS, James Fox, Master, S.S. Heworthy. 16th July 1940. Age 69. Son of Richard and Mary Williams, of Sunderland; husband of Margaret Ann Nesham Williams, of Sunderland. Buried Sunderland (Ryhope) Cemetery.

WILLIAMSON, James Brown, Chief Engineer Officer, S.S. Ashworth. 13th October 1942. Age 57. Husband of Lydia E. Williamson, of Sunderland.

WILLIAMSON, William Tweedy, Third Engineer Officer, M.V. King Lud. 8th June 1942. Age 37. Son of William Tweedy Williamson and Sarah Williamson, of 2 Croft Avenue, Sunderland.

WILLIS, Hector Rayment, Master, S.S. Empire Comet. 19th February 1942. Age 40. Son of William Rayment Willis and Ada Dent Willis; husband of Ethel Irene Willis, of Sunderland.

WILSON, George Mckenzie, Engineer Officer in the Merchant Navy. 14/03/1943. Age 45. Son of William Campbell Wilson and Mary Hannah Wilson. Of 1 Appleby Terrace, Roker, Sunderland.

WILSON, Thomas Richard, Donkeyman, M.V. Athelcrest. 25th August 1940. Age 39. Son of Thomas Christopher and Catherine Wilson; husband of Ellen Wilson, of Sunderland.

WILTON, Thomas Kirby, Chief Engineer Officer, S.S. Ouickstep. 12th January 1942. Age 56. Husband of Sarah Hannah Wilton, of Roker, Sunderland.

WINTERS, Andrew Patrick, Able Seaman, S.S. Stangarth. 16th March 1942. Age 57. Husband of Catherine Winters, of Sunderland.

WRIGHT, Robert, Chief Engineer Officer, S.S. Harmala. 7th February 1943. Age 46. Son of Robert and Catherine Wright; husband of Catherine Wright, of Fulwell, Sunderland.

WRIGHTSON, Gilbert James, Third Officer, S.S. Penolver. 19th October 1943. Age 31. Son of Gilbert Geiselheart Wrightson and Florence May Wrightson, of Sunderland; husband of Florence Mary Wrightson, of Lambley, Northumberland.

YOUNG, Harry, Steward, S.S. Kirkpool. 10th April 1942. Age 34. Son of Tom and Ellen Young; husband of Isabella Young, of Sunderland.

YOUNG, Sydney, First Mate, S.S. Empire Chaucer. 17/10/1942. Age 32. His father lives at 2 Leamington Street, Sunderland. Posthumously commended for brave conduct.

YOUNGER, William Henry, Carpenter, S.S. Empire Gilbert. 2nd November 1942. Age 28. King's Commendation for Brave Conduct. Son of Harry and Mary Younger; husband of Esther Younger, of 7 Eden Street, Newcastle Road, Sunderland.

ZAMMIT, Raymond, Chief Steward, S.S. Empire Dryden. 23rd April 1942. Age 44. Son of Paul and Elizabeth Zammitt; husband of Mary Victoria Zammit, of Sunderland.